FARM ACCOUNTS IN RURAL EUROPE

c. 1700–1914

Boydell Studies in Rural History

Series Editor
Professor Richard W. Hoyle

This series aims to provide a forum for the best and most influential work in agricultural and rural history, and on the cultural history of the countryside. Whilst it is anchored in the rural history of Britain and Ireland, it also includes within its remit Europe and the colonial empires of European nations (both during and after colonisation). All approaches and methodologies are welcome, including the use of oral history.

Proposals or enquiries are welcomed. They may be sent directly to the editor or the publisher at the email addresses given below.

Richard.Hoyle@reading.ac.uk
Editorial@boydell.co.uk

Previous titles in the series are listed at the back of the volume.

Farm Accounts in Rural Europe, c. 1700–1914

"To Better Know One's Own?"

Edited by Nathalie Joly and Federico D'Onofrio

THE BOYDELL PRESS

First published 2025
The Boydell Press, Woodbridge

ISBN 978 1 83765 100 9

The Boydell Press is an imprint of Boydell & Brewer Ltd
PO Box 9, Woodbridge, Suffolk IP12 3DF, UK
and of Boydell & Brewer Inc.
668 Mt Hope Avenue, Rochester, NY 14620–2731, USA
website: www.boydellandbrewer.com

Our Authorised Representative for product safety in the EU is
Easy Access System Europe – Mustamäe tee 50, 10621 Tallinn, Estonia,
gpsr.requests@easproject.com

A CIP catalogue record for this book is
available from the British Library

CONTENTS

ILLUSTRATIONS

Figures

Tables

CONTRIBUTORS

Fulgence Delleaux is Professor of Modern History at the University of Namur. He specializes in the economic, social, and emotional history of European rural areas (France, the Netherlands, and Switzerland), primarily in the eighteenth century.

Federico D'Onofrio is Associate Professor at the Institute for Social and Economic History of the University of Vienna, where he studies the history of data and economic thought. He leads the European Research Council starting grant 'Leading the first data revolution in European agriculture 1870–1945'.

James D. Fisher is a historian of work, knowledge, and capitalism in early modern Britain. He joined the University of Exeter as Lecturer in Early Modern History in 2023. He is the author of *The Enclosure of Knowledge: Books, Power and Agrarian Capitalism in Britain, 1660–1800* (Cambridge, 2022).

Laurent Herment is Directeur de recherche at CNRS Paris (CRH-EHESS). He works on agrarian systems and agro-industry in north-western Europe during the nineteenth and the beginning of the twentieth centuries, with a special focus on fertilizers and starch production. He also works on the starch global commodity chain, specifically on potatoes and cassava.

Richard Hoyle was Professor of Rural History at the University of Reading, then Professor of Local and Regional History at the Institute of Historical Research. He now holds an honorary (visiting) chair at the University of Reading. He was for two decades editor of *Agricultural History Review*.

Nathalie Joly is Senior Lecturer of Rural Sociology at L'Institut Agro Dijon and an Associated Researcher at the French National Institute for Research on Agriculture, Food and Environment (INRAE). Her research focuses on the writing and calculating cultures of the French peasantry, addressing their social framing by scholars, rural elites, and education.

MARKUS LAMPE is Professor for Economic and Social History at Vienna University of Economics and Business, and Visiting Professor at the University of Gothenburg. His areas of research include the history of international trade and trade policy, agricultural history, and the history of real estate markets.

PETER MOSER is the founder (2002) and since then Director of the Archives of Rural History in Bern (AHR, www.agrararchiv.ch). He is President of the European Rural History Film Association ERHFA (www.rural-films.eu) and, since 2022, member of the Executive Committee of the Agricultural History Society in the USA.

FRIEDERIKE SCHOLTEN-BUSCHHOFF studied History and English/American Studies at the University of Münster. She earned her doctorate at Münster in 2020. She currently works as an analyst for global Crop Protection markets and as a freelance historian.

PAUL SHARP is Professor of Economic History at the Historical Economics and Development Group, University of Southern Denmark. He works on topics relating to Danish agricultural and economic history.

ACKNOWLEDGEMENTS

Edited volumes require an immense amount of work and editors and authors inevitably incur debts of gratitude to large numbers of people and institutions. Some people open paths. For their benevolent companionship, Nathalie Joly would like to thank Nadine Vivier, Yannick Lemarchand, Patrick Fridenson, and Jean-Marc Moriceau, and for enriching joint writing, Thomas Depecker. Federico D'Onofrio would like to thank, in particular, Martin Giraudeau, Harro Maas, Niccolò Mignemi, Giulio Ongaro, and the DATAREV team (Marina Chuchko, Myriam Lichani, and Mariia Romanova) for their stimulating insights on (farm) accounting.

We realize that we have taken far too much of our authors' time and really tested the limits of their patience over the course of the three years since we invited many of them to the fifth biennial conference of the European Rural History Organization that was scheduled for Uppsala in May 2021 and finally took place the following year. Thank you for bearing with us.

The editors want to express their particular gratitude to Richard Hoyle for his help with the editing process and to Caroline Palmer at Boydell and Brewer. Heartfelt thanks to Robin Jenny who edited the bibliography and to Teresa who had to endure this book for two consecutive summers.

The realization of this book has been supported by the European Research Council, Starting Grant 'Leading the first data revolution in European agriculture' (DATAREV, grant number 940722).

1

Introduction[1]

Nathalie Joly and Federico D'Onofrio

In the wake of the cultural approach to the Industrial Revolution,[2] historians have investigated the intellectual and social origins of the sustained growth of European agriculture in early modern and modern Europe. In particular, they have stressed the significance of 'useful knowledge' in underpinning technological progress. Did an 'Agricultural Enlightenment' of the eighteenth century metamorphose into an 'Agricultural Revolution'?[3] What were the effects of the 'agromania' that swept through Europe after the Peace of Aachen and reached even Europe's remote peripheries?[4] Dissemination and emulation issues, along with discussions of competing institutional frameworks facilitating innovation and technological adoption, have become central themes in

1 The project that led to this publication has received funding from the European Research Council (ERC) under the European Union's Horizon 2020 Research and Innovation Programme (Grant Agreement no. 949722) and MSCA 833546: FARMACCOUNTA. This funding has enabled the Introduction and Chapter 9 of this volume to be published Open Access under the licence CC BY-NC-ND.

2 Deirdre McCloskey, *The bourgeois virtues: Ethics for an age of commerce* (2006); Joel Mokyr, 'The intellectual origins of modern economic growth', *Journal of Economic History* 65 (2005) pp. 285–351; David S. Landes, 'Culture makes almost all the difference', in Lawrence E. Harrison and Samuel P. Huntington (eds), *Culture matters: How values shape human progress* (2000), pp. 1–13.

3 Peter M. Jones, *Agricultural enlightenment: Knowledge, technology, and nature, 1750–1840* (2016), pp. 31–2.

4 Istvan Hont, 'Correcting Europe's political economy: The virtuous eclecticism of Georg Ludwig Schmid', *History of European Ideas* 33 (2007), pp. 390–410; Koen Stapelbroek and Jani Marjanen, 'Political economy, patriotism and the rise of societies', in Stapelbroek and Marjanen (eds), *The rise of economic societies in the eighteenth century: Patriotic reform in Europe and North America* (2012), pp. 1–25.

the historiography.[5] Historians have investigated the impact of scientific knowledge on farming practices. Modernising elites and experts engaged in spreading innovation – both by setting an example to be emulated and actively advocating new techniques through propaganda, education, and even coercion. Calculative practices were an integral part of the effort of the innovators, especially when, in the second half of the eighteenth century, as Keith Tribe has argued, 'a new discursive formation came into being, one whose structure is constituted by a specific conjunction of concepts of capital, profit, exchange, production and distribution'.[6] Once the farm came to be seen as a unit of production comparable with other economic units, arguments concerning rational management became central. Accounting could thus serve as a means to gather essential farm-related information. From the eighteenth century and well into the twentieth, European elites adopted an ideal model of an accounting farmer meticulously recording economic transactions, seeing tidy book-keeping[7] as being the basis of sound management and the adoption of new techniques.

By investigating the invention of the accounting farmer as an emblem of modern agriculture, this book draws together two poorly connected areas of historical research in the social sciences: on the one hand, a body of scattered investigations devoted to agricultural accounting in different countries and, on the other, the more substantial body of work on the process of agricultural modernisation in Europe between the eighteenth and twentieth centuries. What exactly is there to connect? First, we have the materials, observations, and analyses which are already available and which span the three centuries we consider. Since knowledge is held in silos, period by period, country by country, researchers are often unaware of each other and hardly ever discuss and compare their findings. We believe that the juxtaposition of different periods, historiographies, and objects of agricultural accounting studies can produce unexpected results and prompt the study of hitherto neglected subjects. Second, it is necessary to make better connections between our knowledge of accounting, whose development is seemingly associated with modernity and capitalist rationality, and the analysis of the economic and cultural mechanisms of

5 Jones, *Agricultural enlightenment*, ch. 4; Frank Uekötter, *Die Wahrheit ist auf dem Feld: Eine Wissensgeschichte der deutschen Landwirtschaft, Umwelt und Gesellschaft* (2010); Jonathan Harwood, *Europe's Green Revolution and others since* (2016).

6 Keith Tribe, *Land, labour, and economic discourse* (1978), p. 5.

7 We have used the form 'book-keeping' in preference to other possible variants throughout the book.

the transformation of European agriculture which progressed in fits and starts from the late seventeenth century onwards.[8]

Following Latour, we may contend that accounting reports became key 'representations' to produce economic and managerial knowledge.[9] To paraphrase the French sociologist, no new man suddenly emerged who thought differently from the inhabitants of the pre-industrial agricultural world.[10] This volume puts forward a more mundane explanation of change in economic practice, by considering accounting as a means of 'Drawing Things Together' in a particular calculative manner. It thus strives to trace how the actors who were concerned, whether directly or 'at a distance'[11] – be they estate owners, their bailiffs and stewards, scholars in the field of agronomy and political economy, financial investors, professional organisations, or state agencies – developed representations of rational, profit-orientated agriculture. As varied as the works gathered here are in their analytic framework, they share the idea that accounting could be performative for decision-making and management.[12] The aim is, then, to determine in what ways and to what extent accounts and accounting might have influenced the development of agriculture, as it has industry and commerce.

This volume originated in a panel organised at the fifth biennial conference of the European Rural History Organisation (EURHO), Rural

8 A good definition of agricultural modernisation in terms of technological, social, managerial, and ecological change can be found in Margot Lyautey, Léna Humbert, and Christophe Bonneuil, 'Introduction', in Lyautey, Humbert, and Bonneuil (eds), *Histoire des modernisations agricoles au XXe siècle* (2021), pp. 5–6.

9 In his seminal reflection on the role of inscriptions as ways of representing things and to know them, both for scientific thought and everyday life thought as well, Bruno Latour, 'Visualization and cognition', *Knowledge and Society* 6 (1986), pp. 1–40.

10 This sentence paraphrases Latour speaking of modern scientific culture: 'No "new man" suddenly emerged sometime in the sixteenth century, and there are no mutants with larger brains working inside modern laboratories who can think differently from the rest of us. The idea that a more rational mind or a more constraining scientific method emerged from darkness and chaos is too complicated a hypothesis.' Latour, 'Visualization and cognition', p. 1.

11 For a theoretical focus on quantification and action at a distance, see Keith Robson, 'Accounting numbers as "inscription": Action at a distance and the development of accounting', *Accounting, Organizations and Society* 17 (1992), pp. 685–708.

12 Inspired by the seminal works of Michel Callon. Michael Callon (ed.), *The laws of the markets* (1998); Donald MacKenzie, *An engine, not a camera: How financial models shape markets* (2006). The literature on the performativity of accounting is now too large to be discussed here.

History 2021 in Uppsala.[13] The papers presented in these sessions stimulated a discussion concerning the spread of agricultural accounting during three centuries of European history. At the heart of our exchanges was a questioning of the reasons that led rural elites and scholars to invest in the adoption of agricultural accounting.[14] We also looked at the growing role played by the state through incentives and educational policies, in tandem with the professional organisations that sprang up across Europe in the second half of the nineteenth and early twentieth centuries. We hope that this volume marks an important step in the understanding of how accounting became constitutive of new calculative reasonings and managerial practices in agriculture. Chiapello and Gilbert have reminded us that management techniques 'prescribe action formats, building a unity of action within a work collective'.[15] But this role expands far beyond organisations. Management techniques are also influential in the making, on a day-to-day basis, of the economic system and market mechanisms. By studying accounting in both its institutional genesis and its embodiment in the social figure of the accounting farmer, we can make a new contribution to the analysis of the integration of agriculture into the industrialising societies of Europe. This book sets out to do just that.

In this introduction, we begin by reviewing the historiography of agricultural accounting. We stress the importance of considering accounting as a social practice. Here we make reference to the research of the school of 'new accounting history'.[16] Then we present the main achievements of earlier work on agricultural accounting. We look at accounting successively through textbooks and practices, a perspective which reflects, we think, the two dominant analytical orientations taken by researchers. Our review makes no pretension to being exhaustive. The literature on farm accounting, while still relatively limited, spans too many disciplines and countries for us to be able to encompass it all. We aim instead to elicit the major approaches to farm accounting and the debates which the chapters collected here respond to and complement. Following this overview, we will outline the chapters of the book. To conclude, after we have asked ourselves 'who has written and who is

13 Entitled 'Farmers that count: Standardisation and stewardship in farm accounting, eighteenth to twentieth century'.

14 The composition of rural elites, and their role in the spread of accounting, vary according to the political and economic contexts of the countries studied here. For a more general view of the role of elites in agricultural progress, see Nadine Vivier (ed.), *Élites et progrès agricole: XVIe–XXe siècle* (2009).

15 Ève Chiapello and Patrick Gilbert, *Sociologie des outils de gestion* (2020), pp. 29–30.

16 Peter Miller, Trevor Hopper, and Richard Laughlin, 'The new accounting history: An introduction', *Accounting, Organizations and Society* 16 (1991), pp. 395–403.

writing'[17] the history of agricultural accounting, we pave the way for future developments.

I

The term 'accounting' did not have a stable meaning in the period considered in this volume. The chapters therefore reflect changes in meaning and usage over time, with nuances depending on the country. Accounting historians have highlighted the gradual shift from the term 'book-keeping' to 'accounting'. Parker pointed out that the first term appeared in English-language book titles at the end of the seventeenth century, and became a widespread expression in the eighteenth, evoking the probable Dutch origin (*'boekhouden'*) of the term. The German expressions *'buchhalten'* and *'Buchhaltung'* appeared much earlier, in the sixteenth century.[18] In France, the term *'tenue des livres'* became part of the vocabulary of treatises published in the nineteenth century. Without going into the details of semantic evolutions, we may adopt Labardin and Nikitin's view that in both England and France the term 'book-keeping' has been gradually relegated to a subordinate status (the 'practical' part of accounting) which can be undertaken with little or no training. It is the act of recording individual transactions. Its demotion is closely linked to the appearance of formal accountancy training and the demand by accountants for recognition of their professional status in the second half of the nineteenth century. Accounting came to be defined as a 'science' responsible for the rational creation and coordination of accounts relating to an activity and the analysis of changes in capital.[19] In fact, the actual meaning and significance of accounting and book-keeping appear to have been actively negotiated in the historical cases discussed in this book.

II

What do accounts offer historians that justifies their reading of austere registers and ledgers? To answer this question, it is convenient to draw a fairly clear, yet simplistic, distinction between the two ways farm accounts have been used in the historiography. The most common approach is to

17 Questions precisely raised in Yannick Lemarchand and Robert Parker (eds), *Accounting in France: Historical essays/Etudes historiques* (1996).

18 R. H. Parker, 'Finding English words to talk about accounting concepts', *Accounting, Auditing and Accountability Journal* 7 (1994), pp. 70–85; idem, 'Reckoning, merchants' accounts, book-keeping, accounting or accountancy? The evidence of the long titles of books on accounting in English, 1543–1914', in B. Carsber and S. Dev (eds), *External financial reporting* (1984), pp. 109–22.

19 Pierre Labardin and Marc Nikitin, 'Accounting and the words to tell it: An historical perspective', *Accounting, Business and Financial History* 19 (2009), pp. 149–66.

consider them as a source. Historians (and other researchers) usually read a farm's accounts to learn about its situation in the local or global economy and to look at its productivity and financial performance.[20] The accounting archive that the historian treasures can also shed light on the 'ways of doing things', either the daily or seasonal pattern of work (and so employment), the sale of crops, investment or the long-term strategies employed by the farmer.[21] Records are rarely solely confined to the management of income and expenditure. They give the valuation of assets and calculations of the profitability of the crop or livestock speculations.[22] They can help to capture the decisions of landowners and farmers and their attitude towards innovations. They also provide otherwise scarce information on the social relationships forged in the setting of farming activity. Using farm accounts, historians handle 'the little numbers',[23] count, interpret, and deepen their knowledge of the farm operations by making careful cross-checks. It is also possible to take advantage of

20 Bethanie Afton, 'Investigating agricultural production and land productivity: Methodology and opportunities using English farm records', *Histoire & Mesure*, 15 (2000), pp. 233–45.

21 Michel de Certeau distinguishes two degrees of agency in these ways of doing things: 'strategies are capable of producing, squaring and imposing types of operations, whereas tactics can only use, manipulate and divert them'. Michel de Certeau, 'L'invention du quotidien: 1. Arts de faire', *Gallimard* (1990), p. 51.

22 In the modern era, farm registers vary widely in content. Very often, they mix everyday information with accounts and, sometimes, private memoranda. For a recent analysis of these heterogeneous writings, see Fulgence Delleaux (ed.), *La plume et la terre: Écrire sur son exploitation agricole en Europe occidentale (1650–1850)* (2021) and in particular the following chapters: Reiner Prass, 'Les écrits personnels de paysans et l'histoire économique: Pour un tour d'horizon dans l'historiographie de l'Allemagne préindustrielle', pp. 7–46; Jean-Marc Moriceau, 'A travers les comptes des grands fermiers du bassin parisien (1689–1884): Modèle de gestion ou mémorial familial?', pp. 99–124; Rosa Congost and Enric Sauger, 'Mémoires humbles: Les écrits des travailleurs agricoles comme témoignages du changement social (région de Gerone, Catalogne, XVIIIe siècle)', pp. 143–65. These literacy and numeracy practices were extended in the nineteenth and twentieth centuries through the keeping of diaries, specially designed to encourage farmers to write a daily account of their activities and their expenses and receipts. See here Nathalie Joly, 'Écritures du travail et savoirs paysans: Aperçu historique et lecture de pratiques: Les agendas des agriculteurs' (PhD Thesis, Université de Paris X: Nanterre, 1997); Philippe Madeline and Jean-Marc Moriceau, *Un paysan et son univers de la guerre au marché commun: À travers les agendas de Pierre Lebugle, cultivateur en Pays d'Auge* (2010).

23 To take up Annie Antoine's phrase in her reflection on the use of eighteenth-century accounts kept by small tenant farmers, Annie Antoine, 'Entre macro et micro: Les comptabilités agricoles du XVIIIe siècle', *Histoire & Mesure* 15 (2000), pp. 247–70.

non-accounting information, such as that relating to the hiring of labour,[24] in order to analyse labour relations and the place of bargaining in the relationship between farmer and labourer.[25] This down-to-earth approach using simple accounts has proved its worth, with research demonstrating how micro-economic descriptions can bring nuance to,[26] and even correct, some of the certainties established by long statistical series.[27]

A second way of studying accounts is to consider them as an object of investigation in themselves. The representativeness of the surviving accounts, though, may be extremely problematic.[28] Those who decide to address these questions – and they are few and far between – must have a taste for interdisciplinary dialogue. Since accounting is framed within social, organisational, and political contexts, they may find it necessary to invest in an array of concepts from different disciplines and new conceptual thinking. This is the case, for example, with the use of the core concept of 'practice', which tends to be deployed in a taken-for-granted manner while conceptual clarification is useful for analysing

24 Joyce Burnette, 'Seasonal patterns of agricultural day-labour at eight English farms, 1835–1844', in John Hatcher and Judy Stephenson (eds), *Seven centuries of unreal wages: The unreliable data, sources and methods that have been used for measuring standards of living in the past* (2018), pp. 195–225.

25 Rachel Pintus, 'La main d'œuvre d'une ferme du pays d'Ath: Le livre de comptes des Martin-Scaillez (fin XVIIIe–XIXe siècle)', in Delleaux (ed.), *La plume et la terre*, pp. 167–81.

26 Among others, M. E. Turner, J. V. Beckett, and Bethanie Afton, *Agricultural rent in England, 1690–1914* (2004); Jean-Marc Moriceau and Gilles Postel-Vinay, *Ferme, entreprise, famille: Grande exploitation et changements agricoles: Les Chartier, XVIIe–XIXe siècles* (1992).

27 Notably to counter the unreliability of statistical data at a national or provincial level and to revise established ideas about the backwardness of agriculture in a given place: Ramon Garrabou, Enric Saguer Hom, and Pere Sala López, 'Formas de gestión y evolución de la renta a partir del análisis de contabilidades agrarias: Los patrimonios del Marqués de Sentmenat en el Vallés y Urgell (1820–1917)', *Noticiario de historia agraria: Boletín informativo del Seminario de Historia Agraria* 5 (1993), pp. 97–125; María Teresa Pérez Picazo, 'Riqueza territorial y cambio agrícola en la Murcia del siglo XIX: Aproximación al estudio de una contabilidad privada (circa 1800–1902)', *Agricultura y sociedad* 61 (1991), pp. 39–96.

28 'The historian is constantly aware that transmission cannot be complete. What he is less aware of, however, because it is a barely perceptible fact, is the inequality of these losses. The consequence of this is not only that the quantity of our knowledge is reduced, but also that the proportions of our knowledge are distorted. We like to assume that a little of everything has reached us, as if it were impossible for whole, coherent parts, whole continents, to have sunk.' Arnold Esch, 'Chance et hasard de transmission', in Jean-Claude Schmitt and Otto Gerhard Oexle (eds), *Le problème de la représentativité et de la déformation de la transmission historique: Les tendances actuelles de l'histoire du Moyen Âge en France et en Allemagne. Actes des colloques de Sèvres* (1997), p. 15.

the relationship between social norms and the rule-structured practice of the individuals. The study of accounting reports may also call on highly specific methodologies such as codicology[29] or the ethnography of writing.[30] In short, the history of accounting, either agricultural, commercial, or industrial, is basically a way of *establishing dialogues* between different social sciences and, for those who take interdisciplinarity a step further, a chance to practise the art of comparison.[31]

The 'Foucauldian' or 'Critical' School of accounting history (also called 'New Accounting History') illustrates this multi-disciplinary fruitfulness. Building upon Michel Foucault's work on disciplines of the self and technologies of governmentality, a body of work from a number of researchers has re-examined the process through which accounting has assumed its modern forms.[32] Many aspects of the social functioning of accounting have been analysed through the lens of the influence of socio-political contexts on practices and techniques (and the other way round), and by studying the organisations that regulate and standardise accounting. Research on agricultural accounting is informed in various ways by these directions of analysis. As stressed by Massimo Sargiacomo *et al.*, the governmentality perspective can be applied to agriculture, 'thus echoing the prior Foucauldian interest in Physiocratic perspective'.[33] We therefore propose to take stock of agricultural accounting research at the junction of farming objectives and organisations and policy issues.

29 Claire Bustarret, 'Usages des supports d'écriture au XVIIIe siècle: Une esquisse codicologique', *Genesis. Manuscrits – Recherche – Invention*, 34 (2012), pp. 37–65.

30 From the seminal work of Jack Goody to the approaches of the 'New Literacy Studies', there is a well-established tradition of research in Britain, North America, and France, see David Barton and Uta Papen (eds), *The anthropology of writing: Understanding textually mediated worlds* (2010). See also, in the same volume, on the 'Writing farm' and accountability, Nathalie Joly, 'Tracing cows: Practical and administrative logics in tension', pp. 90–105.

31 Instead of juxtaposing investigations between history and anthropology, the historian Marcel Detienne proposes to conduct them jointly to develop an experimental and constructive comparativism. Marcel Detienne, 'L'art de construire des comparables: Entre historiens et anthropologues', *Critiques internationales* 1 (2002), pp. 68–78.

32 Sverre Raffnsøe *et al.*, 'The Foucault effect in Organization Studies', *Organization Studies*, 40 (2019), pp. 155–82. For a recent discussion of the contributions of this academic school, see Stephen P. Walker, 'Revisiting the roles of accounting in society', *Accounting, Organizations and Society* 49 (2016), pp. 41–50.

33 Massimo Sargiacomo *et al.*, 'Accounting and the government of the agricultural economy: Arrigo Serpieri and the reclamation consortia', *Accounting History Review* 26 (2016), pp. 307–31.

III

Accounting literature in the sense of practice manuals and textbooks is a key source for a range of researchers including historians, sociologists, and scholars of management. They can examine the writers' viewpoints and prescriptions for accounting systems as they co-evolve with farming practices and rural societies. They can also see how approaches to costing and valuation or the techniques of record-keeping have varied over time as much as the management of the workforce. Treatises, manuals, and textbooks of the early modern and modern era may be considered both as instruments and symptoms of the role that accounting was gradually acquiring in the functioning of the farm and in its relations with a set of external entities, amongst them state agencies and academia. Historians have noted the development of accounting literature in the first half of the nineteenth century without being able to assess it precisely.[34] The quantification of this literature is made more difficult by the fact that the titles of accounting handbooks do not systematically mention when they contain instructions and recording models specifically intended for agriculture. Economic and agronomic treatises can contain extensive explanations of accounting methods, followed by examples of completed accounts as part of comprehensive surveys of farming practice. In addition, the writings directed at a popular readership have barely been studied, but Joly has demonstrated the potential of studying popular manuals and agrarian catechisms, which offered technical knowledge, instructions as to how to keep accounts, and moral exhortations to practise regular book-keeping.[35] Although much more remains to be done, the historiography has established a number of reliable benchmarks concerning the importance of accountancy literature in different European countries.[36]

It is not surprising that a considerable diversity of accounting systems was recommended over time. Even if we restrict our analysis to the books

34 We have a much better view of the literature dealing with agriculture in general, as rural historians have systematised the study of these sources as a means of learning about innovations.

35 Nathalie Joly, 'Educating in economic calculus: The invention of the enlightened peasant via manuals of agriculture, 1830–1870', *Accounting History Review* 26 (2016), pp. 131–60.

36 For France, see the bibliographic reference database 'French bookkeeping and accounting treatises and manuals from 1657 to 1950' at http://www.msh.univ-nantes.fr/documentation/comptabilite/comptabiliteprivee/; for Italy, see the typology of accountancy literature from 1771 to 1922 proposed by Marie-Lucie Rossi, 'Une comptabilité industrielle: L'entreprise agricole du Pô à l'Arno (1826–1922)', in *Twelfth accounting and management history conference* (2007), pp. 29–30. For Britain, see Parker's inventory of English language treatises on double-entry accounting before 1850, mainly generalist and from the pens of teachers, Robert H. Parker, 'Roger North: Gentleman, accountant and lexicographer', *Accounting History* 2 (1997), pp. 31–51.

that discuss the accounts of estate owners, the purpose and the content of the records which landlords were advised to keep differed according to whether the owners leased out their land or farmed it in hand, a point which has been well illustrated in Edwards' detailed study of English accounting treatises from the seventeenth and eighteenth centuries.[37] In the early modern era, some writers, taking mercantile practice as their reference,[38] were convinced that estate accounting should be based squarely on the principles of Double-Entry Book-keeping (DEB) while others defended Charge and Discharge Accounting (CDA) saying it not only served as a check on stewards, but also generated cash flow information and the assessment of the current financial position of an estate.

The technique of Charge and Discharge Accounting, used since the Middle Ages for manorial administration, gradually fell into disfavour during the period of the so-called 'Agricultural Enlightenment'.[39] We will see in the next section that if CDA ceased to be recommended in the literature, it remained popular in practice. Its persistence in both estate and farm accounting has long puzzled historians. Putting aside the tricky interpretation of the durability of a method considered by many experts to be less suited to the calculation of financial performance, we can note the disagreements among accounting historians over the interpretation to be placed on the decline of the CDA in the accounting literature. There are two opposing views on this point: some consider the evolution of accounting techniques in terms of continuous progress – a teleological thought – and proceeding by 'natural selection', while others emphasise the social component of techniques, incorporating collective and individual issues.[40] For the former, CDA was no longer promoted as soon as DEB was available while, according to the latter, CDA continued to be employed because of a series of intertwined factors, amongst them a lack of economic competition and therefore of incentive to adopt a more complex technology, path dependency, and a possible prejudice against a mercantile method.[41]

37 J. R. Edwards, 'Accounting on English landed estates during the Agricultural Revolution: A textbook perspective', *Accounting Historians Journal* 38 (2011), pp. 1–45.

38 This is the case of the English treatises on double-entry book-keeping, which treat landed estates separately.

39 One must be cautious not to generalise since there are many nuances from one region to another.

40 On this controversial point, see Edwards, 'Accounting on English landed estates' and Yves Levant and Henri Zimnovitch, 'Overview of cost accounting practices in France from the early nineteenth century to the 1880s', *Accounting History* 27 (2022), pp. 576–606.

41 For instance, Lemarchand revealed a prejudice against techniques of mercantile accounting within governmental circles in late eighteenth-century France. This might be also the case in agriculture. Yannick Lemarchand,

Following the studies of Christian Licoppe,[42] Depecker and Joly investigated the evolution of regimes of knowledge in agricultural sciences in the eighteenth and nineteenth centuries. They stressed how the rise of quantification in agronomic science at the dawn of the nineteenth century has affected representations of farming processes.[43] The two sociologists related the development of agronomic accounting to the global evolution of science and dissemination of scientific thought and to the experimentation initiated in the first half of the sixteenth century which gained ground in agriculture during the nineteenth century. Researchers have also looked more directly at the role of accounting in managerial thought and action.[44] Indeed, in the late eighteenth and the first part of the nineteenth centuries, most agricultural writers were scientists attempting to convince large landowners of the superiority of the new agronomic techniques. They were also developing management techniques, since many of these authors managed at the same time model farms, and, for some of them, such as Thaer in Northern Germany and Mathieu de Dombasle in France, were the directors of agronomic training institutions. The search for optimal profitability required the setting up of experiments – on tillage, crop rotation, livestock feeding and so on – and simultaneously, the designing of sophisticated accounting systems.[45]

A well-known hypothesis, traditionally associated with prominent sociologists such as Werner Sombart and Max Weber and with the economist Marx, connects the use of DEB with the birth of 'capitalist spirit'.[46] Historians of farm accounting have also linked the advocacy of new accounting practices by the likes of Arthur Young with the rise

'Double entry versus charge and discharge accounting in eighteenth-century France', *Accounting, Business and Financial History* 4 (1994), pp. 119–45.

42 For a landmark work on the history of science experiments, see Christian Licoppe, *La formation de la pratique scientifique: Le discours de l'expérience en France et en Angleterre (1630–1820)* (2013).

43 Thomas Depecker and Nathalie Joly, 'Agronomists and accounting: The beginnings of capitalist rationalisation on the farm (1800–1850)', *Historia Agraria* (2015), pp. 75–94.

44 Nathalie Joly, René Bourrigaud, and Fabien Knittel, 'Administrer une ferme-modèle au xixe siècle: Deux expériences d'agronomes entrepreneurs ruraux, Mathieu de Dombasle et Rieffel', *Entreprises et histoire* 3 (2017), pp. 21–36.

45 Thomas Depecker and François Vatin, 'Taking stock to yield a return: Agricultural accounting, agronomometry and chemical statics in the early-nineteenth century', *Accounting History Review* 26 (2016), pp. 107–29; Markus Lampe and Paul Sharp, 'A quest for useful knowledge: The early development of agricultural accounting in Denmark and northern Germany', *Accounting History Review* 27 (2017), pp. 73–99; Thomas Depecker and Nathalie Joly, 'La terre et ses manufacturiers: L'introduction d'une raison gestionnaire dans les domaines agricoles (1800–1850)', *Entreprises et histoire* 79 (2015), pp. 12–23.

46 For more on Sombart, Weber and Marx's views on the birth of capitalism and the invention of double-entry bookkeeping, see Eve Chiapello, 'Accounting

of capitalist farming.[47] In fact, if DEB does not seem so obviously and intrinsically connected to a business-like attitude, it nevertheless enables the rationalisation of both the technical means of production and the social relations in farming, as Depecker and Joly have stressed. Hence Carruthers and Espeland consider the advocacy for DEB essentially as powerful rhetoric: it gave legitimacy to capitalist farming and by doing so, might have profoundly altered the way actors interpreted and understood their economic operations and results.[48]

At any rate, it seems that agricultural accounting historians have given disproportionate importance to double-entry book-keeping, although some of them have pointed out the existence of widespread doubts on the practicality and effectiveness of this technique.[49] This penchant has created a degree of bias in the literature.[50] Textbooks that advocate single-entry book-keeping have received very little attention, especially those originating from non-academic writers. In her study of the popular manuals that received prizes from the French Ministry of Agriculture during the July Monarchy, Joly has shown the existence of a body of 'enlightened landowners' presenting their views on accounting systems adapted to medium-sized and small properties. These were sometimes only simple income and expenditure accounts supplemented by a few

and the birth of the notion of capitalism', *Critical perspectives on accounting* 18 (2007), pp. 263–96.

47 For Marx, the 'capitalist mentality' pursues the rate of return on capital employed in production by extracting surplus value from the sale of commodities or services produced by wage labour. Taking this definition as a key to analysing the English revolution, Bryer has argued that Marx's prediction came true, as evidenced by English farmers' accounts from the seventeenth to the nineteenth century. Rob A. Bryer, 'The genesis of the capitalist farmer: Towards a Marxist accounting history of the origins of the English agricultural revolution', *Critical Perspectives on Accounting* 17 (2006), pp. 367–97.

48 Rhetoric is defined as 'techniques that are used to make a convincing or persuasive argument'. Bruce G. Carruthers and Wendy Nelson Espeland, 'Accounting for rationality: Double-entry bookkeeping and the rhetoric of economic rationality', *American Journal of Sociology* 97 (1991), pp. 31–69.

49 For an English example, Michael Turner, J. V. Beckett, and Bethanie Afton, *Farm production in England 1700–1914* (2001), p. 49.

50 The English language accounting history literature is relatively abundant in general as is the agricultural history of accounting, which may also contribute to this bias, as DEB had been adopted at an early date by merchants and then transferred to the large estates of England and Scotland. Edwards corrected this view by showing that during the nineteenth century, French writers considerably advanced the study of cost accounting in relation to agriculture, Ronald S. Edwards, 'A survey of French contributions to the study of cost accounting during the nineteenth century', repr. in Yannick Lemarchand and Robert Parker (eds), *Accounting in France: Historical essays/études historiques* (1996), pp. 155–90.

auxiliary books for tracking production, but the methods were apparently being put into practice on their own lands.[51]

Critiques of the DEB technique began to increase in the second half of the nineteenth century. The French controversy surrounding Mathieu de Dombasle's accounting model was a striking example: it gave rise to over forty-five articles in the professional press and bitterly divided some fifteen authors (scholars and landowners) over a seven-year period starting in the early 1870s.[52] A similar controversy took place in Switzerland.[53] Debates on the appropriate kind of accounting to be taught to farmers continued into the early twentieth century, with the emphasis on systems of simplified accounting for the use of smallholders apparently growing, especially in the German-speaking countries.[54] While farm accounting theory of the late nineteenth and twentieth centuries has been discussed mostly as part of the broader literature on agricultural economics, itself not very abundant, two topics have nevertheless been highlighted by the historiography of farm accounting: costing, especially in relation to the intricacies of mixed farming, and land valuation.[55] Retrospectively introducing the German debate to his readers in the US, Karl Brandt singled out these two topics as the main battlefield of agricultural economists.[56] Costing, which appeared as a problem in agricultural accounting as early as the eighteenth century, developed from the late nineteenth century and had an obvious impact on decisions about crops and technologies.[57] The importance of the debates on land valuation, a large part of the farm's capital, was stressed by Walter Achilles and more recently by D'Onofrio,

51 Joly, 'Educating in economic calculus'.

52 Yannick Lemarchand, Yves Levant, and Henri Zimnovitch, '"Schisme à Grignon": Autour de la comptabilité agricole, durant les années 1870', *Entreprises et histoire* 88 (2017), p. 37.

53 Juri Auderset and Peter Moser, *Die Agrarfrage in der Industriegesellschaft: Wissenskulturen, Machtverhältnisse und natürliche Ressourcen in der agrarisch-industriellen Wissensgesellschaft (1850–1950)* (2018), p. 61.

54 See, for instance in the classic texts: Sigmund von Frauendorfer, *Ideengeschichte der Agrarwirtschaft und Agrarpolitik im deutschen Sprachgebiet: Von den Anfängen bis zum ersten Weltkrieg* (1957) and Joosep Nõu, *The development of agricultural economics in Europe* (1967).

55 Roger Juchau and Paul Hill, 'Agricultural cost accounting development in Britain: The contributions of three men from Wye: A review note', *Accounting, Business and Financial History* 8 (1998), pp. 165–74.

56 Karl Brandt, 'Land valuation in Germany', *Journal of Farm Economics* 19 (1937), pp. 173–87.

57 According to Lemarchand, Levant, and Zimnovitch, agricultural accounting books published at the beginning of the nineteenth century in France had 'a level of reflection and a degree of sophistication exceeding what we then encounter in industrial accounting manuals', Lemarchand, Levant, and Zimnovitch, '"Schisme à Grignon"', p. 38.

who showed how valuation theory underpinned the political position of German landowners and Italian fascists.[58]

This dynamism in accounting thought may seem, however, to be in contrast with actual practices. The question of whether accounting books were read outside the limited circle of agronomists, large landowners, and professional accountants is difficult to answer, but James Fisher's analysis of agricultural books can be applied more generally to the literature of accounting of the early modern and modern period.[59] In both cases, the aim was to reform rural practices, that is to impose the views of an intellectual elite on the mass of practitioners. Such a project was obviously bound to cause misunderstandings and even rejection. There is also an epistemological question that relates to 'the technical difficulties in the development and use of written knowledge, requiring the translation from practice to text, then back into practice; both the codification of a practical art and the decoding of written instructions'.[60] It may be argued that accounting techniques, unlike knowledge about crops and nutrients, avoid the problem of adapting generic knowledge to a specific local environment, which is a major difficulty for agronomic knowledge. But the question nevertheless arises of the gap between the logic of design, which aims for an ideal of formal rigour, and the logic of use, by nature idiosyncratic and depending on practical contingencies. The work in the following section provides an insight into the heterogeneous rationales of accounting practice.

IV

A distinction appears in the historiography between the accounting of estate holders and that of yeomen, farmers, or sharecroppers, the former often highly formalised while the latter was more narrative in form.[61]

58 Walter Achilles, 'Betriebswirtschaftliche Leitbilder in der ostdeutschen Gutswirtschaft seit dem Ende des 19. Jahrhunderts', in Heinz Reif (ed.), *Ostelbische agrargesellschaft im Kaiserreich und in der weimarer Republik: Agrarkrise – junkerliche Interessenpolitik – Modernisierungstrategien* (1994), pp. 190–212. For a similar argument: Federico D'Onofrio, 'The microfoundations of Italian agrarianism: Italian agricultural economists and fascism', *Agricultural History* 91 (2017), p. 369. On land valuation, see also the discussion of Ernesto Marenghi, in Alberto Gabba (ed.), *Aspetti evolutivi della scienza estimativa: Seminario in onore di Ernesto Marenghi* (1995).

59 James D. Fisher, *The enclosure of knowledge: Books, power and agrarian capitalism in Britain, 1660–1800* (2022).

60 Ibid., pp. 15–16.

61 The difference between yeomen, farmers, and sharecroppers relates to their different land tenure. Yeomen are farmers who work on their own land, farmers in this restricted sense are renting the land by paying a monetary rent, while sharecroppers shared harvest with their landlords.

As Turner, Beckett, and Afton claimed in the case of England in the early modern period (but similar observations can be found elsewhere), farmers produced not only fewer records, but also different records. The authors stressed the correlation between the type of holding and the characteristics of farm records: farm records were 'individualistic' or even 'idiosyncratic' when farmers were autonomously running their farm, but became increasingly formalised with the need for accountability, whenever farmers or farm bailiffs were reporting to an owner or an estate administration.[62]

Accounting historians have therefore often focused on the relatively sophisticated accounting systems of complex, market-oriented estates. They have insisted that the new calculative mentalities and practices were inscribed in the general transformation of European agriculture that began, arguably, in the late seventeenth century.

Large aristocratic estates of this period were often managed from a distance and thus developed a variety of forms of record keeping and control mechanisms.[63] Scholars have examined the accounting practices associated with the evolution of the manorial system and of the relationships between the landlord, the bailiff, or the tenant at the turn of the agricultural revolution. Performance measurement was twofold: it focused on the estate's production and on the agent's behaviour, as the latter was accountable for his decisions.[64] Thus the study of accounts and their associated correspondence provides information on the ways in which supervision was exercised (and how the agent tried to protect himself from supervision), as much as on the productivity of the land, the amount of the rents, the surplus, and a variety of daily concerns. The study of sharecroppers' accounts held by landowners in western France during the eighteenth century confirms the relationship between surviving records and reporting. Annie Antoine found it was landowners who kept accounts and naturally they focused on the owner's share. Accounts therefore appear as part of the informative infrastructure of

62 Turner, Beckett, and Afton, *Farm production in England, 1700–1914*, p. 51. A similar connection between accountability and the abundance of records due to tenancy systems was detected in early modern and modern Tuscany by Reginaldo Cianferoni, 'Gli antichi libri contabili delle fattorie quali fonti della storia dell'agricoltura e dell'economia toscana: Metodi e problemi della loro utilizzazione', *Storia dell'agricoltura* 13 (1973), pp. 47–76.

63 David Oldroyd, *Estates, enterprise and investment at the dawn of the industrial revolution: Estate management and accounting in the north-east of England, c. 1700–1780* (2017); Valerio Antonelli *et al.*, 'The roles of accounting in agro-pastoral settings: The case of the landed estates of Prince Sambiase in the mid-eighteenth century', *Accounting Historians Journal* 46 (2019), pp. 1–18.

64 P. D. A. Harvey, 'Manorial accounts', in R. H. Parker and B. S. Yamey (eds), *Accounting history: Some British contributions* (1994), pp. 91–115.

tenancy.[65] In Italy and Spain, sharecropping contracts created the conditions for the production and survival of the complex accounts of the large estates of the nineteenth and twentieth centuries.[66]

While some of these estates adopted double-entry book-keeping, a majority of the farm businesses which have been studied kept single-entry registers. In England, for instance, charge and discharge accounting remained usual and dominates the surviving accounts.[67] In nineteenth- and twentieth-century Spain and Tuscany, in the context of large commercially oriented estates, single-entry books prevailed amongst the sources. In the case of Tuscany, as well as Catalonia, whilst the accounts could be analysed in order to reveal the profitability of farms and crops, their main role seems to have been to track the relations between the different actors of production: landlords, administrators, farmers, in line with the person-focused accounting systems of the period. Even where double-entry book-keeping was adopted, it was part of a broader system of record-keeping. Antonelli *et al.*, for instance, highlight the use of tallies on the southern Italian domains of the Prince of Sambiase, whose administration employed both very advanced and very primitive tools for record-keeping.[68]

The questions posed by the accounting records of farmers who did not report to a landlord are distinctive. The idiosyncratic nature of their book-keeping may well have hindered their study by economic historians. The absence of basic information, deemed unnecessary to be recorded by the farmer (such as hectares owned, number of workers under his roof) makes it impossible to calculate farm productivity and performance. The muddled arrangement of the records frequently makes them difficult to understand and use. Where farm accountants were both scholars and scrupulous managers, as much as they were writers and fervent prescribers, accounting practice loses some of its obscurity, making it possible for the historian to employ exceptional sets of records such as those of the model farms of Moëglin, Roville, Hofwyl, Sampford Hall,

65 Antoine, 'Entre macro et micro'.

66 Jordi Planas and Enric Saguer, 'Accounting records of large rural estates and the dynamics of agriculture in Catalonia (Spain), 1850–1950', *Accounting, Business & Financial History* 15 (2005), pp. 171–85; Riccardo Mussari and Michela Magliacani, 'Agricultural accounting in the nineteenth and early twentieth centuries: The case of the noble Rucellai family farm in Campi', *Accounting, Business and Financial History* 17 (2007), pp. 87–103; Marie-Lucie Rossi, 'Une entreprise agricole à la recherche du profit optimum: La Casa Spalletti en Italie au XIXe siècle', *Comptabilités: Revue d'histoire des comptabilités* https://journals.openedition.org/comptabilites/1349; idem, 'Les archives agricoles de la Casa Spalletti en Italie (1821–1922): Conserver pour entreprendre', *Gazette des archives* 213 (2009), pp. 103–17.

67 Harvey, 'Manorial accounts'.

68 Antonelli *et al.*, 'The roles of accounting in agro-pastoral settings'.

and so on.[69] The accounting records of the ordinary farmer, by contrast, remain difficult to get to grips with, and somewhat bewildering.[70] Turner, Beckett, and Afton have also questioned the farmers' commitment to financial accounting:

> Evidence of a pragmatic attitude of farmers to their records can be found in the printed account books. While these provided space for all aspects of agricultural production, many farmers felt no obligation to fill in the columns and pages. Thus, even these printed volumes demonstrate the fact that farm records are highly individualistic documents.[71]

The accounts (1697–1745) of an English yeoman farmer discussed by Lee and Osborne are representative of these overly complex sources.[72] The jumbling of debit and credit entries in a ledger kept over two generations disturbed the two historians. Noting the chasm that separates this day-by-day account entry from the standard bilateral recording form, they see it as a form of 'primitive accounting', whose main interest lies at a socio-historical level rather than an economic one.

In fact, this does not mean that independent farmers were necessarily less profit-oriented than estate-holders but they gave additional functions to their records, for instance recording goods and services paid for by barter,[73] deferred payment agreements with partners, discounts

69 Respectively by Albrecht Thaer, Matthieu de Dombasle, Philipp Emanuel von Fellenberg, and Arthur Young.

70 Unlike the historian, the ethnographer can benefit from the commentary of living authors to decipher the inscriptions of ordinary records and to penetrate the cognitive reasoning based on them. For example, Joly has shown how farmers build up a routine calendar by noting their work activities and the weather, through discussions of the contents of diaries (kept around the mid-twentieth century) with their owners, Nathalie Joly, 'Écrire l'événement: Le travail agricole mis en mémoire', *Sociologie du travail* 46 (2004), pp. 511–27.

71 Turner, Beckett, and Afton, *Farm production in England, 1700–1914*, p. 62. Similar remarks, underlining the informal, idiosyncratic, unsystematic character of surviving accounts of independent farmers (and the importance of *Anschreibebuecher*) can be found in Walter Achilles, 'Landwirtschaft in der frühen Neuzeit', in *Landwirtschaft in der frühen Neuzeit* (2010), pp. 76–7; Thijs Lambrecht, 'Reciprocal exchange, credit and cash: Agricultural labour markets and local economies in the southern Low Countries during the eighteenth century', *Continuity and Change* 18 (2003), pp. 237–61.

72 Geoffrey A. Lee and Richard H. Osborne, 'The account book of a Derbyshire farm of the eighteenth century', *Accounting, Business and Financial History* 4 (1994), pp. 147–62.

73 For Densmore, given the prevalence of barter in the rural economy in early nineteenth-century America, 'it is hard to imagine how any farmer or artisan could have functioned without a bookkeeping system'. Christopher Densmore, 'Understanding and using early nineteenth-century account books', *The Midwestern Archivist* 5 (1980), p. 5.

granted, work done or to be done, and so on.[74] For example, the ledger of a moderately wealthy French farmer, François Jacques Maret, who was running a wide range of activities (farming, vineyards, fish, services) in the eighteenth century, reveals an entrepreneur well aware of his profits and losses. He wanted to know exactly how much he was able to borrow (and repay) from various creditors to support his speculations in sheep farming.[75]

Indeed, it is other branches of history (rural history and cultural history) and related disciplines (rural sociology and ethnology) which have extensively studied farm accounts in all their diverse forms and functions. Today, we have solid evidence of practices that spread throughout agriculture as literacy levels rose, with accounts kept in narrative form first by intermediate social groups (ploughmen) during the eighteenth century, then by the broadest strata of the peasantry from the second half of the nineteenth century. Scholars have scrutinised the contents of the *livres de raison* (France),[76] the *Anschreibebücher* (Germany),[77] the *ricordi* and *ricordanze* (Italy),[78] and the the day-books or diaries (America and other countries)[79] kept by farmers. Mouysset reminds us that these genres of

74 For a stimulating reflection on the possible uses of the ordering of words and things into farm registers, see Sylvie Mouysset, 'Penser/classer: La passion de la liste dans quelques livres de raison du Midi de la France à l'époque moderne', in Michel Cassan, Jean-Pierre Bardet, and François-Joseph Ruggiu (eds), *Les écrits du for privé: Objets matériels, objets édités: actes du colloque de Limoges, 17 et 18 novembre 2005* (2007), pp. 151–66.

75 Bernard Bodinier, 'Un journal paysan du XVIIIe siècle: Le livre de recettes et dépenses de François Jacques Maret, laboureur et vigneron à Bueil (Eure), de 1730 à 1761. 1ère partie', *Histoire & Sociétés Rurales* 40 (2013), pp. 97–154.

76 In France, the syntheses available do not specifically focus on the landowners' *livres de raison*. However, historians have offered monographic studies of examples of these documents found in public or private archives. For a review of these works, see Nathalie Joly, Thomas Depecker, and Julie Labatut, 'L'entreprise agricole et sa gestion: Ethos, structures et instruments (XIXe–XXe siècle)', *Entreprises et Histoire* 88 (2017), pp. 6–20.

77 Hopf-Droste proposed this term of 'Anschreibebuch' to describe a mode of writing usually adopted by peasant farmers, as much as in the merchants' profession since the fifteenth century with the keeping of the 'Memorial', that is a document which recorded transactions chronologically, without any thematic ordering. Marie-Luise Hopf-Droste, 'Vorbilder, Formen und Funktionen ländlicher Anschreibebücher', in Helmut Ottenjann and Günter Wiegelmann (eds), *Alte Tagebücher und Anschreibebücher: Quellen zum Alltag der ländlichen Bevölkerung in Nordwesteuropa* (1982), pp. 61–84.

78 Raul Mordenti, *I libri di famiglia in Italia, II, Geografia e Storia* (2001) and idem, 'Les livres de famille en Italie', *Annales, Histoire, Sciences Sociales* 59 (2004), pp. 785–804.

79 For America (southern Minnesota in the years 1856–76), see Rodney C. Loehr, 'Farmers' diaries: Their interest and value as historical sources', *Agricultural History* 12 (1938), pp. 313–25; Everett E. Edwards, 'Agricultural records; Their

writing obey 'a set of writing rules established in the fifteenth century and maintained until the nineteenth century, from Pacioli to Napoleon, permanently shaping the writing of accounts'.[80] In fact, the *livre de raison* was organised in a similar way to the *brouillard*.

> In the *brouillard* or *memorial*, also called main-courante from the end of the eighteenth century (*memoriale* or *squartafolio* in Italy, *memorial* or *borrador* in Spain, *waste book* in Great Britain), all transactions are recorded in chronological order and in narrative form, without necessarily worrying about the accounts concerned and how they will be moved.[81]

By examining eighteenth-century trade dictionaries, Joly demonstrated that

> ... the use of the compound words '*agenda-mémorial*' or '*agenda-brouillard*' reflected traders' habit of recording their transactions in a pocket-sized document, the *agenda*, and this use made its way into agriculture, with treatises on rural accounting of the nineteenth century recommending to keep a waste book.[82]

The historiography on peasant diaries is relatively extensive throughout Europe.[83] It sparked a discussion concerning the specific nature of 'daily accounts', which has been more recently revived by studies of 'moral accounting' as a tool for improving character and regulating behaviour based on objective calculations.[84] To encourage this daily writing habit,

---

nature and value for research', *Agricultural History* 13 (1939), pp. 1–12. See B. H. Slicher van Bath, 'Accounts and diaries of farmers before 1800', *Afdeling Agrarische Geschiedenis Bijdragen* 8 (1962), pp. 5–33.

80 Sylvie Mouysset, *Papiers de famille: Introduction à l'étude des livres de raison (France, XVe–XIXe s.)* (2007), p. 37.

81 Yannick Lemarchand, 'Journal-livre journal (XVIIIs.)', in Didier Bensadon, Nicolas Praquin, and Béatrice Touchelay (eds), *Dictionnaire historique de comptabilité des entreprises* (2016), pp. 389–90.

82 Nathalie Joly, 'L'organisation comptable dans les grandes exploitations françaises (XVIIe s.-milieu XIXe s.)', in Bensadon *et al.* (eds), *Dictionnaire historique de comptabilité des entreprises*, pp. 438–41. For an account of French agricultural treatises recommending the use of the 'livre de raison' from the end of the fifteenth to the eighteenth centuries and their role in the private economy and in regulating the conduct of daily life, see Jean-Marie Barbier, *Le quotidien et son économie* (1981), pp. 19–54.

83 German works have been well considered in Klaus-Joachim Lorenzen-Schmidt and Bjørn Poulsen (eds), *Bäuerliche Anschreibebücher als Quellen zur Wirtschaftsgeschichte* (1992). For a more recent overview, see Prass, 'Les écrits personnels de paysans et l'histoire économique', in Delleaux (ed.), *La plume et la terre*, pp. 27–46.

84 Harro Maas, '*Letts* calculate: Moral accounting in the Victorian period', *History of Political Economy* 48, suppl. 1 (2016), pp. 16–43; idem, 'Monitoring

almanacks and pocket diaries were made widely available. Agriculture was not left behind. As early as the end of the nineteenth century, publishers and agricultural unions began distributing inexpensive books in these formats specifically designed for farmers and their wives.[85] Their success continued unabated throughout Europe during the twentieth century.[86] Although the dissemination of these tools is part of a desire to discipline economic behaviour, it is not limited to it (a point elaborated in chapter seven in this volume on 'Women that Count'). The 'chronicles' that the use of an agenda or almanack encouraged on the farm gradually became 'a way for learning about and reflecting on farm work'.[87]

We would like to insist on the distinction between practices and models. As Hoggart established with regard to the working class and its reception of instructions from the mass media,[88] landowners and farmers paid only 'oblique attention' to the models of accounts proposed to them. Their conduct revealed a casual adherence to prescriptions, with some of the recommended techniques being readily adopted while others were kept at arm's length or even rejected outright. Moreover, the uses that rural elites and scholars saw for book-keeping were not the same as those that motivated landowners to keep accounts. Christopher Napier suggested that for aristocratic landowners accounting was subservient to the maintenance of patterns of conspicuous consumption, rather than a means for the assessment of profit.[89] Certainly maintaining accounts did not prevent aristocrats from overspending and in some cases going bankrupt. For middling and small farms, with little room for manoeuvre, and more subject to fluctuations in harvests, labour costs, and crop prices, their accounts could well be seen as a safeguard against dishonesty in commercial transactions, as payments were rarely made immediately in cash but at the end of periods of credit. And for

---

the self: François-Marc-Louis Naville and his moral tables', *History of Science* 58 (2020), pp. 117–41.

85 To take a French example, 'the nascent and soon powerful *Union du Sud-est des syndicats agricoles* (1892) took over the publishing of an almanack, whose circulation reached 20,000 the following year and which sold at 10 centimes'. The number of copies produced annually soared to several hundred thousand. Nathalie Joly, 'Shaping records on the farm: Agricultural record keeping in France from the nineteenth century to the Liberation', *Agricultural History Review* 59 (2011), p. 71.

86 In Italy, see Manuel Vaquero Piñeiro, 'Readings for farmers: Agrarian almanacs in Italy from the eighteenth to the twentieth century', *Agricultural History Review* 63 (2015), pp. 243–64.

87 Nathalie Joly, 'Vaches et blés sur le papier: Socialisations à l'écrit du monde agricole', *Communication & Langages* 1 (2009), pp. 77–90.

88 Richard Hoggart, *The uses of literacy: Aspects of working-class life* (1967).

89 Christopher J. Napier, 'Aristocratic accounting: The Bute Estate in Glamorgan, 1814–1880', *Accounting and Business Research* 21 (1991), p. 164.

those who wanted to round out their assets, consolidate or improve their income, and then invest, accounting was certainly one of the surest ways to success. Plus, the social respect conferred by well-kept accounts may also have motivated those with entrepreneurial ambitions, as in the case of François Jacques Maret, the ploughman mentioned earlier. Ultimately, accounting norms seemed to be fully integrated into the pattern of lives and social experience.

Efforts to spread formal accounting through the educational system at all levels gained momentum throughout the nineteenth century (particularly in its second half) and into the early twentieth century.[90] The historiography of the modernisation of agriculture tracks these efforts, stressing the role of farmers' associations and extension services.[91] Scholars tend to postulate the adoption of these new practices as an element in the productivity increase that characterised the 'first European green revolution' from the late nineteenth century onwards.[92] Nevertheless, this reasoning has been reversed by Daan Hendrikx and Oscar Gelderblom, who questioned the actual contribution provided by formalised accounting practices (DEB in particular) to the growth of agricultural productivity and claimed that smallholders, unlike estate owners, 'kept track of operations through mental accounting, as often as not supported by simple recordings in private notebooks or the accounts kept by local shopkeepers, artisans, and other suppliers'.[93] If the utility of accounting for the management of small farms can be questioned, how do we explain its importance in the thinking of experts and farmers' leaders?

Accounting historians have underlined the growing role of organisations and institutions outside the farm or the estate. Studies of nineteenth-century estates in Italy have shown the importance of legally mandatory prescriptions (*libretto colonico*), but the role of the government seems to have generally grown, not only in Europe and not only through direct regulations. As part of the general effort to 'govern the rural',[94]

90 On the Tuscan Colle Meleto, Rossano Pazzagli, 'Scuole d'agricoltura e poderi sperimentali: Agronomia, istruzione e progresso tecnico nella prima meta dell'800' (Thesis Fiesole, European University Institute, 1989).

91 Harm Zwarts, 'Knowledge, networks and niches: Dutch agricultural innovation in an international perspective, *c.* 1880–1970' (Thesis, Wageningen University, 2021), p. 109, who also defends the usefulness of accounting for farmers, relying on the work of Peter Jones on Scotland, Paul Sharp and Markus Lampe on Denmark, and Merijn Knibe and Marijn Molema on Frisland.

92 Lampe and Sharp, 'Quest for Useful Knowledge', p. 74.

93 Daan Hendrikx and Oscar Gelderblom, 'Accounting for agricultural development? The case of the Netherlands, 1840–1940', *Agricultural History Review* 70 (2022), pp. 23–48.

94 Liesbeth van de Grift and Amalia Ribi Forclaz (eds), *Governing the rural in interwar Europe* (2017).

policies increasingly required farmers to keep accounts in order to receive subsidies and participate in the broader processes of economic centralisation. Stephen Walker thus highlighted the importance of farm accounting in supporting the policies of the New Deal,[95] while Hendrikx and Gelderblom stressed the importance of government pressure, rather than the internal managerial needs of the farm, as a driver for the adoption of financial accounting practices amongst the middle strata of Dutch farmers. According to them, it was the introduction of an income tax that generalised the use of tools to calculate profit. More radically, Martha Lampland, looking at socialist Hungary, has argued that recording practices may be useful even when the numbers returned are false, because of their significance within the system of planning.[96]

There are thus contrasting analyses of the links between the development of accounting and the modernisation process, and dissenting interpretations of the roles of social actors. This volume covers the whole range of different approaches.

V

The chapters collected in this book are grouped in three sections. Together they track changes in the literature about accounting and the spread of new practices between the eighteenth and the twentieth centuries. They cover a period marked by great transformations in agricultural practice: the social and technical innovations of the seventeenth and eighteenth centuries, with the adoption of new farming systems on the large estates of western Europe, and 'the first green revolution', characterised by the 'marked rise of the small family farm' and the spread of artificial fertilisers between 1870 and 1914.[97] These two so-called revolutions are but the most evident episodes of broader modernisation processes that moulded European agriculture. This edited volume tries to shed light on the role of accounting in these processes, and stresses the emergence of the accounting farmer as the ideal agent of agricultural change.

The first part of the book shows the remarkable complexity of the models proposed to farmers by advocates and practitioners of accounting since the eighteenth century. In the wake of pioneering works on the capitalist rationalisation of the farm published at the dawn of the

95 Stephen P. Walker, 'Accounting and rural rehabilitation in New Deal America', *Accounting, Organizations and Society* 39 (2014), pp. 208–35.

96 Martha Lampland, 'False numbers as formalizing practices', *Social Studies of Science* 40 (2010), pp. 377–404.

97 Jan Luiten van Zanden, 'The first Green Revolution: The growth of production and productivity in European agriculture, 1870–1914', *Economic History Review* 44 (1991), pp. 215–39.

nineteenth century,[98] the chapters track the process of rationalisation initiated at varying speeds across Europe from the late eighteenth century onwards, with a focus on accounting. Fisher evokes the classic principal–agent problem, by showing how accounting, in the work of Arthur Young and William Marshall, was meant to enable a closer control of the workforce and of the bailiffs, and locates such practices in the context of the capitalist transformation of English agriculture in the eighteenth century. In his Marxist perspective, capitalism corresponds to a particular configuration of labour relations. Improved accounting represented a key technique for labour management. The quest for an improved efficiency of farming, though, did not only affect the relationships between owners, managers, and workers but extended to the relations between managers and labourers.

Indeed, the accountability of farm or estate managers to the landlord, whether the English gentleman or the German aristocrat, emerges as a main driver not just of accounting theory, as in Young and Marshall, but also of the actual practice. Scholten-Buschhoff puts the *Rentmeister* at the core of her analysis of the rationalisation and formalisation of the management of manorial estates in Germany. Through the examination of the records of five aristocratic estates in Westphalia and Rhineland between 1650 and 1850, Scholten-Buschhoff tracks the managerial innovations which led to greater transparency and uniformity in the administration of the estate. In particular, she stresses how rationalisation and formalisation accelerated from the eighteenth century, with the establishment of double-entry book-keeping and commercial accounting. She restates the importance of interpreting accounts within a broader constellation of sources, especially correspondence, by showing how the reporting of manager to landowner intensified and landlords tried to exert a stricter control over their properties.

In Hoyle's chapter we see instead another aspect of the rationalisation of farming, namely the experiments conducted by Young. As a study by Roger Juchau demonstrates, cost accounting was crucial to assess the profitability of different farming systems and the various innovations that Young and other protagonists of the 'agricultural enlightenment' advocated.[99] Hoyle continues by discussing aspects of the advocacy and use of farm accounts in late eighteenth- and early nineteenth-century England, stressing the gulf in practice between common farmers and farms run by bailiffs who accounted to their employers.

The topics of the second part of this book extend well into the nineteenth century and demonstrate that the relationship between modernisation,

98 Depecker and Joly, 'Agronomists and accounting'; Joly, 'Educating in economic calculus'.

99 Juchau, 'Early cost accounting ideas in agriculture: The contributions of Arthur Young', *Accounting, Business & Financial History* 12,3 (2002), 369–86'.

rationalisation, and accounting practices was far from univocal, with multiple needs, amongst them improved farm management, converging in the adoption of sophisticated accounting techniques. Fulgence Delleaux describes the exceptional complexity of the accounting system adopted by the landholding families around Geneva in the early eighteenth century. While he deals with the accounts of some of the major personalities of the city during the Enlightenment, Delleaux explains the extraordinarily intricate and very comprehensive record systems of the patricians in terms of religious needs rather than managerial necessity.

It would be a mistake though to imagine that the *stricto sensu* agricultural business can be insulated from the increasingly industrial society that surrounded it. As Laurent Herment shows in his chapter, farm accounting may reveal the integration of the farm into broader production processes. Its results can therefore only be interpreted in the light of the other interests of their owners. Herment's meticulous examination of the records of two farms owned by Adolphe Dailly over the 1860s enables him to demonstrate that the accounting principles adopted on the farms only made sense when the farms are considered as being integrated into the other parts of Dailly's business empire, including his interests in Parisian public transport.

Nathalie Joly's chapter serves as a link between the first two parts of the book and the third. She shows how the political imperatives of modernising the middling peasantry became pre-eminent in the first half of the nineteenth century in France. The chapter examines the educational literature being circulated, especially that directed to women and girls in farming families from the second half of the eighteenth century to the second half of the nineteenth. It describes how, especially in the 1820s and 1830s, an increasing number of books (authored by both men and women) on the topic of the contribution of women to the economy of the farm provided models of simple accounting techniques in an attempt, Joly argues, to familiarise women with the idea of profit and in turn to adapt and integrate family farms into a modern economy. Such literature, which is overall essentially prescriptive, is, however, not uniform: some writers underpinned the agency of women where others tried to use women to buttress the masculine order of nineteenth-century society.

These publications are therefore to be considered within the framework of a general effort to improve the conditions of the peasantry and transform farming through the moral and technical education of the masses. Unlike the treatises by the great agronomists of the eighteenth and nineteenth centuries, this literature did not target estate holders and administrators, but was aimed at common farmers (including farming women). In this context, handbooks tended to consider double-entry book-keeping to be too complicated and cumbersome for the farmer, whether male or female. It was therefore either discarded altogether or presented as the final, most advanced, step in the progression of the farmer's accounting skills. While this literature proliferated and sold massively, especially in the second half of the century, it remains difficult, as Joly stresses, to ascertain how far its lessons were absorbed and the practices it recommended adopted.

The effort the European ruling classes put into compelling peasants to keep accounts is the thread running through the remaining chapters. In the third part, the chapters by D'Onofrio (on Switzerland and the Netherlands), Moser (on Switzerland) and by Lampe and Sharp (on Denmark) show the growing role of governments and farmers' organisations in efforts to make farming transparent and governable. In all three chapters, we see the active spread of models of accounting through the organisation of courses and the supervision of farmers. Farmers were encouraged to separate book-keeping – the everyday recording of facts – from accounting – as the technique for extracting management information from their records. This division enabled accounting-related tasks to be taken out of the farm and placed in the hands of specialised accounting offices, often created by government.

These chapters respond in part to the questions raised by Hendrikx and Gelderblom on the usefulness of farm accounting for middle farmers and smallholders.[100] Calculative practices appear as part of the organisational requirements of rural life, an element of what Anton Schuurman, in his analysis of Dutch agriculture in the nineteenth and twentieth centuries, called the 'institutional matrix'.[101] Issues of farmers' education, of the diffusion, and adoption of practices by individual agriculturalists are considered to be less significant than the imposition of standard procedures. The structure of incentives and the balancing of the interests of various social groups and actors (governments, unions, experts, farmers) come to the fore.

In the three chapters dedicated to the twentieth century, we see accounting in a broader social role as the convergence point of different interests.[102] What seems to characterise the late nineteenth and the early twentieth centuries is a much more interventionist role for governments and for those farmers' organisations that were established or radically renewed at the end of the nineteenth century. For them, accounting was a tool of direct control and part of the policy-making process, but for the farmers themselves it was a tool of empowerment. It enabled them to

100 Daan Hendrikx and Oscar Gelderblom, 'Accounting for agricultural development?'

101 Anton Schuurman, 'Agricultural policy and the Dutch agricultural institutional matrix during the transition from organized to disorganized capitalism', in Peter Moser and Peter Varey (eds), *Integration through subordination: The politics of agricultural modernisation in industrial Europe* (2013), pp. 65–84.

102 Stuart Burchell *et al.*, 'The role of accounting in organizations and society', *Accounting, Organizations and Society* 5 (1980), pp. 5–27.

regulate their relations with their kin (the division of estates on inheritance features prominently in the Swiss case discussed by Moser). It helped them with tax issues (as stressed by D'Onofrio) and allowed them to be part of complex production systems (Lampe and Sharp). Finally, through their collective organisations, information drawn from farm accounts was turned into statistical data that provided farmers with a voice in public affairs (D'Onofrio).

VI

The chapters collected in this volume do not exhaust the topic of farm accounting. On the contrary, they are intended to open the way for further research. We have identified at least three areas that require deeper exploration. First, there is a need for a reassessment of the role of double-entry book-keeping in prescriptive writings and in practice. Various forms of simplified accounting seem to have dominated accounting practices during the early modern and modern era and well into the twentieth century. In terms of sources, this reassessment requires us to pay renewed attention to the accounting literature aimed at farmers and smallholders, rather than the rarefied treatises of the great agronomists.

Second, besides moving the focus away from DEB, current research shows the promise of adopting comprehensive definitions of accounting, capable of encompassing different calculative practices and forms of inscription that are not necessarily familiar or recognisable to professional accountants. The relationship to the commercial accounting of the same period remains unclear, while the tailoring of accounting systems to suit the needs of the farming business, especially within the framework of educational initiatives, emerges as a crucial topic in this book. Research is therefore required on the different genres of accounting literature and their different publics: educators, professional accountants, farmers.

Third, the relationship between practices and prescriptions also deserves further analysis. Too little is known about the transmission of practices and where models were taught and learned. This points to the need to explore new and often neglected sources for the history of accounting in the early modern and modern era: professional journals with widespread readership, the submissions and jury reports of prizes, the discussions among members of rural societies and academies, and especially in the eighteenth and nineteenth centuries, the records of farmers' associations.

In this way it will be possible to track how the gap between norms and the actual activity of farmers was negotiated and became redefined in different historical contingencies, but we may also be able to see the structure of incentives offered to farmers: improved management, increased control, clearer relations with siblings and extended family members, to mention a few.

VII

Martin Giraudeau saw weaknesses in the history of agricultural accounting, which he explained by the idea of 'a scholarship enclosure', that is a general historiographical bias in the study of agriculture: 'whatever happened in the rural areas was generally understood as a side effect of changes, or even of "revolutions", initiated elsewhere'.[103] This volume has nuanced this viewpoint, by showing that agriculturalists were very active in preparing for their own revolutions. The role of agricultural elites in promoting accounting practices among a vast rural population, in spreading a calculative mentality not only among agricultural businesses but also within agricultural families, is a remarkable achievement. It was made possible by the structure of incentives and obligations that farmers experienced when they pondered the decision to keep more or less formalised accounts: the intersection between farm and family, the special managerial needs that derived from animals, plants, and soil. At the same time, it is important not to forget that agriculture cannot be considered in isolation. Banking regulations, tax laws, business models, and economic policies cut across all economic sectors creating similar constraints and shared practices.

Overall, the following nine chapters describe multiple trajectories and transformations of farm accounting. In the different European countries discussed in the contributions, the accounting farmer, and behind the scenes the accounting woman farmer, as regulatory ideals and a social reality, appear, therefore, as crucial elements of the economic modernisation of agriculture and of its role within capitalist societies.

103 Martin Giraudeau, 'The farm as an accounting laboratory: An essay on the history of accounting and agriculture', *Accounting History Review* 27 (2017), p. 201.

2

Accounting for Labour on Capitalist Farms in Eighteenth-Century England[1]

James D. Fisher

This chapter is a contribution to the social history of agricultural accounting. Specifically, it reassesses the role of accounting in the development of agrarian capitalism in England in the eighteenth century. An ongoing debate in accounting history concerns the extent to which English estate and farm accounts displayed evidence of a growing 'capitalist mentality'. This is usually understood in terms of which accounting methods enabled calculations of profitability to inform decision-making. However, accounting can also be understood more broadly as a technique of labour management, which may encompass but is not reducible to a profit-seeking mentality. The capitalist mode of farming that spread in the eighteenth century was not simply a matter of a new commercial or 'business-minded' attitude, but more fundamentally a distinct set of labour relations, namely the increasing employment of wage labour in large-scale farming. This chapter reviews the relationship between accounting and labour management in farming and estate books published in the eighteenth century.

It sits within the general history of management accounting, or the 'provision of accounting information for management purposes'.[2] It broadly adopts a Marxist perspective to the extent that it rejects the notion of 'efficiency' as a socially neutral objective and focuses attention

1 This research was supported by the European Research Council (ERC) as part of the project 'FORMSofLABOUR: Gender, Freedom and Experience of Work in the Preindustrial Economy'.

2 J. R. Edwards and T. Boyns, *A History of Management Accounting: The British Experience* (2016), p. 2.

on accounting as a managerial technique to control the labour process.[3] The approach here is distinct from many previous studies of agricultural accounting by focusing on the social dimension of accounting as a way of mediating interpersonal relationships, specifically the management of workers; by concentrating on accounting at the level of farms not estates, and therefore on the relationship between farmer and worker rather than between landlord and steward; and by applying theories of how accountability can be extended to those who are counted rather than those who count.[4] The first section presents the theoretical and historical framework, drawing especially on the work of Robert Bryer, advocating that we interpret accounting as a response to the principal–agent problem, which it is argued was effectively extended from estates to farms in the development of capitalist farming in the eighteenth century. The second section offers a brief survey of labour accounting in farm and estate management manuals in the seventeenth and eighteenth centuries, highlighting the key themes of trust, indirect control and asymmetrical knowledge.[5] The third and fourth sections constitute the primary analysis through a study of the two most prolific and influential agricultural authors of the eighteenth century: Arthur Young (1741–1820) and William Marshall (1745–1818). It examines how they understood and deployed accounting

3 C. J. Napier, 'Historiography', in J. R. Edwards and S. Walker (eds), *The Routledge Companion to Accounting History* (2nd edn, 2020, pb 2021), pp. 30–40; Edwards and Boyns, *History of Management Accounting*, pp. 13–15.; R. Bryer, R. Fleischman and R. Macve, 'Smith, Marx or Foucault in Understanding the Early British Industrial Revolution? A Re-Examination of Management and Accounting for Capital and Labour at the Carron Company', *Proceedings of the 28th European Accounting Association Conference* (Göteborg, 2005).

4 For an overview of the historiography on agricultural accounting, see L. Jack, 'Agriculture', in J. R. Edwards and S. Walker (eds), *Routledge Companion to Accounting History*, pp. 389–409; M. Giraudeau, 'The Farm as an Accounting Laboratory: An Essay on the History of Accounting and Agriculture', *Accounting History Review* 27 (2017), pp. 201–15.

5 For studies on accounting manuals, see J. R. Edwards, 'Accounting on English Landed Estates during the Agricultural Revolution: A Textbook Perspective', *Accounting Historians Journal* 38 (2011), pp. 1–45; R. Bryer, 'The Roots of Modern Capitalism: A Marxist Accounting History of the Origins and Consequences of Capitalist Landlords in England', *Accounting Historians Journal* 31 (2004), pp. 19, 33–4; D. Oldroyd, 'Through a Glass Clearly: Management Practice on the Bowes Family Estates, *c.*1700–70, as Revealed by the Accounts', *Accounting, Business & Financial History* 9 (1999), p. 183; K. Tribe, *Genealogies of Capitalism* (1981), p. 86; D. Oldroyd and A. Dobie, 'Bookkeeping', in J. R. Edwards and S. Walker (eds), *Routledge Companion to Accounting History*, p. 122. On the sociology of trust, see O. Schilke, M. Reimann and K. S. Cook, 'Trust in Social Relations', *Annual Review of Sociology* 47 (2021), pp. 239–59.

as a solution to the particular problems encountered by the new tribe of capitalist farmers.

I

Management accounting can be broadly understood as a response to the principal–agent problem, which arises '[w]henever an individual (the principal) has another person (the agent) perform a service on [their] behalf and cannot fully observe the agent's actions'.[6] It occurs in situations of conflicting interests and asymmetric information, since the risk that the agent will act in their own interest is compounded by a lack of information about their actions. Accounting offers a way to ameliorate this problem. As Bryer notes, 'account' has two broad senses, meaning both to count and to explain. That is, to give an account is not simply to provide a calculation, but also to provide a justification for behaviour. Hence 'principals hold their agents to account by requiring a report and explanations of performance'.[7] Accounting enables the principal to exercise control over the agent by rewarding or punishing them for their performance, as measured against a set of objective targets.[8]

In Economics, the principal–agent concept is applied to the relationship between ownership and management, or between management and workers.[9] In histories of agricultural accounting, the owner–manager relation has primarily been applied at the estate level, between the landlord (principal) and their steward (agent) to whom they delegate management of their estate. However, the owner–manager relation also applies to the more specific case between a landowner/farmer (principal) and their bailiff (agent) to whom they delegate management of a specific farm. Further, the distinct manager–worker relationship applies between any farmer (principal) and their servants and labourers (agents) to whom they delegate farm work. Yet historians have tended to neglect the role of accounting in mediating the relationship between farmers and their workers. While the farm accounts produced by a steward or bailiff responsible for managing a home farm served a similar reporting

6 F. Varese, 'Principal–agent Problem', in *A Concise Oxford Dictionary of Politics and International Relations* (2018).

7 R. Bryer, 'Accounting and Control of the Labour Process', *Critical Perspectives on Accounting* 17 (2006), p. 557.

8 R. Bryer, 'The History of Accounting and the Transition to Capitalism in England. Part One: Theory', *Accounting, Organizations and Society* 25 (2000), p. 142.

9 N. Hashimzade, G. Myles and J. Black, 'Principal–Agent Problem', *A Dictionary of Economics* (Oxford 2017). Steven Toms describes the relation between shareholders and managers as a principal–agent problem: S. Toms, 'Capitalism', in Edwards and Walker (ed.), *Routledge Companion to Accounting History*, p. 429.

function as other kinds of estate accounts (e.g. rentals), the accounts kept by tenants or owner–occupiers must have served a different purpose. In a wide-ranging survey of surviving farm records, Turner *et al.* have argued that 'farm accounts were not primarily a measure of accountability', hence '[f]ormalized accounts were of limited use to those farmers who were not accountable to others for the running of their farms'.[10] But accountability can function in two directions: accounts can serve to hold the person compiling them accountable for their performance to the principal to whom they report, or they can serve to hold accountable the people being counted.

As Bryer has discussed (although not in relation to farming), a version of the principal–agent problem arises whenever workers sell their labour power but retain direct control over it. How can the manager (principal) get the worker (agent) to act in the manager's interests? When actions can be 'programmed' – when managers can predict the outcome of specified actions – they can give orders and monitor the actions as they are performed. But supervision is costly and often workers must perform 'non-programmed' actions with uncertain outcomes, leaving managers to rely on 'results' controls.[11] The significance of accounting is that it promises to provide an objective measure of results to aid managerial control over workers. Accounting can function as a form of indirect control by holding them accountable for creating value, which cannot be achieved through the 'traditional compulsions' of increasing work effort through 'authority and supervision'.[12] A similar point has been made from a Weberian perspective by Nathalie Joly and Thomas Depecker, who highlight how the precise measurement of work rates and labour costs by nineteenth-century French agronomists 'went hand in hand with new possibilities of control'.[13]

We can link these ideas to the chronology of capitalist farming by reference to a distinction Bryer makes between merely 'capitalis*tic*' farmers – who employed wage labour but only calculated profit as income minus expenditure – and fully 'capitalist' farmers who aimed to maximise relative surplus value by improving labour productivity and

10 M. E. Turner, J. V. Beckett and B. Afton, *Farm Production in England, 1700–1914* (2001), pp. 50–1.

11 Bryer, 'Accounting and Control of the Labour Process', pp. 555–6. See also Bryer, Fleischman and Macve, 'Smith, Marx or Foucault', pp. 29–30.

12 Bryer, 'Accounting and Control of the Labour Process', p. 564.

13 For Weber, it is the presence of a rational organisation of free labour, together with an account of investments and earnings, that characterise the spirit of capitalism, see Max Weber, *The Protestant Ethic and the Spirit of Capitalism* (2008). T. Depecker and N. Joly, 'Agronomists and Accounting: The Beginnings of Capitalist Rationalisation on the Farm (1800–1850)', *Historia Agraria* 65 (2015), p. 86.

calculating the rate of return on capital in production.[14] This corresponds to a distinction made by Marx to delineate two stages in the transition to capitalism: the 'formal subsumption' of labour under capital designates the moment when a capitalist takes control over production without changing the labour process itself; the 'real subsumption' of labour designates when that control extends to reorganising the labour process in order to maximise labour productivity and therefore maximise the rate of return on capital.[15] The use of accounting as a technique of labour management would therefore be associated with the real subsumption of labour on a fully capitalist farm. According to Bryer's narrative, we are most likely to find indications after the mid-eighteenth century.[16] The best and earliest example of such 'real subsumption' is presented in Tom McLean's case study of the Yorkshire farmer Henry Best (*fl.* 1617–1645), whose farming and memorandum books display a keen interest in the 'measurement and management of human performance' through a detailed 'system of labour planning and control'.[17] McLean argues that, in the absence of any need to produce accounts for external reporting, Best implemented labour accounting in order to 'hold his workforce accountable for their performance'.[18]

While Best's management was perhaps unusual for the early seventeenth century, he was part of a growing minority. Over the next two centuries, more farmers were seeking new ways to hold their workers accountable for the simple reason that they were more likely to be managing higher numbers of workers. This was a consequence of tectonic shifts in the occupational structure of farming in England between the sixteenth and eighteenth centuries.[19] Landownership became more

14 Bryer, 'History of Accounting, Part One, Theory', p. 136.

15 Ibid., p. 153. Bryer does not himself explore the evidence for the 'real subsumption' of labour in any detail, aside from brief remarks about Robert Loder's 'obsession' with labour costs and productivity, and the interesting suggestion that Loder's real subsumption of his servants and labourers was limited by the general labour conditions at the time. Bryer, 'History of Accounting, Part Two, Evidence', *Accounting, Organizations and Society* 25 (2000), p. 374. On Loder's accounting, see J. Freear, 'Robert Loder, Jacobean Management Accountant', *Abacus* 6 (1970), pp. 25–38.

16 Bryer, 'History of Accounting, Part One, Theory', p. 158.

17 T. McLean, 'The Measurement and Management of Human Performance in Seventeenth-Century English Farming: The Case of Henry Best', *Accounting Forum* 33 (2009), pp. 63–4, 70. See also D. Woodward, *The Farming and Memorandum Books of Henry Best of Elmswell, 1642* (1984).

18 McLean, 'Measurement and Management of Human Performance', p. 62. McLean places Best within a long-term development that anticipated 'accounting-based disciplinary controls' in later slave plantations and industrial enterprises (p. 70).

19 Discussed in more detail in James D. Fisher, *The Enclosure of Knowledge: Books, Power and Agrarian Capitalism in Britain, 1660–1800* (2022), pp. 39–46.

concentrated, the average size of farms increased, and farms were increasingly worked with hired wage labour rather than family labour.[20] As substantial farmers hired more servants and day-labourers to work larger farms, they were increasingly able to remove themselves from daily labour and focus on the effective management of profit-oriented farms. The relationship between farmers and workers also changed; a yeoman or husbandman who worked alongside young live-in servants, and who hired supplementary labour from those who had some land themselves, was closer in social position to their workers than a large-scale capitalist farmer who leased a farm in an unfamiliar area and employed teams of landless labourers entirely dependent on wages.

In short, as part of a wider process of rural polarisation, the gap widened between the people performing farm labour and the people who managed farms. Farmers were increasingly distant organisationally, in terms of their practical separation from farm labour; they were increasingly distant psychologically, in terms of their lack of personal experience of farm labour; and they were increasingly distant socially, as diverging classes within the rural economy. Consequently, large farmers were facing similar challenges of exercising control at a distance as landlords had for generations. In one sense, the relationship of accountability between the steward and lord in estate management was replicated at the level of individual farms as a result of new divisions of labour. Hence there are compelling theoretical and empirical grounds for investigating the growth of farm accounting as a means of increasing labour productivity and holding workers accountable to capitalist farm managers.

II

The following is a brief survey of labour accounting in agricultural, estate management and accounting literature before the publications of Young and Marshall in the 1770s. While it was only a minor element, the need for labour accounting arose from the same combination of factors stemming from the principal–agent problem as estate accounting in general. First, a distrust of agents and a fear of being defrauded, which is a prominent

20 L. Shaw-Taylor, 'The Rise of Agrarian Capitalism and the Decline of Family Farming in England', *Economic History Review* 65 (2012), pp. 26–60; H. French and R. W. Hoyle, *The Character of English Rural Society: Earls Colne, 1550–1750* (2007), pp. 30–1. While all studies agree average farm sizes were increasing, there is no agreed definition of a 'large' or 'small' farm, which depended on the type of farming: see J. Whittle, *The Development of Agrarian Capitalism: Land and Labour in Norfolk 1440–1580* (2000), pp. 195–6. Further, attempts to measure sizes face the problem of subletting and distinguishing units of property from units of farming: see J. Rhodes, 'Subletting in Eighteenth-Century England: A New Methodological Approach', *Agricultural History Review* 66 (2018), pp. 67–92.

theme in studies of 'Charge and Discharge Accounting' (CDA), typically characterised as enabling 'a person entrusted with the management of the property of another to render an account of their stewardship'.[21] Second, the need to exercise control at a distance, whether geographical, social or organisational. The long history of book-keeping shows the frequent role that 'distance from events has played in creating agency relationships', stimulating new forms of accounting to fulfil the function of 'holding agents accountable at a distance'.[22] Third, linked to this, was the need to acquire information about or possessed by agents. Indeed, the basic function of most estate accounting was to provide 'access to information *in absentia*' for landowners away from their estates.[23] Yet historians have been preoccupied by the technical methods to garner information rather than the full range of relationships that were marked by an asymmetry in knowledge. When we turn to consider the growing interest in labour accounting in the eighteenth century, we find the same nexus: a need driven by distrust to acquire information from a distance about unsupervised agents in order to exercise greater control over their actions.

The basic function of labour accounting was to keep track of labour costs, which also helped to protect against over-charging by workers. As Roger North advocated in *The Gentleman Accomptant* (1714), a weekly record of the days worked served as a protection against workers who 'shark and spunge (for want of better Gain) Days and half Days Works', i.e. claim they have worked more than they have. North's suggestion that the mere 'Knowledge that such an Accompt as this is kept, is sufficient to keep Men to true Reckoning' indicates how such record-keeping helped to exert control.[24] Yet labour accounting was informed by the notion of a standard or customary level of labour productivity from the early seventeenth century, which provided a benchmark against which to check the performance of hired workers. In 1620, Gervase Markham's farming manual offered a basic model that would be recycled over the next century, offering rough estimates of the quantity of work a man could perform per day in the major farming tasks (ploughing, threshing, etc.).[25] The section was copied with minimal changes by Leonard Meager

21 Oldroyd and Dobie, 'Bookkeeping', p. 101. Edwards and Boyns, *History of Management Accounting*, pp. 44–5. In contrast, discussions of 'Double-Entry Bookkeeping' (DEB) focus on technical aspects rather than its social function: Oldroyd and Dobie, 'Bookkeeping', pp. 103–8. Edwards and Boyns, *History of Management Accounting*, pp. 47–8, 50.

22 Oldroyd and Dobie, 'Bookkeeping', p. 112. See also pp. 99, 105, 109.

23 Turner, Beckett, and Afton, *Farm Production*, p. 44.

24 Roger North, *The Gentleman Accomptant: Or, an Essay to Unfold the Mystery of Accompts* (1714), pp. 261–3.

25 G. Markham, *Markhams Farwell to Husbandry* (1620), pp. 140–7. This section was reprinted at least seven times.

in 1697, described in the title as 'Day-labour computed'.[26] It was adapted again by John Mortimer in 1707, although heavily revised and given prices 'computed according to the Workmens Wages' for summer and winter.[27] It effectively converted between day rates and piece rates for the reader, based on a knowledge of how long particular tasks should take. It is possible that Mortimer's section was the inspiration for the detailed list of prices for work by craftsmen and farm labourers provided in Edward Laurence's estate management manual *The Duty of a Steward* (1727).[28] This constituted a reasonably elaborate pricing system, for example distinguishing rates for ploughing on three different soil types and for three sets of ploughing. A few decades later, in 1761, John Mordant included the same list of prices for work tasks as provided by Laurence, but with higher prices.[29] It is striking that for over a century there was little development of Markham's basic template for labour productivity, even if the link to labour costs was elaborated.

However, from the early eighteenth century we find indications that merely knowing average labour outputs was inadequate and that accounting could be used to measure and improve labour performance. In 1714, North explained how an accurate weekly record of labour

> gives a true Accompt, what the Men can do; and Bargains may be made with them by Lump, or Measure accordingly; the doing which reasonably and well, is the greatest Difficulty in Country Business; the Men that work, know exactly; but those that employ them, cannot know any thing of new Work, nor commonly put out, but by some such Means as this; so the Advantages of Workmen is very great; and as they find the Master Ignorant, they will propose outrageously, which nothing corrects, but a Demonstration, that they and their Work are understood ... .[30]

Here, North drew attention to the potential for labour accounts to be used to measure labour productivity directly. The most striking comment is that the need for such accounting arose from the knowledge disparity between those making the bargain: the person performing the work always knew better than their potential employer how long a task might take. Such labour accounting was therefore a form of data gathering,

26 L. Meager, *The Mystery of Husbandry: Or, Arable, Pasture, and Wood-Land Improved* (1697), pp. 65–7.

27 J. Mortimer, *The Whole Art of Husbandry* (1707), pp. 307–10. This was reprinted in five further editions up to 1761.

28 E. Laurence, *The Duty of a Steward to His Lord* (1727), p. 156.

29 J. Mordant, *The Complete Steward: Or, The Duty of a Steward to His Lord* (1761), pp. 44–54.

30 North, *The Gentleman Accomptant*, p. 263. This was highlighted but with minimal comment in Edwards, 'Accounting on English Landed Estates', pp. 28–9.

whose value was only fully realised when it informed future decision-making. It is this form of accounting as a way of *acquiring* knowledge about farm labour that would grow in importance, as employers hiring wage labour and producing for the market felt the pressure to obtain accurate knowledge about labour performance.

Laurence later addressed the same problem of asymmetric knowledge in a different way. As his standard prices were obviously limited to the tasks listed, he recommended a method for gathering information on labour performance for additional tasks:

> if any new sort of Work is to be done, not mention'd in the following Particulars, the Steward's best way is to hire a good Labourer, and to stand by him the whole Day, to see that he does a good Days-Work, and then to measure the same, in order to know what it is worth.[31]

Hence rather than rely on collecting data on average performance levels, Laurence suggested a mini experiment to provide the master with the knowledge required to control labour costs. This general need for managers to acquire knowledge about labour in order to properly hold their workers accountable was also articulated by Mordant, who stressed that a good steward must have wide-ranging knowledge of farm work – 'how to measure their several works, or what prices they ought to demand' – in order 'to prevent any dishonesty in workmen, the many little low tricks which are too often practised by *masons, carpenters, &c*'.[32]

However, these were relatively marginal aspects of farm and estate management literature in the early eighteenth century. Manuals directed to the typical country gentleman showed minimal concern with detailed labour management or accounting.[33] It is also difficult to find any serious interest in labour accounting in the two most prolific agricultural authors of the first half of the eighteenth century, Richard Bradley and William Ellis. Only from the 1770s do we find an explicit concern with accounting for labour on farms. In Cuthbert Clarke's guide to agricultural education (1777), for example, he included an example table for recording the specific days worked by each labourer, the daily tasks they performed, and the combined daily and weekly costs of their labour, by which a farmer may 'find how much any particular piece of work stood him; what he gained by any bargain … [and] prevent any dispute with his workmen'.[34]

31 Laurence, *Duty of a Steward*, p. 156.

32 Mordant, *Complete Steward*, preface. See also pp. 40–1, 393.

33 For example, G. Jacob, *The Country Gentleman's Vade Mecum* (1717), pp. 44, 46; T. Nourse, *Campania Felix, or a Discourse of the Benefits and Improvements of Husbandry* (1700), p. 210.

34 C. Clarke, *The True Theory and Practice of Husbandry* (1777), pp. 22–4.

III

The growing need for farm managers to hold workers accountable is most evident in the early publications of Arthur Young and William Marshall. Neither should be regarded as typical or representative of all farmers in their period, but rather as pioneers within a wider trend of new kinds of farm management. The gentlemen farmers catered for by Young's books differed sharply from Henry Best, who possessed an intimate knowledge of farm practices and carried out a 'muddy-booted, work-a-day' mode of management, in which he 'exercised direct, personal supervision'.[35] Marshall's management was a closer descendant of Best's, but nonetheless exhibited how even the more experienced improving farmer willing to engage in day-to-day management could not personally supervise all activity and required other means of surveillance.[36]

As the dominant agricultural author of the late eighteenth century, Young's writings on farm accounting and his capitalist mentality have often been discussed or referenced.[37] However, in almost all cases, historians have focused on the methods of accounting Young advocated and neglected his explanations for the role of accounting in mediating labour relations. In particular, Young articulated his feelings about accounting in two of his earliest works, in which we see the fresh reflections of a minor gentleman farmer who had recently taken up farming, keen to advise his peers. In the fifth essay in *Rural Oeconomy* (1770) Young made clear, somewhat unwittingly, that the value of accounting for gentlemen farmers was rooted in their general inexperience and ignorance about the practice of farming. At this time, growing numbers of country gentlemen were directly managing farms themselves and a host of professionals and merchants had taken up farming 'without knowing any of its practice'. In particular, an inexperienced gentleman lacked an intuitive sense of farming costs. Young described a gentleman walking over a 200-acre farm observing various equipment and animals, but 'nothing that gives him any idea of expence'.[38] Yet a gentleman could 'neither labour' themselves 'nor give a constant attention to his business'.

This combination of ignorance and the need for delegation created a fundamental paradox for gentlemen farmers, as manifested in the question of whether to employ a bailiff – a head servant to manage

35 McLean, 'Measurement and Management of Human Performance', pp. 70, 65.

36 With thanks to Laura Sayre for pointing out the importance of this distinction.

37 R. Juchau, 'Early Cost Accounting Ideas in Agriculture: The Contributions of Arthur Young', *Accounting, Business & Financial History* 12 (2002), pp. 369–86; K. Tribe, *Land, Labour and Economic Discourse* (1978), p. 69; Tribe, *Genealogies*, pp. 78–83; Bryer, 'The History of Accounting, Part Two, Evidence', p. 377; Bryer, 'The Roots of Modern Capitalism', pp. 45–8.

38 Arthur Young, *Rural Oeconomy: Or, Essays on the Practical Parts of Husbandry* (1770), pp. 93–5.

day-to-day activities. A gentleman needed a bailiff to assist with decision-making and supervision, but ignorance rendered the farmer especially vulnerable to being deceived.[39] On the one hand,

> a young practitioner in farming must necessarily be so much at a loss about a great variety of matters that come before him, of which he is ignorant, that if he does not keep a bailey, his whole business will infallibly suffer.

On the other hand, the same inexperience made him susceptible to being cheated, as indiscretions would be 'over-looked by a master ignorant of the business' such that a dishonest bailiff could 'defraud his master of more money than twenty labourers or servants'. Consequently, 'one of the chief objections to a bailey is the ignorance of the master', and ideally a gentleman would begin with direct management of a smaller farm to gain experience, before taking on a larger farm and hiring a bailiff.[40]

Crucially, it was in the context of this thorny problem of managing through a bailiff that Young first introduced the importance of accounts, and presented a basic system that provided detailed information about production to the manager, minimised the possibility of being cheated, and held the bailiff accountable for their performance. A minute book was to be kept by the bailiff, recording all farming activities, which a gentleman should check 'every evening, that he may know distinctly every thing his teams and men have that day been employed about'. Indeed, if he already knew the measurements of his fields, then without stepping outside 'he can, at any time, tell if the proper quantity of work of all sorts be executed or not'. This was complemented by the use of a cash book and a ledger, both of which were to be kept by the bailiff but regularly checked by the master, such that he could reward or punish the bailiff as needed and know exactly the profit or loss.[41] Hence for Young the value of farm accounting was inseparable from the agency relationship between a gentleman farmer and his bailiff, since an independent mode of acquiring information and evaluating farms offered a partial remedy to the predicament of relying on untrustworthy servants.

In the same essay, Young indicated how accounting was intimately bound up with the problem of managing farm labour as a whole. A gentleman who did not work alongside his servants and labourers could not directly ensure that instructions were followed to the requisite standard. Young lamented the limited effectiveness of crude coercive measures such as '[s]colding and threats', which led to 'impudence',

39 Young discussed the same problem in A. Young, *The Farmer's Guide in Hiring and Stocking Farms* (1770), pp. 270–1.

40 Young, *Rural Oeconomy*, pp. 98–9, 100–3.

41 Ibid., pp. 103–4, 109–12.

'revenge' or 'deceitful conduct'.[42] In the absence of close supervision, employing labour through piece work was an attractive option and allowed a more precise control over the cost of labour, but had the disadvantage of requiring a means of quality control to ensure 'that *well* doing was never sacrificed to quick doing'.[43]

Young paid greater attention to the problem of quantifying labour discipline and productivity in chapter twenty of *The Farmer's Guide* (1770). In an astonishing display of his enthusiasm for calculation, Young attempted to reduce the relative efficiencies of different management styles to a numerical figure. Whereas the basic price of labour was a relatively straightforward item to enter into accounts, estimating labour productivity was more complicated. He first tried to incorporate the labour performed by a working farmer in his example accounts, but this was only partly 'reducible to estimate'. Since a working farmer could simultaneously perform tasks and act as a manager of others performing tasks with or near him, the 'cost' of the farmer's own labour was not equal to the price to hire the equivalent labour: when ploughing, for example, he 'not only ploughs his own acre, but *sees* that his man does the same'.[44] In contrast, a gentleman could never supervise his labourers as closely, and would therefore lose labour productivity through idleness.

Working farmers were more productive in two additional ways: first, by performing their own tasks at a higher intensity than a hired servant, for example in the harvest 'a farmer who drives his own horses will clear twice the ground that a gentleman's servant will do';[45] second, by using their initiative to eliminate wasted time between tasks, in contrast to a servant who only completed the defined tasks as directed: the

> numerous small articles ... such as carting stubble, wood, herdles, turnips, straw, hay ... [the farmer] will croud them together, and make out a complete day's work; whereas the gentleman's servants will divide them yet more, to have the more broken idle loitering days.[46]

In general, it was axiomatic for Young that a farmer working in their own interest would always be more efficient than hired labourers working in the interest of their employer: 'there is a great difference between a man acting for himself and for another'.[47] Yet Young was not content just to establish the basic principle that small differences in labour intensity and organisation were crucial to profitable farming, he wanted to prove it using accounting: 'If we could reduce it exactly to calculation, what a vast

42 Ibid., pp. 113–15.
43 Ibid., pp. 116–17.
44 Young, *Farmer's Guide*, p. 251.
45 Ibid., p. 253.
46 Ibid., p. 275.
47 Ibid., p. 268.

different *per cent.* in profit would appear!'[48] He went on to offer a series of speculative estimates for the efficiencies of common management (for example, a 32 per cent advantage to the farmer who drove his own plough team).[49] Young even considered placing a figure on the predicted cheating by servants, asking rhetorically: 'But how are we to reduce the honesty of the bailey to calculation?'[50] All together, Young estimated that if only customary methods were followed, a gentleman's profit would be one third lower than a working farmer.[51] A gentleman farmer must seek other advantages, namely the implementation of improved methods monitored through accounting. Young therefore not only used accounting to estimate the higher profitability of different farming methods, but also to estimate the relative cost efficiencies of different styles of management and levels of labour discipline and productivity.

IV

Whereas Young articulated the need for accounting for frustrated gentlemen farmers, William Marshall provided a detailed example of how labour accounting could be applied within a more direct mode of management. He was born around 1745 to a prosperous yeoman farmer in Yorkshire, but like Young he was apprenticed as a teenager into a trade, only turning to farming later in his thirties.[52] In 1774 Marshall took over the management of a 300-acre farm near Croydon and over the next few years compiled detailed notes that he edited into *Minutes of Agriculture* in 1778, which combined a diary-like report of daily activities with summaries of his reflections. The result is an extraordinary text that records the thoughts and actions of a self-proclaimed 'scientific' farmer struggling to rationalise labour on his farm. The diary begins with an immediate confrontation with the Bailiff Paradox as outlined by Young: Marshall initially intended to delegate most of the 'minutial' management to a bailiff, but decided to discharge his bailiff for his lack of farming knowledge.[53] While Marshall did employ a bailiff again after the first year, he frequently returned to his central principle of the 'necessity of self-attendance' or close personal supervision for good farm

48 Ibid., p. 255.
49 Ibid., p. 263.
50 Ibid., p. 268.
51 Ibid., pp. 277–8.
52 P. Horn, *William Marshall (1745–1818) and the Georgian Countryside* (1982); G. E. Mingay, 'Marshall, William (bap. 1745, d. 1818)', *Oxford Dictionary of National Biography* (2004).
53 W. Marshall, *Minutes of Agriculture, Made on a Farm of 300 Acres* (1778), entry for 18 July 1774 (the diary pages in the second half of the book are not numbered and are cited by date).

management.[54] Hence Marshall kept accounts for his own use and was engaged with the direct management of his servants and labourers.[55]

Marshall's simplest use of accounting was to calculate and compare different methods of paying for labour, such as piece rates versus day rates, whether to pay part of wages with beer, or whether to maintain servants within the house.[56] But a more fraught use of accounting was to protect against theft by his workers. On 19 May 1776, he recorded his struggle to use accounting to prevent carters ('thieves to a man') stealing grain. He complained that although he kept 'a regular account of every bushel of every species of grain *made-up*, and of every bushel *fairly vended*', he could 'never make the two accounts tally'. This led him to wonder how much worse it must be for farmers who did not keep accounts: 'What, then must be the fate of those who do not keep a minute account, neither of the yield nor of the vent, and whose servants are aware of this neglect?' Farmers without accounts would not even *know* if their servants were thieving, and thus servants would be confident they could steal without detection.

However, another detailed example with carters, regarding how much hay they fed their horses, shows that Marshall had an expansive idea of 'theft'. On 10 April 1776, he observed with horror that in the absence of close attention his carters had allowed horses to eat 70 bundles of hay in three weeks, which he judged far too great an expense. His solution was to treat hay consumed at home in the same manner as that sold at market, that is by binding and accounting for 'every blade'. Why was it worth spending time binding hay that would simply be consumed in the farm yard? Marshall listed the reasons. First, to track all produce across the farm in order to accurately calculate yields; second, to help avoid any wastage. Third, however, was to regulate precisely the amounts of hay handled by workers and hold them accountable for its use:

> I can allowance each species of stock: I can allow each cart-horse, a truss a-week: the ox-team, half-a-load a-week ... And I find that by thus stinting the quantity, the men become more careful ... if they lavish to-day, they will want to-morrow – Thus the servant imperceptibly learns frugality, while his cattle have their food regularly.

Fourth, it gave Marshall the knowledge required to maintain control: 'I have the satisfaction of knowing how every blade is expended ... and of

54 *Minutes of Agriculture*, 20 Sept. 1775. See also 30 June 1774, 7 Dec. 1774, 10 April 1776, 10 June 1777.

55 Ibid., 18 July 1774. The digest contains a long list of all the issues with servants, ibid., p. 35.

56 See following entries: 21 Jan., 28 Aug., 5 Nov. with note added July 1777; 6 June 1776. On this final issue, he noted pointedly that only a 'Farmer who keeps no accounts imagines he saves by boarding his servants in the house'.

course, my hay and stock accounts (with respect to hay) are reduced to certainty'. Hence Marshall perceived 'theft' as any kind of inefficiency; the carters were not taking the hay from the farm for their own use, but simply using it liberally. He was more explicit about this in a later manual when describing the management of a steward:

> idleness is a crime ... a direct fraud; and a manager should guard against it, with the same care and assiduity, as against pilfering. A day labourer who idles away an hour, robs his employer of an hour's wage; – and thereby injures him as much as if he were to steal a faggot of equal value.[57]

The example of the hay accounts and carters shows how accounting operated as a tool of labour management. A different method of managing a particular resource was combined with keeping accounts of that resource, such that it could be regulated to prevent waste and 'theft' by workers. The management of hay was rendered more suitable for calculations, and these calculations ensured a degree of control. Interestingly, Marshall observed that the very fact of keeping a specific account changed the behaviour of his servants. Hence he was able to hold his carters accountable for the amount of hay they fed horses, without keeping them under constant supervision. Instead, he reorganised the process to ensure that the relevant resource could be counted and monitored at every stage.

The most complex and advanced use of accounting was for the purpose of calculating labour productivity to inform decisions about improving methods. Three examples show Marshall attempting to calculate the relative cost efficiency of ploughing, hay-making and stone-picking. On 16 April 1776, he calculated that two pairs of 'whip-reins' (two horses, one man) was both cheaper and more productive in ploughing a field than three-horse teams (three horses, one man and a boy), estimating a saving of between one half and one third. On 27 April, he calculated the cost per acre of ploughing one field was significantly higher than another, ascribing this mostly to the characteristics of the field; the stiff soil, the cumbersome turns due to its narrow shape, and the distance from the stable. However, he also noted the field was isolated from the rest of his farm and, crucially, he had been busy at the time over two miles away, giving servants 'the favourable opportunity of being idle'. He estimated the loss of labour intensity due to the lack of supervision as equivalent to 'almost one team'. Later Marshall added a note referring to the relevant 'labour-account' for that field, which consisted of a list of dates, tasks and number of teams and men employed, allowing him to calculate that on average teams had ploughed no more than two-thirds of an acre per day – which he believed 'to be very exact'. Hence Marshall's system of

57 W. Marshall, *On the Landed Property of England* (1804), p. 422.

accounting was designed to allow him to measure and compare labour costs and productivity on different fields – apparently with enough precision to show the impact of his own absence.

Marshall took this a step further on 18 July 1776 by analysing the labour process itself in detail, minuting his careful observations and calculations in order to find small gains in efficiency. He took detailed observations on the process of loading, unloading and reloading hay onto wagons for the purpose of exposing it to sun and wind before stacking. This allowed him to estimate that if 'one load takes two men three hours and a-half' then 'two men would re-load three-loads a-day: about 13½d. a-load', which he considered a small sum compared to 'the difference between good hay and bad'. This prompted a reflection on the value of regularly writing observations: 'I am of the opinion, that had not the former part of the Minute been made, the latter, nor the calculation, would have occurred', and from these 'schemes of FUTURE CONDUCT rush upon the mind'. Here we see accounting not as a set of reports at the end of the year, but as an entire logic of management, in which everything should be observed, recorded and reduced to calculation.[58]

These calculations extended to apparently trifling matters such as stone picking. On 21 May 1776, he noted the expense of paying three men, two boys and six horses to spend two days 'collecting and carrying-off the scattered heaps' of stones piled by the pickers, at a cost of 'almost 1s an acre', which was 'as much as for picking'. He resolved in future to adopt a new method: to 'place empty carts in different parts of the field … for the pickers to empty their baskets into', in order to save labour. The following year (14 April 1777), however, he noted that the revised method created new inefficiencies, as the pickers spent 'almost as long employed in emptying their baskets, as filling them'. He therefore revised the work process again. This time, the pickers simply filled baskets, and a man and cart were 'always on hand to *empty* them'. He recorded that '[s]even or eight women boys and girls, one man, one horse, and a light cart, have run-over just forty acres in three days and three-quarters' – a total of 30 shillings, or a rate of 9d. per acre for both picking and carrying off, which he was very pleased with.

In summary, therefore, Marshall's book illustrates the range of ways in which accounting was key to his labour management in the 1770s. Accounting helped to decide the most cost effective way of hiring labour and helped ensure his workers were not stealing from the farm – as it had done for generations of farm managers before him. This sat alongside other traditional forms of management, such as providing incentives to encourage hard work or loyalty. However, more detailed accounting was

58 See further examples of analysing the labour process, which did not always involve detailed accounting: carters, 2 Sept. 1776; sowing and harrowing, 2 Oct. 1776 and seedsmen, 5 Oct. 1776.

also crucial in tracking resources across the farm and holding his workers accountable for any waste. Most significantly, he used accounting to evaluate the cost efficiency of different labour methods, which involved systematically observing, recording and calculating the cost of labour down to the smallest tasks, to provide the information required to reorganise the labour process for maximum returns.

Yet, while there are signs of the kinds of measuring and monitoring of labour that would later be developed in the modern management strategies of Taylorism, there were limits too.[59] This was perfectly summed up by Marshall's general maxim for managing servants: 'Treat them as Men; but not as Intimates; nor yet as Machines', since 'how *Machine-like* soever a Day-Labourer may appear, under the immediate eye of an austere Master, he is a *Free-Agent*, at his own Fire-side'.[60]

This categorisation – neither intimate nor machine – precisely locates the state of labour management at the end of the eighteenth century. On the one hand, hired workers were not trusted helpers in a common enterprise, and therefore the techniques of supervision and accountability Marshall developed were crucial to ensuring they carried out his interests. On the other hand, he could not entirely reduce them to mere instruments, to abstracted bundles of muscles and nerves, but had to engage with them as agents with their own interests and expectations, which limited the degree of control he could plausibly exercise.

V

Why was there a growing interest in the theory and practice of farm accounting in eighteenth-century England? A 'rationalist' perspective offers no explanation at all, as it simply assumes that accounting would be valuable for farmers in running a profitable business – the only trouble is explaining why so few farmers before this period kept regular accounts. Alternative Weberian and Marxist interpretations that instead trace the emergence of a capitalist mentality seeking to calculate profitability offer only a partial explanation. Ultimately, farmers could only pursue that objective through directing others. Hence this chapter has argued that the use of farm accounting must be understood in terms of farm management as a whole, operating in historically specific socio-economic conditions. In short, accounting was driven by the capitalist division of labour as well as profit-maximising attitudes. It was stimulated by the new managerial problems faced by a growing number of English farmers arising from the divisions of labour within the tripartite structure of landowner, tenant

59 Frederick W. Taylor (1856–1915) designed a scientific organisation of manual labour based on the timing of movements and the specialisation of workers' tasks.

60 See 'Digest' in Marshall, *Minutes*, p. 40.

and labourer. These were distinct from the challenges encountered by generations of yeomen and husbandmen, and by landlords and stewards content to collect rents and other estate revenues. In quantitative terms, more farmers were using hired wage labour, and the average number of workers they were employing was rising. In qualitative terms, some farmers were becoming increasingly distant from the daily tasks undertaken on their farms. This group of large, wealthy, commercial farmers therefore faced particular challenges due to their distance from day-to-day management and reliance on subordinates. If they were unable or unwilling to engage in close personal supervision of their workers, and not engaged sufficiently to observe directly how well the farm was performing, they required alternative methods of indirect control to resolve the problems of distrust and uncertainty. In a purely structural sense, therefore, we can see how farm accounting was driven in part by the need to manage wage workers.

This fundamental rationale for accounting was intensified by the social changes that characterised the second half of the eighteenth century, as gentlemen, merchants and lawyers increasingly took over the management of farms with a keen interest in turning a profit but little direct farming experience. As inexperienced 'improvers', they faced a distinctive conundrum created by the interplay of four factors. First, their initial lack of practical experience and knowledge about farming meant that they lacked the capacity to form judgments and make decisions themselves and so were especially reliant on others. Second, their wish to avoid manual labour and manage their farms wholly with a pen meant they were especially distant from the productive activity on their farms. Third, their lack of trust in their workers was compounded when there was a significant socio-economic gap between manager and worker (in terms of wealth and landownership), and when there were no existing local bonds between them (as when a new tenant arrived and hired local workers). Fourth, their desire to implement 'improved' methods to increase output and productivity meant that – even if the former were not significant obstacles – they had the additional challenge of imposing new ways of working and monitoring these for their relative success. Hence there were increasing numbers of farmers who desired greater levels of control over their workers in order to maximise profits, but for whom traditional managerial methods were unavailable or inadequate, such as working alongside their subordinates or using direct physical coercion.

A key response was to develop more extensive and sophisticated forms of accounting. It was a managerial technique that provided farmers with a way to acquire information by recording key quantities at strategic points to ameliorate the need for continuous observation; to create safeguards against the dishonesty of hired workers; to monitor and measure the performance of workers with the aim of increasing labour productivity; and to evaluate overall success in terms of profitability, which could be calculated to inform decision-making, especially when it deviated from the local custom of workers. While the use of accounting for some of these purposes was not new in the eighteenth century, we can discern an important shift from a concern with the honesty of servants to a concern with their productivity. The chronology sketched here based on published literature suggests that a basic concern with labour costs was present from the early seventeenth century, but the first intermittent efforts to measure labour productivity only began in the early eighteenth century, which were elaborated from the 1770s as signalled by Young and Marshall.

This mode of labour management was no doubt encouraged by an underlying trend toward greater quantification in many areas of social and economic life, which continued to intensify in nineteenth-century agriculture.[61] Yet, while we can detect a general enthusiasm for counting, the important question is where such efforts to quantify were directed: *what* was counted, *by whom*, and *for what purpose*? One answer here is that labour accounting became an increasing focus and priority for new capitalist farmers engaged in the 'real subsumption' of labour. Indeed, this is a crucial dimension missing from long-running debates about the imposition of labour discipline in the eighteenth century, which E. P. Thompson famously linked to a new time-discipline established under industrial capitalism.[62] For Thompson, this was largely a shift from irregular task-based farm work to regular clock-based factory work (neglecting the development of capitalist modes of farming). But a more exacting measurement and imposition of time-routines would have been insufficient to achieve greater labour productivity. It was accounting that allowed farm managers to go beyond strict schedules and attempt to actually hold their workers accountable for *how* they used their time. A capitalist farmer needed an account book as well as a clock.[63]

61 As detailed in a French context in Depecker and Joly, 'Agronomists and Accounting'.

62 E. P. Thompson, 'Time, Work-Discipline, and Industrial Capitalism', *Past & Present* 38 (1967), pp. 56–97; P. Glennie and N. Thrift, 'Reworking E. P. Thompson's "Time, Work-Discipline and Industrial Capitalism"', *Time & Society* 5 (1996), 275–99. See also the argument for the earlier roots of time-discipline in rural society in M. Hailwood, 'Time and Work in Rural England, 1500–1700', *Past & Present* 248 (2020), 87–121.

63 On the general link between accounting and time discipline see P. Quattrone, 'Is Time Spent, Passed or Counted? The Missing Link between Time and Accounting History', *Accounting Historians Journal* 32 (2005), pp. 185–208.

3

The Estate Accountant and the Development of Manorial Accounting: The *Rentmeister* in Westphalia and the Rhineland[1]

Friederike Scholten-Buschhoff

It is well known that noble manors did much more than display the owner's origin, status and wealth. Estates were the (country) home for the noble family. They were the location where rents and services were paid. At the same time, they were farms which grew and sold agricultural commodities. In consequence, they served a multiplicity of functions, practised a wide range of agricultural activities including forestry, and often pursued a number of commercial activities: brickworks, sawmills, distilleries and so on. For this reason, manorial estates were important employers. The range of activities and the scale of the enterprises made a good operational organization and structure indispensable. Noble estates invariably had an estate manager or administrator, the *Rentmeister*, and he oversaw the keeping of accounts as well as undertaking the daily management of the estates.

This chapter outlines the development of the administrative structures of five noble estates in the area of Westphalia and Rhineland (north-west Germany) for the period from 1650 to 1850 (Figure 3.1). The focus of the chapter though is on the late eighteenth and early nineteenth centuries. It looks at how changes in the manorial administration took place, how the estates were managed and identifies the contribution of central actors.

1 This chapter draws on my doctoral dissertation: F. Scholten-Buschhoff, 'Verkaufen – Verschenken – Lagern. Adelige Getreidewirtschaft in Rheinland und Westfalen, 1650–1850' (University of Münster, 2020). Research funding by the Deutsche Forschungsgemeinschaft is gratefully acknowledged (Research Grant PF 351/11–2).

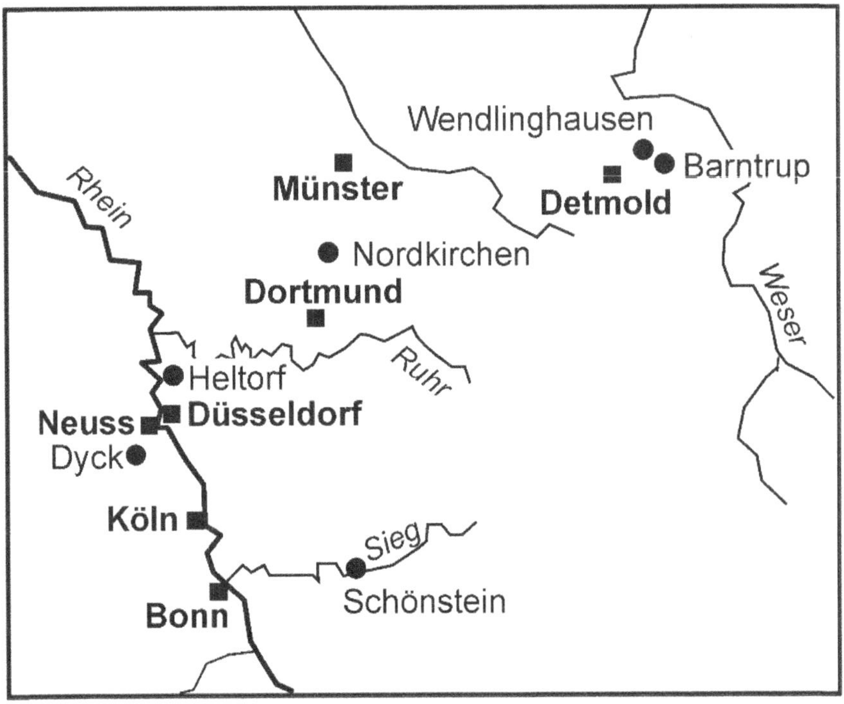

FIGURE 3.1. Westphalia and the lower Rhineland with the estates discussed: circles indicate location of landed estates, squares indicate towns/cities.

After a short introduction to the topic and an explanation of the scope of the study (Section I), the structure of the early accounting in the seventeenth and eighteenth centuries is portrayed (II). From the eighteenth century onwards, accounting underwent significant restructuring and reforms, visible in the form of *rationalization* and *formalization* processes which primarily aimed at greater transparency and uniformity (III). In the course of these processes, a system of commercial accounting was established, double-entry book-keeping was introduced, and the habit of daily correspondence about the management of the estate between landlord and administrator became routine. The drafting of monthly journals became usual and the auditing and scrutiny of accounts by a third party was established practice. The possible reasons and causes for these changes are of particular interest and will be discussed (IV). In the end, this inevitably leads to a closer examination of one of the key figures of noble business management, the *Rentmeister* (V). The recruitment of the *Rentmeister* will be considered (VI), then his freedom of action and supervision by the estate owner. This is read in terms of principal–agent theory (VII). We then consider the flow of information from *Rentmeister* to employer and instructions from employer to *Rentmeister* (VIII). A conclusion follows.

I

My initial intention was to study the operational and market behaviour of rural noble estates based on their administrative records. The study of accounting was merely a means to an end. However, it quickly became apparent that the administration of noble estates was a research topic of its own. Aristocratic estates, specifically their income and expenses, their staff, buildings and possessions, could not be managed without an appropriate system of book-keeping and a responsible administrator – especially when most landlords were absentees for much of the year. The importance of administration is largely independent of the size and location of the noble estates – regardless of whether they have larger or smaller possessions, agricultural properties, sovereign rights, fewer or more political offices or subsidiary businesses. All these parts of the noble estates had to be structured and organized in some way. As a consequence, book-keeping developed into a central part of business management and estate administration became a recognized profession.

The estates which are the focus of this study are representative properties which had either castles or palaces at their head. Only one of the estates, the *Nordkirchen* property of the Plettenberg family, is in the Westphalian region and is located between Dortmund and Münster – two of the bigger towns in the region. The four additional estates which are discussed are broadly distributed throughout the lower Rhineland, taking into account the fertile zones of the Lower Rhine (estates *Dyck*, family von Salm-Reifferscheidt, and *Wissen*, family von Loë) and the districts *Bergisches Land* (*Heltorf*, family von Spee) and *Siegerland* (Schönstein, family von Hatzfeldt), which are less suitable for arable farming and more commercial. However, the size, scope and structure of these properties vary greatly from estate to estate, depending on local conditions, family history and ultimately economic management.[2] Therefore, the estates are also diverse in their profile. However, especially in the context of operational management and accounting, there are a large number of structural similarities.

2 The size of the estates varies greatly. For the manors studied here, we can identify the following sizes: Heltorf, around 4,157 ha., of which 1,554 ha. was agricultural land (1928, much smaller in the eighteenth century); Dyck, 1,727 ha., 447 ha. agricultural land in 1794; Wissen, 1,500–2,000 ha. (assumption by the owner); Wildenburg/Schönstein, 10,750 ha. (1821); Nordkirchen, 2,800 ha., 1,600–1,800 ha. agricultural land in the middle of the nineteenth century). For more details see Scholten-Buschhoff, 'Adelige Getreidewirtschaft', pp. 104–5.

A distinction must be made between the two types of sources employed in this chapter. First, I use account books. They deal with all aspects of the estate. They are often subdivided into account books referring to money, to grain and other natural products such as cattle, and to wood. These three categories represent the different income types of the administration. Second, there is the correspondence between landlords and the estate administrator. The two often exchanged daily letters. Their letters discuss the management of the estate which makes internal decision-making more transparent. Therefore, the letters are essential for an understanding of the evolution of business accounting on these manors. Besides, they are also highly relevant for the analysis of the network of relationships between manager and owner in terms of the principal–agent theorem.

II

Accounts have always been kept in manors as part of the administration (the so-called *Rentei*). In the late sixteenth or early seventeenth century though, the books were barely organized or systematic. Rather, they were merely a loosely written compilation of incomes and expenditures, both in money and in kind, seldom structured by month and arbitrarily supplemented by inserted receipts. But despite their limitations, these books can be regarded as a massive aid to the management of the manors they document and an important tool to guide both planning and decision-making.

From the beginning of the eighteenth century, book-keeping on the manors became better ordered. First, accounts were increasingly structured by income and expenditure. They contain much more detail. On estates in north-west Germany the income of rural aristocratic estates came primarily from four sources:

(a.) Income from land leased to tenants. This was often half of the total estate income.

(b.) Income from feudal rights. These took a variety of forms but were normally paid in money rather than services.

(c.) Money from the sale of farm products, whether grain, cattle, bread, beer or wine, depending on the focus of estate production.

(d.) Income from salaried posts held by the landlord, whether in the military or government.

At this point, the income was not invariably recorded in the accounts according to its source. It was mostly recorded by date of receipt, in a continuous sequence, or by the name of the person making the payment. The same also applied to the expenditure which was also listed chronologically. The highest share of the expenses related to payments to the lord, salaries and wages, the maintenance of the manor's buildings, money lent for improvements, and the household. Both income and expenditure might be received or incurred as money as well as in kind.

Second, every account was now closed with a *computis generalis,* which summarized all income and expenditure over the year of the account. This summary helped the owner to see how the financial year for the estate had turned out. However, the accountants did not take a number of aspects into account: a surplus in the previous year was recorded as income in the second, but a deficit was not necessarily carried over into the new account. In addition, debts and some commercial activities (for instance the brick works found on some estates, even a mineral water business on one) were not always included in the account.

There were three problems that arose out of this form of accounting. First, there was a delay between income being received and expenditure incurred and the book-keeping. This arose from the process of preparing the accounts at the year end. Within the year, the administrator was collecting notes and receipts and generally wrote monthly (sometimes also weekly) journals in which he recorded all income and expenditure. After the year end, he started to write the final version of the account book. But there was often a delay before the account was finished, sometimes even of several years. The long time interval between the end of the accounting year itself and the completion of the account was disadvantageous when transactions were challenged: the longer ago they were, the less likely it was that they could be recalled and doubts about them resolved. The second problem that arose was that the person responsible for the accounts sometimes changed frequently. That also contributed to discontinuities in the accounting. Third, comments and corrections of the entries made by contemporaries also led to difficulties as it was ultimately not clear which entry was finally correct.

So whilst the accounts of the seventeenth and eighteenth centuries show a tendency to become more structured, they have been classified as operating notes or 'concepts ... where much of it is corrected and is presented in a disorderly manner'.[3] They fall far short of the accounts of the nineteenth century. Nevertheless, even these early forms of accounting, which were continuously evolving and to which contemporaries referred again and again in the context of operational processes, demonstrate the developing accountability of the estate managers – at least for the estates in Westphalia and Rhineland. Due to their documentary character, they were of great value for the organization of the manors as they made relevant processes such as sales, leases and payments visible. An overall account, i.e. an account that included all components of the manor

3 Wildenburg A 16040, 'Monita zu den Domänen Wildenburgischen Land Rechnungen von dem Jahr 1750 bis 1796 inclusive' (in private hands). Use via 'Vereinigte Adelsarchive im Rheinland' (hereafter VAR).

(business, household and estate), remained rare until the beginning of the nineteenth century.

III

During the second half of the eighteenth century a structural change took place in all the manorial administrations which have been examined for this study. By the end of this development, which included the *rationalization* and *formalization* of the accounts, the administrations were much more transparent, uniform and clear in their operations. This is most easily visible in the accounts, which have a totally new appearance at the end of the century compared to the beginning.

The process of *rationalization* was fundamental. This was understood as making measurements to optimize the estate's productivity, to increase the manor's income whilst lowering its costs. It contained the idea that all decisions within the administration needed to be justified. This was – at least to a certain extent – a conscious decision to make internal processes transparent and so to optimize them. Within this development, four changes occurred: (a) double-entry book-keeping was introduced; (b) an extensive correspondence about operational processes between landlord and estate administrator was commenced (this will be discussed later); (c) monthly journals, which were presented to the owners for review, were kept; and (d) the ledgers themselves were audited by third parties employed for the purpose or examined by the owners themselves.

All these changes served the purpose of making the entire estate administration transparent to the owners, enabling them to track processes and decisions. The owners demanded 'clear knowledge of the status of the administration'.[4] On the manor of Nordkirchen for example, the *Rentmeister* had to 'submit a comprehensive report on the status of the administration [...] every three months'.[5] This meant that the administrators were obliged to justify their activities to their employer at any time upon request.

As a direct consequence of the '*rationalization*' described above, parallel processes of *formalization* were implemented. This led to the establishment of overall structures and rules that everyone involved in estate administration had to follow. But whereas processes of *rationalization* had already begun in the second half of the eighteenth century, *formalization* had its heyday in the 1830s.

At the core of *formalization* was the increased commercial orientation of estates. Accounts generally became more relevant when estates were developing trading and moving away from being simply the recipients

4 Nor A 3272, #030 (31 Dec. 1866) (use via 'Vereinigte Westfälische Adelsarchive' VWA).

5 Ibid.

of rental income. The accounts evolved from being 'operating notes' towards more precise 'evidence of the funds of things ... that are to be sold or managed' and serve as a media of 'accountability'[6] for the administrator. Sooner or later, this happened on all the estates. On Dyck, the administrator, who was at the centre of these processes, received precise instructions from his landlord for the new accounting organization in 1783:

> In the future, the administrator in Dyck had to divide his annual accounts into main sections according to the following form. (1) The income of the money and the expenditure of his account. (2) The same is purchased as an accompaniment to the grain accounts in the barn and how they are sold. (3) The wood and forestry account. (4) The account of all building materials, such as these are purchased and used in the castles and stately buildings; and finally (5) the wine account, especially since the annual wine harvest is transported from Alfter to Dick ... . Each account section is divided into categories according to the 'formulario' and what cannot be assigned to any category has to be stated in the general sections.[7]

According to these instructions, income and expenditure were no longer accounted by provenance, but by activity. In addition, arrears were listed separately for the first time and a consistent division into target and actual payments was established. Moreover, the balance sheet that used to be at the end of every account changed its appearance: it increasingly contained an overview of the individual categories of the annual in- and outputs of the *Rentei*. At Nordkirchen for instance, the account for 1803–4 closes with a summary page with the title 'Summarische Ausgabe' where the landowner could see at a glance the state of his accounts. This allowed him to see that nearly 25 per cent of expenditure had been used for the maintenance of family members. Salaries for people working on/for the

6 Wildenburg A 16018, 'Ohnamßgebliches Dafürhalten, wie eigentlich eine Rechnung angefertigt werden müße, wie auch Verhaltens-Regeln für Hl. Amtmann Seelbach' (use via VAR).

7 'Der Rhentmeister zu Dick hatte künftig seine Jahrs Rechnungen in Hauptabschnitte nach dem folgenden Formular einzuteilen', also jedoch daß (1) 'der geldempfang und die Ausgabe seine HauptRechnung Auswachs'; (2) 'wird derselben als eine Beilage angeschafft die Früchten Rechnungen auf dem Speicher und wie diese verkaufet werden'; (3) 'die Holzforst und Waltrechnung'; (4) 'die Rechnung von allen Bau Materialien, wie diese angekauft und hieweder an Schlösser und Häuser und Herrschaftlichen Gebäude gebraucht und endlich'; (5) 'die Weinrechnung besonders da die jährlichen Wein-Ernte von Alfter nach der Dick Transport zu werden pfleget [...] Ein jeder Rechnungsabschnitt wird hieweder nach Vorschrift des *formulario* in *rubriquen* eingeteilet, und was zu keiner besonderer *rubrique* einschaut unter die letzere Rechnungs rubrique Emfpangsgeld und Ausgabegeld insgemein gesetzet.' Dyck A 363, #99 (use via VAR).

manor came to 23 per cent of expenditure and improvements 18 per cent. It also becomes clear that the residue of unallocated expenses is enormous (35 per cent). In addition, a fixed cover sheet including information on the author, the currency and measure of capacity valid for the account and a table of contents was introduced.

The aim of this modified, formalized book-keeping was ultimately the creation of a comprehensive annual account. One part of this was the final subdivision of the administration between the public *Rentei* and the private *Ökonomie*. These are more than just contemporary terms – they gave the daily operational business a new structure. While the *Rentei* referred to the administration of the income from rights and possession as well as claims to manorial and personal rights, the *Ökonomie* included the private household of the landlord. A major step in this development was the availability of pre-printed tabular accounting books which came to be used in all the estate administrations. In the case of Nordkirchen, the administrator used a printed form in which categories (income and expenditures) were already laid out. These books also contain a column template about the money or in kind payments that should and actually have been received (*'Soll'* and *'Ist'* payments). The accountant himself only needs to add the single sections, local currencies and measures as well as the information about the payer. These new templates soon became a standard in the account books and contributed to a significantly better overview both in structure and in terms of content.

Despite all the advantages that followed from the 'new types of accounting', a great deal of detail was now admitted from the account books. As a result, there was also a trend towards compiling thematic individual accounts dividing the estate into areas of economic activity. These had existed in the seventeenth and eighteenth centuries, but only occasionally, and they had not been an integral part of book-keeping.

Finally, these *formalization* processes affected almost all branches of the administration. All contracts, be it for leases, sales or services, increasingly followed a uniform, repetitive pattern – both in their implementation and in their documentation.

Both changes, *rationalizations* and the resulting *formalizations*, were not happening on an ad hoc basis within the noble administration, but developed gradually as contemporaries came to accept them. The Hatzfeldt administrator said how 'I have at least used all my diligence and effort as much as I can to finally understand the new way of accounting so that I don't have to struggle with peevishness in this regard for the rest of my life.'[8] In addition it is evident that as complex as the changes were, the reasons why they were introduced were just as multifaceted as the changes themselves.

8 Crottorf A 5417 'Die Jahresrechnung mit Belegen und Nachweisungen pro 1836' (27 Oct. 1837) (private property, use via VAR).

IV

The administrators often discussed the changes. They held that the growing scope and increasing complexity of the estates was the main motivation which lay behind them. At the beginning of the nineteenth century the Nordkirchen administrator even said that complex forms of book-keeping had not been necessary up to the last quarter of the eighteenth century, since the manor's businesses were much smaller and thus easier to organize and handle. 'The course of the business was still extremely simple overall'. But since then the business became more complex and labour intensive due to the 'high income and especially because of more than 500 peasants in the domain [...], constant quarrels, lawsuits, [...], leases, necessary repairs and many other items'.[9]

It was not only the size and the increasing complexity of the manors that were likely to be reasons for these developments. A number of other causes, working in combination, played a decisive role in bringing about change.

(a) Financial pressure. It is well known that the nobility struggled financially. Recent research has come to the conclusion that the landed gentry actively pursued a policy of debt reduction in the second half of the eighteenth century.[10] A combination of high levels of debt and high expenses forced owners to pay more attention to the management of their income, assuming that only the competent management of their estates could ultimately offer the family economic security. The nobles recognized the value of control and support tools as well as *formalizations* as a tried and tested means of increasing income in the short term. This was particularly evident in Nordkirchen: here the *rationalization* and *formalization* of the administration in the last quarter of the eighteenth century and especially in the first quarter of the nineteenth was clearly the result of the high levels of debt carried by the property.[11]

(b) Economic possibilities. Both landowners and estate administrators were conscious of economic developments, in particular, the rising price of grain. Interestingly, the start of the processes of innovation described above coincided with the end of static agricultural prices, after which an increasingly market-oriented agriculture developed. This could have encouraged processes to formalize economic activities such as grain sales as a means of increasing income.

(c) Shift of interest. The landed gentry did not always have the same interest in farming activities. This was not only due to personal preferences, but also simply a result of the large number of activities that they

9 Nor A 13427 (18 July 1800) (use via VWA).

10 S. Solterbeck, *Blaues Blut und rote Zahlen* (2018), p. 318; also H. Reif, *Westfälischer Adel 1770–1860: Vom Herrschaftsstand zur regionalen Elite* (1979), pp. 10–12, 236.

11 See Solterbeck, *Blaues Blut*, pp. 383–7.

had to carry out at the same time. This changed over time, since the French period (and later the agricultural reforms) reduced the number of social and political tasks carried out by the aristocracy and thereafter more time could be spent managing the estates. Many landowners returned to their estates permanently in the nineteenth century and were then able to take over the management themselves.[12] This was related to the change in the standing of the nobility in the nineteenth century. The strategy of staying at the top ('Obenbleiben') included a stronger engagement with the financial basis of the nobility. While the estate was previously only one of many elements in the aristocratic self-image, it was increasingly central to them.

(d) Monetization. The growing availability of money on the estates also played a role.[13] Before the late eighteenth or early nineteenth century, manors often worked 'without money' and a large part of their economic activities were carried out in kind. Orderly book-keeping was less necessary here. It can be observed that there was a long-term shift from payments in kind towards a monetary payment which forced changes in accounting.[14]

(e) Shifts in income. When the manorial system was dissolved, the nobility suffered severe financial losses.[15] As a result, the estate owners looked for other ways to generate income. This was achieved through an expansion of their own agriculture, by the development of forestry and other industrial activities. The prerequisite for this was a correspondingly well-developed operational and accounting system.

(f) Structural changes. The improvements in information networks that took place in the nineteenth century and the slow expansion of the

12 For example, Maria Esterházy-Galantha (1809–61) is the first owner of the estate at Nordkirchen who spent a significant amount of time on her property. She was also actively involved in the management of the estate (and not just by letter). For more details see her diary, also called 'Notizenbuch für Allerhand', covering the years 1846–53 and accessible online via the Universitäts- und Landesbibliothek Münster: https://sammlungen.ulb.uni-muenster.de/urn/urn:nbn:de:hbz:6:1-193019 (last modified April 2023).

13 See M. Giraudeau, 'The Farm as an Accounting Laboratory: An Essay on the History of Accounting and Agriculture', *Accounting History Review* 27 (2017), pp. 201–15; T. Kooijmans and J. Jonker, 'Chained to the Manor? Payment Patterns and Landlord–Tenant Relations in the Salland Region of the Netherlands around 1750', *Tijdschrift voor Sociale en Economische Geschiedenis* 12 (2015), pp. 89–116, sect. 6; J. Bracht and U. Pfister, *Landpacht, Marktgesellschaft und agrarische Entwicklung: Fünf Adelsgüter zwischen Rhein und Weser, 16. bis 19. Jahrhundert* (2020), p. 52.

14 In 1784 on the estate of Nordkirchen only one fifth of the rent of land held by lease was paid in kind. See Bracht and Pfister, *Landpacht*, Table 3.1, p. 50.

15 The manorial system was abolished in the Rhineland during the French Revolution and from 1807 onwards in the rest of Germany. On abolition, rural property was transferred to the farmers in return for compensation.

transport system made it possible for manors to exploit their resources to a greater extent.

(g) Zeitgeist. At the end of the eighteenth century, the overarching process of establishing a market society began in the sense described in Karl Polanyi's *Great Transformation.*[16] Prior to this, it was difficult for manors to act in a profit-oriented manner. For example, when a landlord increased land and grain prices (with the intention of increasing his revenues), it quickly led to a destabilization of the social framework. The reason for this was that all participants, landlord, tenants and buyers, met in different markets at the same time. Those who rented land also bought grain from the manor and/or worked for the landlord simultaneously. These multiple interactions between the manors and villagers in product, labour and land markets, which were closely related to the role of the landowner as patriarch, increasingly dissolved. This finally opened the way for profit-oriented businesses that required sophisticated methods of book-keeping.

Finally, it is interesting that the developments outlined here were not, so far as I can tell, directly influenced by modern approaches to agriculture. Originally it was expected that the professionalization of the management of the manors was the result of the acquisition of knowledge of improved agricultural practices. The landed nobility in the eighteenth and nineteenth centuries may have increased the size of their libraries, but, at least on the estates observed here, without any focus on the subject of agriculture.[17] In concrete terms, this means that neither was there an increased acquisition of so called '*Hausväter- and Kameralistenliteratur*'[18] by the estates, nor has evidence been found of the reception of early works of agronomy. This is surprising as these genres developed central ideas and theories about the promotion of agriculture. Despite this, as will be shown later in this chapter, it turns out that the content of this literature must have been familiar to landlords. But how this knowledge was actually acquired, and how far it was discussed and exchanged between landowners remains unclear at this point.

16 K. Polanyi, *The Great Transformation: Origins of our Time* (2001).

17 See Scholten-Buschhoff, 'Adelige Getreidewirtschaft', ch. 5.

18 Ibid., ch. 5.3.1 and especially Wolf Helmhard von Hohberg and his *Georgica curiosa* (1682). At the core of his analysis is the aristocratic country life: first the general living environment; second his role as a landlord and third everyday life in the family network. Von Hohberg placed the main focus on the behaviour of the landowner within the company. Although he does not explicitly mention the marketing of products, he does mention the sale of beer and annual and weekly markets. The work remained in print for almost a century and appeared in six editions.

V

The history of accounting on landed estates is closely linked to the administrator, the *Rentmeister*. Research shows that every noble landlord employed at least one person to undertake the administration of his manor.[19] I have been able to identify at least sixty administrators who served on three of the noble estates over a period of 200 years. Their periods of employment varied enormously. There are instances of men serving for 40 years and more but others only stayed for short periods of a few years. There is a tendency though for a *Rentmeister*, when appointed, to stay for an extended period.

The need for an estate administrator arose because the landlord had a variety of roles to fulfil which often did not allow him to be present on the estate in person. These included his duties at court, in the military or in politics. Nobles were, for much of the year if not entirely, 'absentee landlords'. In addition, the landowner was not always well equipped to run the administration himself whether because of a lack of aptitude or knowledge. Not every landlord was interested in being involved in the daily administration of his estate.[20] The manors were supposed to give owners a certain standard of living but that did not mean that individual owners attached great importance to profit-oriented management or wanted to invest a lot of time and energy in administration. However, since both the lordship and the manor's interests had to be to be adequately represented and defended, the use of an agent was inevitable.

This is where the *Rentmeister* came into play. All information and responsibilities converged in his position. He was thus the key person in the administration of estates and part of a mediated rule, receiving instructions from his employer but also supplying him with the knowledge on which the owner's instructions could be based. Because of this key position, the steward provides an important gateway into the study of rural noble estates and their administration and rural society generally.[21]

19 The size of the estates has an influence on the complexity of rule and communication. For English estates it is assumed that 'smaller estates were less likely to have resident land agents', J. Theobald, 'Distant Lands: The Management of Absentee Estates in Woodland High Suffolk, 1660–1860', *Rural History* 12 (2001), p. 2.

20 See Scholten-Buschhoff, 'Adelige Getreidewirtschaft', ch. 5.

21 The key position of the administrator or estate steward has been extensively discussed in the English literature. For a selection, see J. V. Beckett, 'Absentee Landownership in the Later Seventeenth and Early Eighteenth Centuries: The Case of Cumbria', *Northern History* 19 (1983), pp. 87–107; idem, *The Aristocracy in England, 1660–1914* (Oxford, 1986); idem, 'Landownership and Estate Management', in G. E. Mingay (ed.), *The Agrarian History of England and Wales, VI, 1750–1850* (1989); Theobald, 'Distant Lands'; D. R. Hainsworth, *Stewards, Lords and People: The Estate Steward and his World in Later Stuart England* (2008); C. Beardmore, 'Landowner, Tenant and Agent on the Marquis of Anglesey's

The *Rentmeister* presided over the *Rentei*, i.e. the institutional and practical administration of the noble estates. It turns out that book-keeping was only one of many tasks that he undertook for his master. On the basis of the contract and instructions landlords gave administrators, it can be shown that the administration was much more than the collection of feudal rents.[22] As early as the seventeenth century, comprehensive catalogues of tasks, so-called 'instructions', were issued as formal contracts between landowners and administrators. They show how extensive the administrative activity was, how heavily it was regulated and how highly bureaucratic it was. The 'instructions' for the administrators were broadly similar on all the manors. They were deliberately implemented to ensure that the administrator was fully aware of his responsibilities when he took up his duties. At the same time, however, they also served to protect the landlord, since the administrator's effective power was guided by a precise catalogue of tasks.[23] As all the instructions were fairly similar over time and place it can be assumed that they were a result of contact between landowners although we have no evidence for this as yet.

The list of the administrator's daily tasks included (a) the writing of the annual (and sometimes monthly) accounts; (b) the administration of leases and the associated concerns and dealing with the complaints of the tenants; (c) the organization of the entire in-kind economy, mainly cattle and grain (this includes the administration of transfers within the estate, the planning and execution of sales, as well as the 'daily supervision, maintenance and measurement of the grain and preparation of

Dorset and Somerset Estate, 1814–44', *Rural History* 26 (2015), pp. 181–99; S. Webster, 'Estate Improvement and the Professionalization of Land Agents on the Egremont Estates in Sussex and Yorkshire, 1770–1835', *Rural History* 18 (2007), pp. 47–69. For discussions elsewhere in Europe, Kooijmans and Jonker, 'Chained'; S. Berghmans, 'The Management of the Estates of the Duke of Arenberg in the Eighteenth and Nineteenth Century' (unpublished paper, Rural History Conference Leuven, 2017) and R. Garrabou, J. Planas and E. Saguer, 'The Management of Agricultural Estates in Catalonia in the Nineteenth and Early Twentieth Century', *Agricultural History Review* 60 (2012), pp. 173–90.

22 See H. Kaak and M. Schattkowsky, 'Herrschaft: Machtentfaltung über adligen und fürstlichen Grundbesitz in der Frühen Neuzeit', in J. Peters (ed.), *Potsdamer Studien zur Geschichte der ländlichen Gesellschaft* (2003), p. xviii.

23 These 'instructions' are therefore a general phenomenon, especially from the eighteenth century onwards, and are found on all the estates. See also Berghmans, 'Management', p. 13. In addition to the service instructions, which have been preserved in many cases (e.g. 'The General Service Instruction of Hofrath Levenhagen in Nordkirchen', Nor A 13200 8 July 1811, use via VWA), the diary of the Nordkirchen administrator Morsbach is another important source. He kept a daily work diary between 1850 and 1859 (NME 8 & 9, use via VWA).

the annual accounts');[24] (d) the management of the services and those employed at the estate (e.g. day labourers, servants); (e) the supervision of the jurisdictions in the villages belonging to the castle; and above all (f) the collection of a whole range of sources of income.

VI

The *Rentmeister*'s responsibilities therefore included accounting, personnel management, administrative organization and general financial management including the keeping of accounts. Probably the most intellectually demanding task was to see the activities of the whole estate 'in the round' It was not enough to 'just' know the business operations in all areas: it meant being able to calculate, plan and develop the estate. The landlords made big demands on their administrators.

In the choice of a *Rentmeister*, the family background might be decisive. There are a number of cases in which the office was passed down through the family. The Nordkirchen administrator Engelbert Morsbach (in service from 1820 to 1859) was taken into service not only because of his good education – he was a trained lawyer – but primarily because he was the son-in-law of his predecessor Sandfort. Sandfort explicitly wanted his son-in-law to succeed him. And Sandfort himself was the son-in-law of his predecessor Schürhof. It is no surprise that positions such as the *Rentmeister* were often inherited within a family. Again and again it is reported that 'individual families understood how to claim those offices for themselves'.[25]

In general, little is known about the social origins of the *Rentmeister*. There is evidence that they often came from educated families. They appear to have been recruited locally, which was appropriate, since local knowledge was essential for their activities. But it is unclear whether they were the 'sons of practical men' as on English estates and had been involved in the 'varied business of land management' since their childhood, that is, whether they had a farming background.

Certainly, a high level of education was necessary. The minimum requirements for this specific work were, first of all, literacy, numeracy, good handwriting, spelling, mathematical and linguistic skills. Many administrators had attended a secondary school. This is documented for the middle of the eighteenth century.[26] In addition, the potential administrator must have been a good householder and economist in the

24 Nor A 3940, #7 (1803) (use via VWA).

25 G. Bloos, 'Die Rentmeister von Düsseldorf', *Beiträge zur Geschichte des Niederrheins* 7 (1893), p. 63. This refers to Mayor's offices as well as estate administrators.

26 This is proven by a school certificate in the estate papers of the Rentmeister Schürhof, see Nor A 7268 'Estate Papers' (17 Dec. 1755) (use via VWA).

spirit of the 'Hausväter-' and 'Kameralistenliteratur'. Prior knowledge of agriculture and forestry was a great advantage. The analysis shows that the educational backgrounds varied from person to person. For a long time there was no uniformity. This is also due to the fact that there was no training tailored to these activities until the nineteenth century. A legal background is common: at the manor of Nordkirchen, *Rentmeister* Sandfort had a doctorate in law ('Justzirechte'). *Rentmeister* Morsbach, on the other hand, had been an 'advocate' and also held the title of the judiciary councillor.

From the second half of the nineteenth century onwards, there were clear efforts to professionalize the work of the administrator. A special school system and the emerging agricultural schools offered an economic–agricultural education that was probably primarily of a practical and less theoretical nature. Graduates then often worked as *Rentmeister*. The Association of *Rentmeister*, established in the 1880s, ultimately organized the profession.

Appropriate professional experience – acquired before taking up administrative work – was also common. Many administrators learned important skills through junior jobs in administrative offices. On the one hand, Max Darup, administrator in Nordkirchen at the end of the nineteenth century, had already worked as an administrator before taking up his position. On the other hand, the *Rentmeister* on the manor at Dyck had usually worked in civil service-like activities before they started working on the estate. They had previously been bailiffs, secretaries, lawyers or court clerks. Two administrators came from a religious background as clergy. At the same time, appointees were apparently not far removed from farming either. It is not uncommon for *Rentmeister* to have managed their own farm or worked on their parents' farms. However, managing a farm whilst working as a *Rentmeister* was almost impossible due to the high workload.

It was therefore no small undertaking for a landowner to find a suitable person who satisfied the complex requirements of the position. In the seventeenth and eighteenth centuries in particular, there seems to have been a lack of qualified candidates.[27]

VI

The *Rentmeister* did not act independently. He would be in daily contact with the housekeeper, estate employees, servants and the day labourers on the estate. The aristocratic owners remained largely invisible to many employees and only dealt with them through the *Rentmeister*. In this way he mediated between the aristocrats and the staff. It required close

27 J. Bremer, *Die reichsunmittelbare Herrschaft Dyck: Die Grafen jetzigen Fürsten zu Salm-Reifferscheidt* (1959), p. 733.

and good coordination and supervision of these sub-areas to ensure that the estates ran smoothly. As the landowners were not only the owners of land but exercised power over both land and people, their authority over both was exercised within the framework of the *Rentei.* Thus, an important task of the *Rentmeister* was to represent the landowner within the community and exercise his power on his behalf in his absence. The relationship of the landowner to his estates was highly complex. At different times it might be marked by cooperation, at others by conflict. A great deal of diplomatic skill might be required on the part of the *Rentmeister* to secure what the landowner sought whilst mollifying the tenants, and vice versa.[28]

However, the 'instructions' did not only contain the duties of the administrator, they also described his role very precisely. He must be 'loyal and trustworthy' and must 'perceive our [owner's] best [interest] everywhere'. At the same time he should 'promote the well-being of the subjects to the best of his ability' and appear with 'law and justice' as well as 'loyalty and integrity'.[29] The reality of the *Rentmeister*'s position is shown by the traditional signature which ended every letter to his employer: 'Your most humble, most obedient servant'.[30] Before he took up his post, the *Rentmeister* also confirmed with an oath that he would fulfil the tasks entrusted to him.

However, the workload of the administrators and its diversity was becoming more and more of a problem. Contemporaries were aware that being a *Rentmeister* was a full-time job – but the workload was sometimes so high that they had difficulties in completing all tasks promptly and well. Around 1813, *Rentmeister* Levenshagen in Nordkirchen described the challenges quite precisely:

> This administration, which he runs under the supreme supervision of the manor, makes up a very important part of his business and, given the quantity, size and partial remoteness of the administered manors, involves no small effort and burden, and with some more or less connected significant cash expenses. The *rentmeister* has to inspect the – often very distant – plots of land himself, has to be mindful of maintaining the lord's justice and improving the manors, has to carry

28 For more about mediation of power within estate management, see V. Hyden-Hanscho, 'Herrschaftsvermittlung in den österreichischen Niederlanden: Léopold Philippe Arenberg zwischen Karl III./VI. und Maria Theresia', in W. D. Godsey and V. Hyden-Hanscho (eds), *Das Haus Arenberg und die Habsburgermonarchie: Eine transterritoriale Adelsfamilie zwischen Fürstendienst und Eigenständigkeit (16.–20. Jahrhundert)* (2019), pp. 183–274.

29 Nor A. 12297, #158 §1 (use via VWA).

30 Nor A. 5350, #1 (1810) (use via VWA), similar in Wildenburg A 6120, #279 'Die Verminderung der Schultheißen und die Anstellung der Renteidiener daselbst' (1830) (private property, use via VAR).

> out sales and leases on the spot, often has to go personally to the courts … appear on behalf of the lord, has to receive money and grain leases in distant places, has to travel in matters relating to the manor, generally also looks after the interests of the manor outside his *Rentei* and place of residence until the landlord takes this over himself or through another employee.[31]

Levenshagen emphasized that the challenge was the diversity of 'sovereign interests', which included interests related to status, business and household, and could therefore only be represented by a single person. Levenshagen's predecessor, Sandfort, wrote to his landowner that 'the management of the Rentei and other businesses in Nordkirchen is not the work of one man'.[32] However, the employment of a second *Rentmeister* is very rare. This only occurred within the course of the increase and expansion of the nobility (e.g. consolidation of possessions in the nineteenth century). If families owned more than one manor, they often hired a separate administrator for each one. However, it was more usual for a *Rentei* to supervised several assets of a family.

The administrative expansion and the developing processes discussed before altered the duties of the administrator. The amount of written work he had to do increased significantly. The volume of the records of administrative acts, show a clear intensification of the written form of business administration from the second or third quarter of the eighteenth century. In the course of these measures, the duties of the *Rentmeister* came to be more and more closely specified.

A central element of the administrative expansion, as an integral part of the *formalization* and *rationalization* processes discussed above, was the increase in the frequency of communication between landowners and administrators. It was the basic assumption that in order to assert

31 'Diese Administration, welche er unter der herrschaftlichen Oberaufsicht führt, macht einen sehr wichtigen Theil seines Geschäftskreises aus, und ist bey der Menge, Größe und theilweisen Entlegenheit der administrierten Güter, sowohl mit nicht geringer Mühe und Last, als auch mit manchen mehr oder minder bedeutenden baaren Auslagen verkauft. Der Rentmeister muß die – oft sehr entfernten Grundstücke bei manchen Veranlassungen selbst besichtigen, muß auf Erhaltung der herrschaftlichen Gerechtigkeiten auf Verbesserungen der Güter bedacht sein, muß an Ort und Stelle Verkäufe und Verpachtungen vornehmen, muß oft persönlich bei den Gerichten … für die Herrschaft auftreten, muß Geld und Kornpächte dem Herbringer gemäß an entfernten Orten in Empfang nehmen, muß in sonstigen herrschaftlichen Angelegenheiten Reisen machen, überhaupt auch außerhalb seines Rentei und Wohnorts des Herrschaftlichen Interesse solange wahrnehmen, bis die Herrschaft dieses selbst übernimmt, oder durch einen anderen dazu Angestellten besorgen läßt.' Nor A 4133 (ad 46 ad num 146) (around 1813) (use via VWA).

32 Nor A 3940, p. 7 (1803) (use via VWA).

rule, orders and instructions must be passed on smoothly to subordinate officials. Given the mediated management and rulership presented here, the transfer of information was the crux of the matter, because the landlord himself could barely control his representatives. The remoteness of the noble combined with the complexity of the operations inevitably meant that the landlords were not directly integrated into local activities. This inevitably created concern on the part of the nobility that the estate was not been managed as it should. In order to keep this danger to a minimum, however, contemporaries established a communication system which primarily served to exchange information, but was the means by which the estate owner monitored and controlled estate activity. The intention was obvious. The estate managers should be deliberately restricted in their freedom by being obliged to regularly report on their activities to the aristocrats and to justify them. Independent decision-making was thus prevented – at least in part. In this way, one tries to prevent situations in which the officers do not act in the sense of the 'sovereign interest'.

VII

The relationship between the landlord and the estate administrator was more than a one-sided relationship of service between employer and employed. Due to the fact that the *Rentmeister* acted as an 'extended arm' of the owner, sometimes even as his deputy, it was a far more complex relationship that was characterized by dependency and control, but also trust and, to some extent, friendship. This is most evident in the full and detailed correspondence between the two that will be discussed below. This shows the degree to which the nobleman was involved in the everyday business life of his estate. The contents of these letters also provide information about how the two actors actually related to each other. The peculiarity of the relationship lies in the social distance between the two actors. The manager had an advantage over the owner due both to his presence on the manor, and his engagement with the local community. The landowner received all of his information from his administrator – i.e. second-hand. Landlords made operational decisions on the basis of what they had been told. But the two actors rarely saw each other, even if they were in contact almost every day.

In the daily business of the estates, important policies were usually agreed in advance with the landlord or were implemented on his instructions. This included, for example, the awarding of contracts. In principle, this meant that the administrator rarely made his own decisions. However, this did not mean that there was no discretion allowed the *Rentmeister*. He always made suggestions or gave his recommendation on the crucial issues (e.g. he would suggest dates for the sale of grain and minimum prices) and it was his assessment of local conditions that formed the basis of the landlord's decision. Thus he exerted a decisive influence over the business. This required a mutual trust between owner and *Rentmeister*. On the one hand, the landowner needed to trust his administrator as he was a 'mediator of power', meaning that he would fulfil his tasks and manage the property in the interests of his employer. The *Rentmeister*, in turn, must have also placed his trust in the lord of the manor – in the sense that he needed to be confident that he would be supported by him and his advice taken.

The administrator's room for manoeuvre only existed as long as the trust on both sides was maintained. Mutual confidence was by no means a matter of course, but must have been built up over time. Administrators gained trust above all through their appearance and actions. It was important to work 'efficiently' and 'according to instructions', to report to the owner regularly about local events (without being asked) and to express the wishes and ideas of the owner, to represent and implement the lord's decisions promptly. And indeed it turned out that the majority of administrators strove to leave no doubt as to their loyalty to their lords.

Even if the administrator's loyalty to their landlords can be assumed, control was an essential part of the relationship. At the end of the eighteenth century, when management of their estates increasingly aroused their interest, the aristocrats began to no longer rely entirely on the promised loyalty. They increasingly asked for written evidence. The control the lord exercised by letter and the frequent reports he demanded were deliberately chosen measures to prevent the power of disposal and the room for manoeuvre of the *Rentmeister* becoming too great, nor the influence and the rule of the landowner too small.

We can read this relationship in terms of principal–agent theory.[33] This is based on the assumption that persons as principals, in this case the landowners, are restricted in their decision-making due to an unequal level of information, in this case because of the absence of the landlord from his estates. They were highly dependent on the actions of others (the agents, here the administrators). But this dependency led to the danger

33 This theory has been current in institutional economics since the 1970s. Relevant for this passage: T. Petersen, *Optimale Anreizsysteme: Betriebswirtschaftliche Implikationen der Prinzipal–Agenten–Theorie* (1989); M. C. Jensen and W. H. Meckling, 'Theory of the Firm: Managerial Behavior, Agency Costs and Ownership Structure', *Journal of Finance Economics* 3 (1976), pp. 305–60; S. Dierkes and U. Schäfer, 'Prinzipal–Agenten–Theorie und Performance Measurement', *Zeitschrift für Controlling & Management* (2008), pp. 19–27; P. Jost *et al.*, *Die Prinzipal–Agenten–Theorie in der Betriebswirtschaftlehre* (2001); M. B. Roiger, *Gestaltung von Anreizsystemen und Unternehmensethik. Eine norm- und wertbezogene Analyse der normativen Prinzipal–Agent–Theorie* (2007); A. Alparslan, *Strukturalistische Prinzipal–Agent–Theorie. Eine Reformulierung der Hidden Action Modelle aus der Perspektive des Strukturalismus* (2006).

of opportunism – i.e. that the agent/administrator uses his knowledge to his own advantage and thus to the detriment of the principal/landowner. This was reinforced by the fact that both persons were ultimately self-interest maximizers and did not have the same utility function. This created a relationship of mistrust between the administrator and the landowner. In part, an attempt was made to circumvent this by agreeing a catalogue of tasks (service instructions) for the estate administrator to carry out. However, this did not change the unavoidable fact that there was always an asymmetry of information, actions or attitudes between the two. The administrator was always going to be better informed than the principal. Theoretically, as an opportunistic actor, the *Rentmeister* could have used this local information to his advantage and, for example, only report to a limited extent – in the sense of hidden knowledge/action. This was particularly the case when selling grain: it was easy for him to secure higher prices, report lower prices to the owner and ultimately keep the difference to himself. Alternatively, there was also the danger of either hidden characteristics, in which the principal was not aware of the properties of the agent (preferences, performance or expectational judgement), or was unaware of the administrator's real intention.

No matter what asymmetry ultimately existed, the challenge was for the owner to control the *Rentmeister*, in such a way that an optimal result was still achieved for the *Rentei*. The aim was to reduce or even negate the natural asymmetry as far as possible. One possibility was to give the agent a share of the profits in order to control his motivation (= incentive). However, there is no evidence that a *Rentmeister* ever received a share of the proceeds from grain sales or any other transactions made on behalf of the estate. His salary, which was significantly higher than that of the other employees, was in itself an incentive which should have motivated the administrator to act in the interests of the aristocrat. In addition, the dense control and information system also served to avoid asymmetries – but only after the conclusion of the contract (*ex post*). This remained the most direct way for the owners to ensure that the *Rentei* was not falling victim to the administrator's high-handedness. However, deceit could not be completely ruled out as there was always the possibility of false accounting by the administrator. If at all, this could only be identified with a great deal of effort.

VIII

The crucial feature of the relationship between the *Rentmeister* and his landlord was therefore the way and the frequency with which they communicated with each other. Initially part of this was the annual (and later sometimes monthly) drafting of accounts and reports which were submitted to the landowners for their approval. Noble accounting was theoretically closely based on the ideas of the 'house father literature'. Wolf Helmhard von Hohberg emphasized in his *Georgica curiosa* of 1682 that book-keeping, as the core of administrative tasks, was a tried and tested means of informing the lord about his estates and at the same time allowed the work of the administrator to be checked.[34] Although, as stated above, there is no real evidence that the nobility was familiar with this literature, it must be assumed that its content was both known and acted on.

Over time the control mechanisms for the administrator's work were increasingly perfected on the manors. Whereas in the middle of the eighteenth century, accounts were the key means of supervision, by the end of the century at the latest a range of new communication tools had been adopted. These included (a) the regular submission of corresponding protocols outlining the processes employed within the *Rentei;* (b) new, detailed forms of accounts as described earlier; (c) a regular exchange of letters between landlords and their estate managers, sometimes even several times a day; as well as (d) the compilation of reports describing the activities of the estate manager in detail. Two types of source show how complex the operational reporting between landlord and administrator on the manors might be.[35]

First there was a regular exchange of letters between administrators and owners, which became increasingly frequent and detailed. A large part of the day-to-day administrative work was discussed in these letters: the correspondence dealt with the entire spectrum of the manorial business. It included many trivial aspects of village life, but also reported on special events, justified business decisions and, above all, sought orders and authorizations (the so-called 'ratification'). The written request for authorizations mainly applied to leases and sales, where the landowner accepted the price recommended by the *Rentmeister*. The letters confirm that the final operational decisions were taken by the landlord himself – despite his physical absence. Hence we have a correspondence between

34 von Hohberg, *Georgica curiosa*, 2. Band, Caput XIX.

35 This is by no means a phenomenon for the selected study area. Such documents in the context of administrative records (e.g. 'wochenzeddeln', letters) also exist on manors in Saxony (see M. Schattkowsky, 'Ein kursächsischer Hofmarschall als Gutsherr: Christoph von Loß auf Schleinitz (1574–1629)', in J. Peters (ed.), *Gutsherrschaftsgesellschaften im europäischen Vergleich* (1997), pp. 300–1 or idem, *Zwischen Rittergut, Residenz und Reich: Die Lebenswelt des kursächsischen Landadligen Christoph von Loß auf Schleinitz (1574–1620)* (2007), pp. 188 ff.); or in Lippe (M. Schulte, 'Rationalisierung in der Landwirtschaft: Johann Friedrich von Reden auf Wendlinghausen (1731–91)', in Staatsarchiv Detmold, *Adel und Innovation: Industriepioniere aus der Familie von Reden* (= Veröffentlichungen der staatlichen Archive des Landes NRW, Reihe D.) (Detmold, 1996), pp. 22–3); and on the Weser (B.-W. Linnemeier, *Ein Gut und sein Alltag: Neuhof an der Weser* (Münster, 1992), p. 272).

the earl of Hatzfeldt and his administrator Hecker in 1832 about the balance of grain stocks that should be at the manor of Crottorf according to the accounts but are not actually in the granary according to the administrator.

The implementation of operational strategies was therefore always associated with high transaction costs (especially distance costs), which made day-to-day operations more complicated. Since it was a matter of communication between unequal persons, it is clear that it was also about the negotiation of dominance.

Through this correspondence, the landowner could obtain the up-to-date information which he needed to inform his decisions, and then these decisions could be communicated back to the estate. He often employed targeted questioning strategies. In turn, the letters gave the administrator the possibility of justifying his work. He always sent his employer his recommendations or reported decisions already made. Especially in times when financial losses were recorded, the administrator was concerned to explain how these were caused less by his management and more by the general economic situation (grain prices, poverty of the population and consequences: unsold grain, rent arrears, sales difficulties in other industries). All of this inevitably meant that the administrative sources such as accounts and journals were always closely related to the letters.

From the first quarter of the nineteenth century there was a new element in this evolving communication system. These were the so-called *revisions*, *monita* or *observates*. Regardless of their exact title, these audits all had the same purpose: they served to check the accounts and thus the activity of the estate administrator. The reports were normally written by a third party, less often by the owners themselves. They allowed the accounts to be tracked entry by entry. The length of these monitoring books (usually several hundred pages long, and covering three to five accounting years) shows how great the need for audit was: arithmetical errors were noted, sometimes also spelling errors or the lack of audibility of transactions. The *Rentmeister* in turn reacted to these observations and revisions by means of a 'response' in which he worked through the complaints point by point. In a comment made in 1837 on the Crottorfer account of two years earlier, the responsible *Rentmeister* remarked in this context: 'The calculator is very happy to admit that, like everyone else, he can make mistakes, but will do everything possible to avoid such a comment.'[36]

The disadvantage of this operational control becomes apparent when we look at the delay between drafting the account and closing it after it had been audited, revised and corrected. This was often five to eight years – even if there were efforts to complete the entire accounting process

36 Crottorf A 5417, 'Monita der Rechnung 1835' (1837) (private property, use via VAR).

within the following year. This time delay was a problem for everyone involved, because after this time lapse hardly any of the participants could remember the individual transactions in detail:

> Your High-Born, it cannot escape the fact that in most cases I can no longer, without making the most laborious and time-consuming investigations, elucidate points of account which have come into question from so long a time, and that it would be an injustice if I should still be held responsible for such obsolete items of account.[37]

The resulting delay in operational processes, as well as the extra work, was constantly being criticized by administrators.

IX

Accounts are a valuable source for the study of rural estates and especially for examining their economic activity. They offer deep insights into the operational and administrative structures, provide information about the everyday life and illuminate the roles of key persons and institutions.

A clear dynamic in the noble administration and especially in its corresponding accounting can be seen in all the manors studied here. While an information network established for the purpose of manorial management only played a subordinate role at the end of the seventeenth and in the first half of the eighteenth centuries, this changed in the second half of the eighteenth century. An increasing *professionalization* in form of *rationalizations* and *formalizations* – visible in the accounts of the manors – began. This did affect not only what was recorded in the accounts, but also the daily work of the estate's manager. His duties became more closely specified, densely documented and closely supervised by correspondence. Contemporaries recognized the growing complexity of manorial management and acknowledged that it required a correspondingly improved apparatus of accounting and reporting.

For the *Rentmeister*, this meant that his role and, above all, his decision-making powers were increasingly limited. He was not an independent manager, but an employee with limited authority. However, the extent of the control and information exchange processes was always curtailed by what was practical, which in turn gave the *Rentmeister* an element of

[37] 'Euer Hochgeborenen kann es nicht entgehen, daß es mir in den meisten Fällen nicht mehr möglich sein kann, ohne die allermühevollsten und zeitraubenden Nachforschungen anzustellen – Aufschluss über Rechnungspunkte zu geben, die von so langer Zeit zur Verwahrung gekommen sind, und daß es eine Ungerechtigkeit sein würde, wenn ich noch für dergleichen veraltete Rechnungsgegenstände verantwortlich gemacht werden sollte', Crottorf A 5014, #1022 'Betreff Revision der Crottorfer und Schönsteiner Rechnungen' (4 Jan. 1849) (private property, use via VAR).

leeway. But their decisions were always liable to be challenged when their accounts were audited. In this respect, the correspondence and other documentation that the *Rentmeisters* generated makes plain their subordination to their employer and the essential insecurity of their position.

4

The Advocacy and Use of Farm Accounts in Late Eighteenth- and Early Nineteenth-Century England

R. W. Hoyle

> The practice of agriculture is in general confined to persons who either have not had sufficient education to keep regular accounts, or who are inattentive and do not choose to be at that trouble, without which it is impossible to ascertain the profits and loss [of the farm], hence they cannot possibly attain the truth.[1]

Accounts are a way of organizing knowledge. At their simplest they formalize and record what the account maker knows. They are a form of memory: they prevent forgetfulness. They serve to prevent fraud and peculation, whether from an employer or a public body. They make it possible to collect arrears by serving as a record of sums owed but not yet paid. Equally by recording payments they are a defence against double payment or claims that a payment has not been made. The flat record of transactions they contain can be analyzed to create new information. So, an account can be used to establish the costs of labour for particular acts, the profitability of one form of production over another, even, in one notorious case, whether men made for better pickers of cherries than women.[2] Accounts which are merely a flat record of transactions are the product of what we might call book-keeping. Accounts which have a higher aspiration and are arranged by type of transaction, the vendor of goods or services to the farm and the purchaser of farm products, or even by individual fields or productive activities are the outcome of

1 George Winter, *A new and compendious system of husbandry* (1787), p. 8 (the text sightly amended).

2 *Robert Loder's farm accounts, 1610–20*, ed. G. E. Fussell (Camden, 3rd ser., 53, 1936), p. 148.

accounting. Book-keeping allows simple calculations of profit and loss to be made. Accounting allows the strategy of the farm to be finessed, unprofitable activities to be dropped and others introduced or their share of farm production adjusted. Book-keeping allows the farmer to see whether he has covered his costs: accounting tells him how he can increase his profit. This is a fundamental distinction and one utilized with profit elsewhere in this volume.

Whilst the utility of accounts does not need to be stressed, it remains an open question whether accounts were invariably made. It would be truly remarkable if an early modern merchant decided not to keep accounts but to rely on memory alone for the record of his transactions, receipts and payments. Public bodies demanded accounts. Parishes maintained long series of accounts to which each successive year's officers contributed. The failure to make accounts and have them declared before the inhabitants, either collectively or before auditors (people appointed to hear accounts), could result in fines or even prosecution. It can also be argued that accounts were fundamental to the English Protestant mind, a way by which men and women recorded their use of the gifts given them by God.[3] So whilst simple accounts and accounting were very familiar, there is a question when it comes to individuals and in particular, farmers, as to whether they kept accounts. They may well have kept pocket books in which they noted debts to them and money they owed to others, the entries of which would be cancelled when each transaction was settled by a payment. But did people who had relatively little money passing through their hands and who were responsible to no one but themselves keep accounts? In the beginning this is a question of literacy and numeracy.[4] But let us assume that farmers could read, write and handle figures. Here we might ponder what Winter is telling us in the quotation with which we opened this chapter. Is he telling us that farmers generally did not keep any accounts at all? Or is he telling us that they did not keep accounts in a format of which he approved? From the larger context, it is probably the latter, but we cannot be certain.

I

So we do not know, and cannot tell, how many farmers kept accounts. One suspects that accounts were, both in the past and today, prone to be destroyed on the death of the farmer, the end of a tenancy or the sale of the farm. They lack attractive personal details of interest to the next generation. They are often scruffy and worn from use. It is noticeable

3 Adam Smyth, *Autobiography in early modern England* (2010), ch. 2 ('Financial accounts').

4 The classic discussion is Sir Keith Thomas, 'Numeracy in early modern England', *Trans. Royal Historical Society*, 5th ser., 37 (1987), pp. 103–32.

that when nineteenth- or early twentieth-century farm accounts pass through the sale room or appear on Ebay, they are priced very modestly. The survival of farm accounts is very poor and we cannot gauge from the numbers which survive how many more there once were.

We can find comments even in the early twentieth century that many farmers did not keep accounts.[5] Instead they relied on what we might call tobacco-jar accounting: if there was money in the tobacco jar on the mantelpiece, then the farmer was ahead: if not then he was doing less well. Of course, farm incomes are often very seasonal so a farmer might, at some times of the year, be carrying high levels of debt with shopkeepers, seed and fertilizer merchants, even for animals bought in. He might also have credits with merchants who had bought his grain, cattle or sheep with days of payment several months in the future. A farmer might not have an exact knowledge of how he stood, just a general sense of his commitments and likely future income. Where credit could not be relied upon was the labour account. It is hard to believe that farm labourers would be willing to wait for payment. As we must envisage that many of them lived hand to mouth, the farmer needed to be sufficiently liquid to pay them weekly and never in arrears.

There are reasonable numbers of farm accounts, especially nineteenth-century ones, held by record offices. Many more remain in private hands. There is therefore a sizeable pool available for analysis and discussion.[6] But many of those extant are not personal accounts kept by a farmer for their own record but accounts kept by farm bailiffs (farm managers) for the scrutiny of their employers. These accounts are normally much fuller and more elaborately structured, for handling other people's money forced a higher standard of accounting. They were doubtless presented in forms which the owner felt satisfied his need to audit the management

5 See also pp. 91–2 below. Masters, conducting fieldwork on the financial performance of farmers in Nottinghamshire in the 1930s, wrote 'Many of the accounts summarised here were probably inaccurate in detail. Working farmers, in particular, generally have little time or patience for book-keeping, some could not be induced to keep accounts and of those who did there were several whose records showed discrepancy on checking, mainly omissions. Where the farmer did not keep accounts the data were assembled by the post-mortem method of checking bills, statements, chequebook stubs and similar sources and these served also to corroborate and amplify available farm records'. S. M. Masters, *The economics of poor land arable farming* (1944), p. 87.

6 The pioneers in the analysis of farm accounts were Michael Turner, John Beckett and Bethany Afton: see their *Farm production in England, 1700–1914* (2001). The major collection is at the Museum of English Rural Life, University of Reading.

of the farm and understand its financial performance as well as to detect any peculation.[7]

Farmers' accounts (as opposed to bailiffs' accounts), when we have them, are often highly personal (or idiosyncratic) in their construction. They record what the farmer thought was important and ignore the remainder. Printed account books were available in the nineteenth century and if employed would have given structure to the accounts but again it is hard to discover how widely they were used. After all, there was no external compulsion that forced a farmer to keep accounts nor any formal training in how to do them: even in the early twentieth century income tax could be paid on rule of thumb premises rather than on the submission of accounts.[8] A general difficulty with them is that they are farmers' accounts rather than farm accounts. So one of the best series of accounts, those of the Brown family of Aldbourne in Wiltshire, contain on the income side income from investments and rents, and on the expenditure side payments for household costs and to family members.[9] The failure to separate non-farming income and household costs from farming costs was a matter of complaint even in the early twentieth century.[10] So the form of farm accounts was decided by the farmer: it was what he wanted to record presented in ways which he found convenient.

II

The extant records tend to fall into several categories, all of which are loosely called farm accounts but which served different purposes. It is helpful to see them as interconnected ways of storing information. Turner, Beckett and Afton, in their pioneering analysis of farm accounts, categorized the sorts of records which farmers kept for their own use into three groups.[11]

7 They are employed in Nicola Verdon, *Rural women workers in nineteenth-century England: Gender, work and wages* (2002). And see her comments at pp. 36–7.

8 Board of Agriculture and Fisheries, Leaflet no. 26, *Farmers and income tax* (various revisions including one of 1908).

9 Museum of English Rural Life, University of Reading, Wil 11, described in *Historical farm records: A summary guide* (University of Reading, 1973), pp. 275–80. This was one of the conclusions of an abortive attempt to draw useful information from them.

10 Board of Agriculture and Fisheries, Leaflet no. 240, *Farm book-keeping* (1911, rev. 1914), p. 3 (which notes that provision consumed on the farm should be treated as a sale).

11 The following account draws on the much fuller discussion in Turner, Beckett and Afton, *Farm production in England*, ch. 2.

(i) Farm account books

Turner, Beckett and Afton suggest that these fall into two broad types. The first are chronological records which could be cast up at the year end to get a simple calculation of profit or loss. The second are more elaborate accounts arranged by client or product. (This, of course, is the distinction between book-keeping and accounting again.) This made it easier to track dealings with an individual merchant for instance and to determine whether all invoices with them had been settled but it required each account to be totalled and then all the totals summed to establish whether the farm had made a profit or loss over the year. A further type of record, but which is not found in the eighteenth century, is the annual farm inventory. Here the farmer calculated the value of his assets. This allowed him to see whether his assets had grown over the year and to calculate the return on his investment.

Turner, Beckett and Afton found that very few farmers had adopted double-entry book-keeping. Where they had, it is possible that they had received training in its use as apprentices or might even have taken up farming as a second career. But in general it was too complicated for farmers and the accounts they made are essentially simple income and expenditure accounts.

We need to allow for the possibility that many farmers used one or more books concurrently and transferred transactions from one to another when time allowed or at the year end. So entries could be made on a daily basis into a cash book and then assigned into separate accounts for individual vendors or purchasers. The difficulty here is that we can rarely be certain that we have the full range of account books maintained by a single farmer. Some may have been selected for retention by the farmer himself or post mortem by family or friends, and others destroyed.

(ii) Labour records

Labour could be paid by the day (or even by the task), or it could be hired on an annual basis (service in husbandry). Where labour worked as the farmer needed to call on it, there was an obvious need to keep track of the number of days that each individual worked, perhaps the tasks they undertook, certainly the sums paid. This might justify the keeping of a wage book for the purpose. Weekly or monthly totals could be transferred from the wage book to other accounts where the granular detail of employment was not needed, only the sums paid. Servants in husbandry posed different problems. Memoranda of the contracts agreed with individual servants can appear almost anywhere.

Turner, Beckett and Afton have discussed the pitfalls encountered in analyzing wage books. Almost by definition wage books only include the costs of day labourers and make no reference to residential servants whose costs were accounted for elsewhere. Day labourers might be a supplement to farm servants so a calculation based on a wage book might underestimate the labour needs of a farm but also the types of labour required for its conduct.

(iii) Memoranda books

This category includes a whole ragbag of records, some of them not accounts at all but records which might inform accounts. They may best be thought of as daybooks or diaries, often small pocket books, sometimes almanacs, in which the farmer noted facts which could prove to be useful in the future. These might be notes of sales of produce with days of payment, dates of ploughing, dates at which cows were put to the bull, notes of the planting of orchards and other improvements, recipes for medicines, and the birth of children.

One would imagine that some of these were notebooks which a farmer might pull from his pocket in the market place (or market inn) to make a note of what had just been agreed. Others were more substantial desk-bound books into which entries were made of things memorable for the future.[12] These were perhaps intended for the instruction of future generations. More specific memoranda books might take the form of cropping or field books which recorded, in effect, the history of a farmer's use of individual fields over periods of years. Whilst these were advocated in the eighteenth century, they only seem to have been used in the nineteenth. Other farmers kept granary books which record the release of corn for threshing and then its use, whether fed to animals or sold.[13] But as much as anything, memoranda books are records of what their compiler thought it was necessary to keep, or was of interest, with the curious and amusing.

There was almost certainly a tendency for the range of record books maintained by farmers to increase over the nineteenth century. By the First World War the farm office might contain a range of books, all interconnected in some way, with information transferred from one to another. In part this reflects a change in the character of the farmer. There

12 For an example of a memoranda book in print, but kept by a gentleman with a home farm, see A. J. Gritt and J. M. Virgoe (eds), *The memoranda books of Basil Thomas Eccleston, 1757–1789* (Record Society of Lancashire and Cheshire, 139, 2004).

13 I exploited threshing books kept by a late seventeenth- to early eighteenth-century Cambridgeshire clergyman who was both farming and collecting tithe. 'Why was there no crisis in England in the 1690s?', in R. W. Hoyle (ed.), *The farmer in England* (2013), pp. 69–100. He also kept orthodox accounts which include both household and farming costs. P. W. Brassley (ed.), *Accounts of the Rev. John Crakanthorp of Fowlmere, 1692–1710* (Cambridgeshire Record Soc. 9, 1988).

was a much greater likelihood that he no longer laboured on the farm in the company of his adult children and hired labourers: instead he supervised and directed a labour force, allocating tasks, setting a strategy and managing the finances of the farm. In this respect he was increasingly a small businessman with a substantial turnover who needed to keep abreast of markets. Keeping accounts was one of the contributions he made to the farm enterprise. In a way, he was much more akin to the farm bailiff on a managed farm than he was to the old-style farmers of the eighteenth century (although it should never be assumed that these men had disappeared. They may even have reappeared in the hard years of the late nineteenth century.)

III

This chapter is concerned not so much with the extant accounts and the forms they take as with the advocacy of account keeping by Arthur Young and others, and the way in which accounts were used in the printed literature. There are three points about Young which need to be remembered.[14] The first is that he had a business background, having been apprenticed to a firm of wine merchants in King's Lynn. Whilst he left at the end of his term, and later in life professed to dislike trade, it is impossible not to think that the training he received there left an indelible mark on his thinking.[15] The second is that perhaps because of his business numeracy, Young was a natural quantifier. His publications are full of acreages, of the numbers of animals, wages, costs and profits. Much of the information is incomplete and so less useful to him (and us) than might be wished. But his instinct to quantify is obvious to the reader. The third is that Young considered the farm to be a business. He had little time for those to whom it was a livelihood. Much of his early writing is aimed not at the farmer but at the investor seeking a farm.[16] (This was the

14 For Young see the obituary in *Oxford Dictionary of National Biography* (ODNB), the full biography by John G. Gazley, *The life of Arthur Young, 1741–1820* (1973) and more generally G. E. Mingay (ed.), *Arthur Young and his times* (1975). For a discussion of his approach to accounts, see Roger Juchau, 'Early cost accounting ideas in agriculture: The contributions of Arthur Young', *Accounting, Business and Financial History* 12 (2002), pp. 369–86.

15 William Marshall also had a commercial background, having been apprenticed in the linen trade, then working in insurance and finally in the West Indies before taking up farming (ODNB). He was not a natural quantifier however in the way that Young was.

16 See his essay, 'Considerations on the oeconomical conduct of such gentlemen as make agriculture either their business or amusement', Arthur Young, *The farmer's guide in hiring and stocking farms* (2 vols, 1770), Essay 5 (pp. 173–245).

'rage for farming' which Marshall identified.[17]) In the introduction to the first edition of his *Farmer's kalendar* (1771), Young says that if the farm is 'properly conducted', the farmer will discover that he gets a better return on his money than from almost any other investment. He will also have the pleasures of the rural lifestyle to enjoy. Farming, he argued, was also ideally suited to the man who had little capital.

> What trade can be set up without introduction or partnership in which a man can employ five hundred pounds? In most he must have nearer five thousand, but in husbandry a young man that is not extravagant, and will mind his business, may on such a farm as £500 will stock, live very agreeably, for it will fix him on eighty or an hundred acres of good land, which will yield him an annual profit of from £100 to £200 a year clear, or from 30 to 40 per cent for his money.[18]

Young then goes on to show how it might be done. He made large claims for the benefits a farmer might receive from his accounts. It is though plain that the advice he gave in his books was aimed at the gentleman farmer employing a bailiff. Detailed accounts were a check on the bailiff's handling of his employer's money but also on the profitability of the farm.

Young's *Rural economy* of 1770 was one of a number of publications by him from around this time which were addressed to the new entrant into farming.[19] This was perhaps life-style farming. Young envisaged that the 'farmer' would come to the farm on a weekend when one of his tasks would be to review and sign off the bailiff's accounts for the previous week. But Young also envisaged that the farmer would be intellectually engaged with his farm. The accounts were the way in which he would come to know his farm, learn how to farm and become equipped to make fine judgments over profitability and techniques.

To enable the farmer to achieve this understanding, Young recommended that a number of account books be maintained. The first was a minute book, 'a regular journal of transactions on the farm', to be kept by the bailiff. This was to be a daily record of agricultural operations, purchases and sales. There was then a cash book, to be balanced weekly. The third book was a ledger. This was to be arranged into accounts, debtor and creditor, for each field, each category of livestock, for wear and tear and all the other activities of the farm. This was to substitute for the journal in double-entry book-keeping which Young thought was too complicated for a bailiff to keep. So, in the examples Young gave, in the account for the 'six acre field', on the one side there would be the

17 William Marshall, *Experiments, and observations concerning agriculture and the weather* (1779), 'Advertisement' [p. 3].

18 [Arthur Young], *The Farmer's kalendar* (1771 edn), unpaginated introduction.

19 For what follows [Arthur Young], *Rural economy or essays on the practical points of husbandry* (London, 1770 edn), pp. 200–16.

expenses, on the other side the sales of hay from the field or transfer within the farm (so 'to the horses'). As this book would be a jumble of small transactions, Young envisaged that the farmer would keep his own ledger in which the entries in the first ledger would be totalled so all payments for manure (for instance) would be reduced to one and a profit and loss for that field calculated. At the end of the year an inventory should be made of each asset at its current valuation.

> By these general methods, a gentleman every year knows, to a shilling, the year's profit or loss and the sum of money he has employed in agriculture.[20]

Young admitted that despite the small outlay of time for the considerable advantages that accounts brought, few kept accounts in such detail. They therefore denied themselves the benefits brought by good accounting.

This style of account suited particular circumstances. Most obviously it was for farms in the hands of a bailiff or manager who could act as the farm's clerk. Less obviously, it was suited to enclosed farms: it was harder to apply to open field farms where the cost centre was smaller and there were more of them. It allowed the farmer to maximize profit – choosing wheat over barley, dairying over fattening – by looking at past profitability. Young maintained that it gave the gentleman farmer an advantage over the 'common farmer' who was forced to guess the profitability of individual fields and farming practices. But whether one in a hundred farmers kept accounts in such detail must be doubted. It is a matter of regret that no accounts from Young's own farm survive so we are denied the opportunity of seeing how far he followed his own advice.

Rural economy had a limited circulation and was never revised nor reprinted. Young's work with the widest circulation – if the number of editions counts for anything – was his *Farmer's kalendar* (first edition, 1771, tenth edition 1815). It may best be thought of as a guide to how to farm arranged by month. In the course of successive revisions it became fuller and fatter. In the introduction to the first edition (1771), Young remarked that previous writers had avoided discussing accounts, but he also drew attention to a recent publication which had tried to adapt merchants' accounts to farming.[21] Young thought that double entry was much too complicated for the farmer to use and suggested a simpler approach.

Young proposed that every farmer should keep a ledger, arranged by each arable field, but with all the grass subsumed under a single heading. Although he does not directly say so, the costs of cultivation were to be split between each field and the value of the produce similarly

20 Ibid., pp. 214–15.

21 For the following, [Young], *Farmer's kalendar* (1771 edn), unpaginated introduction.

allocated in the ledger. So if the tithes of a 400-acre farm were £100, 5*s*. per acre should be attributed to each field according to its size. So too were general overheads such as the bailiff's salary, market expenses, fencing and the like.

Young's purpose in recommending this approach to accounting seems to have been less to establish whether the farm was making a profit or a loss than to see which farming strategies were turning the best profit. To illustrate his method, he offered the example of two ten-acre fields farmed by different rotations. The first – turnips → barley → clover → wheat – made a profit of £126 18*s*. 4*d*. over eight years. The second – fallow → wheat → barley → oats – made £68 16*s*. 8*d*. over the same period. Therefore the first was superior. Young thought that the same approach could be applied to cattle.

So Young's accounts are designed to allow comparisons to be made. They are, in a sense, a dimension of his experimental bent (to which we will turn). And whilst he stressed the simplicity of the system, it has to be questioned whether it was really simple at all. After all, in real conditions one field might be 8½ acres and the other 11¼ acres so that at the least there was a further level of computation required to calculate profit per acre under the two regimes.

Young was not recommending this approach to the ordinary (or, as he called them, the 'common') farmer. Indeed, he was dismissive of them. His method would require too many illustrations to explain it to them. They were ignorant of recent writings on agriculture and so knew nothing of the high profit crops whose adoption Young recommended. So Young's reader was the new entrant to the farming, backed by money, with some business acumen and intellectual curiosity.

In succeeding editions of the *Farmer's calendar*, Young avoided the issue of accounts. In the 1804 edition he did supply a heading under October of 'The farm accounts', and then avoided giving his opinion on what desirable accounts looked like, merely stating what he knew to be true.

> In the arrangement of the business of a farm, this is an object of no inconsiderable importance. The modes of keeping them are almost as numerous as there are farmers in the island. The most plain and simple method commonly used is that of entering all payments on one side of a book and all receipts on the other and balancing [them] when the transactions of the year are ended. This method gives a tolerable idea of the single object of profit and loss. I say *tolerable*, for it is but a tolerable one.[22]

22 Arthur Young, *The farmer's calendar* (new edn, 1804), p. 489, italics in the original.

Under December in this edition, Young published a long essay on farm accounts.[23] In fact this essay was not new, having been first published in *Annals of Agriculture* in 1797.[24]

In it, Young first stated his belief in the importance to farmers of keeping accounts, but he also restated his conviction that few did so.

> There is not a single step in the life of a farmer that does not prove the advantage of his keeping regular accounts and yet there is not one in a thousand who does this. ... A few rough memoranda or figures to yield a gross account of the general receipt or payment are usually the greatest exertions that common farmers, who pretend to keep accounts, make in this line.[25]

Farmers failed to keep the accounts which would be expected in every other business. This might be expected of common farmers but not of gentlemen farmers, and he was critical of the latter whose accounts were often inexact and where claims of profitability based on them were often unsound. Indeed, he argued that the form of the accounts – their very structure – often determined the conclusions that were drawn from them.

The form of accounts that Young recommended were structured around two points. The first was that the individual field should form the basis of the account. He recognized that this was not possible when land was held in open fields or when fields were small. The products of each field were to be treated separately. Likewise, expenses were to be separated into categories and the costs proportionately assigned to individual fields. This was easiest in the case of rents, poor rates and tithes. But careful record keeping was needed to apportion the cost of teams, or manure, to individual fields. And there were other issues which confused matters. There was for instance the question of whether the sheep flock should have the costs of turnips attributed to them and, if so, which costs: turnips in the field or turnips pulled and carted. The choice of price could in this case, and many others, make the difference between profit and loss. Young thought that the sheep account should be for so many weeks on grass, so many on mown grass, so many on clover, so many on ruta baga and so many on turnips, each with its own valuation. Many thought that arable was profitable because they underestimated the cost of maintaining a team, and so the cost of ploughing.[26]

23 Ibid., pp. 533–48.

24 'On the accounts proper to be kept by farmers', *Annals of Agriculture* 28 (1797), pp. 47–64. The essay is discussed at length by Juchau, 'Early cost accounting ideas', pp. 374–8.

25 Young, *Farmer's calendar* (1804 edn), pp. 533–4.

26 These questions of the attribution of costs may be said to derail farm accounting. The question is explored further in Juchau, 'Early cost accounting ideas', pp. 376–8 and see below, p. 82.

This is broadly what Young had recommended in the first edition of the *Farmer's kalendar* and there is little sign that his ideas had changed since. Its roots lie in the experimentation fashionable in the 1760s and later; the conviction that detailed accounts allowed for comparisons between different agricultural regimes. The farmer needed to know whether the better yields came when wheat followed fallow, clover or oats. But this was not a prescription which the majority of farmers could follow.

It was not only 'common farmers' who fell short. Young was touring Sussex at the end of 1789 and in the first weeks of 1790, looking in particular at South Down sheep. He was told that General James Murray of Beauport Park had a flock of 4,000 sheep fed on potatoes. Young invited himself to Murray's house to inspect the flock, but when it came to the profitability of the General's sheep, it transpired that he only kept general accounts and so could not say. Young therefore set about unpicking the accounts over five days, extracting the costs of the flock with the aid of Murray, his bailiff, his flockmaster and his book-keeper. (That Murray kept undifferentiated accounts but had a clerk is itself interesting.) Young concluded that Murray was making a profit of about 17 per cent on his potato-fed sheep.[27] In 1807 Young published a description of the farming of Bernard Howard of Fornham in Surrey which drew on Fornham's farm accounts. Young's claims for the profitability of Fornham's enterprise were challenged by a number of writers in correspondence (which Young published in *Annals of Agriculture*). The questions arose in part from how costs were allocated between accounts. Should the cost of turnips be allocated in its entirety to the sheep account or should a proportion be allocated to the arable account? The profitability of the sheep or the arable depended on how the costs were divided.[28] We have already noted that Young was aware of this.

We do know of a farmer who kept accounts after the fashion that Young recommended. In 1800 the Board of Agriculture published a year's accounts kept by Mr William Dann of Gillingham in Kent.[29] This was variously described as a 'ledger account' or a 'field account'. Dann's method had come to the attention of the Board, who invited him to meet with them and expound his approach to accounts. Dann subsequently provided his accounts for 1797 for them to print.

The account was field by field, of which there were twenty-two on the farm. Costs were given on the left and the crop with its valuation on the right. Both were totalled and the gain (or less often loss) calculated. An explanatory note explains that Dann took the straw and chaff to be equal

27 Gazley, *Life*, pp. 224–5.

28 Ibid., p. 521.

29 [Anon.] (1800), 'Ledger account of the farm of Mr William Dann of Gillingham, Kent, for 1797, with remarks', Board of Agriculture, *Communications to the Board of Agriculture*, II (1800), pp. 433–50.

in value to the harvesting, threshing, carriage and marketing costs and so neither was included in the account. The value of grazing on sainfoin after the crop had been cut was equal to the costs of mowing, making and carrying it from the fields. Nor was the cost of manure or manuring included. In these ways the account was simplified.

What the Board found interesting was that this was a 'field account'. Although advocated by Young most of thirty years earlier, this practice was obviously unfamiliar to the Board's members. They were not uncritical of aspects of the accounts. Some costs included under larger headings should have been charged to the fields, including ploughing costs and manure. The bailiff was treated as a general overhead and his salary was not divided between fields. A close reader of Young's earlier works would have found nothing very novel here. The Board evidently did, suggesting how unfamiliar they were with the writings of their own secretary.

Young was not the only writer to be convinced of the value of keeping accounts by the field. George Winter of Charlton in Henbury (Gloucestershire) was also an enthusiast and he expected that when others tried it, they would find it a revelation.[30]

> Enabled by my own experience, the regular accounts I have kept of each separate field and the observations made on the mode of my neighbours' cultivation, I may venture to assert that many real losses are sustained by improper management, such ... as not allowing a sufficient number of ploughings and harrowings to pulverize and clear the ground of weeds, the application of raw dung unmixed with earth ... or an improper succession of crops.
>
> The produce of several fields of the same kind of grain are frequently stacked or housed promiscuously together. If a farmer is asked why he does not keep them separate, his answer is the hurry of harvest and the unfavourable season prevent such practice, therefore he cannot ascertain the increase of different lands. [Winter suggests a form of sampling] ... the produce per acre of such field may be easily ascertained and this should be immediately minuted in his book. He will soon be convinced of the utility of keeping accounts, he will thereby be best instructed whether two, three or more ploughings, if manured with lime, soaper's ashes, dung or compost, when applied, with the

30 Winter, *New and compendious system*, pp. 8–11 selectively presented here. Little appears to be known about Winter. On the title page of his *New ... system of husbandry* he describes himself as a 'practical agriculturalist'. The anonymous writer who contributed the essay 'A new system of agriculture' to the *New Royal cyclopaedia*, ed. George Selby Howard (3 vols, 1788), II (unpaginated), described him as a 'gentleman of independent fortune who cultivates the land for health, amusement and to serve his unenlightened neighbours', so perhaps a gentleman farmer rather than a working farmer.

> number of loads per acre, the time of sowing and the course of crops preceding are the most advantageous.
>
> ...
>
> By minuting and registering such accounts in a regular manner, they can be referred to at any future period. The Agriculturalist will thereby be enabled to avoid the wrong and to pursue the best and most advantageous method. Such a plan will soon become habitual, amusing, instructive and profitable.

'Habitual, amusing, instructive and profitable'. And yet one has to question whether any of these could be achieved. The data might be fine-grained, but the number of variables introduced surely meant that the farmer, even when highly numerate, could not even begin to assign weights to the various factors that Winter mentions (and he makes no reference to the weather).

We learn a number of things from this discussion. The first is that even quite advanced farmers might not keep accounts which gave them any sense of the profitability of their enterprises – or parts of their enterprises. The second is that there was no agreement as to how accounts should be constructed and when large public claims were made on their evidence, they might well be criticized. For a third, even at the end of the century a farmer who kept accounts on the lines recommended by Young (and Winter) might be regarded as an exceptional figure from whom others could learn.

IV

Young did not have a monopoly on advice to farmers at the end of the eighteenth century. It is therefore appropriate to look at another printed manual to see what it says about how a farmer should keep his accounts.

The *New farmer's calendar* (1800, third edition 1801) was constructed on similar lines to Young's *Farmer's kalendar*.[31] It included a somewhat confused (or confusing) essay on accounts under the jobs to be done by the farmer in December.[32] The farmer should equip himself with a General Stock Book into which he should enter an inventory of his assets and debts. These should be valued at current prices. He should then copy in all his tradesmen's bills in, one assumes, chronological order. He should then draft out two accounts, one for debts and one for credit. On

31 The author was given on its title page as 'A farmer and breeder' but the book is normally attributed to John Lawrence (1753–1839) of Bury St Edmunds.

32 'Conclusion of the year with general account of stock', Lawrence [attrib.] *New farmer's calendar* (1801 edn), pp. 115–18.

the debt side he must enter all the farmer owes, starting with rent, tithe and taxes. On the contra side he should place the valuations of his assets.

But whilst the anonymous author recommended double-entry book-keeping ('the Italian method), he also admitted that it was too complicated for most farmers to manage. Instead they should keep a day book and ledger. The day book was to be a memorandum book which included the dates at which animals were serviced, dates of sowing and the like. As a halfway house, the farmer should enter his accounts into a general stock book without any of the connections inherent in double-entry, and then if he wished to know whether he was making a profit or loss on his stalled oxen or the crop of a particular field, he should pull from the general stock book the transactions concerning that activity and make them into an account.

So whilst the author commended accounts ('the regular taking stock every year [making a capital valuation] and the keeping fair accounts, is, on calculation, attended even with less trouble than the everlasting puzzle, confusion, blindfoldedness and loss, of needless negligence'), but not on the full rigour of double-entry principles. Indeed, he thought that to even recommend that farmers should keep accounts would frighten many of them. A farmer who did would reap considerable advantages.

> Regular accounts and annual valuation will not only afford a man an exact knowledge of his real situation, but wonderfully improve and sharpen his judgment on the real worth of all those articles in which he deals; and in the necessary contemplation of his final accident, he will have the satisfaction to reflect, that all stands fair for the benefit of his family and as little liable as possible to loss or dispute.

V

> Forming experiments in husbandry is so much the taste of the present age.[33]

> As far as a man's fortune will allow him to go, no amusement in the world equals the forming and conducting experiments in agriculture.[34]

We turn now to the role of accounts in experimentation.

Despite the enormous number of reports of experiments in husbandry available in print, there has never been any systematic study of them either for what they tell us about agriculture as an intellectual pursuit or

33 Young, *Rural economy*, Essay X, 'Of experimental agriculture', p. 349.
34 Ibid., p. 355.

improvements in agriculture in the second half of the eighteenth century. This discussion can do little more than draw attention to the subject.

There was a long history of observation in agriculture. Individual wheat plants which cropped well were kept and bred from. There was an enormous amount of farmers' wisdom in circulation based on practical experience. Experimentation however implied not the study and recording of quirky circumstances but the observation of trials set up for the purpose, and most importantly the quantification – both in terms of produce and profit – of controlled experiments. There were complaints by Young that early experiments were poorly expounded and lacked key details.[35] They were rarely repeated to control for the weather. They lacked a comparative element. So whilst experimentation did not start in mid-century, there was probably a much better grasp later in the century of how experiments needed to be constructed and managed if they were going to prove a case. Young outlines the requirements in an essay published in 1770 when his career as an experimentalist was drawing to a close.

> Suppose it to be demanded when mode of sowing barley, the drill or the broad-cast, be most beneficial. For this purpose, two spots of land of equal size, and of a most perfect quality in goodness must be fixed on; the exposure, neighbourhood of ditches, trees etc etc must be the same in both; the preceding crop, the preparatory culture and every other circumstance [must also be the same].

He thought that a test plot of a rood (1,112 m^2) would suffice for each trial and that larger trials, other than the cost, were unmanageable. He also reflected on the costs of managing trials and thought that it was easy for the gentleman with an experimental bent to commit to 'much greater expenses than he can afford'.[36] (He might be speaking from personal experience: his wife thought that Young's experimental work had close to ruined them.[37]) Experimentation though was handicapped by the failure to understand the basic chemical processes which underlay plant grown. Without analytical techniques it was hard to standardize inputs. Manure could vary in nutrient content, and all sorts of industrial waste products were added to the soil to prepare it for sowing. But just as accounts were intended to inform and guide the farmer, so too experiments were designed to evaluate new techniques (notably the drilling of crops) and new forms of animal husbandry (notably the use of turnips and potatoes as animal feedstuffs) to discover what was, and was not, profitable.

In 1770 Young published the results of his five years' work conducting agricultural experiments in two volumes running to just over 1,000

35 Ibid., p. 356.
36 Ibid., pp. 351, 353.
37 Gazley, *Life*, p. 497.

pages.[38] It was a monumental achievement but one which Young came to dislike (he is said to have tried to buy up copies of it) and historians have, if only because of its size, given it a wide berth. It is however a remarkable source book which deserves attention from agricultural historians who really ought to re-analyze Young's data. The discussion of wheat alone runs to 325 pages. We have a chapter on 'Culture and produce in the old method', 'Culture and practice in the new method' and 'Comparison between the old and new husbandry in the culture of wheat'. It then turns to the sowing rates under the old and new agricultural regimes, the times of sowing and a range of minor issues. Similar experiments follow on barley and oats (though not at such great length), then less important crops, including buckwheat, pease and beans, root crops, artificial grasses, grasslands, draining, manures and finally cattle and sheep. It ends with a discussion of implements. Each experiment is accompanied by a full account of the expenditure and income generated. Young also provided a commentary on each experiment, The minute documentation and then discussion of each trial explains the extreme length of the book.[39]

The prime purpose of the book was to examine the old and new husbandries. Young never defines the 'New Husbandry', but the key comparisons in his experiments are between seed broadcast and seed drilled.[40] And whilst he discusses turnips, he never uses them in the rotations described. This represents, in a sense, two approaches to an old-fashioned style of arable farming which was soon to be superseded in many locations. The experiments, though, produced no clear-cut answers as to whether drilled crops brought advantages over broadcast ones. Young's attempt to resolve the question was itself a chapter of over 30 pages in which further trials were reported but no definitive answer emerged: drills, he found, were better suited to beans than wheat.

A reader of *Experimental agriculture* who is familiar with Young's views on accounts will recognize immediately the style of accounts he recommends. All the costs of a field are charged to it. So is the value of the produce and the overall profit or loss is worked out. Here we see Young's method being applied.

If Young failed to come to unambiguous conclusions about the merits of drilling, the question was looked at again by a Mr Amos, an estate steward in Lincolnshire, who published the outcome of his experiments

38 Arthur Young, *A course of experimental agriculture* (2 vols, 1770).

39 Marshall published his own volume of experimental reports, but on a number of fronts it compares poorly with Young's book. William Marshall, *Experiments and observations concerning agriculture and the weather* (1779).

40 On Young's thinking here, see Essay IX, 'Of the new husbandry', in *Rural economy*, pp. 160–78.

with drilling seed in a book of 1794.[41] Again the case for drilling was made by publishing accounts comparing the costs and profits of broadcast and drilled grain. Of the 12 accounts presented, all showed that the advantage lay with drilled crops. These accounts were republished – in the *New farmer's calendar* and then in *The complete farmer*, an encyclopedia for farmers.[42]

Accounts are therefore a familiar feature of the discourse in the agricultural press. There are many instances in *Annals of Agriculture* but here we take examples from volume two (1785), which are representative of a larger body of material. The Rev. Charles Onley of Stitsted Hall in Essex supplied *Annals* with a description of the crop rotations he employed, including accounts for the costs and profits of one acre for the four successive years of the rotation. Mr W. Macro contributed 'an account of the expenses, profits and management of a flock of Ewes', again with specimen accounts. A few pages later John Billingsley of Ashwick Grove in Somerset presented accounts for the 'culture, expense and produce of six acres of potatoes'. Rev. Onley returned to the fray with a discussion of carrots, comparing the cost of keeping horses on carrots with keeping them on oats. H. J. Close of Trimley contributed a piece on 'a new culture of wheat' (horse-hoed wheat), again supported by accounts.[43]

Most of these articles were reports of deliberate experiments rather than simply farming processes which had turned out well. Close calls his account of the horse-hoed wheat an experiment although his account lacks a comparator. His figures were plainly intended to impress those who already knew the likely costs and profits of wheat and therefore did not need comparable figures showing the costs and profits of wheat weeded and hoed by hand.[44] And whilst accounts of innovations in arable practice and crops are a regular feature of *Annals of Agriculture*, it also carried a stream of reports of experiments into animal feeding and fattening, chiefly accounts of cattle, horses or pigs being fed on potatoes or carrots as substitutes for grain.

41 William Amos, *The theory and practice of the drill-husbandry* (1794, 2nd edn, 1802).

42 [Lawrence], *New farmer's calendar*, pp. 293–308; [no author], *The complete farmer, or, General dictionary of agriculture and husbandry* (1st edn, 1766: I have used the 5th edition of 1807 in 2 vols). This is unpaginated but the accounts can be found under 'drill'. The same article also reproduced calculations based on accounts kept by Rev. Close on the savings made by drilling seed rather than sowing it broadcast, taken from a paper in the *Transactions of the Bath and West*.

43 *Annals of Agriculture*, II (1785), pp. 171–7, 427–37, 439–41, 414–17, 451–5.

44 In fact Young found the contribution to be opaque and wrote for further details, which Close supplied, but even then Young was not satisfied.

George Winter's *A new and compendious system of husbandry* (1787) gives a sense of the range of experiments being carried out at the time.[45] The word experiment (or experiments) appears no fewer than five times on his title page. He offered accounts of experiments proving the superiority of drilling seed, of different sorts of grain, on turnips (or rather experiments to combat Turnip Fly) and on the fattening of pigs. Most of the experiments he reports are his own, but he also reprinted reports of experiments carried out by others. One suspects that not all of his experiments were conducted with scientific rigour. His rejection of the 'old mode of cultivation' comes in part from seeing rooks taking seed from a sown field, not any measurement of yield. Like Close he gives no evidence of the productivity of the old methods, instead impressing his readers with evidence of the success of his new methods.

> Of the numerous experiments which I have made on a small scale, and which I have this season extended on a larger one, enable me to say that grain drilled about six or seven inches distance between rows produces the largest crops.

Winter went so far as to develop his own drill which he patented. He offered a challenge to any of his neighbours who was willing to prepare two plots, one to be sown using the traditional method and the other drilled with his machine, to establish which served best.

Another working farmer with literary ambitions was a Lincolnshire farmer, Richard Parkinson. He wrote in the first person, outlining his experiences as a farmer. In a sense the book is part memoir, part autobiography. Parkinson considered himself to be an experimenter and the conclusions he drew from his innovative practices were supported by accounts which served to justify his claims. In this way the soft evidence of the anecdotal and observational was combined with the hard evidence of accounts.[46]

We may seem to have wandered some distance from accounts. But experiments counted for nothing without detailed figures of costs and profits. Accounts became a form of proof, a testimonial to the efficiency and productivity of new farming systems and a guide to the sorts of profits a farmer might expect to gain by adopting new techniques. Only the figures contained in the accounts allowed a farmer to decide whether an innovation was worth pursuing.

45 For Winter see p. 83 above.

46 Richard Parkinson, *The experienced farmer* (2 vols, 1798).

VI

Another way in which accounts were used was to model likely farm costs and incomes, and so show the sorts of profit that a farmer could expect to secure from his investment when he employed certain types of farming regime.

Young excelled at this kind of calculation. It forms the basis of the book in two volumes he published in 1770, *The farmer's guide*. This was directed to the two

> sets of men, gentleman farmers and common ones. Not many of the latter read books but such of them as do [do] not hold all in contempt, but may find in these pages some hints which if they do not instruct, may at least remind them of points of importance in the most critical moments of their lives – when they hire their farms.[47]

It was chiefly directed to the gentleman who either intended to take part of his lands into hand or the new entrant to farming who proposed to buy or rent a farm. So, over the eleven chapters which form the core of the book, Young explained how a man with capital could make the most advantageous investment. Young started with men with only £20 and then proceeded by graduations to a man with £20,000 at his disposal. So, in the discussion of how a farmer could invest between £1,000 and £1,600, we have a total of ten permutations, how to farm with a team of eight horses, a team of six horses, how the farmer could proceed if the soil was good for turnips, how it might be farmed if the farm was mixed ⅓ grass and ⅔ arable, or all grass, or all grass which it was intended to plough, and so on. In every case an account is given, starting with rent, tithes and other outgoings, then implements, livestock, seeds and tillage, labour and sundry articles. The produce is then calculated, a balance struck, interest on the capital deducted from the balance and the return on the investor's capital calculated. The invitation was for the farmer to match a farm to the nearest account.

The farmer's guide served several purposes. Most obviously it is a guide as to how much money an incoming farmer might need to succeed and the returns he might expect to receive. But it was also, in effect, a handbook on how to farm according to size, soil type and farming regime. For the historian it can be read as a guide to how farms worked under different regimes, but yet the copious quantities of data on costs and techniques have been ignored by them. Whether the book was a success at the time might be doubted, for it was never reprinted and certainly not revised or brought up to date later in the century.

47 [Arthur Young] *The farmer's guide in hiring and stocking farms* (2 vols, 1770), Introduction, p. ii.

These were farm accounts, albeit estimated accounts, predicting profits, serving the didactic purpose of informing potential entrants of costs and returns. But the method could be used in other ways as well. In his *Rural economy*, in a discussion of the comparative profit of cultivating different soils, Young published model accounts for land of different rental values. The first was land worth 5s. an acre (which he took to be sandlands, light heathy soils or improved moor lands), land of a rental of 10s. a year, and lands worth 20s. a year to show the potential profitability of each. For an acre of each value of land, he gave the costs over a six-year rotation and the predicted income and then calculated the profit per acre over the six years and annually.[48]

VII

From Arthur Young's time onwards there was no lack of advice available to farmers as to how they should best keep accounts. It would appear that many failed to do so, or if they did, they took simple forms of which the advocates of accounts could hardly approve and at which they often sneered. By the beginning of the twentieth century it would seem that little had changed. An advisory leaflet for farmers entitled 'Farm book-keeping' published in 1911 by the Board of Agriculture began with the following comment:

> No set of books or system of book-keeping can be recommended as the best for farmers under all circumstances. Much depends upon the size of the holding, the class of business carried on, whether there is any retail trade in such things as milk or other dairy produce, or poultry, and, lastly, upon the capabilities of the farmer himself and the amount of time and labour he is allowed to devote to accounts.[49]

It went on to suggest two broad systems of accounts: a 'simple system' which resulted in a profit and loss account, and 'a fuller method' employing a cashbook, a ledger and a labour book which allowed the profitability of the separate 'departments' of the farm to be established. The same leaflet recommended that an annual valuation be made ('essential if the accounts are to show the true financial position of the farmer or the profit and loss of particular departments') although it pondered whether current prices should be used.

Given some of the other essays in this volume, in particular those by D'Onofrio, Lampe and Sharp, and Moser, it is perhaps remarkable that the English farmer was still allowed such discretion as to how he cast his accounts in the years before the First World War. The leaflet stressed that the farmer's choice of accounts might lie in the amount of time that

48 Young, *Rural economy*, essay 7, pp. 269–95.
49 Board of Agriculture, *Farm book-keeping*.

he was prepared to spend on them.[50] Where the farmer worked with his men, then simple accounts would suffice. For the larger farmer, a comparison is drawn with the manufacturer ('knowledge of the exact cost of producing things he sells is just as useful to a farmer'). We see here the distinction between Young's 'common farmer' and his gentleman farmer with a bailiff or clerk, between book-keeping and accounting.

In theory, at least, the farmer who kept fuller accounts was better equipped to deal with changing circumstances. It would be interesting to know whether agricultural depression and the keen need to cut and monitor costs was an incentive to keep more sophisticated accounts and analyze them more fully. To discover whether knowledge really amounted to empowerment requires evidence that the accounts were indeed subjected to analysis. This is currently lacking: perhaps it always will be.

In truth, one wonders how much had changed in the century and more between Young and the Board of Agriculture's circulars of the years before the First World War. Accounts remained a matter of personal preference for the individual farmer and for this reason, the answer may be not very much at all. The breakthrough may well have been the increased recourse to market town accountants who, for a fee, took the farmer's jotting and invoices and made accounts out of them. There is an untold story here, but for another day.

50 There is no suggestion that the accounts might be delegated to his wife (for those who were married) or professional assistance sought.

5

The Fantastic Accounts of the Large Farmers of Geneva in the Long Eighteenth Century[1]

Fulgence Delleaux

In September 2006, I discovered in the State Archives of Geneva, almost by chance, the writings of Jacques-André Mallet (1740–90), who supervised an agricultural estate about fifteen kilometres from the city of Calvin, in Avully. Mallet managed the property on behalf of his mother, Dorothée Favre, who was its owner.[2] He kept a *Journal d'Avully* in which he reviewed monthly, from 1773 to 1789, the agricultural work carried out on the estate and the impact of the climate on it. There are also two account books of Mallet's covering the period 1771–89.[3] These both amazed and astonished me, as Mallet meticulously recorded nearly everything about the various products of his farm and their destinations: the quantity of sowing and yields for each field, the volume and nature of the wine obtained from different plots, the quantity and type of hay (natural, clover, alfalfa, spelt) harvested and consumed by different types of animals (cows, oxen, horses), and the portion of cereals and wine reserved for self-consumption and sale. Moreover, a reading of Mallet's

1 I have borrowed the title of the chapter from Emmanuel Le Roy Ladurie's famous article: 'Les comptes fantastiques de Gregory King', *Annales: Économies, Sociétés, Civilisations* 23 (1968), 1086–1102. This contribution would not have been possible without the active and benevolent support of Jacqueline and Dominique Micheli, Natalie Rilliet, Laurent Christeller and François-Charles Pictet. I would like to express my deep gratitude to them.

2 At that time we only had access to a microfilm copy (Arch. État. Genève, MIB 760). This was of poor quality which sometimes made transcription difficult. The originals were sent to us in February 2009 by their owner François-Charles Pictet.

3 F. Delleaux, 'L'Astronome aux champs: Le journal de Jacques-André Mallet sur son domaine d'Avully en Genevois (1773–1789)', *Histoire et sociétés rurales* 31 (2009), pp. 141–94 and *Histoire et sociétés rurales* 32 (2009), pp. 135–97.

probate inventory revealed that he also kept a *Carnet de notes relatives à Avully* and a *Livre de dépenses d'Avully*, two documents which unfortunately have not survived.[4]

Mallet's accounts bore no resemblance to the account books of the tenant farmers (*censiers*) of French Hainaut, on whom I was working at that time for my doctoral thesis.[5] The latter, akin to most of the registers – we take 'registers' to include notebooks, memorandums and accounts as well – maintained by medium- and large-scale farmers in Western Europe, were found to be incomplete in both their temporal coverage and their documentation of products, as has been shown by a recent survey.[6] Generally, farm accounts only recorded the sales of certain farm products, as well as the hiring and payment of labour, and, even then, mostly in a discontinuous manner.[7] This is entirely understandable, since it made sense for a farmer to keep a written record of his commitments and commercial transactions, especially when payments involved several instalments, spread over several months and therefore difficult to remember, but the same was certainly not true of information concerning, for example, the quantity of wheat harvested. On this point, it was sufficient for the farmer to go to his granaries or barn to evaluate his stocks.

Initially, I thought that Mallet's meticulousness was essentially due to his scientific training and his parallel activity as an astronomer, and that his journal was unique.[8] In April 1790, at a session of the *Société pour l'encouragement des Arts et de l'Agriculture* of Geneva, Professor Picot delivered a eulogy of Mallet which confirmed that 'he observed everything in the moving picture of crop productions; he kept a record of everything with an inimitable accuracy and spirit of order'.[9] I have since discovered that Mallet was not the only one to keep such accounts, since I have encountered similar, and even more detailed, documents kept

4 Private archive of François-Charles Pictet, Inventory of 13 Feb. 1790.

5 F. Delleaux, *Les censiers et les mutations des campagnes du Hainaut français: La formation originale d'une structure socio-économique, fin xviie–début xixe siècle* (2012).

6 F. Delleaux (ed.) with the participation of M. Hermans, *La plume et la terre: Écrire sur son exploitation agricole en Europe occidentale, 1650–1850* (2021).

7 This is frequently the case in England and Germany: J. Broad and R. Ford, 'Quand les fermiers anglais prennent la plume: Une littérature diversifiée (1600–1850)', in F. Delleaux (ed.), *La plume et la terre* (2022), p. 82; R. Prass, 'Les écrits personnels de paysans et l'histoire économique: Un tour d'horizon dans l'historiographie de l'Allemagne préindustrielle', in Delleaux (ed.), *La plume et la terre*, p. 43.

8 J. D. Candaux, S. Capdeville, M. Grenon, R. Sigrist and V. Somov (eds), *Deux astronomes genevois dans la Russie de Catherine II: Journaux de voyage en Laponie russe de Jean-Louis Pictet et Jacques-André Mallet pour observer le passage de Vénus devant le disque solaire, 1768–1769* (2005).

9 Bibliothèque de Genève, Ms Fr. 655.

by other estate owners in the Geneva area between the mid-eighteenth and early nineteenth centuries.[10] The aim of the present contribution is therefore to show the originality of these accounts and above all to explain the reasons for such a singularity.

I

First, the accounts of farmers near Geneva that I discuss here are of the estates of the city's patricians. 'Patricians' were wealthy and powerful families in the city who owned landed property in the country and lived off their income. Their estates were few in number but also larger than most other farms: at the end of the eighteenth century, of all the properties in Geneva, only 5 per cent were larger than 20 hectares. The remainder was made up of small and medium-sized units: almost 30 per cent were smaller than 0.5 hectares in size, 43 per cent were between 0.5 and 5 hectares and 21.7 per cent between 5 and 20 hectares.[11]

These large estates, which were called 'campagnes', were owned by the patricians of Geneva. They generally spent their summers there and returned to Geneva in the autumn, after the harvest.[12] They either managed the estates directly or through a 'granger-vigneron', a sort of sharecropper who provided some of the equipment, and with whom they shared the proceeds of the business. As Annie Antoine has shown with reference to modern France, sharecropping was not always synonymous with absentee landowners and backwardness. This was also the case in Geneva.[13] It was in the owner's interest to invest in the running of the estate alongside their tenant farmer, and carry out improvements. Ultimately, the landowner benefited from half of the grain harvest – after deducting the seeds consumed – and from the entire harvest of grapes. In the case of direct management, which was commonly the case, the owner had a 'country household', i.e. servants, all housed and fed on the estate:

10 The main sources will be the accounts of Ami-Théophile Perdriau and Horace-Louis Micheli (private archives of the Micheli family) and the accounts of Marc, Jacques and Isaac Pictet (Fondation des Archives de la Famille Pictet, APP). The accounts of Philippe Des Arts, André Naville, Jeanne-Andrienne Des Arts and André Jules Pierre Naville have been discussed by D. Zumkeller, 'Les patriciens genevois aux champs et leurs écrits: Les améliorations viticoles au domaine de Villette (XVIIIe siècle)', in Delleaux (ed.), *La plume et la terre*, pp. 253–67.

11 D. Zumkeller, *Le paysan et la terre: Agriculture et structure agraire à Genève au xviiie siècle* (1992), p. 96.

12 I. Ackermann, M. Hans-Moëvi, I. Roland and D. Zumkeller, *Les maisons rurales du canton de Genève* (2006).

13 A. Antoine, 'La légende noire du métayage dans l'ouest de la France (xviiie–xxe siècle)', in G. Béaur, M. Arnoux and A. Varet-Vitu (eds), *Exploiter la terre: Les contrats agraires de l'Antiquité à nos jours* (2003), pp. 457–70.

valets, herdsmen, cowmen, winegrowers and maids. There were also seasonal workers: harvesters, threshers, reapers and grape pickers. This workforce was often drawn from outside the Republic of Geneva, coming from the neighbouring regions of Auvergne, Savoy or even Vaud.

Like that of Le Reposoir in Pregny, which extended over 30 ha, these large estates consisted of a house, seasonally occupied by the 'master household', adjacent farm buildings, cultivated land, meadows, a vegetable garden and an orchard. Occasionally, there was also scrub land – 'teppes' – and woodland. Cereal farming was of primary importance: often almost half of the land on large estates was sown with autumn and spring cereals. These included wheat, buckwheat, oats, rye, messel (a mixture of wheat and rye), barley and even corn.[14] It is difficult to reconstruct the rotation in which all these crops were grown with confidence. The presence of temporary artificial grassland (clover, sainfoin and in French 'esparcette') suggests, in any case, an absence of fallow or a decline in its area.[15] Within the large estates, there was also a significant proportion of permanent grassland, which was partly used to feed cattle for fattening and milk production.

We should not forget wine production. Although vines did not occupy a very large surface area, wine nevertheless provided the bulk of the income of the estates. There were low vines and high vines or 'hutins', so characteristic of the Genevan region. The former produced red and white grape varieties. The latter were fields planted with fruit trees – peach trees, cherry trees, apple trees – in which 'salvagnins', vine shoots, grew. Cereals were also usually grown at the foot of these shrubby vines.

Many of these products were intended for sale. Indeed, the large estates took advantage of the demographic growth of the neighbouring city of Geneva after 1750, and the concomitant increase in demand, to generate a large vendable surplus.[16] We know, therefore, that between 1768 and 1789, consumption of grains rose from 63,492 to 71,370 hectolitres and the total annual wine consumption steadily increased from 32,000 to 54,000 hectolitres between 1700 and 1790.[17] This urban demand also changed: consumption of a finer wine by the elites,[18] of butter instead of walnut oil – whose average annual consumption jumped from 3.8 to 9.0 kg per inhabitant during the period 1768–1821 – and also of milk which,

14 Zumkeller, *Le paysan et la terre*, p. 166.

15 Ibid., pp. 178–9.

16 A. Perrenoud, *La population de Genève (xvie–xviiie siècles): Études démographiques* (1979).

17 A. M. Piuz and L. Mottu-Weber (eds), *L'économie genevoise de la Réforme à la fin de l'Ancien Régime, xvie–xviiie siècles* (1990), pp. 242, 312.

18 D. Hiler, 'Le vin genevois au XVIIIe siècle: Vente et consommation', *Revue du Vieux Genève* 14 (1984), p. 50.

increasingly drunk with coffee, became a common foodstuff, whereas it had previously been reserved mainly for the sick and for children.[19]

As prices continued to rise on the Geneva markets (between 1763 and 1788 alone, the annual growth rate of the price of wheat was 1.01 per cent while the average price of a pound of butter rose from 129 to 182 deniers between 1759 and 1780), the Genevan landowners adapted to maintain their profits.[20] They chose to introduce better quality vines from Vaud.[21] They also decided to sell their calves early in the year and to increase the number of artificial meadows in order to optimise the milk production of the cows.[22] In November 1785, Mallet noted in his *Journal d'Avully* that 'two superb calves were born in August that they intended to raise'.[23] This implies that he usually sold his calves, just like Horace-Louis Micheli, who had an estate in Landecy. According to one of Micheli's registers for the year 1806:

> I have promised all our calves, weighed alive, to Aimé Babel, butcher, at seven sols a pound, discounting one pound for the rope. He will take them at the age of 15 days in our absence and at the age of three weeks when we are at the estate.[24]

These were all operations relating to production and trade that required book-keeping.

II

Where the large farmers of the Île-de-France, who took advantage of the developing urban market of Paris, filled at most one or two account books during their lifetime,[25] the large farmers in the vicinity of Geneva kept up to twenty accounts, and in great detail. This is the case with

19 Idem, 'Permanences et innovations alimentaires: L'évolution de la consommation des Genevois pendant le xviiie siècle', *Bulletin de la Société d'Histoire et d'Archéologie de Genève* 18 (1984), p. 36; A. Radeff, *Du café dans le chaudron: Économie globale d'Ancien Régime: Suisse occidentale, Franche-Comté et Savoie* (1996), p. 155; Piuz and Mottu-Weber, *L'économie genevoise*, p. 341.

20 Zumkeller, *Le paysan et la terre*, pp. 263, 331.

21 F. Delleaux, 'De la paille à la grappe: Mesurer le progrès agricole d'un domaine genevois au xviiie siècle', *Revue Suisse d'Histoire* 68 (2018), p. 266.

22 F. Delleaux, 'La grande exploitation, la ville et les agronomes: Dynamiques et stratégies de production au domaine d'Avully en Genevois à la fin du xviiie siècle', *Histoire, Économie & Société* 34 (2015), pp. 5–26.

23 Archive of François-Charles Pictet, *Journal d'Avully de Jacques-André Mallet*.

24 Archives Micheli, register no. 264.

25 J. M. Moriceau and G. Postel-Vinay, *Ferme, entreprise, famille: Grande exploitation et changements agricoles, xviie–xixe siècles* (1992); J. M. Moriceau, *Les fermiers de l'Île-de-France: L'ascension d'un patronat agricole, xve–xviie siècle* (1994).

Ami-Théophile Perdriau (1729–99), who owned an estate in Landecy, consisting of 21 ha of arable land, 16 ha of meadows and about 10 ha of vines: during his active life, from 1759 to 1799, he began no less than 12 registers and, in addition, continued those of his father Pierre, each of them having a title indicated on the cover or the flyleaf (Table 5.1).[26] These are account books mostly relating to the agricultural domain, more rarely to the master's household alone. Sometimes they include both, as in the case of the *Livre de dépense et recette générale commencé le 1er janvier 1776*.

Table 5.1. Ami-Théophile Perdriau's account books.

Livre de comptes courants de campagne commencé le 1er janvier 1768–1775]
Livre de comptes courants de campagne commencé le 1er janvier 1776[–1781]
Livre de comptes courants de campagne commencé le 1er janvier 1782[–1787]
Livre de comptes courants de campagne commencé le 1er janvier 1788[– 1793]
Livre de comptes courants de campagne commencé le 1er janvier 1794
Livre de dépense et recette générale commencé le 1er janvier 1776[–1784]
Livre de comptes courants commencé le 1er janvier 1785[–1790]
Comptes de dépense et recette de campagne [commencing 1791]
Livre de notes et petits comptes journaliers de campagne commencé le 1er janvier 1792[–1797]
Livre de dépense de ménage commencé en mars 1788[–1792]
Livre de notes sur les consommations tant du ménage des maîtres que celuy des domestiques [commencing 1792]
Carnet de campagne commencé le 1er janvier 1768[–1777]

Source: Archives Micheli.

Among these registers, there are five that are labelled *Livres de comptes courants de campagne*. They cannot be considered as account books in the strict sense of the term. They do not systematically record all the disbursements and receipts related to the farm. In fact, Perdriau first summarised the hiring of the various servants – shepherd, herdsman, winegrower, servant, etc. – and the payment of their wages to the owner. In the *Livres de comptes courants de campagne*, Perdriau drew together information that was scattered through the other account books, such as the *Carnet de campagne commencé le 1er janvier 1768* or the *Comptes de dépense et recette de campagne*, begun in 1791, where the 'transport des déboursés' (expenses) and the 'caisse de campagne' (revenues) were recorded monthly. The same process can be seen when Perdriau summarises, also for each year, in his *Livres de comptes courants de campagne*, the elements relating to the sale

26 Archives Micheli.

of his wines, which are scattered through other account books, among a multitude of other payments: New Year's greetings for servants, payment of workers hired to cultivate the land or of 'people who killed a wolf', as in December 1793, the purchase of oil, etc. It records, for each numbered barrel, the nature of the vintage contained – red, white or salvagnin, the date of its sale, its quantity – indicated in 'setiers'[27] – its price and the name of its buyer. Finally, Perdriau recorded the annual production of his estate in the *livres de comptes courants de campagne* including that of the grape harvest and the cereal harvest.[28] For the various fields, he records the number of tied sheaves, the number of 'coupes' after threshing and the amount of sowing beforehand.[29] For haymaking, he specifies the number of carts for the various meadows and the number of carts given to the horses and cows.

Perdriau therefore carried out an annual accounting exercise for the key agricultural activities on the estate, which he presented in his *Livres de comptes courants de campagne*. With the exception of 1814 – due to an epizootic and the passage of troops – this accounting practice was continued by his son-in-law Horace-Louis Micheli (1776–1846) who took over the reins of the estate on Perdriau's death, as he indicates in the margin of his register entitled *Petites recettes de campagne et petites dépense de notre ménage*.

> My accounts for 1814 were not copied and consisted only of a handbook in which I wrote down everything I spent and what I received. The events of this so memorable year have so greatly changed the details of our life, as well as the essentials, that I accuse myself here of a preoccupation of mind so constant and so unbearable and insurmountable, that I have not followed the details of the order, as I could have done [...]. I return to my accounts, which consist of receipts and expenditures alone. The items of the latter are not separated as I have always done in quiet years. The household expenses, those of the children, my own, and various expenses incurred by such extraordinary circumstances, either in the country or in the city; all this is written in the same book; apologising for such agitated and rare circumstances, I renounce copying all these items to put them in their place, which would be very long; I limit myself to putting below the exact note of what I have received and spent.[30]

27 The 'setier' is a Genevan measure for wine equivalent to 54.05 litres.
28 Archives Micheli.
29 The 'coupe' is a Geneva measure equivalent to 79.3 litres.
30 Archives Micheli.

III

Perdriau and Micheli were not the only ones to carry out this type of accounting. Isaac Pictet (1746–1823), who from October 1768 supervised an estate of about 30 ha, called the Reposoir, in Pregny, and opened up to 20 registers.[31] Their number and content once again testify to the concern of a Genevan patrician to record meticulously all aspects of the operation of his estate. This may be seen for instance in the *Livre du compte de mon grenier commencé le mois de juillet 1770*.[32] On the left-hand page, Pictet registered the annual harvest results – information that he also recorded in his *Livre pour mes semailles et mes moissons commencé en juillet 1770*, indicating in particular the number of carts of manure spread on each field – and, on the right-hand page, what the wheat, rye, oats and chaff harvested during the year in question were used for: food for the servants, the winegrower, the family, the horses, the chickens or for sale to private individuals.

The extreme meticulousness of this type of accounting allows the historian, as is the case with Jacques-André Mallet's estate, to calculate, for instance, the exact proportion of the various grains that the farmer reserved for his own consumption (seeds, food for masters, servants and poultry) and the payment of salaries (those of the seasonal labour force and of the craftsmen whose services he required). All this information makes it possible to go beyond the extrapolations that are usually necessary because of the incomplete nature of agricultural accounts, and to provide an extremely accurate picture of the operation of an agricultural estate, an example of which is given in Table 5.2.[33]

Pictet did not stop at these annual accounting summaries – already remarkable in themselves – since he produced, in a register entitled *Tableau des récoltes en vin et des moissons de Pregny*, a multi-decennial balance sheet of the cereal and wine production of his farm, from 1732 to 1807.[34] To do this, he used the registers left by his grandfather and father as well as his own. In the same way, Jacques-André Mallet, around 1789, in one of his account books, drew up tables showing the evolution of the productivity of his estate of about thirty hectares: grain from 1740 to 1789, vines from 1772 to 1788, fodder from 1773 to 1789, clover, both first and second cuts, from 1774 to 1789, walnuts from 1777 to 1788 with the quantity of oil and its price, and cattle. For the latter, from 1777 to 1787, it presents the number of cattle, the expenses incurred to their breeding –

31 On the history of this domain see N. Rilliet, *Le Reposoir, histoire d'un domaine genevois* (2012).

32 Fondation des Archives de la Famille Pictet, APP E.3.40.

33 Archive of François-Charles Pictet, *Livre de comptes de Jacques-André Mallet*.

34 Fondation des Archives de la Famille Pictet, APP E.3.39.

TABLE 5.2. Production, consumption and marketing of grain at the Domaine d'Avully directed by Jacques-André Mallet, harvest year 1784–5, in hl.

Type	Stock available at the beginning of the year			Self-consumption								
	Previous year	New harvest	Total	Seed	Servants (8 people)	Master's household (3 people)	Animals	Sale	Payment in kind	Expenditure	Remaining at the end of the year	Total
Wheat	8.6	102.6	110.8	23.8	24.9	5.0	0.6 (poultry)	25.4	0.3 (black-smith) 0.7 (harvesters)	80.7	31.1	111.8
Sarrasin		48	48	3.5l	14.3l	4.8	0.8 (pigs) 2.4 (capons) 2.3 (poultry)	16.6	0.0	44.7	3.2	44.0
Rye		18.6	18.6	3.5	14	0.0	0.0	0.3	0.9 (harvesters)	18.7	0.0	18.7
Barley	1.4	4.9	6.3	0.7	2.9	0.0	0.3 (oxen)	0.2	0.0	4.1	2.3	6.3
Vetch		4.3	4.3	0.9	2.9	0.0	0.0	0.0	0.3 (harvesters)	4.1	0.0	4.1

Source: Archive of François-Charles Pictet, Inventory of 13 Feb. 1790 and Journal d'Avully de Jacques-André Mallet.

fodder, bran, salt, the income from sales, and the quantity of butter and cheese produced annually.

These are all unusually comprehensive accounting exercises compared to those maintained by the vast majority of European large farmers at this date. The reasons for this should now be explained.

IV

In a register kept by the owner of the Landecy estate, we find an explanation of the importance of keeping accounts.

> Although a country owner is accountable only to himself for his management, he must always have his accounts perfectly in order, balanced each week, for what can be balanced each week, each month, for what can be balanced each month, and finally settled in full each year. Without this precaution, exact calculations are impossible. One is thrown into the embarrassment of often not being able to account for one's own disbursements and income.[35]

The register, kept between 1778 and 1786, entitled *Conseils et préceptes par Ami-Théophile Perdriau,* is composed of seven notebooks, the first three of which are sub-titled *Principes de conduite économique et morale pour le possesseur de Landecy qui me suivra* ('Principles of economic and moral management for the owner of Landecy who will succeed me'), and the other four *Abrégés et précis d'une existence assez indifférente* ('Summary and report of a very indifferent existence').[36] His various account books enabled him to have a readily accessible, precise and accurate picture of the financial performance of his farm: in other words, to keep the business connected with it in order and to control its administration. In this respect, Perdriau did not hesitate to draw up, at the end of one of his books, entitled *Carnet de campagne,* covering the years 1768–77, a 'general recapitulation of the expenditure and income of the estate in the ten years contained in the present book', a way for him to review the profitability of his business over the long term.[37] Perdriau specifies that 'to know and to know exactly the returns from the estate, it is necessary to add to the year's income the value of what the estate provided to the household annually'. In other words, to the value of the sales of the various products of the estate, it is necessary to add the value of the share of the various productions reserved for self-consumption, namely

35 Archives Micheli.

36 This document has already been used by Anne-Marie Piuz to trace the life of Élisabeth Baulacre, Ami-Théophile Perdriau's grandmother: 'Un aspect de l'économie genevoise au XVIIe siècle: La fabrique de dorures d'Élisabeth Baulacre', *Mélanges offerts à Paul Martin* (1961), pp. 523–40.

37 Archives Micheli, *Carnet de campagne d'Ami-Théophile Perdriau* (1768–77).

a certain quantity of wheat, wine, milk or poultry. Finally, to complete the evaluation, Perdriau considers that it is necessary to 'deduct from the year's expenditure the rents paid to the persons interested in the domain'. He therefore had to draw up an operating account in order to verify the efficiency of his estate, more precisely its capacity to generate a significant profit or 'net product', an exercise recommended more particularly by the Physiocrats.[38]

The agronomists, whose literature was also being disseminated at the same time, tended to recommend – in addition to practical methods for increasing the various agricultural productions – the most detailed book-keeping possible, i.e. a book-keeping system that was not limited solely to the financial aspects just mentioned and which ultimately provides a precise picture of the internal workings of the farm, by presenting, for example, yields in relation to the surface area.[39] The large farmers in Geneva paid particular attention to this agronomic literature, which was mainly French and Swiss, since references to it are regularly found in their inventories after death, but also in the margin of their account books (Table 5.3).[40]

Table 5.3. Agronomic readings of Jacques-André Mallet.

l'Abbé Rozier, *Dictionnaire d'Agriculture.*
Arthur Young (trans. M. de Fréville), *Le Parfait fermier anglais.*
Duhamel du Monceau, *Traité de la culture des terres.*
de Boutrolle, *Le Parfait bouvier ou instructions concernant la connaissance des bœufs et vaches.*
de Béguillet, *Traité des subsistances et des grains.*
de Sarcey de Sutières, *Agriculture expérimentale à l'usage des agriculteurs, fermiers et laboureurs.*
de la Salle de l'Etang, *Traité des prairies artificielles.*
de Jean Bertrand, *Traité de l'irrigation des prés.*
de Jacques de Solleysel, *Le Parfait maréchal.*
de Plaigne, *L'art de faire, d'améliorer et conserver les vins, ou le Parfait vigneron.*
Recueil de pièces oeconomiques et autres curieuses et utiles contenant la meilleure méthode de semer les grains, de faire des prairies artificielles, des engrais de terre, de cultiver la vigne … .

38 Georges Weulersse, *Le mouvement physiocratique en France de 1756 à 1770* (1910).

39 J. C. Perrot, 'La comptabilité des entreprises agricoles dans l'économie physiocratique', *Annales: Économies, Sociétés, Civilisations* 33 (1978), p. 567. For an overview of the agronomic literature, A. J. Bourde, *Agronomie et agronomes en France au xviiie siècle* (1967).

40 Archive of François-Charles Pictet, Inventory of 13 Feb. 1790.

Table 5.3. *cont.*

Mémoires de la société économique de Berne.
Bibliothèque physico-économique.
Observations sur les maladies de bestiaux, sur les dartres.
Sur les maladies de grains.
Sur la culture des pommes de terre.

Source: Archive of François-Charles Pictet, Inventory of 13 Feb. 1790 and Journal d'Avully de Jacques-André Mallet.

In February 1790, after the death of Jacques-André Mallet, the *Mémoires de la société économique de Berne* were amongst the works in his library. In the third volume of this periodical, published in 1762, one of the authors, a member of the Fribourg economic society, in an article entitled 'Réflexions sur les moyens proposés pour faire fleurir l'agriculture en Suisse' ('Reflections on the means proposed to make agriculture flourish in Switzerland'), stated that 'a good farmer must know how to calculate, both for the sale of his foodstuffs, and to keep an exact record of the various operations he carries out on his land'.[41] These are typical elements of the thinking of the Swiss patriot economists. These thinkers from Basel, Bern or Zurich, directly influenced by French physiocratic thought – the Marquis de Mirabeau who took part in the work of the Bern Economic Society[42] or Charles Butré in the Zurich Physical Society – sought to reform agriculture and, more generally, the economy of the country, by approaching all agricultural activities from the point of view of monetary utility, taking into account the possibilities opened up by the markets.[43] To this end, they advocated the education of peasants and, at the same time, the use of the most complete accounting system possible and the introduction of new cultivation methods to maximise profit.[44] Such an approach led, as it did for Mallet or Pictet, to the construction of statistical data presented in tables, relating to agricultural production and its various parameters for which changes were desired. Data thus made it possible to better understand the cost–benefit ratio of the very same changes that patriotic Swiss economists were advocating. According to the Bernese

41 'Réflexions sur les moyens proposés pour faire fleurir l'agriculture en Suisse', *Mémoires et observations recueillies par la Société oeconomique de Berne* 2 (1762), pp. 89–90.

42 A. Bertholet and B. Kapossy, *La physiocratie et la Suisse: Études sur la correspondance du marquis de Mirabeau et Marc Charles Frédéric de Sacconay (1731–1787)* (2023).

43 J. Valarché, 'L'influence des physiocrates en Suisse', *Revue d'histoire économique et sociale* 35 (1957), pp. 337–46.

44 R. Braun, *Le déclin de l'Ancien Régime en Suisse: Un tableau de l'histoire économique et sociale du 18e siècle* (1988), pp. 70–3.

Albrecht Stapfer in 1761, the farmer must constantly ask himself the following questions when considering the possibility of changing his cultivation techniques: 'Won't all this lead to significant unexpected costs (*faux frais*)?' 'Will my income be increased or decreased?'.[45] Clearly, this cost–benefit ratio is 'the common thread in the accumulation of empirical and statistical data' in the records of the large farmers in Geneva.[46] How else can we understand the words of Ami-Théophile Perdriau when he recommends to his successors, in one of his registers, that their

> statements of harvests, wheat, wine, fodder and sowing must be kept with the same accuracy, so that you can say to yourselves: such and such a vineyard and such and such a field have yielded such and such a sum for 10 years, and then lead you accordingly, in order to keep them under the same crop or to change their destination?[47]

This degree of accounting refinement is, let us repeat, not only advocated by the patriotic economists, but also by the Physiocrats and the agronomists. Many of their writings were probably presented and discussed within the *Société pour l'encouragement des Arts et de l'Agriculture de Genève*, created in 1776, in which several large rural landowners of the region participated, including Jacques-André Mallet.

Beyond this scholarly institution, one cannot ignore the existence of family, friendly and professional networks throughout the Geneva region, within which knowledge and practices circulated among enlightened landowners. In the margin of one of his registers, Isaac Pictet notes: 'I lent Mr Aubert Dejournes the son *Les principes de l'équitation* (1769) by Mr Dupaty on 13 October 1780, to Mr Stuart Belisaire on 1 July 1781'.[48] Philippe Des Arts (1686–1754), the owner of the Villette estate in 1725, records in a register 'I have put in the *chapons* [vine shoots that are planted] that Mr Marc Pictet of Pregny gave me.'[49] Marc Pictet is the grandfather of Isaac Pictet. 'I also tried some of the drugs used by Mr Pictet. I sent him a quarter and a half which he had prepared and I sowed in Susorme in the first row and half of the second on the side of the sunset', records Mallet, in his *Journal d'Avully*, in September 1783, about a preparation for wheat seeds.[50] Some of these great farmers even became true agronomists in their own right, such as Charles Pictet de Rochemont (1755–1824), who ran a vast estate of 75 ha in Lancy. Pictet de Rochemont was famous for publishing his own experiments – in particular regarding the introduction of merino sheep – and for running a periodical from 1796

45 Ibid., p. 72.
46 Ibid., p. 72
47 Archives Micheli.
48 Fondation des Archives de la Famille Pictet, APP E.3.54.
49 Zumkeller, 'Les patriciens genevois', p. 264.
50 Archive of François-Charles Pictet, *Journal d'Avully de Jacques-André Mallet*.

onwards, the *Bibliothèque Britannique*, the main organ for disseminating the English agricultural methods that were so renowned at the time.[51]

As noted above, in Perdriau's words, the Genevan estate holders did not keep their accounts for themselves alone. They were bound to facilitate the management of the farm by their descendants. Their registers represented, in a way, the memory of the estate. It was therefore necessary for them to be as clear as possible. We can thus understand the following annotation by Horace-Louis Micheli in one of his account books:

> The expenditure page written next to it had been reserved for the expenditure of January [1808], which is usually larger than that of the other months and cannot fit on a single page. As this was not the case this year, it turns out that the February expenditure was written on this page reserved for the January expenditure and that the following page for the February expenditure remains blank.[52]

Consequently, in the exercise of writing in the private sphere, 'the individual never acts alone, but with and for those around him', as Sylvie Mouysset has written.[53]

Is the desire to obtain a rational management of one's domain, in order to take advantage of the growth and changes in the demand in Geneva, enough to explain such a meticulous accounting entry? Once again, other farmers, notably near Paris, benefited from the same market growth as their Geneva counterparts, and were just as concerned with the profitability of their business, ran estates three or four times larger than the Genevans, and yet, to our knowledge, did not carry out similar accounting. There must have been other motives that explain this cumbersome practice that the large estate holders at the gates of Geneva engaged in. Their motivation undoubtedly went beyond practical goals and probably originated in the Reformed religion to which they belonged.

V

It is known from the study of Weber that a Calvinist was obliged to actively control his conduct in order to avoid falling into the 'instinctive and spontaneous enjoyment' that is common to man.[54] He must adopt an

51 D. M. Bickerton, *Marc-Auguste and Charles Pictet, the Bibliothèque Britannique (1796–1815), and the Dissemination of British Literature and Science on the Continent* (1986).

52 Archives Micheli.

53 S. Mouysset, 'Pourquoi laisser trace de sa vie ordinaire? France-Catalogne (xve–xixe siècle)', in P. O. Jané and P. Poujade (eds), *Memòria personal: Construcció i projecció en primera persona a l'època moderna* (2015), p. 73.

54 M. Weber, *L'éthique protestante et l'esprit du capitalisme* (1967), pp. 148–9; G. Todeschini, 'La comptabilité à partie double et la rationalité économique occidentale: Max Weber et Jack Goody', in N. Coquery, F. Menant and F.

ascetic discipline. In the case of a landowner and farmer, could this not be expressed through the very assiduous keeping of accounts, especially as it would ultimately be an excellent means for him to detect the signs of his fate after death? It should not be forgotten that a Calvinist, believing in the logic of the Reformed dogma of predestination, seeks to demonstrate to himself, through his daily conduct, that God has saved him from birth. The slightest slackening in recording his endeavours can therefore be seen as a worrying sign. For the farmer, disorder in his accounting is seen as a warning from God, a threat to him. Successfully managing his farm and making it flourish would be seen as 'the result of an inner strength from God', knowing that this divine help is only given to those who are chosen, i.e. worthy of going to heaven,[55] and the book-keeping would help to demonstrate this. Even today, when the religious imperative is usually attenuated, 'keeping a chronicle [...] presumes a well-kept operation', as Nathalie Joly states.[56]

It is probably no coincidence that Perdriau refers to his estate as being 'in a state of prosperity'. On another occasion he writes of his

> books from 1768 to 1778 and thereafter, kept in great detail and with accuracy, and in which one will see the annual expenses, their times, their proportions, and in general the whole summary of the operation.[57]

The same is true when Isaac Pictet notes, in June 1804 in one of his registers, that:

> in order to know more exactly what my vines yield, portion by portion, and to be able to judge the less productive ones as well as the bonuses of which they are susceptible, I have imagined drawing up a table [...], which indicates their content, by means of which I can act on almost immediately.[58]

For Calvinists, the uncertainty, not to say anxiety, about the fate that God has in store for them after death will always persist during their earthly existence, despite reassuring signs. Therefore, the keeping of very detailed accounts cannot cease during their lifetime, even if they clearly indicate an improvement in agricultural yields. It is probably in this way that we must understand the remark of Isaac Pictet, who after transcribing in his *Tableau des récoltes en vin et des moissons de Pregny* the

Weber (eds), *Écrire, compter, mesurer: Vers une histoire des rationalités pratiques* (2006), pp. 67–76.

55 S. Kalberg, 'La sociologie des émotions de Max Weber', *Revue du Mauss* 40 (2012), p. 294.

56 N. Joly, 'Vaches et blés sur le papier: Socialisations à l'écrit du monde agricole', *Communication et langages* 159 (2009), p. 83.

57 Archives Micheli.

58 Fondation des Archives de la Famille Pictet, APP E.3.39.

'incontestable proof that to sow less,[59] but to sow well, to leave nothing fallow, by varying the annual products, is infinitely preferable to the old customs', to such an extent that 'in these last fifteen years he has almost doubled the product of the fields', concludes in the following way: 'I cannot recommend this method too highly, and try to perfect it; *this is what I am working on*'.[60] Pictet admits to working tirelessly to improve his cereal productivity.

From 1804 onwards, Isaac Pictet drew up such a 'tableau des moissons de Pregny', accompanied by a commentary.[61] For the years from 1732 until 1807, when he ceased to make entries in this document, he presented for each year the total number of coupes of wheat and rye sown, the number of sheaves harvested afterwards and finally the 'produit', in other words the number of coupes of grain collected after threshing. In addition, he calculated the productivity of the soil, expressed at the time as the number of grains harvested for each one sown. The yield per seed nearly doubled, rising from a ratio of 3.5 to 6.75 from 1732 to 1807. To trace this long-term evolution, Pictet relied on the records left by his predecessors, as well as his own records, which he started in 1770. I have transcribed the results and present them in the form of a graph (Figure 5.1).[62]

To use Weber's expression, the farmer from Pregny could be said to have received a 'psychic reward' from the increase in his grain yields.[63] Pictet's book-keeping and, even more so, the figures that he calculated from his accounts, would be a way for him to counter the religious anguish inherent in his life as a Calvinist. In the words of Mohamed Cherkaoui, the Calvinist 'is condemned to lead his daily life as a never-ending struggle to detect the signs of his grace'.[64] A 'laborious concern' in André Biéler's expression would thus pervade the whole existence of the Calvinist farmer; he would be supposed to participate in the work of God, i.e. to feed his creatures. His work should therefore be considered

59 It is now recognised that a lower seeding rate gives wheat a greater capacity for tillering, i.e. producing several stems – and therefore several spikes – from a single grain. In principle, the reduction in sowing gives the wheat the possibility of better capturing the nutrients present in the soil. Thus, according to Isaac Pictet, before September 1788, when 'a lot was sown', the average volume sown was 3.74 hl/ha: a quantity similar to that reported by the Geneva agronomists in the mid-eighteenth century. From September 1788, the average volume of seed was 2 hl/ha (Fondation des Archives de la Famille Pictet, APP E.3.39). For more details see Delleaux, *De la paille à la grappe*.

60 Fondation des Archives de la Famille Pictet, APP E.3.39, emphasis added.

61 Ibid.

62 I have continued these figures up to 1811, using another register by Isaac Pictet (Archives Pictet, APP E.3.4).

63 Weber, *L'éthique protestante*, p. 155.

64 M. Cherkaoui, 'Le réel et le rationnel: Rationalités et conséquences inattendues chez Max Weber', *Revue européenne des sciences sociales* 42 (2004), p. 76.

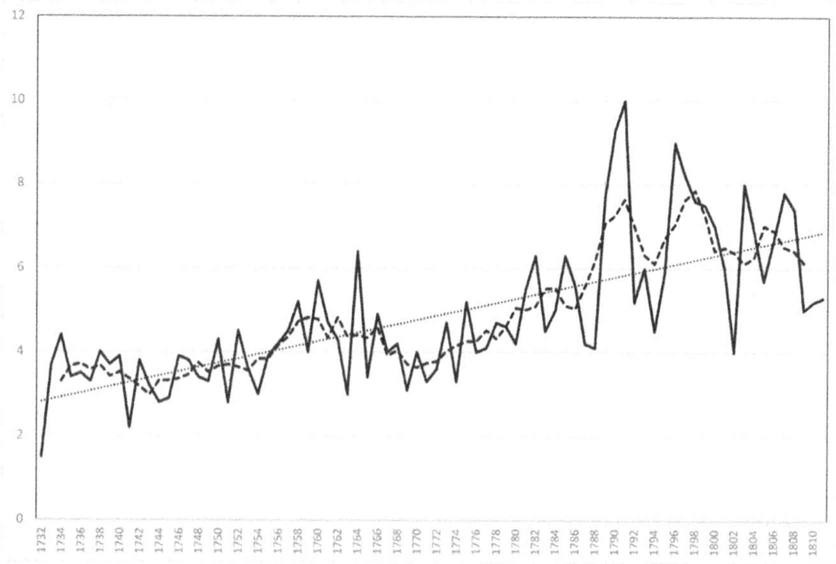

FIGURE 5.1. Wheat yields at Le Reposoir from 1732 to 1811 (with five-year moving average and linear trendline). *Source:* Fondation des Archives de la Famille Pictet, APP E.3.39 and E.3.4.

as a service rendered to Him and not as personal profit.[65] This is probably the meaning of the efforts undertaken by Isaac Pictet, but also by his father Jacques, to increase and make profitable the wine production of their Reposoir estate, and their will to record their success in doing so in one of their registers.

> Some time after the work just read was completed, I chanced to find the product of the vines for 15 years prior to 1746, which I had begun to establish [on the register]. The result proves so clearly the improvement of the vines that I did not hesitate to transcribe it here.[66]

James and Isaac Pictet would de facto be associated with God's work. Consequently, this agricultural performance is not an end in itself: it is subordinate and subject to eternal life. They would then testify to the

65 A. Biéler, *La pensée économique et sociale de Calvin* (1959), pp. 398–400. On this sense of anxiety among farmers in the pre-industrial era, and not only for religious reasons, see F. Delleaux, *Inquiétude dans les champs: Essai sur la gestion des exploitations agricoles dans l'espace francophone, vers 1730–vers 1830* (2022).

66 Fondation des Archives de la Famille Pictet, APP E.3.39. For more details: Delleaux, *De la paille à la grappe*, pp. 240–73.

farmer's 'rationality in value' and not to his 'rationality in purpose'.[67] No doubt the people in charge of worship did not fail to remind him of this.

Daniel Sandoz, a farmer in La Chaux-de-Fonds, this time near Neuchâtel, who kept a register covering the years 1770–1779, noted, after listening to the sermons during the fast on Thursday 9 September 1773, that 'our ministers exhorted us [...] to cultivate our land'.[68] Nine years earlier, some forty kilometres away, Mochard, the pastor of Bévilard, in the Bernese Jura, in his *Essai sur la meilleure méthode pour l'éducation du paysan* ('Essay on the best method to educate peasants'), considered that 'it is appropriate to show, before anything else, how he should be trained in the fear of God'.[69] He added further that

> the zeal of a shepherd for the temporal good of his flock will also engage him to provide those who have the most intelligence with the reading of some good authors who deal with rural oeconomy

which one imagines must have served as an aid to increasing agricultural production.[70] Weber reminds us that 'the pastor exercised an influence that we moderns cannot fathom'.[71] In his register, based on his father David's notes and his own, Sandoz drew up a very meticulous record of the production of spring cereals (barley, oats and barley) on his farm between 1737 and 1780, indicating for each year the area of the plots sown.[72] Does he not also seek to highlight the progress he has been able to make in terms of grain yields? Indeed, a significant increase in yields of 20 per cent can be observed in Sandoz's calculations from the end of the 1760s (Figure 5.2). Could this be the result of a change in agricultural practices? At that time, some farmers in the Neuchâtel area tried to plough

67 M. Weber, *Économie et société. Tome 1: Les catégories de la sociologie* (1st edn 1956), 1995), pp. 56–7; C. H. Cuin, 'Émotions et rationalité dans la sociologie classique: Le cas de Weber et Durkheim', *Revue européenne des sciences sociales* 120 (2001), pp. 86–7.

68 On Sandoz, see S. Ecklin, *Le journal de Daniel Sandoz, 1770–1779: Essai de lecture critique* (Mémoire de Licence de l'Université de Neuchâtel, 1990); S. Ecklin, 'Le journal de Daniel Sandoz, 1770–1779: Chronique d'un système rédactionnel complexe', in R. Chartier and A. Messerli (eds), *Lire et écrire en Europe (1500–1900): Perspectives comparées* (2001), pp. 139–49.

69 M. Mochard, 'Essai sur la meilleure méthode pour l'éducation du paysan, relativement à l'agriculture', *Mémoires et observations recueillies par la Société oeconomique de Berne* 5 (1764), p. 65.

70 Ibid., p. 99.

71 Weber, *L'éthique protestante*, p. 186.

72 Archives de l'État de Neuchâtel, *Journal de Daniel Sandoz* (unlisted).

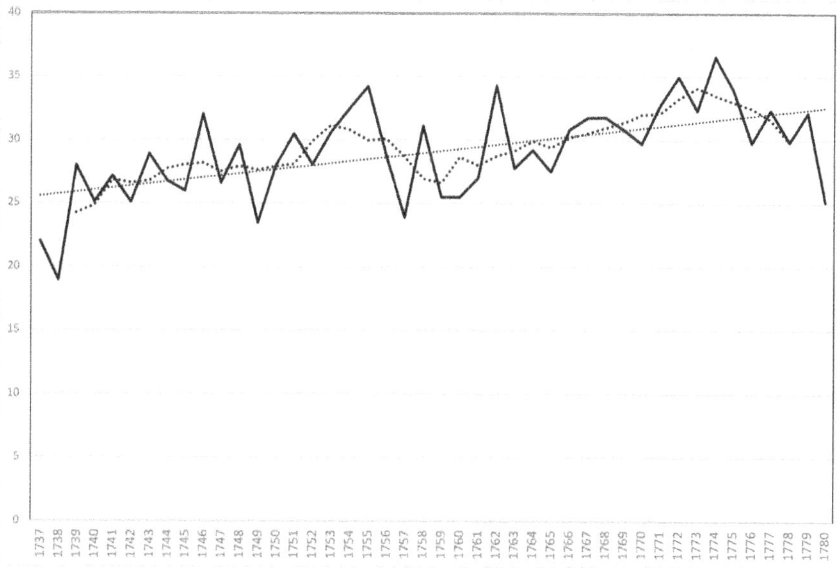

Figure 5.2. Spring cereal yields at David and Daniel Sandoz in La Chaux-de-Fonds from 1737 to 1780 (in hl/ha) (with five-year moving average and linear trendline). *Source:* Archives de l'État de Neuchâtel, Journal de Daniel Sandoz (unlisted).

their fields two years in succession.[73] On Wednesday 1 May 1776, Sandoz mentions that he has 'ploughed very little land without manure'.[74]

VI

In conclusion, adherence to the dogma of predestination and the concomitant conviction that the increase of capital can be both a means of helping God in His participation in economic life, and a tangible sign of obtaining His grace, would lead to two types of behaviour: on the one hand, the agent would do everything possible to achieve this enrichment, practising a kind of professional asceticism aimed at avoiding the temptations of an impure life; on the other hand, in order to expose this profit as clearly as possible, he would have recourse to methodical book-keeping without let-up. These two aspects would be 'psychologically a means of reacting against the religious anguish of the Calvinist caused by the impossibility of knowing God's decree concerning him'.[75] Let us

73 R. Cop, 'Travaux céréaliers et assolements aux montagnes du xviie au début du xixe siècle', *Musée Neuchâtelois* 27 (1990), p. 92.

74 *Journal de Daniel Sandoz.*

75 Cherkaoui, *Le réel et le rationnel*, p. 76.

acknowledge in passing that, in agricultural accounts, it remains difficult to read explicit 'emotives', in the sense of William Matthew Reddy, i.e. statements about emotions or feelings that are both descriptive and performative,[76] because this was probably self-evident for a farmer at the time and it therefore seemed unnecessary to express them on paper. In other words, in their records, Pictet and the other Calvinist estate holders did not expressly mention either their fear of God's plan or the way in which such fear prompted them to seek an improvement in their agricultural productivity in order to lessen it. In any case, we would have in the large Calvinist estate holders the illustration of 'a kind of triangle, as Kaspar Von Greyerz puts it, between self-writing, moral discipline and the dogma of predestination'.[77] Certain productive results, presented in the accounts, would then only be clearly readable within the framework of a religious context which partly conditions them. This is an aspect relatively ignored in the most recent works of which we are aware[78] and which would deserve, a fortiori, to be analysed further, in particular in the other regions affected by the Reformation.

76 W. M. Reddy, *La traversée des sentiments: Un cadre pour l'histoire des émotions, 1700–1850* (1st edn, 2001, 2019 edn), pp. 141–7.

77 K. von Greyerz, 'Écriture de soi et lecture religieuse chez les protestants du monde germanophone en perspective confessionnelle', in Daniele Tosato-Rigo, *Appel à témoins: Écrits personnels et pratiques socioculturelles, xvie–xxe* (2016), p. 56.

78 F. Ammannati (ed.), *Religion and religious institutions in the European economy, 1000–1800* (2012), pp. 331–596.

6

The Accounting Practices of Two Large French Farms in the Middle of the Nineteenth Century: The Farms of Adolphe Dailly[1]

Laurent Herment

In the nineteenth century, French agriculture did not enjoy a reputation for dynamism. Throughout the century, agronomists lamented the underperformance of an agricultural sector dominated by smallholdings. Over the past thirty years however, there has been a reassessment of the backwardness of French agriculture. This has revealed that in some regions, large-scale farming – sometimes characterized as capitalist – was the predominant mode of cultivation.[2] It has also been discovered that small farms could, under certain conditions, achieve higher yields than their larger counterparts.[3] This is not to claim that French agriculture

1 I would like to thank Nathalie Joly and Federico D'Onofrio, the anonymous referees, and Pierre Labardin for their comments. I remain solely responsible for the shortcomings of this text.

2 G. Béaur and J-.M. Chevet, 'Les incertitudes de la croissance: Y-a-t-il eu un modèle français du développement agricole?', in L. Herment (ed.), L'histoire rurale de l'Europe: XVIe–XXe siècle (2019), pp. 271–96; J.-M. Moriceau, *Les grands fermiers: Les laboureurs de l'Île-de-France (XVe–XVIIIe siècle)* (2017); J.-M. Moriceau and G. Postel-Vinay, *Ferme, entreprise, famille: Grande exploitation et changements agricoles XVIIe–XIXe siècles* (1992); G. Postel-Vinay, *La terre et l'argent: L'agriculture et le crédit en France du XVIIIe au début du XXe siècle* (1998), pp. 241–317; idem, *La rente foncière dans le capitalisme agricole: Analyse de la voie 'classique' du développement du capitalisme dans l'agriculture à partir de l'exemple du Soissonnais* (1994).

3 L. Herment, 'Mesurer les performances *céréalières* des petites exploitations du Bassin Parisien durant le premier XIXe siècle', *Histoire et Sociétés Rurales* 36 (2011), pp. 97–136; J-. L. Mayaud, *La petite exploitation triomphante* (1999);

led the way in the scientific and technical advancements of the time, but it enables us to affirm that French farmers, much like their European counterparts, adeptly seized opportunities presented by the market. Two of these opportunities stand out: industrial crops and animal husbandry.[4] Beyond the specific dynamism of farmers, these two types of production significantly benefited from scientific progress over the course of the nineteenth century. This is particularly evident in the case of industrial crops, such as potatoes processed for starch and beet for sugar. These advancements were closely tied to innovations in chemistry and the utilization of selected seeds.[5]

French historiography has also dedicated a great deal of attention to accounting techniques to understand the decision-making of farmers. Yannick Lemarchand's work attests to this research effort, and has resulted in numerous publications on the nature of accounting practices and methods suitable for agriculture.[6] As has been shown by the research of Nathalie Joly, Thomas Depecker, and François Vatin, the agricultural elites of the nineteenth century actively advocated the adoption of accounting techniques to gauge the performance of farms.[7]

R. Hubscher, 'La petite exploitation en France: Reproduction et compétitivité (fin XIXe siècle–début XXe siècle)', *Annales ESC* 40 (1985), pp. 3–34.

4 On husbandry see N. Koning, *The Failure of Agrarian Capitalism: Agrarian Politics in the UK, Germany, the Netherlands, and the USA, 1846–1919* (1994).

5 On the progress of agricultural chemistry and the use of commercial fertilizers see N. Jas, *Au carrefour de la chimie et de l'agriculture: Les sciences agronomiques en France et en Allemagne 1840–1914* (2001); idem, 'Les enjeux scientifiques, techniques et commerciaux du contrôle de la qualité des engrais au XIXe siècle', *Réseaux* 2000/4 (no. 102) (2000), pp. 165–94; L. Herment, *La plus belle firme du monde ne peut offrir que ce qu'elle a* (2021); R. Bourrigaud, *Le développement agricole au 19e siècle en Loire-Atlantique* (1994). There exist only a few works about seed selection at this time. For the development of sugar beet see C. Schnakenbourg, *Histoire de l'industrie sucrière en Picardie (1810–2006)* (2010) and for potatoes for starch production see L. Herment, 'Un Capitulo poco conocido sobre la historia de la patata en la region Parisina durante el siglo XIX', *Obradoiro de Historia Moderna* (2018) https://dialnet.unirioja.es/servlet/articulo?codigo=6954354.

6 See Y. Lemarchand, 'The birth of industrial accounting in France: Some curious paradoxes', *Accounting History Rev.* 29 (2019), pp. 221–41; Y. Lemarchand, Y. Levant, and H. Zimnovitch, 'Schisme à Grignon: Autour de la comptabilité agricole durant les années 1870', *Entreprises et histoire* 88 (2017), pp. 37–52; Y. Lemarchand, *Du dépérissement à l'amortissement: Enquête sur l'histoire d'un concept et de sa traduction comptable* (2013). Beyond agriculture, accounting literature in France was very lively as demonstrated by T. Boyns, J. R. Edwards, and M. Nitkitin, 'The development of industrial accounting in Britain and France before 1880: A comparative study of accounting literature and practice', *European Accounting Rev.* 6 (1997), pp. 393–437.

7 T. Depecker, N. Joly, and J. Labatut, 'L'entreprise agricole et sa gestion: Éthos, structures et instruments (XIXe–XXe siècle)', *Entreprises et histoire* 88

Yet, as Martin Giraudeau noted, '[t]he farm [...] seems like a distant, almost exotic site for accounting'.[8] This author cautions against a hasty reading of agricultural accounting manuals. On one hand, the practices of record-keeping were ancient and varied depending on the locations, time periods, and, of course, the individuals maintaining them. On the other, accounting practices should not be construed as imported directly from industry or commerce. Ultimately, it is essential to consider the objectives of these practices, which, as Giraudeau reminds us again, often have little to do with calculating profit and/or a rate of profit.[9]

First, it is highly likely that only a small proportion of farmers attempted to keep accounts following the principles of double-entry book-keeping or in accordance with the recommendations of the textbook authors.[10] This probability is underscored by the sheer number of farmers and farms in nineteenth-century France, estimated at five or six million, coupled with the scarcity of accounts preserved in the archives. However, the absence of formal accounts does not imply that farmers, both large and small, did not engage in calculations. The evolution of specializations in response to market signals serves as evidence that farmers and landowners knew how to count, demonstrated rational decision-making and capitalized on the financial opportunities inherent in diverse crop choices.[11]

A second remark relates more particularly to the end of the nineteenth century. We know that agricultural unions played a driving role in the modernization of agriculture and in the premises of its industrialization.[12] Despite their influential role, an extensive analysis of union newspapers

---

(2017), pp. 6–20; T. Depecker and F. Vatin, 'Taking stock to yield a return: Agricultural accounting, agronometry and chemical statics in the early-nineteenth century', *Accounting History Rev.* 26 (2016), pp. 107–29; N. Joly, 'Comme le sang dans le corps des animaux: Le capital circulant expliqué à la jeunesse rurale par Louis Gossin (1838)', *Entreprises et histoire* 88 (2017), pp. 182–8; idem, 'Educating in economic calculus: The invention of the enlightened peasant via manuals of agriculture, 1830–1870', *Accounting History Rev.* 26 (2016), pp. 131–60.

8 M. Giraudeau, 'The farm as an accounting laboratory: An essay on the history of accounting and agriculture', *Accounting History Rev.* 27 (2017), pp. 201–15.

9 About the emergence of double-entry accounting and its role in the emergence of capitalism, see E. Chiapello, 'Accounting and the birth of the notion of capitalism', *Critical Perspectives on Accounting* 18 (2007), pp. 263–96.

10 See P. Labardin, *L'émergence de la fonction comptable en France* (2008), pp. 63–4, 150–4.

11 L. Herment and N. Mignemi, 'La especialización agrícola en la historia rural europea: Recursos, mercados y espacios (siglos XVIII–XX)', *Mundo Agrario* 22 (49) (2021), pp. 163–80. L. Herment and A. Antoine, 'Specialisation in rural history: Towards a definition', in A. Antoine (ed.), *Agricultural Specialisation and Rural Patterns of Development* (2016), pp. 13–45.

12 Herment, *La plus belle firme*; N. Mignemi, *Coopératives et mondes agricoles: France et Italie (1880–1950)* (Rennes, 2017).

published from 1884 onward reveals that accounting did not take a central position in the acculturation of the peasantry to the processes of agricultural industrialization and capitalism. Articles dedicated to accounting were notably scarce, if not entirely absent, from the majority of these publications.

A final observation is imperative. In considering the acculturation of farmers to accounting practices, it is crucial to underscore that acculturation processes are multi-dimensional and bi-directional, as scholarship on this subject has evidenced.[13] The proliferation of manuals aimed at acquainting farmers with accounting undeniably addressed a specific need; however, this does not imply that readers uncritically adopted the principles outlined in these guides for incorporation into their account books. It is highly probable, if not certain, that farmers constructed accounts tailored to their resources and expectations. While some may have endeavoured to adhere more or less to the principles of double-entry, the majority almost certainly did not. Indeed, a significant portion of small-scale farmers may not have maintained any records, not simply because of the lack of any legal requirement to do so, but also owing to a perceived lack of utility.

Nevertheless, as Gilles Postel-Vinay reminds us, some large-scale farmers were subject to commercial law and this compelled them to keep formal accounts. Their decision to seek this legal status was intricately connected to the pursuit of capital for financing ventures such as the

13 This remark about the non-unidimensional and unidirectional character of the processes of acculturation agrees, at least partially, with the observations of Martin Giraudeau. For the 'Berry box', see J. W. Berry, 'Immigration, acculturation, and adaptation', *Applied Psychology* 47 (1997), pp. 5–68; idem, 'The acculturation process and refugee behavior', *Context* 10 (1989), pp. 1–12. For critics of the process of acculturation as one-directional, see among others C. Ward, 'Thinking outside the Berry boxes: New perspectives on identity, and intercultural relations', *International Journal of Intercultural Relations* 32 (2008), pp. 105–14. Although these works referred to the process of acculturation of migrants, it seems they can be applied to the process of acculturation of peasantry faced with a multipolar expertise (economic, chemical, biological, etc.). Gibson defined the process of acculturation as a 'process of culture change that occurs when individuals with different cultures come into contact'. M. A. Gibson, 'Immigrant adaptation and patterns of acculturation', *Human Development* 44 (2001), pp. 19–23. On the process of acculturation of French peasantry at the end of the nineteenth century, see Herment, *La plus belle firme*.

establishment of a distillery, sugar factory or starch factory.[14] It is amongst these farmers that we might expect to find double-entry book-keeping.

I

Advocates of farm accounting have long recognized the challenge involved in getting the principles of double-entry accounting accepted within the agricultural sector, even after 1945 when efforts were made to compel farmers to keep accounts. As noted by Lemarchand *et al.*, the difficulties in translating ideal forms of agricultural accounting into practical applications sparked intense debates at the close of the nineteenth century.[15] Notwithstanding these challenges, the claims of scholars, such as Nathalie Joly, Thomas Depecker, and François Vatin, who have linked the emergence of accounting in nineteenth-century France with a developing capitalist ethos, raise several questions, the answers to which shed light on accounting practices in the rural milieu:[16]

(a) There are a whole range of questions relating to the emergence of a capitalist ethos within the rural realm and the forms it took.

(b) More mundane questions are to be asked regarding the range of accounting practices and techniques employed by farmers, including double-entry book-keeping, cash accounting, patrimonial or cost accounting, and more.

(c) The question of the diverse, but not necessarily conflicting, objectives behind the implementation of accounting. These might range from profit calculation and crop viability assessment to understanding production cycles and means of improvement, as well as maintaining management oversight.

Within the limits of this chapter, it is impossible to respond to, or even discuss, all these questions. By investigating a specific example, I shall illustrate the impossibility of establishing a singular technique or practice as a universal rule. Depending on the specific purposes of each accounting document, either cost or profit calculation might be adopted. Conversely, meticulous assessment of cash inflows and outflows might

14 It is interesting to discover that during the second part of the nineteenth century, a good number of the Parisian merchants, shopkeepers, and craftsmen did not keep account books or kept them in a defective manner, despite legal requirements. See P. Labardin, 'Accounting prescription and practice in nineteenth-century France: An analysis of bankruptcy cases', *Accounting History Review* 21 (2011), pp. 263–83.

15 Lemarchand et al., 'Schisme à Grignon'.

16 N. Joly, 'Educating in economic calculus: The invention of the enlightened peasant via manuals of agriculture', T. Depecker and F. Vatin, 'Taking stock to yield a return'.

also be deemed crucial in other instances. In some cases, the periodic valuation of assets, including debts and credits, took precedence in the accountants' endeavours.[17] The monetization potential of assets and credits, along with the term of debts, became central concerns in other circumstances. Moreover, the chosen accounting technique may vary even within documents originating from the same source. In some instances, the double-entry system appears to be more or less adhered to, while in other cases, considering its objectives, the clerk applied more rudimentary yet equally relevant techniques.[18]

In the examination of the accounts of the farms of Bois d'Arcy and Trappes, both under the ownership of the Dailly family, a methodological imperative arises – to engage with the source, not simply as a passive reader, but rather to understand the process the accountants went through in making the account. In essence, this entails the meticulous reproduction of the clerk's work, while respecting the document's integrity. Only through a quintessentially historical approach, by delving into the materiality of the source, understanding the conditions of its formation, and subjecting it to thorough and critical scrutiny, can one unravel the objectives of the clerk who drew up the account, discern the owner's intentions for the farm, and unearth the source's potential contributions to historical understanding. This is the analytical framework I employ in scrutinizing three accounting documents pertaining to the farm owned by Adolphe Dailly (1816–87) in the Paris Region during the late 1850s.[19]

In the next section of this chapter (II) I provide a succinct presentation of the social and economic standing of Adolphe Dailly, the proprietor of the Trappes and Bois d'Arcy farms, along with an overview of the characteristics of the sources utilized in this investigation. Subsequently, in the third section, a detailed analysis is presented of the cash ledger for the farms of Trappes (1858–9) and Bois d'Arcy (1859–60). The fourth section employs the inventory ledger of the Bois-d'Arcy farm (1859–60) to show how these two farms were integral components of Dailly's larger

17 From this perspective, the probate inventory could be seen as an accounting document, see L. Herment, *Les fruits du partage: Petits paysans du Bassin Parisien au XIXe siècle* (2012), pp. 129–60, 225–329.

18 As was argued by Pierre Gervais for the early modern period, it is necessary to not consider accounting practices in the past as precursors of contemporary practices. See P. Gervais, 'Comptabilité et profit: Comment saisir les pratiques comptables de l'époque Moderne', *Comptabilités* 14 (2021), idem, 'Why profit and loss didn't matter: The historicized rationality of early modern merchant accounting', in P. Gervais, Y. Lemarchand, and D. Margairaz (eds), *Merchants and profit in the age of commerce, 1680–1830* (2014).

19 This chapter forms part of a larger work in progress. Here I only examine in detail three of the documents in the Dailly archive.

enterprises. Consequently, this necessitates a similar analytical treatment of the accounting documents for each farm.

II

Adolphe Dailly, the owner of the two farms, was a prominent figure in French agronomical and industrial circles. He succeeded his father, Gaspard Dailly, at the head of Omnibus de Paris and he was one of the founders of the Crédit Foncier (1853), a bank devoted to the financing of the purchase of real estate. At the same time, he also had roles in the administration, and was in charge of the publication of the agricultural survey of 1867 for three French departments.[20] From an agricultural standpoint, Adolphe Dailly transcended the conventional role of a farmer, concurrently managing a starch factory, which used potatoes as input, and a distillery using beet cultivated on the same farms.[21] He employed farm managers (*régisseurs*) to oversee the operation of his farms. Dailly was far from representative of the millions of small-scale French farmers but was part of the wealthiest agricultural elite. Consequently, our discussion and the analysis presented here are applicable only to an extremely narrow range of farmers.[22]

The extant records of these farms, now accessible at the *Archives du monde du travail* in Roubaix, northern France, are significant for three reasons, at least. First, these documents provide invaluable insights into the accounting methods used on large-scale farms. Second, they enable us to have a glimpse into the objectives underpinning such accounting practices. And third, these records serve as valuable primary sources for comprehending rural and agricultural history. Moreover, the interest of these books is increased by the fact that Dailly's father served as a member of the Jury for the competition organized by the *Société royale et centrale d'agriculture* to give prizes to the best accounting manuals intended for farmers. Dailly's father was no theorist and his direct involvement in financial and industrial business distinguishes him from

20 The départements of Haute-Marne, Côte-d'Or, and Saône-et-Loire (Champagne and Burgundy). Beside the farms of Trappes and Bois d'Arcy, Dailly owned a third farm in this region, the farm of Etuf (in the département of Yonne).

21 The farm of Trappes was by far the largest. The crops covered more than 210 hectares at the beginning of the 1850s and more than 250 hectares at the end of the 1860s. The acreage of the farm of Bois-d'Arcy was nearly 100 hectares.

22 It is highly likely that the farms of the Dailly family, like their other companies , were subject to commercial law. However, at this stage of my research we cannot say for certain. It would explain why the accounting records of the farms are so thorough.

Mathieu de Dombasle, another early proponent of such practices in French agriculture.[23]

(a) Sources

It is not my intention on this occasion to present a comprehensive survey of Dailly's farms and enterprises. The Dailly archives encompass more than seven metres of archival materials, comprising over seventy items, each further divided into a number of individual files. For the purposes of this chapter, I focus on examining three specific files all for the year 1859–60: the cash ledger of the Trappes farm, which was paramount in the family's agricultural ventures;[24] the cash ledger of the Bois d'Arcy farm and, finally, the inventory ledger of the Bois d'Arcy farm for the same year. There is also a monthly inventory of the Bois d'Arcy farm which will not be drawn on here.[25] This is only a small sample drawn from a substantial archive on which it would be possible to work for years. Preliminary work shows that the accounting practices described here persisted over an extended period, spanning at least from the early 1850s to the early 1890s.[26]

The cash ledgers illuminate a substantial portion of the daily operations of the two farms. Each farm was a distinct entity, with the distillery, the starch factory, and the Poste aux chevaux (Dailly's transport company) forming additional entities within the overarching Dailly empire. The accounting practices were consistent across both farms. These apparently dull records provide insights into the underlying logic of the Dailly enterprises and hold significant potential for historians specializing in the rural domain.

Each month, the manager of each farm, often assisted by a clerk, typically the local schoolmaster, began a new ledger to document the farm's expenditures and sales. Unlike a conventional 'double-entry' book, this document itemized cash expenditures for each account, such as lucerne, potatoes, the sheep flock, and the cowshed, among others. If two columns appeared on the right-hand side of the page, their purpose was solely to aggregate the amounts when the manager needed to total expenses for a particular account. Unlike traditional double-entry

23 About Mathieu de Dombasle see F. Knittel, 'L'Europe agronomique de C-J-A Mathieu de Dombasle', *Revue d'histoire moderne et contemporaine* 57 (2010), pp. 119–38; N. Joly, R. Bourrigaud, and F. Knittel, 'Administrer une ferme-modèle au XIXe siècle: Deux expériences d'agronomes entrepreneurs ruraux, Mathieu de Dombasle et Rieffel', *Entreprises et histoire* 88 (2017), 21–36.

24 *Archives nationale du monde du travail*, fonds Dailly, 19 AQ 46.

25 The last three records can be found in fonds Dailly, 19 AQ 41.

26 I have also begun to explore the records for the 1860s and the beginning of 1890s.

accounting, there were no separate columns for 'credit' and 'debit'. In accordance with this structure, the managers entered all the sales for the month at the end of the document. This form of accounting resembled a cash ledger or a record of charges and discharges. However, it did not provide a means to assess the farm's overall profitability or the profitability of specific activities, as will be demonstrated. For the year 1858–9 at Trappes, I counted 1,183 items of expenditure and 153 sales transactions, while for Bois d'Arcy in the year 1859–60, there were 891 and 56 respectively.

To convert what initially appears as a cash ledger, used by the farm owner to oversee his managers, into a double-entry accounting system, it is essential to reference the names of each account. This transformation into a typical double-entry accounting structure is straightforward.[27] At the beginning of the month, the account indicated whether the farm is a creditor or debtor; after recording all expenses and sales during the month, the farm manager calculated the financial position at month-end. Subsequently, the sums of expenses and sales are reconciled against the manager's financial position each month.

As we shall see, the cash ledger served not as a mechanism for calculating the profitability of various activities, but rather as a tool to ascertain precise cash expenditures for each category of crops or accounts. It also served a secondary purpose: the farm manager documented interactions with individuals and businesses with whom the farm maintained periodic relationships, such as hired labourers and suppliers. Monthly salaries of shepherds, carters and day labourers, along with the corresponding number of work-days allocated to each task, were also recorded. In certain instances, payment for workers occurred not on a daily basis but for specific tasks (what in nineteenth-century French corresponded to the work of a *manouvrier* or an unskilled worker). The range of suppliers encompassed wheelwrights, smiths, masons, millers, seed suppliers, grocers, and others. While the ledger facilitated an understanding of relationships with these individuals, it did not function as a ledger of debts and receivables: for instance, debts were only recorded upon settlement.

The second document, the general ledger (*Inventaire*), delineates various types of operations. Two of them require special attention. The first documented the flow of products between accounts, recording transactions such as what the *engrais* (fertilizers) account received from the *vacherie* (the cowshed) account,1 or what the *écurie* (the stable) account contributed to the *engrais* account. In the following, this document will be utilized to assess the flows received and disbursed by the starch factory, distilleries, and, most notably, the 'potatoes' and 'sugar beet' accounts.

27 Indeed, what is missing is the general ledger from which the information was drawn. But it is not a problem because the information available allows us to reconstitute it more or less precisely.

The second category of operations was associated with the general management of the farm, involving accounts such as *frais généraux* (general expenses) and *dépenses* (expenditures).

This document – a part of the farm's general ledger that I have been so far unable to locate – traces material flows and converts them into monetary units. Operating under a double-entry logic, this document manifests a semblance of cost accounting principles. To complete my investigation into the Bois d'Arcy farm, I have also examined the monthly inventory for the year 1859–60. While this complements and enhances comprehension of information derived from both the cash ledger and the general ledger for inventory, it will not be utilized in this study due to a lack of pertinent information.

If the initial document (the cash ledger) served Dailly in overseeing his manager's activities and the second (the general ledger of inventory) facilitated an assessment of material flows between accounts, the third document enabled meticulous tracking of material flows, both internal and external to the farm, on a monthly basis.

Eve Chiapello's scholarly insights into the emergence of capitalism as a concept offer a conceptual framework for interpreting Dailly's pioneering exploration of applying double-entry accounting within agriculture. This interpretation goes beyond viewing accounting merely as a functional aspect tied to the entrepreneur's actions, instead emphasizing its role as a form of representation.[28] Moreover, these documents not only monitored monetary flows but also meticulously traced material flows, as the observations made by Thomas Depecker and François Vatin remind us.[29] Nevertheless, in contrast to some of their contemporaries, Dailly and his managers did not seek an alternative overarching standard of measure beyond cash. The inseparable connection between the two realms – action and representation, as well as monetary and material flows – underscores the sophisticated nature of Dailly's accounting practices.

(b) The cash balance of the farms

The cash ledger functioned as a vital instrument for the farm owner to evaluate his manager's activities and overall farm management. However, understanding Dailly's managerial decisions necessitates a broader framework that considers the interrelationships among various entities under his ownership: the Starch Factory, the Distillery, *Poste aux chevaux*, in addition to the farms.

The accounting year, commencing in July and ending in June the following year, not only captured the daily routine and agronomic

28 E. Chiapello, 'Accounting and the birth of the notion of capitalism', *Critical Perspectives on Accounting* 18 (2007), pp. 263–96.

29 Depecker and Vatin, 'Taking stock to yield a return'.

imperatives of the farm but also accounted for additional activities related to the three areas of operation, as we shall explore in detail. The cash ledger at Trappes comprised forty-seven accounts, while that at Bois d'Arcy had forty. One point ought to be made. There was no general account for each type of crop but rather two distinct accounts: one for the preceding year and another for the current year. For instance, at Trappes, accounts exist for 'winter wheat 1858' and 'winter wheat 1859', with the former incorporating all expenses and receipts associated with wheat sowed in the autumn of 1857 and harvested in the summer of 1858. Conversely, animal husbandry features a single account for the entire year, encompassing all expenses and receipts associated with the cattle herd between July 1858 and June 1859, noted in the account 'Vacherie 59' (cowshed 59, '59' being the year of the account).[30]

In addition to the accounts that recorded farming operations, three other categories of accounts were identified. The first encompassed activities closely linked to the farm of Trappes, including the *fabrique de fécule* (starch factory), *distillerie* (distillery), *batterie* (the machinery used for processing sugar beet and potatoes), and the *poste aux chevaux*. The second category involved accounts dedicated to specific tasks, such as the *engrais* (fertilizers) account. The third category encompassed general expenses and those related to the managers' and permanent staff's livelihood (*dépenses, frais généraux, bâtiments, appartements, impôts,* etc.). Tables 6.1 and 6.2 illustrate the expense and receipt structures for the farm of Trappes during the year 1858–9, while Table 6.3 depicts the main accounts' expense and receipt structures for the year 1859–60 at the farm of Bois-d'Arcy.

For Trappes, expenditures exceeded the turnover by 2,500 francs, suggesting that the farm might not have been profitable. Beyond this initial observation, it is noteworthy to emphasize the significance of the 'flock' (*troupeau*) account and the 'cowshed' (*vacherie*) account in the turnover, representing 40 per cent and 10 per cent of the turnover respectively.[31] The sale of wheat, while substantial, accounted for only 20 per cent of the turnover, whereas oats, lucerne, rapeseed, potatoes, and beetroots were either absent from the account or virtually so.

The situation at the farm of Bois d'Arcy was similarly challenging, with sales amounting to 45,520.60 francs and expenses totalling 46,729.37 francs. As illustrated in Table 6.3, only the flock and winter wheat proved to be profitable.

30 The term 'vacherie' in contemporary French means 'nasty remark'. I translate the term used in the accounts, which include all the expenses devoted to the herd of cows by cowshed.

31 The flock account was called 'troupeau' at Trappes and either 'troupeau' or 'bergerie' at Bois d'Arcy.

Table 6.1. Total expenses, Farm of Trappes. Cash ledger, year 1858–9 (francs).

Account	Expenses	%
Flock	22,745.9	16.4
Starch factory and distillery	22,070.77	15.9
Poste aux chevaux	14,716.68	10.6
Stable	10,811.8	7.8
Overheads	9,492.12	6.8
Cowshed	7,835.5	5.7
Lucerne	6,457.74	4.7
Winter wheat	6,390.08	4.6
Other	38,067.07	27.5
Total	138,459.83[?]	100.00

Table 6.2. Total turnover, Farm of Trappes. Cash ledger, year 1858–9 (francs).

Account	Turnover	%
Flock	53,749.00	39.5
Poste aux chevaux	33,180.00	24.4
Winter wheat	27,144.80	20.0
Cowshed	13,647.35	10.0
Starch factory and Distillery	5,482.92	4.0
Others	2,806.55	2.1
Total	136,010.62	100.00

Table 6.3. Main expenses and receipts for the Farm of Bois d'Arcy 1859–60 (francs).

	Expenses	Receipts
Flock	16,226.95	22,810
Poste aux chevaux		10,500
Winter wheat 59	2,758.96	10,170.5
Stable	5,358.26	
Lucerne 59	3,888.28	
General costs	2,515.98	
Taxes	2,351.81	
Oats 59	1,781.01	

Within the confines of this chapter, it is impossible to examine all the issues these documents bring to the fore. I shall therefore focus exclusively on the potatoes and sugar beet to gain deeper insights into Dailly's accounting practices. The most striking discovery here is how surprisingly meagre the returns from the starch factory and distillery were. At Trappes, their combined contribution to the total turnover stood at a mere 4 per cent, while their expenses constituted 16 per cent of the total expenditures. If we add the 'batterie' account, these industrial concerns accounted for nearly 17 per cent of the expenses recorded in the cash ledger for the farm of Trappes. The perplexing question arises: why did one of the most renowned French farmers persist in producing starch and alcohol that exhibited such paltry profitability?

Furthermore, the accounts for potatoes and sugar beet showed no or virtually no receipts, both at Trappes and Bois-d'Arcy. Where do potatoes and beetroots feature in the farm's financial records? Addressing this question provides valuable insights into the overarching purpose of such accounting practices, revealing that the farms were integral components of a broader network of enterprises with interconnected ties. This exploration underscores the assertion that the cash ledger does not serve as a reliable tool for estimating the farm's profitability.

To justify this conclusion, I will analyze the potato and sugar beet accounts, along with the 'starch factory' and 'sugar refinery' accounts, but the flock or *poste aux chevaux* accounts could have provided equally relevant examples.

III

The Trappes and Bois d'Arcy farms served as integral components within the broader framework of Dailly's enterprise. Functioning as pivotal contributors to the distillery, starch factory, and the *poste aux chevaux*, they supplied potatoes to the starch factory and sugar beet to the distillery. Despite the critical role played by these supplies, they were not recorded in the cash ledger of either farm. Similarly, the cash ledger of the Trappes farm omitted the sales of the starch and alcohol produced by the factories, even though this farm bore a significant portion, if not the majority, of the expenses incurred by them, including salaries and equipment maintenance. Furthermore, both farms contributed fuel and straw to the *poste aux chevaux*. The precise transfer prices in this remain elusive. Here we will only explore the connections between the Bois d'Arcy farm and the factories.

To appreciate all these points, it is necessary to scrutinize the inventory ledger. This document, detailing the material flows between accounts in the farm of Bois-d'Arcy and elucidating the ties between the farm and the factories during the year 1859–60, serves as a crucial complement to the cash ledger. Through this exploration, a more nuanced understanding of the internal operations of the farm and its role in the broader scope of Dailly's enterprises can be attained.

Through the inventory ledger, one gains insight into the material flows between accounts throughout the accounting year at Bois-d'Arcy. This provides the means to quantify the kilograms of sugar beet and hectolitres of potatoes delivered by the farm to the factories. Equally significant is the opportunity to discern the transfer prices governing the exchange between the farm and the factories, thereby allowing us to estimate the profitability of potatoes and sugar beet. It is crucial to emphasize that my intention is not to assert a precise measurement of profitability but rather to elucidate the technical accounting choices involved.

An examination of the cash ledger reveals that the expenses of the farm of Bois-d'Arcy for 'potatoes 59' (i.e., potatoes harvested in autumn 1859) totalled 462.12 francs, while the expenses for 'potatoes 60' (i.e., potatoes planted for harvest in autumn 1860) amounted to 101.68 francs. Notably, these sums do not encompass the valuation of the potatoes planted in autumn 1859. Similarly, the expenses for 'beet 59' totalled 588.53 francs, and those for 'beet 60' amounted to 483.10 francs. However, it is noteworthy that no income from sales of either beetroots or potatoes was recorded.

While the cash ledger remains silent on the connections between the Bois d'Arcy farm and the factories, the importance of these ties becomes evident through insights derived from the inventory ledger. It reveals that Bois d'Arcy played a pivotal role, supplying the starch factory with potatoes and the distillery with beetroots. During 1859–60, approximately 1,147 hectolitres of potatoes were dispatched to the starch factory at a valuation of 2.50 francs per hectolitre.[32] The same year, the farm delivered 315,000 kilograms of beet to the distillery, valued at 22 francs per ton. The cumulative value transferred between Bois d'Arcy and Trappes amounted to 2,867.50 francs for potatoes and 6,300 francs for the beet, totalling 9,167.50 francs.[33] Despite the considerable economic transactions, these activities find no mention in the cash ledger. And there is an absence of references to potatoes and beetroots in the monthly inventory as well.

To evaluate the balance between cost and sales of these two crops it is possible to make the following calculation. Table 6.4 illustrates the remarkable profitability of potatoes and beet, recognizing the imprecision inherent in these calculations due to the inclusion of some expenses and

32 It is also necessary to take into account 108 hectolitres of potatoes that the farm of Trappes sent to the farm of Bois d'Arcy to be planted and which were valued at 3 francs/ha.

33 Not including the 108 hectolitres supplied by the farm of Trappes (324 francs) and the price of the unloading of potatoes (24.60 francs).

negative transfers pertaining to the current year, despite the fact that the potatoes and beetroots sent to the factories were planted in 1859. Nevertheless, I consider the final figures to be reliable enough.

TABLE 6.4. Balance between the estimated costs and sales of potatoes and sugar beet for the year 1859–60 at the Farm of Bois-d'Arcy (francs).

	Potatoes	Beetroots
Transfers (credit) for [18]59 and [18]60 (from the inventory ledger)	2,902.10	6,973.30
Sales	–	–
Expenses [18]60	–84.68	–431.10
Expenses [18]59	–426.12	–640.53
Transfers (debit) for 59 and 60 (from the inventory ledger)	–1,138.45	–852.84
	1,252.85	5,048.83

Ultimately, a comprehensive understanding of the farm's financial landscape emerges when we consider the transfers between accounts. This nuanced perspective not only leads to reassessing the profitability of certain productions but fundamentally alters the portrayal of the farm. The driver of this change lies not in the fluctuating profitability of specific outputs but in the revelation that key products – potatoes and sugar beet – were omitted from both the cash ledger and monthly inventories. They need to be reintegrated into the accounts in order to gain a realistic assessment of profitability. In essence, the farms manifest themselves as integral components of the larger Dailly enterprise, and their profitability emerges as inseparable from the conglomerate activities of Dailly. These observations extend beyond specific accounts, such as 'flock', 'oats', and 'straw'.

Interpreting the farm's accounting documents necessitates viewing them as facets of a broader enterprise. The farm's cash ledger, traditionally seen as a tool for Dailly to supervise farm operations and stewardship, appears to transcend this role. It not only evaluates crop profitability but also gauges the farm's capacity to contribute to the operations of the factories and the *poste aux chevaux*. In a sense, the two farms function as cash and agricultural output generators in the service of the factories. And so, a more in-depth exploration of the extensive Dailly enterprise is needed to achieve a complete understanding.

For the managers of the two farms, the cash ledger served a different purpose. It functioned as a tool to ascertain their precise financial standing, whether as debtors or creditors in relation to the owner. As the managers reconciled predominantly negative receipts and expenses, the owner incurred an interest payment on capital, sourced either to finance the working capital of farms or to support various enterprises within Dailly's ownership. This preliminary investigation, however, leaves this aspect of Dailly's enterprise open to further research.[34]

IV

The accounting practices evident in the cash ledger of Dailly's farms deviated from the conventional double-entry system. While the records potentially allow for the implementation of double-entry accounting, Dailly deliberately opted for a system that did not adhere to the canonical double-entry accounts framework. To understand why requires us to assess the intentions of the enterprise's owner, his managers, and, to some extent, understand the role the accounts were intended to play.

Through the cash ledger, Dailly could supervise the managers' activities on the farms. This document enabled him to evaluate all the work conducted within the farm during a given year. Additionally, in the case of the Trappes farm, it allowed him to ascertain the costs associated with the operations of the distillery and the starch factory. The inventory ledger, functioning as a double-entry cost accounting system, enabled both the manager and Dailly to monitor the value and cost transfers within the farm and between different entities of the enterprise, particularly the factories.

In summary, the forms of accounting described in my analysis deviate from the numerous prescriptions found in the agricultural accounting textbooks. And whilst this analysis could be extended further, one overarching conclusion emerges. Dailly's primary focus in establishing accounts was not to gauge the profitability of various farm productions or the individual profitability of each farm. Rather, it appears that his foremost concern centred around overseeing and managing cash flows and material flows between the various components of his business.

34 The cash ledger of the farm mentions the payment of interest to 'Baron père' and other people.

7

Women that Count: The Missing Link in the Modernization of Agriculture in Nineteenth-Century France[1]

Nathalie Joly

Women have an undeniable role in the prosperity of the farm, albeit one that is difficult to define. It is certainly for this reason that the agents of agricultural progress never entirely ignored women, with at least some writers in all periods taking up the pen to educate 'the gentler sex' in their role on the farm. For if women participated actively in the production and reproduction of farm capital, why should they not be instructed, like their husbands, in methods to increase the profitability of their own activities and those of the family as a whole? Why not train women to handle numbers and take an active part in the management of the farm?

This chapter sheds light on the social construction of women's role in the running of the farm over the 'long nineteenth century'.[2] It is intended as a contribution to the history of agricultural accounting from a gender perspective. The instructional literature I will use is considered to be a powerful producer of norms. It allows us to see how women's conduct has been framed in terms of their economic role on the farm, beyond their role in the household, or 'the province belonging to them' to use the hackneyed phrase of domestic manuals. Accounting activities such as record-keeping, listing, tabulating, drawing up a balance sheet, and so on situate women within the division of labour. The aim here is to consider

1 My gratitude goes to Thierry Bonnaud for his unwavering interest and support. I am also indebted to Laura Sayre for her much appreciated translation work. This chapter appears OA with funding from the Institut Agro Dijon (CESAER), under the licence CC BY-NC-ND.

2 Following E. Hobsbawm, I take this to be 1789–1914, E. Hobsbawm, *L'ère du capital (1848–1875)* (1994).

what degree of *agency* is attributed to them within discourses pertaining to the appropriateness and value of instruments of measurement.

Hopwood has stressed the importance of placing accounting practices within the cultural and interpretative contexts in which they were embodied and given their effectiveness.[3] Calculation, typically austere in nature, necessarily requires an element of rhetorical motivation, but it is above all important to look at the institutional aspects of this rhetorical process. This perspective, which constitutes the theoretical foundation of 'The new accounting history',[4] proposes to identify the institutional and legitimatized practices and forms of discourse that share a common vocabulary and set of objectives, as outlined in Foucault's archaeological approach.[5] For instance, Miller and O'Leary have located the construction of standard costing and budgeting strategies in the wake of a wide range of calculation programmes and techniques which emerged in the first three decades of the twentieth century and which came together to regulate the lives of individuals at work.[6] The authors have highlighted how accounting 'assisted in rendering visible certain crucial aspects of the functioning of the enterprise' by routinely raising questions of waste and inefficiency in the employment of human, financial, and material resources. In close connection with a series of diverse strategies such as the development of scientific management, the creation of intelligence tests, and the rise of industrial psychology – to recap the authors' demonstration – cost accounting and budgeting contributed to a regulation of 'the individual person[,] to make her accountable by reference to [a] prescribed standard of performance'.[7]

The first half of the nineteenth century saw the emergence of a popular economic discourse aimed at the inhabitants of the countryside, at the very moment when France was looking to small and medium-sized farms to modernize their agricultural practices. The guiding hypothesis of this chapter is that the rational education of rural women and girls is part of a familialist strategy driven by scholarly elites and the state. Actors must acquire new knowledge to adapt to new economic circumstances, including mounting calls for increased productivity and the mobilization of more capital in agriculture. They also need to subscribe to a 'set of beliefs associated with the capitalist order that help to justify this order and to support, by legitimizing them, the modes of action and the devices

3 A. G. Hopwood, 'Accounting and Everyday Life: An Introduction', *Accounting, Organizations and Society* 19 (1994), pp. 299–301.

4 P. Miller, T. Hopper, and R. Laughlin, 'The New Accounting History: An Introduction', *Accounting, Organizations and Society* 16 (1991), pp. 395–403.

5 M. Foucault, *The Archaeology of Knowledge and the Discourse on Language* (1972).

6 P. Miller and T. O'Leary, 'Accounting and the Construction of the Governable Person', *Accounting, Organizations and Society* 12 (1987), pp. 235–65.

7 Ibid., p. 241.

that are consistent with it'.[8] To paraphrase Weber, it is necessary for them to acquire values and psychological responses in 'elective affinity' with the capitalist economy emerging at this period.[9] It is this educational work, and the institutional dimension of its rhetorical process, that I will specifically consider here. My objective is to examine what kind of knowledge the historian may gain from employing a gender perspective, and conversely what is lost when the role of women is ignored within the process of change.

In the remainder of this chapter, I will offer a view of the ideal vision of the woman farmer's role and skills in the economy of the farm, including accounting and the many other tasks women were encouraged to perform, both independently and together with their husbands.[10] I will draw on both academic and popular literature targeting a female audience and give a brief historical contextualization of this literature. The first section describes the beginnings of economic education in the second half of the eighteenth century. The second focuses on the 1820s through to the 1850s, when popular literature for women began to gain ground and the ambition to teach women to keep the farm accounts, or even to specialize in this task, was more clearly articulated. The third section describes the institutionalization of a new discourse on women's role in agriculture and the codification of female accounting practices, as evidenced by a major work by Cora Élisabeth Millet-Robinet, author of a highly popular farming handbook which played a key role in reshaping rural and domestic economic models. The fourth section is a discussion of the rhetorical strategies used to address farm work and accounting practices. In conclusion, I will assess how the gender perspective helps us understand the processes and implications of the social framing of economic behaviours as an element of agricultural modernization.

I

> If the outside, the forceful work, in a word, the whole of a Farm and Market essentially concern the Farmer, one will agree that the interior detail is particularly the responsibility of the Woman Farmer; it is she who is the principal agent, and is always present, the necessary supervisor of the Backyard and of the Domestic realm; it is to her, finally, it

8 L. Boltanski and E. Chiapello, *Le nouvel esprit du capitalisme* (1999), p. 46.

9 M. Weber, *L'éthique protestante et l'esprit du capitalisme* (Paris 1964).

10 I use the terms 'woman farmer' and 'farm woman' (women farmers, farm women) in this chapter to express the French word 'fermière'. In either language, the point is to recognize the woman's role as an economic agent on the farm, not simply her status as the 'farmer's wife'.

is to her care, to her vigilance, to her capacity that the prosperity of the Farmer is most often due.[11]

Imbued with the educational spirit of the Enlightenment and the precepts of the French economists known as Physiocrats, Louis Rose's *La bonne fermière ou éléments économiques utiles aux jeunes personnes destinées à cet état*, published in Lille in 1767 and apparently the first French agricultural manual directed at a female audience, clearly asserts the significance of the woman's economic role on the farm. Deploring that nothing has yet been written about these 'ménagères par excellence',[12] these 'meritorious women',[13] while the 'celebrity women, the scholars, the devotees, the *précieuses*, the little mistresses, the gallants, etc. have received a thousand literary tributes',[14] Rose offers to rural girls an 'Economic Code'[15] to prepare them for their future roles as Farm Women. His introductory speech does not show any particular originality, since it merely repeats the clichés of the moment, the views held by the Physiocrats (a group of eighteenth-century French economists) on the essential role of agriculture for society, of science as an enlightening force and the need for large landowners to implement at their own expense 'what genius & sagacity can suggest of better'.[16] On the other hand, Rose defends the idea of women's economic role and their skills on the farm which is much more innovative. The opening chapters of the work ('The good Woman Farmer in her household, in her kitchen', and so on), again, lack originality, situating the work in the tradition of home economics books listing the wide range of knowledge and skills a well-informed woman should possess and which allow her to fully hold her rank at her husband's side. But when the author comes to describe women's agricultural activities, to which he devotes two-thirds of his book, his prescriptions come from practice – the practices of the women he has observed in his immediate circle and of whom he offers the small details, the reasonings, and sometimes the little 'secrets'. Observation, calculation, and prudence guide her management of the barnyard as well as the particular care she takes to fatten the oxen. Thus, 'the slightly educated farm-woman knows

11 Louis Rose, *La bonne fermière ou éléments économiques utiles aux jeunes personnes destinées à cet état* [The good farmer woman, or economic elements useful to young people destined for this state] (1767), pp. 11–12. Rose described himself as county magistrate of the city of Béthunes.

12 Rose, *La bonne fermière*, p. aij. The term refers to the tasks of farm management and administration, as consecrated by Olivier de Serres in his *Théâtre d'agriculture et Mésnage des champs*.

13 Ibid., p. iv.

14 Ibid., p. aij.

15 The capital letters here and in subsequent citations are in the original.

16 Rose, *La bonne fermière*, p. aiv.

that animals that are too old can fatten up easily'[17] and it is up to her to establish the animals' feed ration as carefully as possible, adjusting the different ingredients according to the needs of the animals at a given moment. If the animals sell better at Easter, the 'intelligent woman fattener' can even hold them until Whitsunday.

> If she calculates the cost of fertilizer, the farm woman expects to find her account. This will depend on the year, the quantity of grain and the cost of fat. For the great science of a woman farmer who understands her household well is to think long and hard about all her needs, in order to make the supplies in time.[18]

She can use her sagacity to 'apply herself only to the species of livestock where she will feel more profit'.[19]

In this first 'ode' to 'La bonne fermière',[20] Louis Rose claims that the Farmer's prosperity is fully dependent on his wife's contribution. Combining example with argument, he describes the case of a prosperous farmer, 'very intelligent and very diligent', who holds a farm of about three hundred acres on a rather difficult soil and whose wife, 'a true housewife and excellent farmer [...] earns more money with her farmyard and by her thriftiness, than he amasses with his crops and sheep'.[21] Although supplied in the form of an anecdote, this marks a change whereby formal recognition is given to the woman's pre-eminent role in the agricultural economy, thanks to her specialized skills and her specific management abilities. No elaborate recording techniques are provided, simply the recommendation to keep a register 'where everything is written' accompanied by the observation that it is 'the Farm Woman, often enough, who keeps it, because she is more usually at home'. In passing, he cautions the reader against any negligence: 'if she is late in annotating, she forgets her bonuses and loses them: she must be paid for them with accuracy .... To sell at home and in cash is the safest and best method on a farm.'[22] Anticipating the possibility of widowhood, the author recommends that information be shared between husbands and wives: 'the Farmer will sometimes take his wife on a walk to the field, the woman Farmer will ask him from time to time to pass by her Dairy'.[23] The result is a perfect union, in the mutual interest of the couple: 'everything

17 Ibid., p. 138.
18 Ibid., p. 142.
19 Ibid., p. 146.
20 Manuals referring to the 'Fermière' or the 'Ménagère' (in the agricultural sense) in their titles were regularly published throughout the nineteenth century.
21 Rose, *La bonne fermière*, p. 12.
22 Ibid., p. 40.
23 Ibid., p. 42.

will be weighed and considered, the husband will always be the master, the wife the mistress and reason their sovereign'.[24]

It was not until the first half of the nineteenth century that accounting techniques and the spirit of quantification invaded agriculture, becoming the alpha and omega of economic conduct.[25] But the 'Bonne Fermière' prefigures a model of family economic conduct that will be taken up and reinforced in later writings. It also raises a pioneering question of interest to the history of agricultural accounting: how much do women earn for the farm? As long as they do not keep their own accounts, this question cannot be answered, thus hindering our understanding of their exact role in the farm economy. A few decades later, as we will see in the next section, accounting education took on a new dimension, which in turn provides insight into the farm woman's economic contribution.

II

During the revolutionary period, books were considered to be 'an instrument of integration and conditioning to Christian and civic morality, as well as to economic activity'.[26] Beginning in the 1830s, the availability of books adapted to working farmers' reading skills and knowledge requirements became a key issue in conjunction with a political consensus that sought to balance the needs of large and small farms,[27] whilst putting the instruction of the rural masses on the agenda.[28] From this point on, all rural accounting or agronomic treatises devote at least some space to questions of small-farm economics and agricultural accounting. Likewise all of them present calculation as the best means of reforming and improving peasant routines. Double-entry book-keeping was deemed too complex for small farms. Instead, more simplified

24 Ibid., p. 24.

25 T. Depecker and N. Joly, 'Agronomists and Accounting: The Beginnings of Capitalist Rationalisation on the Farm (1800–1850)', *Historia Agraria* 65 (2015), pp. 75–94.

26 N. Richter, *Du conditionnement à la culture: L'offre de lecture des Lumières à la Troisième République* (2003), p. 20.

27 C. Gaboriaux, 'Entre innovations agronomiques et pratiques paysannes: La figure de "l'agriculteur pratique" au 19e siècle', in C. Bonneuil, G. Denis, and J-. L. Mayaud (eds), *Sciences, chercheurs et agriculture: Pour une histoire de la recherche agronomique* (2008), pp. 45–60.

28 Municipalities with over 500 inhabitants were obliged by the Guizot Law of 28 June 1833 to maintain a primary school at their own cost. A circular of 30 July 1836 required that 'the basic principles of agriculture [be] taught in rural primary schools'. T. Charmasson, A.-M. Lelorrain, and Y. Ripa, *L'enseignement agricole et vétérinaire de la Révolution à la Libération* (1992), p. 28.

book-keeping, or at the very least the use of an *agenda* or pocket-sized notebook, was recommended as a way of recording daily operations.[29]

At first glance, one could believe that the woman farmer was not touched by this didactic literature. A competition run by the Council of Agriculture between 1837 and 1840 for the design of 'small manuals, clear, simple and accurate, in which one can find, next to the description of excellent agricultural practices, moral precepts of order and economy'[30] targeted only the working class of '*cultivateurs*'. In an earlier study of the content of these textbooks I found that the award-winning authors wrote only for men.[31] The woman farmer seems to have been relatively invisible within the burgeoning popular farm management literature perhaps because of the large number of home economics manuals aimed at them.[32]

The purpose of this section is thus to counter the idea that women were left behind in the effort to control on-farm economic practices. While there is undoubtedly an institutionalized discourse that posits the enlightened farmer as the hero of rational management, parallel discourses strove to define the conduct of the 'Bonne Fermière'. This is the case with authors who wrote for a mixed public, framing their moral and practical instructions in terms of a collaboration between husband and wife. This is also the case with authors (generally female authors) dealing with domestic economy and providing specific managerial instructions for rural women. Indeed, one can see a similar desire for rationalization in

29 N. Joly, 'Shaping Records on the Farm: Agricultural Record-keeping in France from the Nineteenth Century to the Liberation', *Agricultural History Review* 59 (2011), pp. 61–80.

30 Charmasson, Lelorrain, and Ripa, *L'enseignement agricole*, p. xxviii.

31 N. Joly, 'Educating in Economic Calculus: The Invention of the Enlightened Peasant via Manuals of Agriculture, 1830–1870', *Accounting History Review* 26 (2016), pp. 131–60.

32 This editorial strategy complicates the identification of works that may have contributed to farm women's economic and accounting education. Thus, the corpus for the present study includes a set of generalist home economics books: in total, 97 home economics and agricultural textbooks addressed to farm women and published from 1804 to 1899. By way of comparison, a previous analysis I made of the content of agronomy manuals and agricultural catechisms targeting a male audience was based on 130 original titles published between 1830 and 1870. Joly, 'Educating in Economic Calculus'.

French,[33] English,[34] and American[35] domestic manuals from the 1820s onwards, including a consistent rhetoric aimed at shaping women's economic imagination and their ability to act as accountants, all while providing 'easy-to-handle techniques and tools to help the housekeeper in her management'.[36]

Writing for the peasant family could even seem exciting. In the introduction to his agricultural booklet, *Le petit producteur français*, the polytechnician Charles Dupin already foresaw the multiplier effects of a book useful to 'four million families' while at the same time committing 'their twelve million children [...] to push further the improvements begun by their fathers'.[37] Showing that he was aware of C. J. A. Mathieu de Dombasle's accounting formulae, model farm, and pioneering agricultural training institute,[38] Dupin suggested proceeding step by step in the teaching of double-entry accounting, beginning with the farmers, who then 'will give this knowledge to their children, their wives and their daughters'. In commercial and industrial establishments, Dupin notes, the wife or daughter of the house keeps the accounts; thus he hopes that once she is educated, the farm woman could do the same 'with the greatest success'.[39]

33 Scholarly analysis of textbooks published in France has focused primarily on the period 1880–1914, ignoring works from the first half of the nineteenth century – i.e., the non-school form of this teaching. It was only in 1882 that home economics courses were officially introduced into primary education and this new obligation was accompanied by the publication of dedicated school textbooks. Agricultural home economics education also dates from the end of the nineteenth century, see L. L. Clarke, *Schooling the Daughters of Marianne: Textbooks and the Socialization of Girls in Modern French Primary Schools* (1984); S. Roll, 'De la ménagère parfaite à la consommatrice engagée: Histoire culturelle de la ménagère nouvelle en France au tournant des XIXe–XXe siècles' (PhD dissertation, Université de Marc Bloch Strasbourg II, 2008); T. Depecker, 'La loi des tables: Quantification du besoin alimentaire et réforme des conduites de vie (XIXe–XXe siècles)' (PhD dissertation, EHESS Paris, 2014).

34 S. Walker, 'How to Secure Your Husband's Esteem: Accounting and Private Patriarchy in the British Middle Class Household during the Nineteenth Century', *Accounting, Organizations and Society* 23 (1998), pp. 485–514.

35 T. Le Texier, 'Homemade Economics: The Managerial Rationalization of Women's Everyday Life in America, 1820–1920' (2012). http://www.letexier.org/article.php3?id_article=107

36 Ibid.

37 This text is part of a series of cheap publications (75 cents a copy) devoted to the economic and technical education of the small manufacturer and the female worker as well as to farm women.

38 N. Joly, R. Bourrigaud, and F. Knittel, 'Administrer une ferme-modèle au XIXe siècle: Deux expériences d'agronomes entrepreneurs ruraux, Mathieu de Dombasle et Rieffel', *Entreprises et histoire* 88 (2017), pp. 21–36.

39 Dupin, *Le petit producteur français*, II, p. 20.

This familialist strategy is strongly reflected in the work of Jacques Bujault, a printer, bookseller, and lawyer who also became a farmer of his family property. This popular moralist used fiction to bring 'instruction to the most remote farm, and to the most obscure roof',[40] in the manner of the English women economists Jane Marcet and Harriet Martineau in the 1820s and 1830s.[41] With humour and originality, Bujault portrays a wise old man aged 106 speaking to an audience of villagers on a variety of subjects relating to agriculture, rural life, family, and religion.[42] Among the topics discussed in these village meetings is that of young rural girls' education. Bujault composes a fanciful story 'on the nice way to make little girls into housewives, and the older ones too, ha-ha!' in which we learn that the chatelaine of the village decided to teach her two young daughters how to do the housework. The edifying result is not long in coming.

> The girls paid, received, sold, bought the small household goods, and never spared themselves. They kept a register and wrote everything down. They raised three times as many chickens, sold four times as many eggs, not to mention 30 small pigs.[43]

The author concludes his story, as usual, with a proverb: 'in the long run, a small amount of money makes a big profit'. In the more academic part of his work, composed of memoirs, letters, and petitions that intertwine rural economics and politics, Bujault pleads for a gradual elevation of the peasantry's knowledge level, with a central role for women and children. This view is consistent with the observation that rural France at this point is still largely illiterate.[44] Children who have been to school thus

40 J. Bujault, *L'agriculture populaire ou méthode générale et nouvelle pour l'enseignement et l'amélioration de l'agriculture* (1831), p. 11.

41 P. Bouche, 'Vulgariser, convaincre: Les *"femmes économistes"* en Angleterre dans les années 1830', in F. Vaton and N. Edelman (eds), *Économie et literature: France et Grande-Bretagne 1815–1848* (2007), pp. 141–59.

42 These fictions complement the content of the *Maître Jacques,* a popular almanac in the West of France established in 1834 by Jacques Bujault, who claimed that 500,000 copies were printed each year. Bujault bequeathed significant funds to perpetuate its publication. The renowned agronomist Jules Rieffel made a compilation of Bujault's works, *Œuvres de Jacques Bujault* (1845).

43 Ibid., p. 116.

44 Literacy levels in France rose steadily between the eighteenth and nineteenth centuries, under the impetus of the State and the ruling classes. The Guizot law (1833) was the first step towards mass schooling for young French people, but it did not make schooling compulsory and did not apply to girls. Based on Inspector Maggiolo's retrospective survey in 1879–80, Furet and Ozouf point to significant regional variations in literacy rates, the legacy of long-standing social and economic inequalities: 'From the end of the 17th century to the second third of the 19th century, the Saint Malo–Geneva line

begin to take on the tasks of keeping up correspondence between family members or reading the newspaper. This figure of 'the child delegated to writing'[45] is extended in Bujault's work to include the 'child accountant for the family'. To fulfil this role, girls and boys must be introduced to the principles of political economy, learn them by heart at school and become the educators of the whole household: 'these little babblers will be able to shout their principles into everyone's ears, even the grandfathers'.[46] Recommending that husbands should hold their wives in high esteem ('Everything prospers under the hand of an active and careful wife'), Bujault likewise gives them instructions for mobilizing young hands: 'Have your children write down the proceeds of your harvests, your purchases, your sales, and your expenses'.[47]

In the introduction to a manual for the Young Farm Woman, the demand for education is put into the mouth of the interested parties: 'Why do we only take care of these *damned* men? as if they were the only ones in the countryside to make the land worthwhile! and what about us? We are nevertheless *something* on the farm.'[48] In a mirror to these aspirations in another classic textbook, Jeanne explains to her cousin in the city, Henriette, how to keep the farm accounts because 'Daddy wants us to know as exactly as possible what each thing costs and brings in'.[49] Fields, livestock, barnyard, orchard, garden, household items – the diligent girl describes the books to be kept and their organization, a writing job that takes her no more than a quarter of an hour each day. If it is an expense to properly fertilize a field, to apply the necessary improvements, to drain it, 'my book will tell me at the end of the year if the harvest compensates for all these expenses'.[50] The author of this manual, a teacher, describes in

separated two Frances in terms of literacy. A France of the North-Northeast, with relatively high rates of spouses knowing how to sign their marriage certificate, and a France that includes the western Armorican region, the Massif Central and the entire Aquitaine and Mediterranean Midi, with very high illiteracy rates.' F. Furet and J. Ozouf, *Lire et écrire: L'alphabétisation des Français de Calvin à Jules Ferry* (1977), p. 37. Despite these findings, it is important to emphasize the existence of a practical mastery of basic writing and arithmetic skills linked to the professional life and a non-school form of socialization, see N. Coquery, F. Menant, and F. Weber (eds), *Ecrire, compter, mesurer: Vers une histoire des rationalités pratiques* (2006).

45 J. Hébrard, 'La lettre représentée: Les pratiques épistolaires dans les récits de vie ouvriers et paysans', in R. Chartier (ed.), *La correspondance: Les usages de la lettre au XIXème siècle* (1991), pp. 279–365 at p. 290.

46 Bujault, *L'agriculture populaire*, p. 36.

47 Ibid., pp. 38–9.

48 *Manuel de la Jeune Fermière ou dialogue campagnard entre le curé-laboureur et la mère Matinotte sur l'économie domestique agricole* (1850), p. 2.

49 M. Piètrement, *Le bonheur au foyer domestique: Livre de lecture courante pour les jeunes filles* (1887), p. 218.

50 Ibid., p. 218.

various ways the economic awakening of the apprentice farm woman; for example, as she looks ahead to the results of her poultry breeding: 'when the broods are made, it does not take more time to look after a hundred fowl than fifty, and it is on the quantity that one has the profit'. Nor does she fail to observe at the markets her customers' preferences and 'the goods which sell well'.[51]

The horizon of a new agrarian economy – investing in inputs, intensifying production, marketing more aggressively – goes hand in hand with the orderly and prudent conduct of young girls and mothers who must get used to calculating and measuring profit. From one book to another, the propagandists' pens repeat and reinforce the idea that the peasant family's happiness and progress is in the hands of its women, shaping an ethos in affinity with the desired prospect of the social ascension of the middle peasantry. It thus emerges that the construction of economic and managerial norms was directed primarily at peasant families, even if the models were borrowed with reference to bourgeois figures.[52] Indeed, reflections on how upper-class rural women should be educated only emerged in the second half of the nineteenth century, and led to institutionalized education, as I will describe in the next section.

III

In the middle of the nineteenth century, Cora Élisabeth Millet-Robinet's audacious project was to create a *Maison rustique des dames,*[53] the feminine version of the compilation of agronomic knowledge published in the successive editions of the *Maison rustique*. Millet-Robinet was well-positioned to comment on the conditions of agricultural progress and in particular on the role of farm women. Managing, together with her husband, a property in the Vienne region of France, she gained recognition both as a scientist, having developed a new breed of silkworms, and as a writer. In 1856 she became the first woman elected as a national correspondent to the French Imperial and Central Society of Agriculture. Her purpose with the *Maison rustique des dames* was to draw the attention 'of the government and [others] to the serious subject of women's agricultural education'.[54] Placing agricultural instruction on the same level as the study of grammar, arithmetic, or history, she deplored the insignificant role society assigned to women, inviting them instead to take their place on the farm as full partners with their husbands. None of the knowledge

51 Ibid., p. 244.

52 F. El Amrani-Boisseau, *Filles de la terre: Apprentissages au féminin (Anjou 1920–1950)* (2012).

53 C.-E. Millet-Robinet, *La maison rustique des dames* (11th edn, 1880), I, p. vii. The work first appeared in 1840 but was regularly republished.

54 Ibid., p. vii.

offered to men should be denied to women: since the latter have to plan all the diverse activities of the farm, from planting to harvesting, they must be trained in all the necessary details. Volume 2, Chapter 5 of *La maison rustique des dames* assembles all the available scientific knowledge and technical details relating to farming activities specifically under women's control. The economic importance of poultry, to which no fewer than 143 pages are devoted, is clearly stated. The author has taken care to begin this chapter with the 'Statistics of the production and export of eggs', followed by about twenty pages on chicken breeds and ending with an analysis of the 'Comparative advantages of each breed'. Breed improvement is an important topic, and the chapter concludes with 'The duties of the poultry girl'. The key points of her management – counting the animals twice a day, culling hens which were poor layers – provide an opportunity for the author to chastise 'the reluctance of peasants to try new things: for the hen of a new race to be found good, in a country where she is imported, she would have to lay golden eggs'.[55]

The *Maison rustique des dames* is also notable for stressing the importance of records for farm management. The book-keeping is to be done in the morning or the evening, with the mistress of the house 'devoting herself irrevocably to this little work which, once organized, can be finished in a quarter of an hour or at most in half an hour a day'. As in all accounting manuals, there are firm instructions on the regularity of record-keeping, 'negligence leading to immense inconvenience'.[56] But the originality lies in the attention given to note-taking. Moreover, the titles of the six recommended accounting books (notebook, kitchen books, general receipts and expenses, workers' accounts, miscellaneous notes, and correspondence) testify to a broad understanding of what accounting is. It is recommended to 'always carry in one's pocket a notebook to record temporarily all receipts, all expenses', and 'even notes extraneous to accounting'. Examples of completed documents then guide the organization of the notes and their contents. Millet-Robinet argues that the female assistant–steward has a large degree of autonomy in her decision-making, in addition to decisions taken in concert with her husband, and so has need of a solid theoretical training to complement her practical experience. Transcribing and archiving daily events is part of this knowledge-building experience,[57] and for this Millet-Robinet draws on women's specific skills. Hence the advice given on what to write down and the possible uses of such writings:

> One writes in it [the *livre de notes*] the various notes that may be useful to remember, for example the day when a beast gives birth, the number

55 Ibid. (1856 edn), II, pp. 435, 458, and 484.

56 Ibid. (1873 edn), I, p. 24.

57 Joly, 'Shaping Records on the Farm'.

> and sex of the newborns, and so on. In this same book, certain work can also be recorded daily, the dates of which one wants to remember, for example, sowing dates, so as to know whether the sowing operations took place at the appropriate time and to benefit from the experience when other sowing operations will take place. In a way, one makes – in this book – a very concise account of the events of the day. It is very easy to refer to these notes which concern a multitude of things the memory cannot cope with.[58]

Speaking to the wealthy strata of the peasantry, Millet-Robinet extended the views of her predecessor, Marie Armande Jeanne Gacon-Dufour, who could likewise pride herself on delivering advice gathered from her own experience.[59] The *Maison rustique des dames* attests to the rise of a new agrarian economy, enjoining its enlightened readers to seek profit in their farming activities in a methodical way. It is no longer enough to tell the farm woman, as Gacon-Dufour did, that 'with little, she can do a lot, thanks to her attention to the smallest details, even those that may seem at first glance to be of slight importance'.[60] Rather, she must learn how to spend efficiently and calculate the gain of a new method, a new material, or an improved breed. The record-keeping tools are provided for this purpose. The model of accounting proposed in the *Maison rustique des dames* was so successful that virtually all manuals of domestic and rural economy from 1860 to 1914 were inspired by it or indeed simply reproduced it.

The agricultural 'modernity' of Millet-Robinet's writings has received little attention from historians.[61] Many still classify her as an author of domestic economy (in the restrictive sense), probably because the first volume is largely devoted to home care and cooking (including nearly 300 pages of recipes), while the second volume has two long chapters on domestic medicine and gardening. The agricultural knowledge introduced

58 Millet-Robinet, *La maison rustique des dames* (1873 edn), I, p. 28.

59 Gacon-Dufour mentions in her first *Bibliothèque Physico-Economique, instructive et amusante à l'usage des villes et des campagnes* (1802) that she was responsible for the breeding of a flock of 200 ewes. Following the success of her practical instructions for the mistress of a rural house, the author went on to publish her *Recueil pratique d'économie rurale et domestique* (1804).

60 M.-A.-J. Gacon-Dufour d'Humières, *Recueil pratique d'économie rurale et domestique* (1804), p. 29.

61 Millet-Robinet also composed a fictional dialogue in 1860, 'an agricultural and moral story, very moral' as she put it (p. 3), which she hoped would be read and reread like a fairy tale. Centred on the two opposing characters of Pierre Routine and Jean Progress, the tale follows the growth of their children, including one of the educated daughters taking up book-keeping in order to take her place with the more enlightened son. C. E. Millet-Robinet, *Guide pratique du fermier et de la fermière: La routine vaincue par le progrès. Histoire agricole et morale: Annexe à La maison rustique des dames* (1860).

in the second volume and the accounting model presented in the first, despite their consistency and novelty, are somewhat overwhelmed by this other material. It is true that Millet-Robinet's text is conservative in other respects (the relation of the woman to her husband and to her children, the relation between masters and servants) and that the traits of modernity pointed out here are relative. Pierre Michel, reading the *Maison rustique des dames* as a work of domestic edification, finds in it the elements of a morality which, as the pages go by, shapes an agricultural utopia 'torn from capital and its monsters'. He sees in the construction of the poultry house, in particular, the dream of an economy as 'the reserved domain of the woman, the true rustic boudoir', evacuating the very real stakes of what was a lucrative activity for women.[62] This model of the *mater-familias* is posited however as an advance: 'Until now, female power was nothing. Without wanting to be everything, it will be satisfied to be something.'[63]

Other writers in this period are inclined to glorify the woman's role on the farm, although at times this seems like a purely rhetorical exercise, since no particular knowledge is ascribed to her, with the good housewife being defined primarily in terms of her opposite, the bad mistress. Upper-class women who fail to uphold their responsibilities on great estates are subject to particularly harsh criticisms.[64] Noting that he neglected to mention the importance of women in his famous *Cours d'agriculture*, published between 1844 and 1848,[65] the Comte de Gasparin (Minister of the Interior and Acting Minister of Industry, Agriculture, and Commerce in 1839) made up for it by unabashedly pointing out the consequences of their misconduct:

> we have often seen run-down farms with an excellent tenant, but whose wife was mean, fussy, negligent; while a mediocre tenant prospered if, by her activity, good manners, and skill, the wife knew how to inspire

62 P. Michel, 'La maison rustique des dames, ou l'édification domestique', in S. Micaud (ed.), *L'édification: Morales et cultures au XIXe siècle* (1994), pp. 105–15 at p. 107.

63 Ibid., p. 106.

64 One finds this criticism as well in the case of family trade. As Pierre Labardin and Paulette Robic have shown, 'when the wife fulfils her obligations properly, silence surrounds her work. But, in the event of bankruptcy, the failures are noted.' P. Labardin and P. Robic, 'Épouses et petites entreprises: Permanence du XVIIIe au XXe siècle', *Revue française de gestion* 188–9 (2008), pp. 97–117 at p. 110.

65 A. de Gasparin, *Cours d'agriculture* (6 vols, 1844–8). The early volumes do not mention women's work but the fifth volume (in the 1851 edition), in a section devoted to 'Intelligent supervision', deals with 'the education of agricultural stewards, inferior agents of agriculture, and the role of women in the agricultural profession'. But 'Des femmes dans le profession agricole' fills only three and a bit pages. *Cours d'agriculture*, V, pp. 444–7.

> zeal for his interests. The servants, before accepting a position, inquire especially about the character of the housekeeper, and if she has a bad reputation, the farm finds only the scum of the earth who cannot be placed elsewhere. We would gladly offer a variation on the well-known proverb and say: 'As much as the woman is worth, so much is the land'.[66]

Given the importance of what they have to know, plan and control, rural women occupy a more prominent position in the household than women who live in the city. During the second half of the nineteenth century, the desire to shape and institutionalize their role as farm managers was well underway. Primary schools performed part of this function from 1836, and even more under the Third Republic. This investment in women's education is not without a political motive, for it is a way of attaching the economic elites to the land. The theme of blossoming housewives in the countryside does little to conceal the fact that the rural exodus was a social problem. To fight against the boredom experienced by young girls from good families, who are likely to 'divert their husbands from their rural business to go to the city', the solution is to 'find them occupations'.[67] Pierre Euryale Cazeaux hints at this in his plea for a women's rural institute:

> What teases, what annoys in a bourgeois household, in the midst of the tumult of the cities, fades away within a larger administration, in the calm of country life [...] The farmer's wife, if we consider her only under the wide-brimmed hat of the housewife, sees her personal action expand and grow. She has a real budget to regulate, estimates of consumption to draw up, a concordance to establish between payments and the timing of income. She is generally assigned, for her own use, certain parts of the farm that are productive of food and money, such as the farmyard, a few cows, the orchard and the vegetable garden. She will find there material for profit: and if she is intelligent and careful, she will know how to take advantage of it in such a way as to increase the well-being of the personnel, and even to form there some reserves of *ecus* for the family's wardrobe.[68]

In a bibliographical note on Saintoin-Leroy's accounting manual, Édouard Lecouteux, the editor-in-chief of the *Journal d'agriculture pratique*, explained that Saintoin-Leroy taught accounting courses in a boarding

66 This formula is based on two proverbs passed down from generation to generation by country writers: 'As much as the peasant is worth, so much is the land' and 'As much as the woman is worth, so much is the family and society'.

67 Gasparin, *Cours d'agriculture*, p. 447.

68 P.-E. Cazeaux, *Du rôle des femmes dans l'agriculture: Esquisse d'un institut rural féminin* (1869), pp. 63–4.

school for young girls whose parents were farmers in Beauce. Lecouteux's judgment of this initiative reveals his views on the importance of the couple and the role of women:

> The idea is good. There is already more than one good farm which owes its prosperity to the cooperation that the woman farmer knows how to give to the work of her husband, and something not less happy! Enriched farmers have the good spirit not to aspire to matrimonial alliances with city families. The city dwellers inoculate themselves against the rural spirit […].[69]

The famous rural economist continues, describing the importance of providing young rural women with accounting skills, less for their own management and agency than for keeping their rank close to their husbands:

> Our farmers, whether owners or tenants, will gain excellent clerks because these clerks will be directly interested in the results of the enterprise. The evenings on the farm will resemble the evenings of trade and industry: the fathers and mothers will speak in knowledge of their serious business, which always have charm when paternal foresight knows how to attach all the future of a young family to it. In such a case, the figures themselves have their poetry, and accounting takes a good place in the home. Thus it will happen with the work of Mr. Saintoin-Leroy: the author has worked for the family, the family will accept it.[70]

The polytechnician Dupin, writing in 1827, advocated the acquisition of accounting skills by women. Writing about commercial and industrial establishments with which he was familiar, he enjoined farmers to pass on their knowledge of double-entry book-keeping to their wives and daughters, a recommendation that few propagandists would urge later on. Being resolutely associated with an entrepreneurial and capitalist conduct of agriculture, the double-entry technique continued to be considered suitable only for men.

IV

Whether aimed at a popular readership or a higher-class audience, the instructional literature discussed in this chapter honoured women's economic conduct while striving to reinforce their managerial role in farming. The authors played a key role as transmitters as well as prescribers of experience, albeit in varying proportions according to what they felt women and girls should learn to improve and fully perform their

69 É. Lecouteux, 'Notice sur le manuel de comptabilité agricole de Saintoin-Leroy', *Journal d'agriculture pratique, 1861*, Tome 1, p. 623.

70 Ibid., p. 623.

role on the farm. Thus, the first point of discussion here will be the social agenda these writers have for family farm women. Then I will ask to what extent the 'good practices' given as models correspond to reality. In the next section I will consider the impact of these instructional writings, including the question of women's agency in the process of agricultural modernization.

(a) The 'assistant–steward' versus the 'secretary–accountant'

The advice offered in these writings varies considerably in its socio-economic significance. Some authors provided instructions accompanied by many practical illustrations, such as Rose in his *La bonne fermière*, or Millet-Robinet with the remarkable knowledge contained in her *Maison rustique des dames*. Rose claimed to portray farm women's activities and management in practical ways, using details provided by experienced women whose names he did not bother to mention.[71] Millet-Robinet drew on her own knowledge and personal experience of agriculture, pleading for women to be educated and given responsibility on an equal footing with men. Both intended not merely to teach accounting techniques, but to transmit the most efficient and economic ways of managing those areas of production which were in women's hands. This first group of authors presented the woman as 'the assistant–steward' on the farm, performing a specifically economic role in tandem with her husband. The way they described women's activities helps us understand their place within the division of agricultural work and knowledge. It acts to disperse 'the darkness by which the history of women in agriculture was shrouded' as Heide Inhetveen pointed out.[72] But women's own experience was only valued for a short period. When agriculture came to be regarded as a science and as a trade just like all others in the course of the nineteenth century, female experience-based knowledge was eclipsed by science-based knowledge crafted in the laboratory, a place women would not be allowed to enter for almost half a century.

Other authors offered writings with a strong normative and moral flavour. They moved directly to advice-giving and tended to reduce women, as spouses, to management tasks. Their aim was to explain what

71 Studying the role of farm women in science, Heide Inhetveen noted that the earliest agricultural literature appearing in vernacular languages in the sixteenth century across Europe contained detailed depictions of the tasks that housewives had to perform on large farm estates. But she deplored the fact that women were treated anonymously and not given credit for their knowledge by the male authors. H. Inhetveen, 'Women Pioneers in Farming: A Gendered History of Agricultural Progress', *Sociologia Ruralis* 38 (1998), pp. 265–84.

72 Ibid., p. 268.

should be counted and how. This second group of writers supported a model of the farm wife as 'secretary–accountant'. Simple techniques of recording and balancing the accounts were taught to women and even to young girls. Double-entry book-keeping, which agronomists in scholarly circles were discussing throughout this period, was rarely made available to a female readership. Indeed, helping to concretize the principles of political economy, the double-entry technique appeared both as a masculine technique and as an emblem of the farmer–entrepreneur. It was therefore up to the father to introduce his successor to the subtle details of this technique.[73] In any case, this pattern of male transmission of knowledge was already being practised by the keeping of the 'livre de raison' on large estates.[74]

Writings addressed to young girls were particularly edifying. Appealing to common sense and sometimes in a tone of admonition, they distilled simple advice meant to leave a lasting impression on the mind. A few eloquent little stories or proverbs, as the moralist Bujault excelled in offering, were supposedly sufficient to regulate parents' and children's conduct: 'In the long run, a small amount of money makes a big profit'; 'Have your children write down the proceeds of your harvests, your purchases, your sales and your expenses'. By contrast, writings directed to highly educated women used more elaborate arguments, putting the discourse of political economy at the service of philanthropic and moral instruction. This second range of writings, which became dominant in the second half of the nineteenth century, were prescriptive rather than descriptive in any simple sense. Writers portrayed the farm or the estate as a place for making money. They considered farming activities as entirely calculable and entrusted these calculative tasks to the care of women and girls, providing them with detailed instructions for setting up accounts. This literature should be studied more closely to achieve a fuller understanding of its empirical and moral advice.

(b) Did norms rule practice or vice versa?

The view of female agency this literature conveyed was not disconnected from reality. The observations we have of women's work on estates and family farms support the idea that the respective positions of men and women within agricultural knowledge and decision-making systems were

73 For a published dialogue between a landowner and his son on double-entry accounting which was awarded a prize by the Royal and Central Academy of Agriculture, see N. Joly, 'Louis Gossin. Comme le sang dans le corps des animaux: Le capital circulant expliqué à la jeunesse rurale (1838)', *Entreprises et histoire* 88 (2017), pp. 182–8.

74 S. Mouysset, *Papiers de famille: Introduction à l'étude des livres de raison (France, XVe–XXe siècle)* (2007).

complex. Only rarely do they provide us with information on women's role in accounting, except in some isolated cases. For instance, we know that Anna, Electress of Saxony (1532–1587), skilfully managed the Prince of Saxony's estates and contributed to two treatises on agronomy that originated at the court of Dresden. Ursula Schulde, who documented the financial management skills of this remarkable woman, pointed out that early modern books on the education of princesses spread the ideal of the 'house-keeper princess', who understood and supervised agriculture.[75]

It has been generally asserted in the literature that elite practices spread downward as education levels rose in rural countries. Scarlett Beauvalet considered that the ability of women to sign official documents was indicative of them securing a role in the exploitation and management of accounts. As she noted, in the last third of the sixteenth century, 'very few women were literate at the time of marriage. After 1720, there were none who could not at least sign their name, and one saw more and more women farmers multiplying their accounting entries, and the farmers delegating great responsibilities to them.'[76] Sometimes, accounting practices are mere presumptions, in the absence of sources. Studying the accounts of Robert Loder's estate in southern England for the years 1610–1620, Jane Whittle wondered whether his wife kept accounts on her own, for there is no mention of the fruits of the wife's activities in the accounts kept by the husband. Her work therefore appeared 'as an empty space, a silence in the records, and their activities must be reconstructed from circumstantial sources'.[77] Observations closer to the period examined in this chapter confirm women's familiarity with writing and counting. Schlumbohm's study of Dutch couples who, in the seventeenth and eighteenth centuries, emigrated to many parts of Germany to farm in the dairy sector reported that 'their wives had a certain level of education that enabled them to cope with accounting and written exchanges with

75 These were texts from Christian Oeconomy, books on marriage and texts known as the Mirror of Princess, see U. Schulde, 'Cultiver selon "les bonnes règles et avec profit": La création d'un savoir agricole à la cour de l'électeur et de l'électrice de Saxe à Dresden', in Nadine Vivier (ed.), *Élites et progrès agricole* (2009), pp. 59–81 at p. 71.

76 S. Beauvalet, 'Les femmes dans le monde rural à l'époque moderne, XVIe–XVIIIe siècles', in Nadine Vivier (ed.), *Ruralité française et britannique, XIIIe–XXe siècles: Approches comparées* (2002), pp. 89–116 at p. 96.

77 J. Whittle, 'Le travail des femmes dans les ménages ruraux anglais, 1450–1650: Trois approches alternatives', in Vivier (ed.), *Ruralité française et britannique*, pp. 77–87 at p. 83.

the authorities'.[78] He also stated that the wives of these farmers demonstrated their skills when they found themselves in charge of the farm as widows.

In nineteenth-century France, wives were commonly said to 'Faire et défaire les maisons' ('Make or break the household'), a way of bringing Xenophon's words up to date, when he described the mistress of a large estate as the 'mother-bee' or the 'garrison commander'. At the dawn of the agricultural revolution, women of middling farm households held an important status and many responsibilities in the cooperation that took place within the farm, as shown by Martine Segalen. The sociologist recorded proverbs that, from one region to another, deployed a 'varied metaphorical range to affirm the importance of economy in the female management of the household'[79] and of women's qualities at work: 'a thrifty woman makes a good house' (Champagne), 'a brave woman in a house is worth more than a farm and livestock' (Gascony). In line with Walker's analysis of English working-class households, Ségalen found that the farm woman had a stronger influence on the husband when the household lived essentially from self-subsistence. It was then she who decided how to spend the money her activities brought in – particularly from the sale of milk, butter, eggs, and poultry – the main resources for daily life: 'holder of the purse strings, dispenser of small sums from day to day, she could mistreat her servants and ridicule her husband in the eyes of the village community'.[80]

Two conclusions can be drawn from these all too rare observations. On the one hand, the model of the 'assistant–steward' took over actual women's practices and spread throughout the social body at different periods and in different countries. As with merchants' manuals in the modern era,[81] this type of writing selected knowledge both from predecessors' books and from the surrounding environment. On the other hand, the model of 'the secretary–accountant' was fostered as a means of social monitoring for women in the second half of the nineteenth century. Indeed, faced with the threat of rural exodus and its political issues, French conservatives and religious movements actively promoted the home and the image of the mother–wife to the detriment of the wife who worked in partnership with her husband. This ideological framing, endorsed by the

78 J. Schlumbohm, '"Zu Schreiben und die ganze Beschaffenheit der Sache": Signierfähigkeit und Schriftgebrauch bei Bauern und Heuerleuten des Kirshspiels Belm, ca. 1770–1840', in H. E. Bödeker and E. Hinrichs (eds), *Alphabetissierung und Literalisierung in Deutschland in der Frühern Neuzeit* (1999), pp. 163–80 at pp. 170, 172.

79 M. Ségalen, *Mari et femme dans la société paysanne* (1980), p. 131.

80 Ibid., p. 130.

81 P. Jeannin, 'La diffusion des manuels de marchands: Fonctions et stratégies éditoriales', *Revue d'histoire moderne et contemporaine* 45 (1998), pp. 515–57.

literature reviewed here, was expounded in elementary schools,[82] with a hands-on introduction to book-keeping. Then it progressed, during the first half of the twentieth century, into agricultural domestic training and women's circles of the Jeunesse Agricole Catholique.[83] The pivotal point of this mentoring was the invention of 'a separate feminine sphere' used for the glorification of domestic womanhood.

The great majority of the writers also reflected these dominant social representations. Both male and female authors put an emphasis on feminine virtues: the farm woman's active zeal for work, the special attention she gave to detail, her sense of moral duty. In doing so, they echoed the Catholic Church's conception of feminine nature as expressed throughout Europe in the early nineteenth century. Thus, woman was seen as

> a new social subject, free from all political passion, gifted with religious sentiments [...] with a soul different from and complementary to the male soul [...] and as a reserve of civilizing resources.[84]

Once it had been established that their bodies did not govern their minds, as previously thought, women's nature could be positively requalified and partly reoriented in the direction of management and business. So it was with the glorification of their so-called innate temperance. Women were thus considered as agents taking more rational decisions because they were better able than men to detach themselves from their emotions. In line with Max Weber's analysis of the 'spirit of capitalism', we may think that temperance became a valuable female trait as it held an elective affinity to the spirit of capitalism. Indeed, moderation counters the human drive to maximize profit and allows the renewal of opportunities for gain in a rational manner. In farming business, calling for temperance at a period when investments were highly valued but somewhat risky was a subtle strategy: thus women could be seen as apt partners to discuss with their husbands how to spend the farming surplus. As this suggests, narratives on female nature deserve more attention in the agricultural history of accounting. Although historians and feminist scholars have solidified the thesis of feminine nature as a stigma, gender narratives may also have shaped women's conduct in a positive sense by fostering their agency in some domains.

82 Clarke, *Schooling the Daughters of Marianne*.

83 For analysis of this ideological shaping see, for France, M. Perrot, 'La jaciste: Figure emblématique', in Rose-Marie Lagrave (ed.), *Celles de la terre. Agricultrice: L'invention politique d'un métier* (1987), pp. 34–60; for Belgium, E. Gubin, 'Un rempart contre le désordre: Les paysannes belges au tournant du XXe siècle', *Enquêtes rurales* 10 (2004), pp. 137–58.

84 M. de Giorgio, 'La bonne catholique', in G. Fraisse and M. Perrot (eds), *Histoire des femmes en Occident: Le XIXe siècle* (1991), IV, pp. 203–39 at p. 204.

V

Once we move beyond enthusiasm for the agricultural enlightenment model and recognize its overemphasis on the influence of books in the dissemination of knowledge of advanced agriculture,[85] we may wonder what effect the literature examined in this chapter actually had on women's conduct. Compared to books published on agriculture and new agronomic techniques, writings on economics and accountancy aimed at a female audience are more practical and have a stronger moral tone. They provide easy-to-manage techniques and behaviourist advice. Would their ostensible claim to be within the reach of all women, even from an early age, offer a gain in efficiency? Would the moral lessons embedded in the practical advice provide an effective means of communicating with their target audience?

The idea of 'order' provides the principle of coherence for this literature. Thus, it can be linked to other fields of social prescription: order in industrial work and within working-class families, for example in hygiene and childcare practices. Steered by the upper classes, the popular agricultural writings I have studied have a modus operandi that hardly differs from those of the manuals on hygiene for women of the working class.[86] Their objectives of social control may seem strangely similar. It is whispered in the ears of women on small and middling farms that their orderly conduct and good book-keeping can be a guarantee of their families' upward mobility, just as it is hammered into working-class women that they can escape poverty by managing the household economy in an orderly fashion. In the Foucauldian approach to the control of the domestic sphere, an approach that focuses on the proliferation of techniques for disciplining the body, health, food, and housing,[87] women are allies of the state and reformers, capable of containing obscurantism, combating immorality, and imposing authority on husbands and children. This raises the question of whether rural women, by receiving an accounting education for the farm, were 'externally acted' agents rather than 'self-acting' actors of modernization. In other words, would accounting education help make them 'governable agents', or conversely, give them more agency?

In several respects, I have highlighted the social control project to which women were subjected in the literature studied here. This tends to support the thesis of a domestication that confines women's role to the social project and the limits defined by the upper classes and the state.

85 As pointed out by James Fisher, with a fresh approach to rethinking books, knowledge, and labour, in *The Enclosure of Knowledge: Books, Power and Agrarian Capitalism in Britain, 1660–1800* (2022).

86 L. Bolstanski, *Prime éducation et morale de classe* (1969).

87 J. Donzelot, *La police des familles* (1977).

But I would like to conclude by pointing out some weaknesses of this interpretation. Indeed, accounting has also been theorized in terms of agency, from both a cognitive and a moral perspective. Drawing on Jack Goody's seminal work[88] and other theoretical reflections on accounting, writing, and power,[89] one can surmise that keeping accounts enhanced women's capacity for reflexivity and rationalization. It was for this very purpose that women farmers were advised in some writings to keep notebooks or diaries in addition to accounts. For Rebecca Elisabeth Connor, the recording of financial accounts in pocket books in eighteenth-century England expressed 'a growing cultural expectation that women document what they had, what they owed, and what they were owed'.[90] Beyond the cognitive reasoning tied to the act of making lists, tabulating, or balancing accounts, the daily practice of writing was supposed to have an effect on willpower. It was a form of self-discipline. As stressed by Harro Maas, 'moral accounting was not a property of the mind, but a tool-based practice with normative consequences for one's personal life'.[91] As claimed by promoters of daily planners and diaries, writing in everyday life, whether numbers or facts, was a way to improve the self along several dimensions – financial, social, and personal. It is thus important to bear in mind that the 'real value' of record-keeping extended well beyond statements of gain and loss, as some of the authors examined here clearly expressed in their emotive pleas for accounting. We don't have the women's words nor their practices for the long nineteenth century. But we can at least put forward the idea that the accounting education they received may have enabled some of them to better negotiate their autonomy and gain agency. This argues for a reversal of perspective. The use of figures, the advocacy for accounting and even the historical work (accounting history is a masculinized academic sub-field)[92] all bear the hallmarks of a gendered approach, in which men play the leading if not the unique role. We still need to make room for women's accounting role in documenting the process of agricultural modernization, in which they have so far remained the missing link.

88 J. Goody, *The Domestication of the Savage Mind* (1977).

89 K. Hoskin and R. Macve, 'Writing, Examining, Disciplining: The Genesis of Accounting's Modern Power', in A. Hopwood and P. Miller (eds), *Accounting as Social and Institutional Practice* (1994), pp. 67–97.

90 R. E. Connor, *Women, Accounting and Narrative: Keeping Books in Eighteenth-Century England* (2004), p. 2.

91 H. Maas, 'Letts Calculate: Moral Accounting in the Victorian Period', *History of Political Economy* 48 (1996), pp. 16–43 at p. 32.

92 S. Walker, 'Accounting Histories of Women: Beyond Recovery?', *Accounting, Auditing and Accountability Journal* 21 (2008), pp. 580–610.

8

Did Farmers Want to be 'Rational'? The *Landøkonomiske Driftsbureau* and the History of Danish Farm Accounting

Markus Lampe and Paul Sharp

In 1918, the *Landøkonomiske Driftsbureau* (Bureau of Agricultural Economics, henceforth *Driftsbureau*) was established as the outcome of a joint venture between the major Danish agricultural societies and the Government's Department for Statistics. The initiative came from two committees set up in 1910–11 by the Royal Agricultural Society of Denmark, one on the provision of good agricultural literature and another on accounting. Their aim was to prepare specialized handbooks and forms for accounting on small and medium-sized farms, a guide to good farm management, an account of the cooperative movement and a history of Danish agriculture.[1] In the same vein, the main motive behind the establishment of the Bureau was to improve farming practices by, inter alia, increasing the awareness among farmers of income, expenses and cost structures, thereby to improve economic reasoning, thrift and prudence. Participating farmers were to complete the prescribed forms and receive assistance from accounting consultants in converting them into accounts. These accounting consultants worked for so-called accounting associations founded through regional agricultural societies, who received government subsidies for their collaboration with the *Driftsbureau*. The *Driftsbureau* received a selection of the accounts and worked them into annual reports that informed the Department of Statistics, agricultural science, the agricultural press, extension services and the participating farmers.

1 H. Hertel, *Det Kgl. Danske Landhusholdningsselskabs Historie*, II, *Selskabets Historie i Tiden fra 1869–1918* (1920).

The initiative stands in a tradition of 'agricultural enlightenment' in Denmark that goes back to the agricultural reforms of the late eighteenth century and the sense-making of new opportunities for commercial agriculture in the first half of the nineteenth century. In this process, accounting, initially practised only by a very small elite, became a central element in the debate over how to use agricultural resources, mostly livestock, to take advantage of growing demand from Denmark and abroad, especially from industrializing Britain.[2] This project had its roots in a Danish variety of Albrecht Thaer's 'rational farming'. The elite group that proposed it advocated accounting as a way to convert farms into rational, efficient and market-oriented units of production.[3] Elsewhere we have described this group as an epistemic community that, during a period when the future of agriculture and systematic knowledge about it were subject to considerable uncertainty, aimed to use accounting as a way to legitimize their view of agriculture.[4] They argued that the action of accounting was a step towards rationalizing production, and their published accounts served to legitimize accounting as well as to publicize best practices, providing comparison and benchmarking that accounting made possible.

Danish agricultural accounting as a tool to establish rationality and efficiency is thus one version of the general trend followed by elites in most of the Western world in the nineteenth century to either establish efficiency as a social goal and/or use 'governing by numbers' to establish what was presented as 'rational' management of people and resources.[5] It is the success – or not – of this programme of accounting and

2 M. Lampe and P. Sharp, '"Rational" farmers and the emergence of modern accounting in Danish dairying', *EHES Working Papers in Economic History* 115 (2017).

3 M. Lampe and P. Sharp, 'A quest for useful knowledge: The early development of agricultural accounting in Denmark and Northern Germany', *Accounting History Review* 27 (2017), pp. 73–99.

4 Lampe and Sharp, '"Rational" farmers'; see also P. M. Haas, 'Introduction: Epistemic communities and international policy coordination', *International Organization* 46 (1992), pp. 1–35.

5 R. Nimmo, 'Auditing nature, enacting culture: Rationalisation as disciplinary purification in early twentieth-century British dairy farming', *Journal of Historical Sociology* 21 (2008), pp. 272–302; J. Auderset and P. Moser, *Die Agrarfrage in der Industriegesellschaft: Wissenskulturen, Machtverhältnisse und natürliche Ressourcen in der agrarisch-industriellen Wissensgesellschaft (1850–1950)* (2018), ch. 1; cf. S. Burchell, C. Clubb, A. J. Hopwood, J. Hughes and J. Nahapiet, 'The roles of accounting in organizations and society', *Accounting, Organizations and Society* 5 (1980), pp. 5–27; B. G. Carruthers and W. N. Espeland, 'Accounting for rationality: Double entry bookkeeping and the rhetoric of economic rationality', *American Journal of Sociology* 97 (1991), pp. 31–69; P. Miller and T. O'Leary, 'Governing the calculable person', in A. G. Hopwood and P. Miller (eds), *Accounting as Social and Institutional Practice*

benchmarking and the accompanying rhetoric of rationality, thrift and control over the different elements of the farm that we refer to when we ask whether farmers want to be 'rational' or not. Were they convinced of the benefits promised? And even if they might have been in principle, did they think the benefits were worth the intellectual toil of keeping and consolidating their books?

In the late nineteenth century, accounting did indeed spread to larger parts of Danish agriculture, the accounting-backed recommendations of the 1850s and 1860s proved economically successful, and thus accounting became a key element in Danish agricultural education and practice. Numbers were gathered and compared mainly through the rise of cooperative creameries, breeding associations and crop rotation competitions. Cooperative creameries, for example, required their managers to keep accurate accounts of milk deliveries per member and the revenues and expenses of the creamery for control by its board.[6]

Accounting in different forms thus had manifold and changing uses in agriculture. The focus was, however, on dairying and the most efficient use of existing assets like cows or land. It was less concerned with representing the totality of the farm in numbers, the ultimate aim of double-entry book-keeping.[7]

Although monetary values were involved in many of these calculations, the systemic view of double-entry book-keeping, the consolidation of the available information into profit and loss statements, balance sheets and return on capital invested for the entire farm was much less frequently used and referred to, although landowning elites and university professors vividly stressed their advantages. This reflects what had already become apparent: farm accounting, in contrast to that by for example banks, merchants or industrial firms (even the aforementioned cooperative dairies), is simply more costly and difficult to maintain. It requires abstract conceptualization of, for example, prices for items which have no, or poorly signalled, market prices, such as grass for grazing, milk fed to calves, or manure produced by animals. It requires an understanding of the systemic and circular nature of organic agriculture, whereby manure produced by cattle helps to grow crops which in part feed those self-same cattle. And it requires accurate measuring of a wide variety of inputs and outputs.

(1994), pp. 98–115; P. Miller, 'Governing by numbers: Why calculative practices matter', *Social Research* 68 (2001), pp. 379–96.

6 P. Sharp, S. Henriques, E. McLaughlin, X. Tsoukli and C. Vedel, 'A micro-level analysis of Danish dairy cooperatives: Opportunities for large data in business history', *Enterprise and Society* (2023), pp. 1–29; M. Pedersen, 'Landbrugets Regnskabsføring', *Ugeskrift for Landmænd* (1919), pp. 415–16.

7 Auderset and Moser, *Die Agrarfrage in der Industriegesellschaft*, pp. 49–69.

Thus, although the agricultural intelligentsia were of no doubt that accurate book-keeping and accounting were a necessity for what they propagated as rational production, individual farmers might find the fixed costs of implementing such a strategy prohibitive. They might just be convinced that comparing milk yields and feeding practices was useful for their day-to-day practices, but calculating a return on capital employed was not. Lack of enthusiasm for accounting among farmers did not stop its proponents, since Danish agricultural science required information from many farmers in order to be able to provide prescriptive teaching of best practice. The lack of accounts from this perspective can be seen as a market failure, and support offered to farmers through the *Driftsbureau* sought to address this, and hoped – in the process – also to raise enthusiasm for accounting, once the practical or rhetorical benefits would become apparent to participating farmers and their neighbours.

When describing accounting practices, we use the classical distinction between book-keeping and accounting and refer to book-keeping as the recording of data on the farm, in monetary terms (e.g., revenues and expenses in the cash book), and, more importantly, in daily activities (work, land use and harvest, feeding and milking of cows, in the produce and labour accounts, etc.). Accounting is then the processing of these figures into data for certain purposes, which can be 'partial' and 'product oriented', that is, for a certain activity (e.g., dairying) or 'total' for the entire farm (the profit and loss statement, balance sheet, etc.). While Danish farmers traditionally focused on the former, the *Driftsbureau* and its collaborators promoted the latter.[8]

In the following, we first provide a brief overview of the co-evolution of agricultural book-keeping and accounting, agricultural modernization and livestock-oriented specialization until the First World War. We then examine the establishment of the *Driftsbureau*, its system of accounts and logic of collection, and the intentions of experts and authorities behind them from the establishment of the bureau to the German occupation of Denmark in the Second World War. Our next step is to try to understand why farmers – who were not obliged to keep books and draw up accounts for tax purposes – participated in this endeavour. Consistent with the market failure described above, these discussions reveal implicit resistance to or at least pervasive disinterest in 'total' accounting of the *Driftsbureau* kind, but nevertheless widespread use of 'partial' traditional accounting for productive and benchmarking purposes. The testimonials of those who did accounts, statistically more intensive and self-declaredly more conscientious farmers, highlight how accounting improved systemic

8 See P. K. Thordal, 'Udviklingerne i Landbrugets Regnskabsføring og dertil hørende Konsulentvirksomhed', *Ugeskrift for Landmænd* (1942), pp. 315–17; T. Bro Pedersen, 'Driftsøkonomisk Vejledning paa Grundlag af Regnskabsresultater', *Ugeskrift for Landmænd* (1942), pp. 318–21.

understanding of the farm, could serve as a diagnosis tool in critical times, and was overall associated empirically and narratively with better and 'more rational' farm management.[9]

I

The origins of systematic agricultural accounting in Denmark can be traced back to the early 1800s, to the colourful character of Carl Frederik Gyllembourg (1767–1815), who, exiled from Sweden, published in 1808 his *Forsøg til et Landbrugs-Bogholderie* ('Attempt at an Agricultural Book-keeping') in Copenhagen.[10] This soon received the official approval of the Royal Agricultural Society of Denmark and the circle of 'rational farming' followers of German agronomist Albrecht Thaer. They formulated the Society's official recommendations with the aim of transforming agriculture into a modern, scientific enterprise in the tradition of the enlightenment. In 1805, Gyllembourg had presented his work to the Society to be considered for a prize, and it was hailed as 'the scientific arable farming's non plus ultra'. In fact, Crown Prince Frederik refused to award the prize, because Gyllembourg had been involved in the conspiracy behind the assassination of Swedish King Gustav III in 1792.[11]

In his *Forsøg*, Gyllembourg proposed an array of connected tables to record and process all sorts of internal and external transactions on a (large) farm and, most importantly, not only to record material flows and quantities produced on a farm for scientific purposes, but also to calculate monetary returns, since without the latter it was impossible to know which form of production was economically optimal. He stressed that 'accounting has two aims: the scientific and the mercantile',[12] and should thus be made in a way that enabled comparisons between farms.[13]

9 Note that similar issues of self-selection in accounting (and publishing accounting results) were an important element in discussions about dairy accounts and the profitability of dairy unit leases as early as the 1860s (Lampe and Sharp, '"Rational" farmers'; N. E. Hofman Bang, 'Om Meieriregnskaber og Forpagtningsforhold', *Ugeskrift for Landmænd* (1862), pp. 213–28).

10 This section is based on a summary of Lampe and Sharp, 'A quest for useful knowledge'; Lampe and Sharp, '"Rational" farmers'; M. Lampe and P. Sharp, *A Land of Milk and Butter: How Elites Created the Modern Danish Dairy Industry* (2019).

11 L. Krusius-Ahrenberg, 'Carl Fredrik Gyllembourg-Ehrensvärd som dansk lantbruksekonom', *Svenska litteratursällskapet i Finland historiska och litteraturhistoriska studier* 23 (1947), pp. 284–369 at p. 335. Gyllembourg was only allowed to publish his book in 1808, after he had convinced the Danish Crown Prince that his involvement had been minor.

12 C. F. Gyllembourg, *Forsøg til et Landbrugs-Bogholderie* (2 vols, 1808), II.

13 C. F. Gyllembourg, *Forsøg til et Landbrugs-Bogholderie*, I.

In the turmoil of the Napoleonic Wars and the post-war agricultural crisis, the push for rationalization of Danish agriculture lost momentum, but in the wake of the crisis, new actors acquired large Danish farms and brought a new wave of agricultural modernization. Its central figure at that time was Edward Tesdorpf (1817–89), son of a Hamburg merchant who bought the estate of Orupgård on the island of Falster south of Copenhagen in 1840. Over the following decades he converted it into the centre of a large agricultural conglomerate. He was one of the presidents of the Royal Agricultural Society from 1860 to 1888 and is credited with the introduction of modern agricultural practices, the establishment of Denmark as a major dairy exporter, the establishment of a modern sugar beet factory and various other initiatives. On his estates on Falster and in the Agricultural Society, he employed and promoted a group of experts who were major protagonists in the 'second wave' of agricultural accounting in Denmark.[14]

A speech by Tesdorpf at a regional agricultural society on 'Should milk cows be fed with concentrates?' discussed whether it made sense to feed cows with grain through the winter in order to obtain more dairy products and more manure to fertilize the land, or whether grain should be sold on the markets and cows kept on the typical minimum diet during the winter and mostly produce milk while on pasture from spring to autumn.[15] Based on the dairy accounts of his estates, he answered in the affirmative, and sparked a vibrant, accounting-based debate about animal husbandry that lasted well into the 1860s.[16] Different authors followed Tesdorpf's logic and confirmed that feeding concentrates in winter did indeed lead to more manure and thus higher overall returns. Some, however, cautioned that one should not forget about quality, value and marketability of the produce. Others continued the discussion to compare the 'profitability' (in terms of income and manure obtained)

14 The most prominent expert from Tesdorpf's circle was Thomas Riise Segelcke, who became the first dairy consultant of the Royal Agricultural Society in 1860 and cooperated closely with Tesdorpf for decades. After 1874, he taught at the Royal Veterinary and Agricultural College, becoming professor in 1892. He taught agricultural and dairy accounting there for 27 years, and transcripts from his classes are preserved in its library (Lampe and Sharp, '"Rational" farmers'; Lampe and Sharp, *Land of Milk and Butter*; M. Lampe and P. Sharp, 'Accounting for the wealth of Denmark: A case study of Smithian growth using the emergence of modern accounting in Danish dairying', *European Journal of the History of Economic Thought* 26 (2019), pp. 659–97; Det Landøkonomiske Driftsbureau, *25 Aars Undersøgelser over Landbrugets Driftsforhold, 1918–43* (1943), ch. 7.

15 E. Tesdorpf, 'Er det rigtig at give Malkeqvæget et kraftigt Foder?', *Ugeskrift for Landmænd* (1856), pp. 81–5.

16 Lampe and Sharp, *Land of Milk and Butter*, ch. 5; Lampe and Sharp, 'Accounting for the wealth of Denmark'; Lampe and Sharp, '"Rational" farmers'.

from milk cows vs. beef cattle, discussed whether the use of commercial fertilizers like guano made sense or whether new dairy machines and procedures were worth the farmer's investment. Despite disclaimers regarding regional differences, cow breeds, etc., this literature evolved into a consensus of accounting-backed best practices for modern 'scientific farming'.

As a side effect, the lively discussion of the non-standardized accounts and profit calculations of individual farmers led to a set of standardized accounts for the Danish dairy sector, at least on estates with separate dairy units. From the second half of the 1870s, agricultural experts at the Royal Agricultural Society collected these accounts every year and published them in the Society's journal *Tidsskrift for Landøkonomi*. These reports are suitable for analysis with modern quantitative research methods.[17]

Note, however, that such detailed accounts exist almost exclusively for large estates where, presumably, the fixed costs of accounting proved easier to carry. In an attempt to spread accounting to smaller producers, by the 1880s a broad range of guides and tables were available for interested farmers, mainly focusing on dairying, but also for other parts of the farm. The focus of accounting in publication and practice was on the technical and economic efficiency of production. In the second half of the nineteenth century, we find many examples of book-keeping separated by productive activities and, based on them, certain partial accounts of, most prominently, the value of the milk incorporated in dairy products or crop rotations and harvest records. Overall, it is not fully clear how prevalent book-keeping and accounting actually were in Denmark before 1900, although debates occasionally include data from 'normal farms'.[18] However, at a meeting in 1886 of expert stakeholders about accounting guides for small farms, Johannes Friis, one of the central figures in scientific improvement from the 1850s, suggested that relatively few of them were of actual practical use.[19]

17 See I. Henriksen, M. Lampe and P. Sharp, 'The role of technology and institutions for growth: Danish creameries in the late nineteenth century', *European Review of Economic History* 15 (2011), pp. 475–93; Ibid., 'The strange birth of Liberal Denmark: Danish trade protection and the growth of the dairy industry since the mid-nineteenth century', *Economic History Review* 65 (2012), pp. 770–88; M. Lampe and P. Sharp, 'Just add milk: A productivity analysis of the revolutionary changes in nineteenth-century Danish dairying', *Economic History Review* 68 (2015), pp. 1132–53.

18 e.g., N. P. J. Buus, 'Om Køernes Udbytte i 1864', *Ugeskrift for Landmænd, 1865*, I, pp. 179–93.

19 See the report on the meeting in *Ugeskrift for Landmænd 1886*, I, pp. 47–9. On Friis see Lampe and Sharp, '"Rational" farmers', pp. 15–16.; ibid., n. 23, collects references and book reviews for accounting guides up to 1878. Landøkonomiske Driftsbureau, *25 Aars Undersøgelser*, pp. 7–9, surveys the situation until the early twentieth century.

Discussions about the profitability of agriculture were thus framed in terms of the production, prices and demand for specific goods, or what we have termed 'product accounting', and not based on overall profitability measures. This approach also fits well with the accounts by cooperative creameries that needed to be kept to inform their members about production and explain how butter prices were converted into milk delivery payments. Although such accounts also informed financial results, these again refer by and large to only one product, butter, and thus fit well with the single product efficiency approach.[20]

In the same spirit, local 'control associations' for ordinary farmers (*Kontrolforeninger*) emerged from 1895 in the regional agricultural societies.[21] They allowed farmers, with the help of subsidized agricultural consultants, to systematically keep, standardize and compare accounts of, for example, milk yields, milk fat content and fodder compositions for participating farmers. This provided important material for the diffusion of best practice at the local level and beyond, since many control associations published comparative reports and cooperated in an umbrella organization, *De danske Kontrolforeningers Landsudvalg*, that produced annual reports from 1932 to 1979 in parallel to those of the *Driftsbureau*. These reports provide an overview of milk yields (average and top), fat content, feeding practices and the like. Table 8.1 gives an overview of membership in the control associations, which from 1900 to 1947 increased from 6,600 to 70,400 farms with up to 800,000 cows, covering more than a third of all farms owning half of all cows in the country. On the eve of the First World War, there were more than 500 control associations, about half as many as there were cooperative creameries at the same time, but an order of magnitude more than accounting associations (see below). Similarly, competitions for cultivation schemes and crop rotations collected accounts for land use.[22]

By contrast, regarding data on the profitability of *individual* farms, we are more or less left with the singular find by S. P. Jensen, who describes in detail the preserved accounts of one particular farm, Porsager near Stevns (south of Copenhagen), for the period 1870 to 1914. He calls these accounts, preserved in the diary of Hans Christian Sørensen from 1868 to 1918, quite exceptional because of their detailed content. They

20 Sofia Henriques, Eoin McLaughin, Paul Sharp, Xanthi Tsoukli and Cristian Veddel, 'Opening the black box of the Danish dairy cooperatives: A productivity analysis' (European Historical Economics Working paper 203, 2020).

21 Sammenvirkende danske Landboforeninger, *1895–1920: Kontrolforeningerne og deres Arbejde gennem fem og tyve Aar* (1920); Z. D. Lando, 'Landøkonomisk Oplysningarbejde', *Handelsvidenskabeligt Tidsskrift* 4 (1940), pp. 188–207.

22 J. C. Overgaard, 'Kejsernes nye Klæder', *Ugeskrift for Landmænd* 61 (1916), pp. 161–2.

TABLE 8.1. Control associations, affiliated members and associated cows in Denmark, select years, 1903–45.

Year	Associations	Total members	Total cows	Proportion of the national herd (%)
1903–4	280	6,600	111,900	10.3
1908–9	449	9,584	167,483	13.1
1913–14	587	12,757	208,013	15.9
1918–19	614	13,393	179,111	17.2
1924–5	1,013	27,689	431,901	31.0
1929–30	1,467	44,463	598,852	36.7
1934–5	1,588	50,376	669,088	40.6
1939–40	1,817	68,032	791,128	49.8
1944–5	1,785	71,050	795,971	50.7

Source: T. Andersen, 'Oversigt over Regnskabsresultaterne i De danske Kontrolforeninger (15. Oversigt) 1946–47'. Slagelse: Sorø Amtstidendes Bogtrykkeri.

were preserved more or less by chance by the brother of Sørensen's daughter-in-law.[23]

For a more general picture, we lack sources into the early twentieth century, as evidenced by Einar Jensen's attempt to reconstruct 'accounts of production and financial returns on the representative farm from 1871 to 1929', roughly by decade.[24] In his methodological considerations, Jensen explains that there are no actual data from individual farms going back much before the First World War,[25] so that he had to combine information from agricultural censuses, harvest statistics, price data, and further sources on median farm size, median production regimes (land

23 S. P. Jensen, 'Landbrugets systemskifte 1870 til 1914 belyst gennem dagbøger og regnskaber fra en enkelt gård', in S. P. Jensen (ed.), *Fra stilstand til vækst: Studier i dansk landbrugs udvikling fra 1682 til 1914* (2007), pp. 215–49 at p. 216.

24 E. Jensen, *Danish Agriculture: Its Economic Development. A Description and Economic Analysis Centering on the Free Trade Epoch, 1870–1930* (1937), ch. 9, pp. 254–75; Appendix III, pp. 403–8.

25 Ibid., pp. 255–7. Note that according to the *Driftsbureau*, Ivar Dokken's attempt to link the accounts of 12 member farms of Odense Omegns Landboforeining from 1911–12 to 1921–2 published in its *Periodiske Beretninger I* (1924) forms the only available series that goes back to before the First World War (Landøkonomiske Driftsbureau, 25 *Aars Undersøgelser*, p. 4). Dokken was accounting consultant at the Odense society before he joined the Driftsbureau (O. H. Larsen, 'Det landøkonomiske Driftsbureau og dets Arbejde gennem de første 10 Aar', *Ugeskrift for Landmænd 1928*, pp. 769–72, 785–8).

use, livestock kept), median yields and produce, median labour requirements, and median prices and costs of inputs and outputs. He uses these to construct the receipts and expenses from what one might call a synthetic representative farm, approximated by a 'full-sized "Gaard" [family farm] of 28 hectares [...] located in Sjælland, the largest of the Danish islands'. Table 8.2 (Jensen's Table 10) gives an overview. Following the path of the leading estates of the 1850s and 1860s, and relying on cooperative creameries and slaughterhouses, Jensen's representative farm obtained an increasing share of its revenues from dairy production (rising from 8.6 per cent in 1871 to 41.1 per cent in 1912 and 35.4 per cent in 1929) and its by-products: beef, pork (using returned skimmed milk) and eggs (together forming 20.6 per cent in 1870, 37.4 per cent in 1912, 46.9 per cent in 1929). Crop farming products declined from 51.7 to about 16 per cent over the period. We should, however, not overlook that grain – as outlined above – featured heavily as an input into dairy production, which actual in-depth records of such internal flows would reveal much more clearly than Jensen's synthetic data.

Table 8.2. Einar Jensen's historical record of financial returns on the representative farm, 1871–1929.

	1871	1881	1891	1901	1912	1929
Receipts						
Cereals	1,693	1,509	958	645	1,004	2,206
Peas	70	60	48	—	—	—
Potatoes	32	44	27	66	188	264
Seed	—	—	—	—	135	350
Butter	299	761	1,457	2,101	3,288	6,161
Beef	336	383	422	551	863	1,372
Pork	378	448	723	1,199	1,842	5,852
Lambs	260	180	126	120	75	—
Wool	28	21	22	15	11	—
Eggs	—	—	40	115	282	945
Horses	375	375	350	300	300	250
	3,471	3,781	4,173	5,112	7,988	17,400
Expenses						
Hired labour	455	615	700	836	1,087	3,425
Concentrates	—	108	206	335	681	2,365
Grain	—	120	129	176	648	1,712
Fertilizer	—	12	18	38	113	700

TABLE 8.2. *Cont.*

Seed	—	50	100	150	220	360
Machinery repairs	75	100	120	200	300	500
Building repairs	—	—	—	100	120	190
Veterinarian, etc.	10	20	25	75	100	175
Insurance	50	45	90	120	140	250
Light and power	—	—	—	—	—	200
Miscellaneous	25	20	20	20	130	215
Real estate tax	270	270	320	320	290	700
Mortgage interest	950	950	1,200	1,250	1,250	1,250
	1,835	2,310	2,928	3,620	5,079	12,042
Net spendable income	1,636	1,471	1,245	1,492	2,909	5,358

Note: in current Danish kroner
Source: Jensen, *Danish Agriculture*, Table 10.

II

It was into this context that the *Driftsbureau* was to emerge. Already before the First World War, and arising out of the control associations, a movement developed to encourage more comprehensive farm accounting. The first of these accounting associations (*Regnskabsforeninger*) was founded in 1910 in Samsø (a smaller island North of Fyn in the Kattegat), and a dozen more followed soon after, embedded into the local network of agricultural societies and smallholder associations, and building on the spread of the control associations.[26] In October of the same year, the Royal Agricultural Society established a committee of experts to create the guidelines for a unified agricultural accounting guide. In 1913 the committee delivered a draft guide that included trial accounts, annual returns and four basic books for cash, general accounts, livestock and labour. Based on daily records, farmers were supposed to start keeping these books and then receive assistance from accounting consultants to produce annual balance sheets, profit and loss statements and key financial indicators. The official history of the *Driftsbureau* describes the first attempts as not very promising: participating farmers filled in the cash book quite consistently, but the actual detailed book about

26 This and the following paragraphs are based on Landøkonomiske Driftsbureau, *25 Aars Undersøgelser*, pp. 9–21.

agricultural activities, instrumental to understanding the farm economy, was seldom kept. The Society thus decided to connect with the existing control associations (for livestock) and cultivation competitions (for land use). In 1914, O. H. Larsen, a newly appointed professor at the Danish Veterinary and Agricultural College, was commissioned to prepare a plan for the organization of periodic, representative and systematic accounting data on the relevant aspects of Danish agriculture.

This plan was formally adopted in 1916, perhaps not coincidentally a time of crisis for Danish agriculture due to wartime conditions,[27] and led to the foundation of the *Driftsbureau*. Larsen explicitly mentioned the work of Professor Laur in Switzerland and the institution he founded (*Schweizerisches Bauernsekretariat*, 1898, and *Abteilung für Rentabilitätserhebungen*, 1901)[28] as inspiration alongside more recent initiatives in Norway, Sweden and Finland. The Bureau was to be financed in the first two years by the Royal Agricultural Society and subsidized by the government from 1918. Its board was made up of representatives from the Royal Agricultural Society, the Joint (Regional) Agricultural Societies, the Joint Smallholder Societies, the Cooperative Commission (representing the cooperative creameries), the government's Statistical Department and Professor Larsen, who was co-opted by the other members. J. C. Overgaard, head of the prestigious Ladelund agricultural school, became first head of the Bureau. He immediately embarked on travels to Norway, Finland and Switzerland to study their existing structures. Actual and prospective accounting consultants and association initiators met at a course at Ladelund in February 1916 to establish common ground and build on the existing practices, not least those of the control associations and cultivation competitions.[29] Similar meetings were held in 1917 and subsequent years.

The plan was to build on and multiply the existing Accounting Associations, overcoming the cost barriers to entry by providing them with instructions and a free guide to data collection and processing. Government-subsidized local accounting consultants and assistants were to process and forward the accounts to the newly established Bureau which would select, process and arrange them into annual reports, taking into account regional variations and differences in farm size as well as land use, livestock intensity, etc. Free accounting courses (including travel expenses), blank books and guides, as well as copies of the annual

27 Although Denmark remained neutral during the First World War, the important British market was often cut off, as were the supplies of coal which fuelled many parts of the rural economy, including the butter factories.

28 Auerset and Moser, *Die Agrarfrage in der Industriegesellschaft*, pp. 64–99. Laur's experience is discussed in D'Onofrio's and Moser's chapters in this volume (chs 9 and 10).

29 J. C. Overgaard, 'Kejsernes nye Klæder', *Ugeskrift for Landmænd*, pp. 161–2.

reports, were to be provided to participants, and anonymity in processing and publication of the accounts was guaranteed. In a retrospective, Larsen justified this bottom-up approach based on existing agricultural organizations and voluntary participation as a cost-saving way of obtaining accounts and broad and sustained participation in comparison to a model where the Bureau would have directly recruited a sample of farms into their survey.[30] From the beginning, however, this voluntarist model also raised questions regarding the self-selection of participants and thus their representativeness.

Even before data collection formally started, Overgaard had published a pilot report with data for 1916–17, covering 75 accounts from all over Denmark that contained the necessary data for the Bureau's system, collected by accounting consultants during the early days of the establishment of the Bureau.[31] The report on the 1917–18 production year then contained 235 accounts from 17 accounting regions.[32] From then on, annual reports titled *Undersøgelser over Landbrugets Driftsforhold: Periodiske Beretninger* were published until after the Second World War. Other periodical reports from the Bureau were provisional (earlier) yearly results (based on data for about half the farms), data on agricultural wages and on prices of the main products and inputs into agriculture, all starting in the early 1920s. From 1923, the Statistical Department of Denmark included the results from the *Driftsbureau* surveys into its official statistics. By 1926, the annual accounts included numbered 671,[33] and in 1940, around 1,000 accounts were processed out of 7,660 submitted to the accounting consultants of 78 accounting associations, although there was still some imbalance between large and middle-sized farms and smallholders. For the latter, information was comparatively scarce.[34] If this implies an element of failure, in terms of geographical reach, the

30 Larsen, 'Det Landøkonomiske Driftsbureau'.

31 J. C. Overgaard, *Undersøgelser over Landbrugets Driftsforhold*, I, *Nogle Regnskabsresultater fra danske Landbrug i Aaret 1916–17* (1918).

32 O. H. Larsen and I. Dokken, *Undersøgelser over Landbrugets Driftsforhold*, II, *Regnskabsresultater fra danske Landbrug i Aaret 1917–18* (1919).

33 J. Pedersen, 'Det landøkonomiske Driftsbureaus Beretning', *Nationaløkonomisk Tidsskrift* III, 35 (1927), pp. 90–101.

34 Statistics Denmark, *Agriculture and Danish Farm Returns through 100 Years: 1916–2015* (2017), ch. 4.1; P. K. Thordal, 'Udviklingerne i Landbrugets Regnskabsføring og dertil hørende Konsulentvirksomhed', *Ugeskrift for Landmænd 1942*, pp. 315–17. In general, in Denmark in the 1910s to 1930s, farms under 10 ha were classified as 'smallholders/cotters', farms between 10 and 50 ha were seen as either 'small' (10–20 ha), 'middle-sized' (20–30 ha) or 'large' (30–50 ha) family farms. Farms larger than 50 hectares were seen as middle-sized (50–100 ha) or large (over 100 ha) units in the tradition of former landed estates and subsequently emerging large farming operations. Most of the land belonged to family farm-size units, see, for instance, Larsen and Dokken, *Undersøgelser*, pp. 17–18.

Figure 8.1. Map with dots for all farms contributing in the sample for the 1940–1 accounting year. Source: Landøkonomiske Driftsbureau, *25 Aars Undersøgelser*, p. 34. Reprinted with permission from Institut for Fødevare- og Ressourceøkonomi, https://ifro.ku.dk/.

Driftsbureau achieved comprehensive coverage of the country (Figure 8.1). Overall, more than 16,000 accounts were processed and reported by the Bureau from 1916 to 1940.[35]

The first official accounting guide by the *Driftsbureau* was published in 1918, and revised editions were issued in 1926 and 1938. The 1926 version

[35] Landøkonomiske Driftsbureau, *25 Aars Undersøgelser*, p. 31.

is 50 pages long and explains the logic of data collection and processing, as well as the key indicators to be calculated.[36] Two versions of accounts were collected: Accounts type 'A' (intended for smaller farms) represent the minimum including external interactions of the farm and key figures on the farm's business. Accounts type 'B' add more information on internal material and work flows on the farm, which make it possible to reconstruct, for example, the 'classical' value of cow dung as fertilizer used on the fields,[37] but also the more precise use of hired and family labour in the different areas of operation on the farm. In both accounts, the following four elements appear: (a) an account of assets, including land, capital, etc.; (b) cash accounts on payments coming into and going out of the farm over the year; (c) produce and labour accounts, covering the flow of work and produce from the farm to other businesses, the farmers' household and private uses; and (d) an annual balance sheet that reflects the result of the business of the farm and its farmer. Type 'B' accounts add and/or separate out (e) accounts for livestock, with sub-accounts by type of animal, normally: horses, cattle (separated into milk cows, calves and bulls, and possibly beef cattle) and pigs, with possibilities for chicken, sheep or goats; (f) accounts for labour and fields (detailed by field and labour use on them); (g) household accounts (flows between farm and household, including in-kind consumption by family members while working on the farm); and (h) more detailed annual balances for different activities.

Assets were to be valued by their approximate market value, although for real estate often the taxable value (*ejendomsskyldværdi*) was used. Typical positions here include land, improvements, plantations, buildings (including the farmers' dwelling), livestock, tools and machines, all with adequate depreciation deductions, inventory, debt/credit bills and, on the passive side, capitalized outstanding payments for 'old part' (*Aftægt*), which were to be treated as capitalized annuities for life. The cash accounts were to include all types of income and expenses, including tax payments, building reparations, wages paid, sales and purchase of produce and inputs, etc.

For produce, work and field accounts, either relatively summarized accounts could be kept ('A') or very detailed diaries for labour use, field work and production ('B') could be consolidated into annual accounts. Livestock books would record daily production (especially of milk) as well as all sorts of feedstuffs converted into feed units (FU), normalized to barley. The accounting guide lists 90 different kinds of feed (for cows) ranking from boneless meat feed (*benfrit kødfodermel*, at 0.6 FU)

36 Larsen and Dokken, *Vejledning*.

37 See above, and Lampe and Sharp, 'Quest for useful knowledge', and *Land of Milk and Butter*.

to *runkelroetop* (a fodder beet derivative, at 15 FU). Grazing is valued at between 3 and 5 FU per day, depending on the weight of the animal.[38]

For the annual balance, the key figures to be calculated were the gross revenues (*bruttoudbytte*) as the aggregate market value of all produced and self-consumed output. From this, operating costs (*driftsomkostninger*), including a management payment for the farmer and remuneration for family labour, taxes, depreciation, etc., were to be deducted. These two figures served to calculate net revenue (*nettoudbytte*) and rate of return (*forrentningsprocent*) as a sort of return on capital (based on the initial asset valuation).[39] Detailed example tables on how to do this were provided in an eight-page appendix to the actual guide.

Accounts of type 'B' also made it possible to dive deeper into the net revenue from different operations, like the cost of horses, the net income from dairying (accounting for the use of on-farm produced feed, etc.), the value of cow-produced fertilizer, the cost of labour in different operations, the cost of labour days, etc. For these, specific consumption equivalents were referred to and reported in some of the annual reports (e.g., a 4-year-old child accounted for 0.4 of a grown man aged 15 years and older; a woman and a 12–15-year-old boy accounted for 0.8 of a grown man, and so on).[40]

The annual reports provided summary statistics on the key indicators, generally by region and farm size: total production and its value, harvest results, capital assets and their distribution by capital type,[41] prices, gross income and its components,[42] total expenses and their components, as well as net income and business percentage. For those farms with

38 Larsen and Dokken, *Vejledning*, pp. 16–17.

39 Thordal, 'Udviklingerne', claimed that he introduced the 'business percentage' measure into the literature, in a 1913 report on the accounting results of members of the Copenhagen County Agricultural Society for which he worked as an accounting consultant, see *Ugeskrift for Landmænd 1915*, I, issues 10–12.

40 Larsen and Dokken, *Undersøgelser*, p. 93.

41 For example, in 1917–18, farms had on average a capital value of 2,351 Danish kroner per ha, ranging from 1,661 in Western Jutland to 2,965 on Falster and Møen, and also varying in an inverted U-shape when tabulated by farm size. On average 68% of the capital value consisted of land and buildings, 24% of animals (of which 12% were cattle) and 5.5% of machines, tools, inventory, etc., again with considerable variation by farm size and region (Larsen and Dokken, *Undersøgelser*, pp. 24–9). Distribution by farm size *and* region was not reported.

42 For example, in 1917–18, not a good year for dairying (Henriques *et al.*, 'Resilience'), 69% of all income came from animal husbandry, of which 31.3% was from milk, 14.5% from other cattle products, 12.6% from pigs, etc., and only 11.9% from grain production – although we should highlight that self-produced grain was used to feed livestock. The share of income from animal husbandry varied again considerably across regions (from 60 to 85%) and

accounting 'B', further detailed statistics were provided (in 1918/19, these made up between 75 and 156 of the 275 farms, depending on the item covered). Where possible, comparisons to similar publications were made (e.g., from Skåne, Finland and different parts of Norway);[43] such comparisons became institutionalized through the agricultural economics section in the Nordic Association of Agricultural Scientists (*Nordiske Jordbrugsforskeres Forening*). There were also book exchanges with similar institutions in Europe, Canada and the US.[44]

The annual reports do provide micro data for all farms, although these are somewhat difficult for modern researchers to use, and are probably not useful for contemporary benchmarking exercises, because all figures appear either nominalized per hectare or in per cent. This form of presentation is probably attributable to the principle of anonymity in processing and publication guaranteed to participating farmers.[45] Contemporary observers nevertheless criticized the lack of absolute numbers and the non-replicability of the summary tabulations by size and region from the very beginning.[46]

The immediate use of the data collected is clear. They informed experts as well as the government and other stakeholders about the conditions of agriculture in Denmark. Interim and final reports and reports on prices were picked up by the agricultural press and informed farmers about the general state and probable evolution of business. In 1923, the *Driftsbureau*'s statistics became part of the data handled by the government's Statistical Department, and in consequence are still available on the website of Statistics Denmark and in anniversary publications of

was highest for farms below 20 ha (74–75%) and lowest for farms over 100 ha (47.9%); Larsen and Dokken, *Undersøgelser*, pp. 35–8.

43 Ibid., p. 39.

44 Larsen, 'Det landøkonomiske Driftsbureau og dets Arbejde gennem de første 10 Aar', p. 788.

45 However, the original sheets (from 1916 to 1976) have been preserved in more than 800 boxes in the Danish national archives. Mikkelsen/Nørr, *Efter bemyndigelse*, pp. 312–16, contains an image of such an account from 1957 featuring the name of the owner and location of the farm and describes the source as 'documenting the operating conditions on identifiable properties'. We thank Kenn Tabersen from the Danish National Archives for this information, and Marina Chuchko for discussions leading to the inquiry.

46 K. J. Kristensen, [Review of] 'Det landøkonomiske Driftsbureau: Undersøgelser over Landbrugets Driftsforhold, I, Nogle Regnskabsresultater fra danske Landbrug i Aaret 1916–17 ved J. C. Overgaard. 38 S.', *Nationaløkonomisk Tidsskrift*, III, 27 (1919), pp. 587–90, at p. 590; Pedersen, 'Landøkonomiske Driftsbureaus Beretning', pp. 99–100, 92–3, shows that for some years in the 1920s the corresponding tables seem to have been published with less detail, blaming austerity and misplaced cost savings. Larsen, 'Landøkonomiske Driftsbureau', p. 788, stresses the small staff and difficult financial situation of the Bureau in the late 1920s.

the *Driftsbureau*.[47] From this official status came official uses of the data: legislation in 1933 on communal real estate taxes and in 1938 on interest payments by state-sponsored smallholders (*Staatshusmænd*) introduced a business-cycle adjusted approach to payments based on the farm account data processed for the Ministry of the Interior.[48]

Danish agricultural history textbooks rely on the data for the period covered here. For example, Erik Helmer Pedersen's textbook account reports the rates of return from 1917 onwards, as well as wages, and incomes, expenses and further data from books and articles that used the farm accounts, such as the work by Jørgen Pedersen, whose main results merit attention as an example of contemporary scientific use of the farm accounting data.[49] Initially, Pedersen had been one of the main critical voices questioning the farm accounts, both in terms of data collection and regarding the usefulness of key indicators like the business percentage for macroeconomic questions beyond agricultural (micro)economics.[50] In his quantitative account of overall incomes in and demand from agriculture between 1922 and 1936, an attempt to make sense of the role of agricultural demand in the Danish Great Depression, he nevertheless argues that the data from the *Driftsbureau* provide a valuable source to compute aggregate agricultural incomes, not least because tabulated tax returns cover only a small percentage of all farms reliably, and with tax bases that are only adjusted with a lag and never to the full extent to actual conditions in a given year.[51] He assumes that while levels might be overstated (although less than was often claimed), general tendencies can be extracted from the farm accounts, and he welcomed the *Driftsbureau*'s rigorous attempts to assure representativeness across regions and size classes in the face of self-selection by the more ambitious farmers.[52] He devised strategies to aggregate the data into macro series.[53] His interpretation focuses on the demand side and reveals that farmers' (nominal)

47 Statistics Denmark, *Agriculture*; Landøkonomisk Driftsbureau, *25 Aars Undersøgelser*; H. Vitting Andersen, *Landbrugets økonomi i 50 år: 1918–1968* (1968).

48 Landøkonomisk Driftsbureau, *25 Aars Undersøgelser*, pp. 27–8.

49 E. H. Pedersen, *Danske landbrugs historie*, pp. 27–30; Pedersen, *Undersøgelse.*

50 J. Pedersen, 'Landøkonomiske Driftsbureaus Beretning', pp. 94–7.

51 J. Pedersen, *En Undersøgelse af Indtægtssvingningerne i Landbruget i Perioden 1922–36 og deres Indflydelse paa andre Erhverv* (1938), pp. 8–9, 21–6.

52 Kjeld Bjerke, in his '[Book review of] J. Pedersen, *En Undersøgelse af Indtægtssvingningerne i Landbruget i Perioden 1922–36 og deres Indflydelse paa andre Erhverv* (Studier fra Aarhus Universitets økonomiske Institut, Nr. 2, Kbhvn. 1938, 50 S.)' in *Nationaløkonomisk Tidsskrift*, III, 46 (1938), pp. 345–7, maintains that the Driftsbureau sample contains a significant upward bias in levels (see nn. 41 and 42), but concurs with Pedersen on its use for annual changes and judges Pedersen's method favourably.

53 Pedersen, *Undersøgelse.*

incomes and expenses fell after 1926, with an enormous decline after 1931. Larger farms suffered more in the crisis (but also benefited more in booms). In terms of expenses, the most severe cutting back was in terms of demand for large new investments, but also the tax adjustments seem to have made a difference. Payments to hired labour also declined continuously from 1929–30 to 1932–3, but much less in magnitude than the collapse in farm incomes and total expenses and the decline in investments. His conclusion, based on special reports from the *Driftsbureau*, was that since wages were more flexible in agriculture than in other sectors, the decline in the total wages adjusted for the decline in the wage level corresponded to a comparatively mild decline in employment by about 12 per cent from 1929–30 to 1932–3.[54]

III

In 1942, Christian Jervelund, the owner of a 37-hectare family farm with 22 or 25 cows in northern Fyn, began his reflections on the lessons he had learnt from 40 years of his own agricultural accounting by stating that 'accounting was never the Danish farmer's strong point'.[55] Indeed, as we have seen, while at the end of our period more than a third of Danish farmers were members of control associations, only 7,600 of Denmark's more than 200,000 farmers, less than 4 per cent, were active members of accounting associations,[56] a slight improvement from 2.5 per cent in the early 1920s.[57] It is possible that some farmers after initial training and participation left the organizations and the reliance on accounting consultants,[58] but available anecdotal evidence suggests that this was not common. Apart from the only slowly growing numbers of accounts available to the *Driftsbureau*, we can also mention here the private accounting extension initiative by Captain Martin Petersen, a former navy officer turned model farmer. From 1917 to 1922, based on his own accounting guide and books, Pedersen and his associates held inexpensive short courses for primary school teachers on how to teach agricultural accounting. In turn, the teachers then organized evening courses in their schools for local farmers. Petersen's methods combined the promise of improvement through accounting with an unequivocal

54 Pedersen, *Undersøgelse*, pp. 39–42.

55 C. Jervelund, 'Hvilke Fordele har jeg som praktisk Landmand haft af ca. 40 Aars Regnskabsføring?', *Ugeskrift for Landmænd* (1942), pp. 321–3.

56 Landøkonomiske Driftsbureau, *25 Aars Undersøgelser*; Statistics Denmark, *Agriculture*, ch. 4.1; Lando, 'Landøkonomisk Oplysningarbejde', p. 202; Thordal, 'Udviklingerne'.

57 I. Bang, 'Regnskabsføring i Landbruget, med særligt Henblik paa Skatteansættelsen', *Nationaløkonomisk Tidsskrift*, III, 31 (1923), pp. 194–205.

58 Landøkonomiske Driftsbureau, *25 Aars Undersøgelser*, p. 32.

military style of prescribing definite practices to get there. The initial plan was to reach and convince 80 per cent of all Danish farmers to adopt Petersen's methods. The courses are reported to have reached 1,500 teachers and 40,000 farmers, but with little long-term impact.[59] At the same time, in discussions about the quality of accounting teaching at the Royal Agricultural and Veterinary College, contributors highlighted that agricultural accounting done well, i.e., in a systematic double-entry fashion, was much more complicated than the double-entry practised in trade or industry, due to the many internal transactions that require keeping track of internal flows and devising strategies to attach internal prices to them.[60] Such complications and the time and monetary costs of accounting, although small, might have disincentivized most farmers in normal times from engaging in full accounting, reflecting earlier issues highlighted above.

Crucially, the main reason for farmers having to make a full set of accounts in other countries, the obligation to do so for tax assessment, was more or less absent in Denmark. The strong farming lobby constantly managed to keep farms, except a small share at the top, excluded from mandatory tax accounting, unlike artisans and other freelance professionals and formal enterprises, sparking occasional discussions about tax fairness.[61] Therefore, although accounting consultants[62] and accounting farmers indeed stressed that accounting helped to provide peace of mind regarding tax matters, they also stressed that it did not necessarily pay off financially, and could be not the main motivation.

In the relatively less elitist agricultural journal *Ugeskrift for Landmænd,* we find explicit discussions of the benefits of accounting for farmers on two occasions, first in 1932, when austerity measures threatened to lower the subsidies agricultural societies received for employing the accounting association's consultants and their assistants, and then in 1942, when the periodical asked its readers to write accounts of their experiences with accounting.

59 L.O., 'Kursus i Regnskabsføring i Hadsten og Omegns Landboforening', *Ugeskrift for Landmænd 1918,* pp. 280–2; M. Pedersen, 'Landbrugets Regnskabsføring', *Ugeskrift for Landmænd 1919,* pp. 415–16; Hansen, 'Regnskabsføring'; Thordal, 'Udviklingerne'; A. Milthers, 'M. Pedersen', in S. C. Bech (ed.), *Dansk Biografisk Leksikon* (1979–84). Online at https://biografiskleksikon.lex.dk/M._Pedersen (version of 18 July 2011).

60 Landbrugskandidat N., 'Skovduen eller Skaden?', *Ugeskrift for Landmænd 1916,* 451–4.

61 I. Bang, 'Regnskabsføring i Landbruget'.

62 C. Jervelund, 'Hvilke Fordele har jeg som praktisk Landmand haft af ca. 40 Aars Regnskabsføring?', *Ugeskrift for Landmænd 1942,* pp. 321–3; H. Bay, 'Hvilket Resultat giver et gennemført Regnskab efter 30 Aars Forløb', *Ugeskrift for Landmænd 1942,* pp. 359–61; Thordal, 'Udviklingerne'.

The 1932 contributions stressed that especially in bad times – like the post-war uncertainty that coincided with Captain Pedersen's accounting initiative and the rollout of the accounting associations – farmers turned to the overall (lack of) profitability of their businesses and needed to be able to identify where their individual business approach could be improved. In times of crisis, the variance in business outcomes appears to increase, prompting farmers to shift their focus from technical issues to individual strategies. Accounting consultants could then serve as business consultants and identify the strengths and weaknesses of individual farms, by focusing on the revenues and expenses of individual activities and comparing them to those of similar farms with better economic results or to a benchmark acquired through years of practice. In reality, accounts can reveal much more than the simple visits to the farm and technical assistance that agricultural consultants have to rely on in their absence. Accounting-based consultancy, however, always had to take into account the local conditions for agriculture and build on the relationship of trust between farmer and consultant.[63] One accounting consultant argued that accounting comparisons are akin to experiments, as similar versions of the same business can exhibit differences in some aspect, and the consequences can be traced back to the overall business outcomes.[64]

In a similar way, accounting farmers like Jervelund stressed that full accounting had indeed provided him with decisive advantages and insights beyond those from the product-based approach of the control association in which he also participated. He was enabled to do more comprehensive planning beyond the inputs into and outputs of a specific activity, both regarding cultivation strategies and labour management on a daily basis. He stressed that this had led him to a more intensive crop rotation with less grassland and more profitable crops than he had practised before, leading to more feed units for his cows, while the control association information would only have enabled him to decide on a more efficient feed mix. Such decisions made his farm more productive and more profitable, but ultimately understanding the inner workings of the farm in more detail provided him with greater satisfaction (and presumably made him a better farmer).[65]

Similarly, H. or W. S. Bay of Rolykkegarrd – the exact identity of the author is uncertain but he appears to have trained at the Royal Agricultural and Veterinary College in double-entry book-keeping before the First World War – stressed in 1942 that accounting had provided him with valuable information for farm management and, in his case,

63 A. P. Jacobsen, 'Regnskabsfører og Driftskonsulent', *Ugeskrift for Landmænd 1932*, p. 397; Thordal, 'Udviklingerne'; Bro Pedersen, 'Driftsøkonomisk Vejledning'.

64 Bro Pederson, 'Driftsøkonomisk Vejledning'.

65 Jervelund, 'Hvilke Fordele'.

had enabled him to calculate profitability over the previous 30 years to provide others with a yardstick for their farms or investment plans. His modern, well-equipped farm of 132 hectares, about 115 of them cultivated, and 65 cows on the island of Lolland brought an average of 16,500 kroner per year to its owner.[66] Like Jervelund, Bay highlights the pleasures of accounting in almost poetic fashion:

> Accounting has both a questioning and moral meaning for the practitioner. Many times when the clouds threatened outside the business, either in the form of rain in the busy time of autumn or whatever other unpleasantness life can bring, accounting with what goes with it is a distraction that brings peace to the mind and after a few hours gives a completely new attitude and desire to take hold again.[67]

So, much in line with the rhetoric of accounting and rationality in the nineteenth century, the proponents of accounting stressed that – while having some costs and probably no immediate pay-offs – it converted the farmer into someone more aware of his farm, more capable of navigating difficult times (possibly with the help of consultants) and more capable of actively formulating cultivation strategies. Added to this, even farmers who only kept a cash book were said to discipline their spending more effectively.[68] Accounting farmers provided material for diagnosis and comparison that could be used by themselves, by consultants and by experts to understand and improve agricultural business management. Returning to the beginning of this chapter, its practitioners present accounting as a way to become more conscientious, rational, self-aware and capable farmers. It is, of course, possible, and indeed likely, that the reverse was also true and even more relevant, i.e., more capable and/or successful farmers were more likely to account.

Statistically, the results of the self-assessment of representativeness of the sample in every publication of the *Driftsbureau* underline that there was a bias, be it due to self-selection or the treatment effect of accounting. Contributing farms in each size bracket used their land more intensively, held more cattle and obtained better harvests and higher milk yields than the corresponding average farm in the more comprehensive official statistics, although the extent to which this was the case might have diminished somewhat over time.[69] Also, smallholders were less likely to submit accounts, but again somewhat less so over time, maybe due to institutional incentives regarding their farm payments.[70]

66 Bay, 'Hvilket Resultat'.

67 Ibid., p. 361.

68 Bro Pedersen, 'Driftsøkonomisk Vejledning'.

69 Larsen, 'Landøkonomiske Driftsbureau'; Statistics Denmark, *Agriculture*, ch. 4; Landøkonomiske Driftsbureau, *25 Aars Undersøgelser*, p. 35.

70 Larsen and Dokken, *Undersøgelser*, pp. 15–18.

Thus, although the statements quoted above certainly indicate that those convinced of accounting replicated the rhetoric of the earlier epistemic community regarding its benefits, the practice spread much less than expected. It seems that the *Driftsbureau* was never completely able to compensate for the market failures which meant that farmers would not internalize the wider benefits of submitting accounts. Whether its monetary incentives were too low or there was a failure to convince the vast majority of farmers that accounting would actually help them understand their farm better is a question we cannot resolve with the material at hand.[71]

IV

The collection of farm accounts gathered and processed by the *Driftsbureau* provide fascinating insights into Danish agriculture, data production and the use and meanings of accounting.

On an institutional level, the Danish case provides an interesting study: the *Driftsbureau* and its collection was effectively a private–public partnership. It was set up at the initiative of key agricultural organizations and the government, and built on non-governmental accounting associations founded by farmers from within their established regional associations, employing government-subsidized accounting consultants and assistants who helped farmers and forwarded selected accounts to the Bureau. This was seen as a cost-saving approach consistent with the overall culture of rural Denmark, in which farmers displayed strong agency and a general scepticism towards centralized government activities.[72] The consequences were that participants were self-recruited and the sample of accounts balanced *ex post* rather than being purposefully constructed *ex ante*. However, given the evident lack of interest of the vast majority of farmers in farm-level accounting – as opposed to accounting for individual productive activities, especially dairying – and the absence of (tax) legislation that forced them to do so, this was probably the only viable strategy.

The resulting figures provided new and detailed insights into Danish agriculture and could be used for government administrative purposes, in economics and agricultural sciences. They were also used by consultants to establish what best practice looked like, not only technically, but financially, and formed the basis of a more informed extension service. In the inter-war period, this seems to have been most useful in times of crisis and uncertainty, but we can assume that the kind of comparison

71 cf. Auderset and Moser, *Agrarfrage*, ch. 1.

72 cf. N. Boberg-Fazlic, P. S. Jensen, M. Lampe, P. Sharp and C. V. Skovsgaard, '"Getting to Denmark": The Role of Agricultural Elites for Development', *Journal of Economic Growth* 28 (2023), pp. 55–69.

and benchmarking described by consultants and accounting farmers also benefited the extension services and their clients in normal times. The extent to which crisis management relied on actual accounting data – beyond the use of prices for agricultural goods also collected by the *Driftsbureau* – remains unclear and warrants further investigation. Unlike in other countries,[73] the accounts themselves were not envisioned as part of a political programme and remained largely uncontroversial in public debates. This might have been the case because agricultural parties dominated Danish politics in the inter-war period. They defended the unusual but powerful narrative of Denmark as an agricultural country – often combined with very clear sectoral policy, and controversies about agriculture thus took place elsewhere.[74]

Thus, while accounting farmers could identify themselves as possessing a more systemic understanding of their farms, a more informed ability to act and react, and as being closer to an epistemic community of experts (including publications in widely circulated periodicals), they provided a valuable service to their non-accounting counterparts. They fed data into an extensive system of agricultural research, public debate and local extension services that all other producers could also rely on through the dense network of agricultural associations. This wide network was, in the words of Lando, 'work on agricultural enlightenment' that transmitted the essence of 'rational' agricultural practice across rural Denmark, even if most of its members did not go through the pain of enlightening themselves in the way Jervelund or Bay describe.[75]

Such 'enlightenment by proxy' might have been marginally less effective than the full programme, but jointly with the collective power of agricultural associations and the farmer-based party Venstre and Radikale Venstre representing the smallholders, it provided a framework for the spread of good agricultural practices and a safety net for bad times. *Plus ça change*... Gyllembourg never completed his 1808 farm accounting guide, but it nevertheless stands as an impressive achievement. Under the *Driftsbureau*, farmers collectively did not become rational, but many did, and individuals and the entire sector benefited at a time when central government was not prepared, or able, to force the process.

73 cf. Auderset and Moser, *Agrarfrage*, pp. 89–95.

74 P. Boje, *Vejen til velstand: Marked, stat og utopi*, II: *Hvorvor blev Danmark riget – og ikke rigere. Tiden 1850–1930* (2020), pp. 579–601, 626–9.

75 Lando, 'Landøkonomisk Oplysningarbejde'; Jervelund, 'Fordele'; Bay, 'Resultat'.

9

The Intentional Spread of Farm Accountancy Offices in Switzerland and the Netherlands, 1890–1940[1]

Federico D'Onofrio

The spread of accounting and book-keeping has been famously linked to the advance of capitalism.[2] The historian of accounting R. A. Bryer dated the appearance of agrarian capitalism in England to the emergence of the rate of return on capital as a leading indicator of success in the seventeenth century.[3] Indeed, as has been shown by various chapters in this volume, estates and large farms developed accounting and book-keeping practices to rationalise their administration, enter new capital markets, try new forms of control of labour, and integrate agricultural and urban enterprises.[4] In fact, though, the family farm, rather than large capitalist estates, has been identified as the backbone of the 'First Green Revolution' that shaped the European countryside from

1 The project that led to this publication has received funding from the European Research Council (ERC) under the European Union's Horizon 2020 Research and Innovation Programme (Grant Agreement no 949722) and MSCA 833456: FARMACCOUNTA. This funding enables this chapter to appear Open Access under the licence CC BY-NC-ND.

2 This hypothesis, which ultimately has its roots in the work of Max Weber and Werner Sombart, has been critically reviewed and inverted by Eve Chiapello, 'Accounting and the Birth of the Notion of Capitalism', *Critical Perspectives on Accounting* 18 (2007), pp. 263–96.

3 R. A. Bryer, 'The History of Accounting and the Transition to Capitalism in England. Part One: Theory', *Accounting, Organizations and Society* 25 (2000), pp. 131–62.

4 See in this volume the chapters by Friederike Scholten-Buschhoff (ch. 3), James D. Fischer (ch. 2) and Laurent Herment (ch. 6).

the last decades of the nineteenth century onwards.[5] Here the take-up of accounts, especially double-entry accounts, has been shown to be slower.

For such farms, it is not clear whether the growing complexity of farm operations really necessitated the adoption of time consuming and cumbersome formal book-keeping (even as single-entry book-keeping). Controversially, Daan Hendrikx and Oscar Gelderblom, for instance, have claimed that 'mental accounting' would have probably satisfied the needs of Dutch farmers of the late nineteenth and early twentieth centuries.[6] Other historians, instead, have insisted on the powerful effect of productivity on systematic accounting information.[7]

What explains, though, the diffusion of accounting and book-keeping to family farms that took place over the course of the twentieth century in Europe?[8] By examining the case of the Netherlands and Switzerland, this chapter shows that the spread of farm accounting was the result of an intentional, concerted effort by agricultural experts, economists, extension officers, farmers' leaders and, more generally, the rural elites. It therefore only partially responded to the managerial needs of farmers, and served instead other goals.

The elite's zeal in favour of book-keeping has been widely discussed in the literature as part of a campaign to educate farmers to become more rational and effective: the accounting farmer appeared as an ideal of sound agronomic practices.[9] This chapter adopts a different approach. Jiri Auderset and Peter Moser have recently underlined the crucial role

5 J. L. van Zanden, 'The First Green Revolution: The Growth of Production and Productivity in European Agriculture, 1870–1914', *Economic History Review* 44 (1991), pp. 215–39.

6 D. Hendrikx and O. Gelderblom, 'Accounting for Agricultural Development? The Case of the Netherlands, 1840–1940', *Agricultural History Review* 70 (2022), pp. 23–48.

7 M. Lampe and P. Sharp, 'A Quest for Useful Knowledge: The Early Development of Agricultural Accounting in Denmark and Northern Germany', *Accounting History Review* 27 (2017), pp. 73–99.

8 This includes socialist Europe, as the work of Martha Lampland on Hungary shows: M. Lampland, 'False Numbers as Formalizing Practices', *Social Studies of Science* 40 (2010), pp. 377–404; idem, *The Value of Labor: The Science of Commodification in Hungary, 1920–1956* (2016).

9 T. Depecker and N. Joly, 'Agronomists and Accounting: The Beginnings of Capitalist Rationalisation on the Farm (1800–1850)', *Historia Agraria* (2015), pp. 75–94; N. Joly, 'Educating in Economic Calculus: The Invention of the Enlightened Peasant via Manuals of Agriculture, 1830–1870', *Accounting History Review* 26 (2016), pp. 131–60; P. Labardin and P. Gervais, 'Marketing the Past over the Long Run: Uses of the Past in French Accounting Textbooks, 17th–19th C.', *Journal of Historical Research in Marketing* 14 (2022), pp. 90–110.

of accounting as the *lingua franca* of agricultural economics and policy.[10] Building on their contribution, this chapter shows that, for the rural elites of the early twentieth century, book-keeping was not only indispensable for improved management of the farm, but also, increasingly, as a tool of the government of agriculture as a whole and thus played – to use the terminology of New Accounting History – a broad 'societal function'.[11]

In particular, this chapter analyses the role of meso-level institutions, such as farmers' unions of varying kinds and orientation, in promoting accounting. The literature has recognized the importance of the dense network of associations and co-operatives that covered the European countryside in the modernization of the continent's agriculture.[12] Literature on Switzerland and the Netherlands has particularly stressed this role of farmers' organizations, focusing on the integration of agriculture in industrial society (in the case of Switzerland) or the complex scientific and institutional matrix underpinning agricultural development (in the case of the Netherlands).[13] The chapter argues that, through the establishment of accounting offices, they were essential not only in providing cheap accounting services but also in turning book-keeping into an element of the collective action of farmers.

Family and farm budgets (also called surveys) had been collected by interviewers (often agricultural economists), who interviewed peasant families, since the beginning of the nineteenth century. These had been

10 J. Auderset and P. Moser, *Die Agrarfrage in der Industriegesellschaft: Wissenskulturen, Machtverhältnisse und natürliche Ressourcen in der agrarisch-industriellen Wissensgesellschaft (1850–1950)* (2018), p. 94.

11 S. Burchell *et al.*, 'The Roles of Accounting in Organizations and Society', *Accounting, Organizations and Society* 5 (1980), pp. 5–27; N. M. Gandhi, 'The Emergence of the Post-Industrial Society and the Future of the Accounting Function', *Journal of Management Studies* 13 (1976), pp. 199–212.

12 J. L. van Zanden, *De economische ontwikkeling van de Nederlandse landbouw in de negentiende eeuw, 1800–1914* (1985), p. 246.

13 P. Moser, J. Auderset and B. Baechi, 'Die agrarisch-industrielle Wissensgesellschaft im 19. / 20. Jahrhundert: Akteure, Diskurse, Praktiken', in B. Brodbeck, M. Ineichen and T. Schibli (eds), *Geschichte im virtuellen Archiv: Das Archiv für Agrargeschichte als Zentrum der Archivierung und Geschichtsschreibung zur ländlichen Gesellschaft* (2012), pp. 21–38; Auderset and Moser, *Die Agrarfrage in der Industriegesellschaft*; A. Schuurman, 'Agricultural Policy and the Dutch Agricultural Institutional Matrix during the Transition from Organized to Disorganized Capitalism: Integration through Subordination: The Politics of Agricultural Modernisation in Industrial Europe', in P. Moser and P. Varley (eds), *Integration through Subordination: The Politics of Agricultural Modernisation in Industrial Europe* (2013), pp. 65–84; M. Molema, 'Collective Organisation of Knowledge in the Early Phase of the Dutch-Friesian Dairy Industry (*c.* 1880–1914)', *Historia Agraria* 73 (2017), pp. 91–118; H. Zwarts, 'Knowledge, Networks, and Niches: Dutch Agricultural Innovation in an International Perspective, c. 1880–1970' (PhD Dissertation, Wageningen University, 2021).

used as a tool for interpreting and governing the countryside, developing from the pioneering work of social reformers, such as Frédéric Le Play, into the big enquiries of the early twentieth century.[14] But accounting offices involved farmers in the production of data that entered the policy-making process. Most of all, farm accounting offices became part of a constellation of activities and services that farmers' associations, co-ops, co-operative banks and local government offices offered to farmers. The spread of farm accounting was therefore inscribed in the broader role played by farmers' organizations and their leadership as 'defenders of agriculture' vis-à-vis the industrial interest, urban workers and governments.

The first section of this chapter describes how accounting and bookkeeping emerged as a policy question in various continental European countries in the wake of the agrarian crisis of the 1870s and 1880s. The second and third sections analyse two different institutional models for the organization of accounting services: the Dutch – in particular the organization created in the provinces of Friesland and Groningen – and the Swiss. The fourth section finally shows how farm accountancy data emerged as a form of representation of farmers' interests within European countries and in the rising international arena.

I

There is a clear link between the creation of farm accounting offices and the political activism of agriculturalists in the last decades of the nineteenth century. The actual impact of the 'agricultural crisis' of the 1870s and 1880s is debated. While some economic historians have questioned the reality and significance of the crisis, other have insisted on a 'European grain invasion' that dragged down prices and triggered a long depression.[15] In any case, it is certain that the crisis spurred a lot of discussion about the 'American threat' among the European rural elites

14 Among the extensive literature on Le Play, see T. Porter, 'The Engineer and the Sage: Le Play's Quest for Social Renewal and the Reconstruction of Observation', *History of Observation in Economics Working Paper Series* 2 (2009). On budget surveys in enquiries, F. D'Onofrio, 'Making Variety Simple: Agricultural Economists in Southern Italy, 1906–9', *History of Political Economy* 44 (2012), pp. 93–113; F. D'Onofrio, *Observing Agriculture in Early Twentieth-Century Italy: Agricultural Economists and Statistics* (2016), chs 3 and 6.

15 T. W. Fletcher, 'The Great Depression of English Agriculture, 1873–1896', *Economic History Review* 13 (1961), pp. 417–32; K. H. O'Rourke, 'The European Grain Invasion, 1870–1913', *Journal of Economic History* 57 (1997), pp. 775–801. D. Pilat, *Dutch Agricultural Export Performance (1846–1926)* (1989), p. 29 questions the impact of the crisis on Dutch agriculture.

and stimulated investigations of North American agricultural competition.[16] The perceived crisis also led to a renewed political activism, as witnessed by the creation of new farmers' associations or the reactivation of older ones across Europe, often with the goal of mobilizing farmers around a protectionist agenda. Switzerland and the Netherlands were no exceptions to this trend.

The Swiss Farmers Union was created in 1897 as part of the wave of foundations of new societies, with a clear protectionist programme following the blueprint of the German *Bund der Lanwirte*. In the Netherlands, instead, the geography of farmers' organizations was more complex, divided according to productive specialisms and on religious and ideological lines. Of the two societies discussed in the next section, the Friesland Society of Agriculture had a quasi-monopoly of agricultural representation in the province. Its farming members were mostly butter exporters who rejected protection.[17] In Groningen, farmers' organizations had a tormented history, witnessed by many name changes, and saw harsh disputes over free trade and protectionism that culminated with the resignation of its influential president Derk Roelf Mansholt in 1884, a supporter of protection.[18] At the national level, the regional *Landhuishouding Congresses* of the 1840s and 1850s, which concentrated on technical improvement and forbade discussion of trade policy, were superseded by the creation of a permanent national *Landbouw-Comité* in 1884 to coordinate the action of the government and the provincial agricultural societies.[19] Nevertheless, the *Landbouw-Comité* encompassed proponents of a protectionist reaction to the crisis as well as free-traders who favoured productive specialization ahead of overseas competition.

Organizations established in this period were divided over the importance to be accorded to tariff protection, but an interest in improved farm management was common ground for agricultural experts. The ideal of a tidy, well-administered farm appealed to both those who supported protectionist measures and those who preferred specialization within the international division of labour. For the free-traders, accounting and other managerial technologies improved efficiency. Its adoption was crucial to

16 S. Beckert, 'American Danger: United States Empire, Eurafrica, and the Territorialization of Industrial Capitalism, 1870–1950', *American Historical Review* 122 (2017), pp. 1,137–70.

17 Molema, 'Collective Organisation of Knowledge', p. 98.

18 H. M. L. Geurts, *Herman Derk Louwes (1893–1960): Burgemeester van de Nederlandse landbouw* (2002), p. 56; N. G. Addens and H. D. Louwes, *Gedenkboek, 1837–1937* (1937).

19 Schuurman, 'Agricultural Policy and the Dutch Agricultural Institutional Matrix'; idem, 'Het Nederlands Landhuishoudkundig Congres van 1846–1896: Forum en showroom van de Agrarische Republiek', in T. Engelen, A. Janssens and O. Boonstra (eds), *Levenslopen in transformatie: Liber amicorum bij het afscheid van prof. dr. Paul M. M. Klep* (2011), pp. 318–35.

enable managers to compete. These kinds of arguments in favour of the spread of book-keeping motivated the free-tradist *Landhuishouding Congresses* in the Netherlands during the 1850s and 1860s, or the *Deutsche Landwirtschafts-Gesellschaft,* in Germany, which created its accounting office in the 1890s. On the other hand, protectionists did not disagree with this fundamental function of accounting but added a new layer of importance to it. For them, farm accounting was crucial to understanding which policies, especially concerning tariffs, the farmers most needed in order to maintain a stable rate of profit, and it was a tool in the struggle for government attention. As we will see below, Ernst Laur and the organization he led, the SBV, based their actions on this conviction. To them, accounting was not an internal issue of the farm, but opened the way to a representation of the whole of agriculture in policy making. In these two fundamental goals, we see the origins of the alternative models of accounting office discussed in the following sections.

For both groups, how to convince small and medium farmers to endure the pain of keeping systematic and reliable records of the life of their farms in an accounting framework remained a key issue. Hendrikx and Gelderblom have stressed how farmers had informal systems of accounting – what they call 'mental accounting' – while Nathalie Joly has explored, instead, the conscious spread of almanacs, agendas and other kinds of publications that provided material support for the recording of facts concerning the farm as an alternative to formal systems of book-keeping. Experts often displayed a paternalistic attitude towards farmers and denied any validity to these informal records. They claimed that formal accounting was essential to help farmers acquire an economic mentality and turn into entrepreneurs.[20]

In fact, though, it would be wrong to frame the contrast between experts and farmers in the old schemes of post-modern critique that stressed the struggle between 'modern' top down schemes and grass-roots resistance.[21] It is more interesting, instead, to focus on accounting offices as the site of a broad – although far from universal – coincidence of interests between farmers and experts. In the next two sections, we discuss two examples of the institutional channels through which the co-operation between experts and farmers was achieved in Western Europe, with a particular focus on accounting offices. Whereas the cases of the Netherlands and Switzerland are neither wholly typical nor representative, they show how farm accounting offices could originate from different purposes and be either business- or policy-oriented.

20 Hendrikx and Gelderblom, 'Accounting for Agricultural Development?'; N. Joly, 'Shaping Records on the Farm: Agricultural Record Keeping in France from the Nineteenth Century to the Liberation', *Agricultural History Review* 59 (2011), pp. 61–80.

21 Y. Kotsonis, *Making Peasants Backward* (1999).

II

Agricultural associations in Groningen and Friesland relied on co-operation to provide farmers with cheap and effective accounting services. In 1886, the agricultural crisis convinced the Dutch parliament and government to establish the State Enquiry on the Condition of Agriculture, as happened elsewhere in Europe in the same period.[22] The State Enquiry dedicated a great deal of attention to the issue of accounting.[23] In the vast majority of the 95 municipalities (*gemeenten*) that it surveyed, the enquiring commission reported that either 'books were not kept' or that 'no regular books' were kept. The commissioners concluded:

> It has been found that almost nowhere is proper accounting done by farmers. With few exceptions, even the great advantages of book-keeping are not recognized. Some reporters point out these disadvantages emphatically. The peasants do not know the net yield of their fields.[24]

The focus on improved accounting and book-keeping systems was in general part of the renewed attention on the cognitive elements of agriculture, which encompassed schools, research institutions, and the circulation of information. Farmers' organizations played a major role in this three-fold system. J. M. G. van der Poel has described the creation in the nineteenth century of provincial agricultural societies in the Netherlands, first as *commissiën van landbouw* and eventually as *maatschappijen van landbouw* (agricultural societies) with their national umbrella organization the *Landbouw-Comité*.[25] These organizations, composed of farmers but also other agricultural stakeholders (who, nevertheless, were often farmers themselves) such as government officials, members of parliament and experts, strived for a directive role over local agriculture and represented its interests. Provincial agricultural societies were bulwarks of the local liberal elite, 'notables and gentlemen farmers' (*herenboeren*), but by the later part of the nineteenth century, they were in competition with newly founded associations of farmers based on religious orientation. Across the country, many smaller farmers were members of local, independent agricultural societies rather than of the provincial ones.[26] Overall, farmers' organizations had thousands of

22 For an overview of European state-sponsored agricultural enquiries, see the papers collected in N. Vivier (ed.), *The Golden Age of State Enquiries: Rural Enquiries in the Nineteenth Century. From Fact Gathering to Political Instrument* (2014).

23 A. Schuurman, 'The Agricultural Enquiry of 1890 in the Netherlands: Bringing the State Back In', in Vivier (ed.), *Golden Age of State Enquiries*, pp. 239–54.

24 Staatscommissie tot onderzoek naar de toestand van de Landbouw, *Uitkomsten van het onderzoek naar den toestand van den landbouw in Nederland* 4 (1890), p. 69.

25 J. M. G. van der Poel, *Heren en boeren* (1949).

26 Geurts, *Herman Derk Louwes*, p. 56.

members: in 1905, the members of the various farmers' organizations of the Netherlands numbered 100,328 (of whom 32 per cent were members of the provincial agricultural societies) and by 1920, membership had grown to 195,503 (of whom 36 per cent were members of the provincial agricultural societies).[27]

Although this membership was far from encompassing all farmers or even a majority of them, it was large enough to give organizations a critical mass to undertake action. Farmers' organizations ran accounting courses to respond to what they perceived as the needs of their members. In contrast with the courses that were taught in schools, these courses addressed adult farmers, who actually managed their farms. In some cases, the teacher also taught in agricultural schools of the regions, but in other cases, it seems that accountants were hired who worked independently.[28] At the same time, societies fostered the creation of standardized and simplified book-keeping aids. With a view to the dissemination of best practices, some societies employed a system of prizes similar to that already used by improvement societies of the eighteenth century: they launched a competition with anonymous submissions, collected contributions, and contracted the winning author.[29] In other cases, they directly contacted professional accountants and commissioned from the model forms.

In 1881, the *Genootschap van Nijverheid in de Provincie Groningen*, an organization that had just emerged from the merger of the *Groningen Maatschappij van Landbouw in de Provincie Groningen* and the *Genootschap ter bevordering der Nijverheid te Onderdendam* and which, for simplicity, we will call the Groningen Society of Agriculture, ordered an enquiry among its almost 1,500 members on their desiderata concerning accounting. The answers revealed a widespread interest in accounting courses and pre-printed account books especially adapted to the needs of Groningen farmers.[30]

The situation was similar in Friesland, a province in the north-west of the Netherlands that specialized in dairy farming and particularly in the production of butter. In 1886, like similar organizations, the Friesland Agricultural Society began organizing accounting courses, as part of its effort to relaunch butter production and improve the competitiveness of farmers.[31] Moreover, towards the turn of the century, the society decided

27 Ibid., p. 297.

28 Hendrikx and Gelderblom, 'Accounting for Agricultural Development?', p. 31.

29 Hist. Centrum Overijssel te Zwolle, Overijssel Maatschappji van Landbouw, 0330.1 984.

30 Addens and Louwes, *Gedenkboek, 1837–1937*, pp. 365–6.

31 Established in 1852, the Society brought together farmers, landowners, various notables and officials, see Molema, 'Collective Organisation of Knowledge',

to create a simplified system of book-keeping and commissioned two accountants, Keestra and Zijlstra, to prepare one. Book-keeping systems, though, were not simply accepted. They appeared in a competitive environment and had to persuade. Some members of the society, for instance, recommended an alternative system developed by the director of the winter school in Groningen, J. Heidema, and promoted by the Groningen Society of Agriculture.[32]

The Friesland Society printed, therefore, some experimental account books for the different parts of the farm in 1900 based on Keestra and Zijlstra's system. They consisted of the following books and lists: (a), a Profit and Loss Account; (b), Cash Book for receipts and expenses; (c), Hay and cattle list; and (d), Milk and fat content list of the cattle. Keestra and Zijlstra had clearly adapted their book-keeping system to the specific needs of the local business, dairy farming. Their lists, therefore, absorbed most of the sector-specific elements, such as the hay and cattle list and the milk and dairy fat list. Their stated purpose was really to offer each farmer an easily understandable track record of their own farm in a world of increasingly commercialized agriculture. As they put it in the presentation of their model books: 'The purpose of these accounts is to enable the practical herder to keep a record of the most important things in his business in a simple manner, and at the same time to give him an overview of the financial progress or decline of his business.'[33]

These books were tried out by 25 pastoral and 14 mixed farms, for the year 12 May 1900 to 12 May 1901 and the generally positive (but not uncritically so) experience of the participating farmers was recorded by the Secretary of the Society. The surviving documents show the Friesland Society continued printing account books for an unknown number of farmers and held courses to teach them book-keeping. The plan for a course in book-keeping (probably held in 1900) announced that

p. 101. It also promoted the creation of a Dairy School and employed dairy consultants to spread Danish methods. B. van der Burg, 'Een en ander over zuivelbereiding in Nederland: Openbare voordracht gehouden ter opening van de lessen in de zuivelbereiding aan de Rijks Hoogere Land-, tuin- en Boschbouwschool te Wageningen den 28 September 1914', *Mededeelingen van de Rijks Hoogere Land-, Tuin- en Boschbouwschool en van de daaraan verbonden instituten* 7 (1914), pp. 101–21. For the courses organised by the Friesland Society in 1909, Tresoar, Leeuwarden, 144.952 and for previous ones 144.824.

32 On Heidema's system, J. A. Kuperus, 'Boekhoudingen op nederlandse Landbouwbedrijven voor 1900: Ceres en Clio: zeven variaties op het thema landbouwgeschiedenis: geschreven ter gelegenheid van het vijfentwintigjarig bestaan van de Studiekring voor de Geschiedenis van de Landbouw', in *Agronomisch-historische bijdragen* 6 (1964), pp. 89–90.

33 Tresoar 144.824, 'Toelichting van Landbouwboekhouding op veerzoek van het Dagelijks Bestuur der Friesche Maatschappij van Landbouw samengesteld door P. Keestra en A. Zijlstra' (my translation).

accounting should provide the farmer with a 'photograph of his whole farm'. The course, free for members of the Society, was open to 'actual farmers and those men and women who were expected to take over a farm soon'.[34] In 1915, the Friesland Society published a new system and new forms adapted to the calculations required by the income tax introduced that year. The social reformer Anne Melles Rauwerda created the new forms (the 'methode-Rauwerda') which were eventually printed in a run of 1,000 copies to be distributed among the Society's members who attended book-keeping courses.[35]

In this context, Dutch agricultural societies tried very hard to establish the figure of the 'book-keeping farmer' to promote a tidy and effective agriculture, and, while the number of farmers involved remained small compared to the large rural population, the archives of the Frisian and other agricultural societies witness the existence of a demand for an accountancy service (and a corresponding offer to meet this demand by the societies and professionals), in the early twentieth century.

Nevertheless, simplified book-keeping did not solve the problem of accounting analysis. In 1900, when the Groningen Society of Agriculture (actually named at this point *Groningen Maatschappij van Landbouw en Nijverheid*) launched a new enquiry on book-keeping among its membership, along the lines of the enquiry of 1881, the enquiring committee did not stress so much the necessity of book-keeping courses. This time, it expressed, instead, the wish that the needs of its members for accounting 'be met by what is called in Germany *Buchführungsgenossenschaften* [accounting co-operatives, German in the original], whereby the members send their notes to the *Genossenschafts* [co-operative, German in the original] accountant for elaboration'.[36] It was a sign of the growing awareness of the advantages of separating accounting from book-keeping among advocates of the new managerial techniques. To some of the members of the Groningen Agricultural Society, formal accounting, especially double-entry accounting, clearly seemed too complex for the necessities and capabilities of the farmers.[37]

Keeping the books according to simplified rules was one thing, but the analysis of such books and inventories, that is, accounting proper, required more technical skills than most farmers possessed. Side by side with the 'book-keeping farmers', therefore, accounting offices appeared

34 Tresoar 144.824, 'Leerplan voor 'n curssus in 't landbouwboekhouden' (n.d.) (my translation).

35 Tresoar 144.824 various documents; on Rauwerda, see J. J. Kalma, 'Rauwerda, Anne Melles', https://socialhistory.org/bwsa/biografie/rauwerda.

36 Addens and Louwes, *Gedenkboek, 1837–1937*, p. 366.

37 When, in 1913, they discussed again the topic of farm accounting, the members of the Society stressed that 'rekenen met de puut' or 'counting with the purse' had its advantages in term of simplicity.

that collected farmers' books in order to produce financial reports, thus allowing farmers to delegate the analytical task to a professional consultant.

In the same year, the leadership of the Friesland Society of Agriculture discussed the examples coming from Germany, where different forms of accounting offices had been created either by private individuals or by agricultural associations.[38] However, it was in the wake of the introduction of income tax for farmers in 1914 that the problem of accounting became really pressing for Dutch farmers' organizations. In order to calculate the correct tax payment, farmers needed professional accountants to calculate their real income and draw up detailed inventories.[39] The Frisians and the Groningers tried two different approaches to the problem.

In 1915 the Groningen Society of Agriculture (at this point called the *Groninger Landbouwbond* after merging with other organizations) discussed the creation of a Central Bureau for the Accounting of Farm Businesses. Such a Central Bureau, as observers reported to the Friesland Society of Agriculture, was intended to provide farmers with

> simple and practical registers for recording the daily receipts and expenditures. On the basis of these registers and of inventories to be drawn up [by the accountants], the Central Bureau will then compile a complete Balance Sheet and Loss and Profit Statement for each farmer once a year.

This was explicitly connected to income tax. 'Now that farmers will soon be assessed in income tax, it is considered all the more important that they know their operating profit.'[40]

In fact, the Central Bureau was actually an accounting firm hired to assist members of the Groningen Agricultural Society (actually named *Groninger Maatschappij van Landbouw*, GMvL, after 1925) with their

38 For instance, they discussed the special offices of the DLG, whose modernizing and moderately anti-protectionist attitude appealed to Frisian farmers and which opened an accountancy office under the direction of Friederich Aereboe in 1896. Friedrich Aereboe, *Buchführung: Anleitung für den praktischen Landwirt* (1896).

39 It must be noted, though, that not all, or even not many farmers were required to fill in the tax form, since this was required only from individuals who had a minimum income of 2,000 fl. or who owned assets worth at least 16,000 fl. V. S. Ohmstede, *Wet op de inkomstenbelasting 1914, benevens wet op de vermogensbelasting, wet op de dividend- en tantièmebelasting, wet op de Raden van beroep voor de directe belastingen* (2nd edn, 1918), p. 118.

40 Tresoar, FMvL 824, Van Cor. Visser (?) to the Bestuur of the FML, 15 Apr. 1915.

accounts for a reduced fee agreed in advance.[41] To the members who asked for information, the Groningen Agricultural Society responded by sending a 'rapport' and suggesting that they keep track of their revenue and expenses and should also come to see the accountant ('on Tuesdays') for the farm inventory. In June 1918, the Groningen Agricultural Society was listing subscribers ('abonne's') with the indication of the size of their farms. For farms up to 50 hectares the cost in 1918 was 30 florins, but was raised to 40 in 1919–20.[42] Subscribers were not small farmers, since they exceeded the minimum threshold for a tax form. In that year, the new subscribers managed farms with an average size as large as 46.7 hectares, significantly larger than the average in the province.[43] They thus represented better-than-average agricultural entrepreneurs, but not the largest landowners of the province, who probably did not need the collective arrangement.

The Friesland Society followed a different path. Leeuwarden and its countryside had a pioneering tradition of co-operation. Instead of hiring an accountant, the Friesland society, therefore, sponsored in 1917 the creation of a co-operative accounting bureau for its members, the *Cooperative Centrale Landbouwboekhouding* (CCLB). On Friday, 4 May 1917, the conference hall above the Cooperative Dairy Bank in Leeuwarden hosted a gathering of a 100 people interested in the creation of the accounting co-operative. The meeting was presided over by Tj. Kuperus, administrator of the Bank, P. van der Meulen of the Inspectorate for Direct Taxation, and J. van der Meer, secretary of the Friesland Society of Agriculture. Van der Meulen had originally launched this initiative to establish collaboration between the tax authorities and the farmers. The new income tax, he claimed in his speech, made it necessary for farmers to 'break with the old habit of not keeping books', and Kuperus went as far as to say that 'Many people have experienced this firsthand, especially through taxes, that bad and good book-keeping can produce results.' Despite some opposition, the assembly approved the idea to charge a committee, including Kuperus, van der Meulen, van der Meer, and Rauwerda, with the task of preparing the statutes of the new institution.[44] The new co-operative was created with the goal of fostering agricultural book-keeping, printing model books and forms, and helping

41 Groninger Archieven 405, Groninger Maatschappij van Landbouw (1), 1837–1991, 3.02.

42 Groninger Archieven 405, 5.200, circular letter from the Secretary of the GMvL to abonne's, 17 Apr. 1919.

43 Groninger Archieven 405 5.200, 1921: Abonne's landbouwboekhouding 1919–1920, Nieuwe Abonne's; average size of farms larger than 5 ha. according to landbouwtelling of 1921, reported in E. W. Hofstee, 'De ontwikkeling van de groote der landbouwbedrijven in de provincie Groningen', *Tijdschrift voor economische geographie* 38, pp. 6–7 (1947), p. 136.

44 Tresoar 144.824, Onderlinge Coop. Centrale Landbouwboekhouding, s.d.

farmers with their inventories, books and accounting, especially for fiscal reasons. It became one of the constituent parts of the Friesland Society of Agriculture. Already in 1918, curious journalists or accountants were writing from Geeldria, Holland and as far as South Africa, asking details about the arrangements.[45] By the 1920s, the CCLB had 1,569 members.[46]

While the Central Bureau established in Groningen and the Co-operative created in Leeuwarden differed in institutional structure and legal status, they both served to separate book-keeping from accounting: farmers kept their everyday records at home, but the accounting and the inventories were done by professionals. Moreover, both tried to create economies of scale to lower the cost of professional accounting and thus to make accounting accessible to a broader share of the farming population. As we will clarify below, other provincial societies, but also private companies, created or tried to create similar institutions through the Netherlands over the course of the 1920s.

The approach adopted in Switzerland since the late nineteenth century, instead, despite similarities, had fundamentally different goals since policy making was, from the very beginning, its main (but not exclusive) purpose. Only over the course of the 1920s, and not without resistance, did the accounting offices that had sprung up in the Netherlands in the wake of the implementation of income tax begin aggregating their data for policy purposes.

III

From the 1880s, the Aargau Agricultural Society of Aarau, in Switzerland, had organized a 'winter school' for farmers who wished to learn book-keeping.[47] The economist Ernst Laur came to teach on this course at the end of the 1890s. The goals of the winter school were not dissimilar from those of the accounting courses in the Netherlands, namely, improving farm management. In his first manual of simplified book-keeping for farmers, Laur stressed that in the modern world, where the farm produced for the market and the farmer's goal was to make money, new techniques were needed to assess the success of the farm and the value of the soil. He highlighted that 'the difficulty of the problem (of running a profitable farm) completely excludes the possibility to solve

45 Tresoar 144.824, various letters.

46 Tresoar 144.377, Secretary of the FMvL to Riksfoerbundet Landsvygdens Folk of Stockholm, unreadable date.

47 The Aargauische landwirtschaftliche Gesellschaft was founded in 1838, Aargauische landwirtschaftliche Gesellschaft (ed.), *Die Landwirtschaft im Kanton Aargau: Festschrift zur Feier des 100jährigen Bestehens der Aargauischen landwirtschaftlichen Gesellschaft* (1911).

the computations mentally and keep all the different cases in mind'.[48] Modern farm management, in a commercial society, required therefore the adoption of some form of recording system. 'Through book-keeping' – Laur continued – 'the farmer will be able for the first time to judge his own economic action and draw from the experiences of the past useful conclusions for the future'.

Book-keeping was a discipline of self-observation for farmers.[49] For Laur, the experience of book-keeping would transform the farmers themselves and their mentality and it would divert them from old habits:

> Let us not forget the high educational value of agricultural accounting ... Book-keeping stimulates observation and reasoning. It sharpens economic sense and frees agriculturalists from the impressions left by past times and condition that still obscure their gaze.[50]

It was a crucial component of agricultural modernity.

Laur became Professor of Agricultural Economics at the Federal Polytechnical School in Zurich and head of the Secretariat of Swiss peasants of the Swiss Farmers' Union (SBV). He thus combined an academic position with a political role at the helm of an interest group representing thousands of farmers across the country (almost 93,000 in 1906).[51] His goals expanded accordingly. The Swiss parliament funded the accounting office of the Union in order to 'collect materials and conduct preliminary studies for an effective representation of farmers' interests'.[52] Laur used such funds to establish in Brugg the accounting office of the SBV, whose task was to assist and instruct Swiss farmers in book-keeping and accounting. While farmers recorded sales and expenses for their own purposes, therefore, the Swiss Farmers Union was also collecting precious data: thousands of account books, which it intended to use to describe the economic situation and interests of Swiss farmers.

Laur's PhD advisor in Leipzig, Hermann Wilhelm Howard, had established a *Buchführunggesellschaft* (accounting society) in the 1870s. Laur's model for this data-collecting activity, though, was the famous Saxon and then Prussian statistician Ernst Engel. Howard had focused on the profitability of the individual farm and in general preached a business-centric approach. Engel instead had underlined the importance of book-keeping

48 E. Laur, *Die Buchhaltung des Schweizerbauern* (1898), p. 4.

49 On the connection between observation and observance: K. Park, 'Observation in the Margin, 500–1500', in L. Daston and E. Lunbeck (eds), *Histories of Scientific Observation* (2011), pp. 15–44.

50 Laur, *Die Buchhaltung des Schweizerbauern*, p. 6.

51 Secrétariat des Paysans Suisses, *Statistiques et évaluations agricoles* (1923), p. 25.

52 *Botschaft des Bundesrates an die Bundesversammlung betreffend das Budget für das Jahr 1898*, 5 Nov. 1897, p. 269.

for broader goals of statistical surveillance and practically demonstrated its potential for research. He had aggregated the data provided by the family budgets collected by the Belgian statistician Édouard Ducpétiaux to identify regular relations between the different measures and had thus discovered that the share of food expenses over total expenses, as a rule, decreased when income increased.[53] In 1882, in a lecture he gave on the 'Housewife's accounting book and its place in the economic life of the nation', he envisaged the possibility of an institution to collect all the accounting books kept by housewives across Germany in order to centralize them and obtain 'instruments to measure the welfare of the nation'.[54] Laur had been in contact with Engel when he studied in Leipzig and he clearly recognized the potential of aggregated accountancy data.

In the first years of the century, somewhat more than 100 farmers per year could enrol in the course of the SBV, but many more than this applied. In 1903, for instance, the newspaper of the SBV, the *Bauernzeitung*, reported that only half of the applicants to the book-keeping course could be admitted.[55] In 1904, only 126 out of 216 applications could be accepted.[56] The *Bauernzeitung* claimed that the farmers who took the course were well satisfied by it, and this was confirmed by the high proportion of them who, after keeping accounts for a year, returned their ledger books to the accounting office in Brugg. In 1901, for instance, the newspaper claimed that a majority of participants had been so happy with book-keeping in the first year that they continued keeping accounts for the following ones and only 6 farmers had decided to drop out, for health issues or other justified problems.[57]

Even more than in the Dutch case, this number was very small compared to the number of farmers in Switzerland (there were 243,000 farms in 1905 and 238,000 farms in 1929 in the country), even compared

53 E. Engel, 'Die vorherrschenden Gewerbszweige in den Gerichtsämtern mit Beziehung auf die Productions- und Consumtionsverhältnisse des Königreichs Sachsen', *Wirtschaft und Statistik* 73 (1857), pp. 126–36; idem, 'Die Lebenskosten belgischer Arbeiter-Familien früher und jetzt – Ermittelt aus Familien-Haushaltrechnungen und vergleichend zusammengestelt', *Bulletin de l'Institut International de Statistique* IX (1895), pp. 1–124.

54 E. Engel, *Das Rechnungsbuch der Hausfrau und seine Bedeutung im Wirthschaftsleben der Nation: ein Vortrag* (1882), pp. 36–7. I am indebted to Max Ehrenfreund for stressing the importance of this citation.

55 'Buchhaltungkurses des schweizerischen Sekretariates', *Bauernzeitung* 3 (3) (Mar. 1903), p. 11.

56 'Buchhaltungkurs des schweizerischen Bauernsekretariates', *Bauernzeitung* 2 (4) (Feb. 1904).

57 'Die Rentabilitaetserhebungen des schweiz. Bauernsekretariat', *Bauernzeitung* 5 (1) (Nov. 1901), pp. 19–20.

to the broad membership of the SBV.[58] Considering the significant commitment implied by the course, though, such participation testifies to an expanding kernel of highly motivated farmers. What were their motives to attend the courses and open their books to the SBV? The reasons the documents mention include farmers' concern that they did not overpay for land and their need for precise accounts and inventories to calculate the shares that belonged to different heirs.[59] Laur underlined how the need for the SBV accounting assistance was mostly felt by young farmers who had just inherited their farm. He remarked that they rarely continued account-keeping for more than three years and even then often limited themselves to cash-receipts and disbursements after they stopped submitting their records to the central office of the SBV.[60]

While the farmers' individual needs were essential to motivate farmers, from the very beginning, the SBV accounting office intended to use the data to foster the Union's political objectives.[61] By aggregating farm accountancy data, Laur was able to speak about trends that involved the entire agricultural sector and could use his surveys of profitability to establish collective agency for Swiss farmers. On the columns of the *Bauernzeitung*, for instance, the Swiss Farmers Union amplified the message of its annual reports on the accountancy data survey and explained how policy proposals concerning health insurance schemes or tariffs affected farmers' income. The growing membership of the SBV must have been aware of the importance that this data had in enabling them to achieve the collective goals of the organizations. The enemies of the SBV, on the left and on the right, clearly saw the crucial role of these numbers. As late as 1952, Laur's opponents wrote sarcastically that:

> when the figures from Brugg [the seat of the accounting office of the SBV] march in, all mere assumptions and opinions retreat into a quiet corner in the face of this erudition and are ashamed of their impertinence, which is not verified by any science, to have spoken out at all in such a circle.[62]

58 Number of farms in 1905: Secrétariat des Paysans Suisses, *Statistiques et évaluations agricoles*, p. 5; number of farmers in 1929: International Institute of Agriculture, *The First World Agricultural Census* (1939), III, p. 315.

59 Walter J. Roth, 'Farm Accounting Investigations in Switzerland', *Journal of Farm Economics* 13 (1931), p. 561.

60 Ibid., p. 558.

61 Laur, *Die Buchhaltung des Schweizerbauern*, p. 6.

62 Schweizerischer Verband für Wohnungswesen, 'Die Rentabilitätserhebungen des schweizerischen Bauernsekretariates im Lichte statistischer Wissenschaft', *Wohnen* 27 (1952), pp. 213–14.

IV

Laur's approach attracted considerable interest in Europe and Laur himself was an indefatigable promoter of his own achievements. He transformed individual account ledgers into precious data, key tools for agricultural economists and policy makers. The peculiarity of the activity of the Swiss Peasant Union was evident to farm accountancy experts abroad. Georg Stieger, who headed the accounting office of the DLG in Germany, remarked upon it in 1909. He observed that Laur sought to provide the government with a solid basis for its price policies, so that the government could identify by how much prices must rise (or the costs fall) in order to guarantee the farmers a remuneration of 4 per cent on their assets. This was the reason – Stieger continued – why Laur was interested in the statistical treatment of data (the approach which his teacher Howard had rejected).[63]

In the countries of Northern, Central and Eastern Europe especially, agricultural organizations began discussing and then imitating the accounting office of the SBV. Since 1911, drawing on the Swiss experience, the Finnish Confederation of Agricultural Associations began collecting farm accountancy data. The programme was eventually transferred to the government-led Agricultural Board in 1915.[64] In Denmark a similar office appeared before 1918.[65] Similar offices are reported in Sweden, Norway and the Kingdom of Poland over the course of the 1910s. Emulation was favoured by an active policy of the SBV to keep the accounting office in Brugg open to visitors from all over Europe: many generations of agricultural economists from all over Europe and the USA came to Brugg.[66]

In 1913, when Laur attended the General Assembly of the International Institute of Agriculture (IIA), he read a report on Farm Accountancy Data Statistics that was received with great interest. At the end, the Austrian delegation proposed that the Institute collect information on farm accountancy offices in order to be able to 'use the results of accounting institutions for its own statistical and economic research'.[67] An article by

63 G. Stieger, 'Moeglichkeit und Bedeutung landwirtschaftlicher Produktionskostenberechnungen', *Jahrbuch der Deutschen Landwirtschafts-Gesellschaft* 24 (1909), pp. 950–81.

64 H. Järvelä and A.-M. Aarnio, *Maatalouden kannattavuustutkimus 75 vuotta* (1987), p. 116.

65 See Lampe and Sharp, 'Quest for Useful Knowledge'.

66 H. Haumann and W. Baumann, '"... Um die Organisation des typischen Arbeitsbetriebes kennenzulernen": Zu Aleksandr Čajanovs Schrift "Bäuerliche Wirtschaft in der Schweiz"', *Schweizerische Zeitschrift für Geschichte/Revue Suisse d'Histoire/Rivista Storica Svizzera* (1997), pp. 1–26.

67 Institut International d'Agriculture, 'Séances plénières de l'Assemblée Générale – Séance du samedi 10 Mai', *Actes de la quatrième Assemblée Générale, 6–12 Mai 1913* (1913), p. 59.

Laur in the Institute's journal followed shortly afterwards in which he proposed a standardized nomenclature.[68] The Institute assigned to the Italian agricultural economist Ernesto Marenghi the task of surveying all the existing farm accounting offices of Europe.[69] The work was resumed after the war, with the General Assembly of 1920, and led to the publication of a book by the IIA.[70] In 1924, the IIA promoted the creation and/or reorganization of accounting offices in its member countries in order to collect data on a standardized questionnaire, devised by Paul Deslarzes, Laur's man in Rome, using the nomenclature invented by Laur.

We can see the influence of these efforts in the Netherlands. Dutch accounting offices, such as those created in Friesland and Groningen, had emerged out of the necessity for farmers to have precise accounts of the profitability of their farms in the wake of the income tax reform,[71] but, following the Swiss example and the suggestions of the International Institute of Agriculture, they also began aggregating their data. By 1921–2, at the latest, the Directorate of Agriculture at the Ministry of Internal Affairs had begun collecting accountancy data from the network of the government's agricultural consultants (*Rijkslandbouwconsulenten*), an institution created to foster the adoption of new technologies and management techniques.[72] The data, though, were scarce and unsystematic.[73] Thus, in 1925, the *Landbouw-Comité* decided to create a Union of the Farm Accounting Offices (*Vereeniging Landbouwboekhouden*) that had come into existence after the introduction of income tax in the 1910s.

On 21 March 1926, the Secretary of the Landbouw-Comité, Dr H. Molhuysen, and J. A. Stoop, a tax inspector from Tiel, welcomed the representatives of farm accounting offices in the Hague. Stoop proposed

68 E. Laur, 'Basis of International Statistics of Agricultural Book-keeping', *Monthly Bulletin of Agricultural Intelligence and Plant Diseases* 5 (1914), pp. 171–85.

69 E. Marenghi, 'Organizzazione ed importanza degli uffici di contabilità per lo studio dell'economia dell'azienda agraria', *Rivista Italiana Di Ragioneria* (1914), 4, pp. 162–75; 5, pp. 201–4; 6, pp. 241–6; 7, pp. 289–301; 8, pp. 329–38; 9, pp. 386–90: E. Marenghi, 'Gli uffici di contabilità agraria nei diversi paesi', *Atti della Reale Accademia dei Georgofili* 99 (1921), pp. 100–12.

70 Institut International d'Agriculture, *Les offices de comptabilité agricole dans les différents pays* (1924).

71 The effect of the income tax has been stressed in particular by Hendrikx and Gelderblom, 'Accounting for Agricultural Development?'.

72 On the crucial importance of the *consulenten* and the winter schools they ran in educating Dutch farmers, see Zwarts, 'Knowledge, Networks, and Niches', pp. 105–9.

73 Nationaal Archief ten Haag, Directie van de Landbouw: Afdeling Landbouw-Economische Aangelegenheden: Landbouwboekhouding 1923–1930, 2.11.08.02-6.

they join forces and standardize their accounting methods.[74] If, initially, the stated objective was to establish co-operation between tax inspectors (*het fiscus*) and farmers to overcome some of the problems caused by the income tax, in April 1926, Stoop and the agricultural economist Geert Minderhoud (former Secretary of the Groningen Society of Agriculture) introduced the idea of using the data for statistical purposes. They believed that accounting offices would be a much better source of information than the agricultural consultants. Stoop insisted therefore on the necessity to homogenize account books and inventories.[75] The offices were asked to anonymize the information they collected from their members and transmit it to the Directorate of Agriculture, thus transforming private accounts into public data. Minderhoud explained that the models were to be the German Agricultural Council (*Landwirtschaftsrat*) and the Swiss Peasant Union.[76] In this way, accounting offices that had been created for the sake of helping individual businesses could be turned into elements of the governance of agriculture.

Significantly, the Friesland Society of Agriculture and the CCLB (which, according to the members of the *Landbouw-Comité*, gathered half of the total number of farm accounts in the Netherlands)[77] decided not to join this Union. In response to pressure from Stoop, the secretary of the Friesland Society of Agriculture clarified its position in November 1926, saying that they feared centralization, rejected too close a relationship

74 Nationaal Archief ten Haag, Circular letter from Molhuysen, No. 75/651 Onderwerp: Vereeniging Landbouwboekhouden, 7 Oct. 1926, Vereniging Landbouwboekhouden. 'Vereniging Landbouwboekhouden: Oprichting', n.d. 2.19.042.49-1. Apart from the *Landbouw-Comité*, the founding members of the Union were the accounting offices of the agricultural societies of Drente, Holland, Utrecht, Gheldria and Overijssel, Groninengen, North-Brabant and Zeland. The Union of Cheese Producers joined in 1927. Nationaal Archief ten Haag. Vereniging Landbouwboekhouden. 'Vereniging Landbouwboekhouden: Toetreding Leden', n.d. 2.19.042.49-2. Molhuysen to Stoop, 25 Feb. 1927.

75 Nationaal Archief ten Haag, Summary of the meeting of the heads of provincial accounting offices held in the Hague, 22 Apr. 1926, Vereniging Landbouwboekhouden. 'Vereniging Landbouwboekhouden: Oprichting', n.d. 2.19.042.49-1.

76 Nationaal Archief ten Haag, Notule van de vergadering van het bestuur en de commissie van toezicht van de vereeniging 'Landbouwboekhouden' of diensdag 30 Apr. 1929, Vereniging Landbouwboekhouden. 'Vereniging Landbouwboekhouden: Correspondentie, Geregistreerd in Numerieke Dossierorde in Volgorde van Aanhangigmaking. 1929–1930', 2.19.042.49–10.

77 Nationaal Archief ten Haag, Summary of the meeting of the heads of provincial accounting offices held in The Hague, 31 Mar. 1926, Vereniging Landbouwboekhouden. 'Vereniging Landbouwboekhouden, n.d. 2.19.042.49-4: Ingekomen vergaderstukken van het Koninklijk Nederlandsch Landbouw-Comité.

with the tax authorities, adding that they really saw no need for the proposed uniformity.[78] Although the CCLB over the course of the 1930s provided anonymized figures to the government, its managers firmly refused to bend the accounting methods devised for the private benefit of their members to the standards required by nationwide statistical analysis.

Internationally, Laur's project of an international statistics of farm accountancy data seemed to bear fruit after 1928, when the IIA started collecting farm accountancy data for the statistical series *Recueil de statistiques basées sur les données de la comptabilité agricole*, which ran until the end of the 1930s. This statistical enterprise was underpinned by the broad support which Laur's proposal received from European rural organizations, which strove to standardize farm accountancy data according to the principles established at the Bucharest International Congress of Agriculture in 1929. In the wake of the congress, Laur shared a circular letter to the directors of accounting offices and professors of agricultural economics across Europe proposing a standardized terminology for farm accountancy data – a terminology adopted by the Dutch Union of Farm Accounting Offices, among others.[79] Over the course of 10 years, the IIA was thus able to publish accountancy data from a number of countries, ultimately 25 in all.

Despite growing criticism on the side of statisticians (who questioned the actual representativeness of the surveys),[80] farm accountancy data remained an important tool of agricultural policy in the inter-war period. The most important agricultural economist in the USA, Henry C. Taylor – whose relationship with Laur was always polemical – insisted on the complementarity of accountancy data to general production and consumption statistics, focusing on their importance to the new system of quotas. He stressed how they permitted the establishment of natural advantage in production.[81] In 1938, after the foundation of the *Office Centrale de la Comptabilité Agricole* at Soissons, France, the agricultural economist Michel Augé Laribé could affirm the importance of farm accountancy data to establish 'a general index of economic activity for

78 The response of the Frisian Society was summarized by J. A. Stoop to Molhuysen, 30 Nov. 1926, Vereniging Landbouwboekhouden. 'Vereniging Landbouwboekhouden: Toetreding Leden', Nationaal Archief ten Haag, n.d. 2.19.042.49-2.

79 Laur to the Mssrs the directors of the accounting offices and the professors of agricultural economics, 15 Aug. 1929, Archivio dell'Accademia dei Georgofili, Fondo Tassinari, p. 66.

80 C. Gini, 'Il progettato trasferimento degli uffici di statistica agraria, Allegati ai verbali delle sedute nella sessione del 1926, Dicembre 1926 – V', *Annali di Statistica: Atti del Consiglio superiore di statistica, serie VII* (1930), pp. 238–45.

81 The State Historical Society of Wisconsin, Henry C. Taylor Papers, 1896–1968, letter dated Rome, 9 Nov. 1934 to Hobson.

agriculture'.[82] Finally, in 1965, the European Economic Community, under the impulse of the Dutch Commissioner Sicco Mansholt of Groningen, decided that the 'development of the Common Agricultural Policy' required 'that there should be available objective and relevant information on incomes in the various categories of agricultural holding and on the business operation of holdings coming within categories which call for special attention at Community level'. The Farm Accountancy Data Network was established to co-ordinate the activity of the various national farm accounting offices that existed or were to be established.[83]

V

Since the eighteenth century many writers on agriculture, as extensively shown by the other chapters of this volume, have preached the virtues of well-kept accounts. But it is really only the twentieth century that witnessed institutionalized efforts to spread book-keeping among small and medium farmers and to provide services for accounting at relatively low fees or for free. The bulk of this effort was done by the local and national farmers' associations that emerged in the second half of the nineteenth century or that were dramatically reorganized in reaction to the agrarian crisis of the 1870–80s. Attempts at spreading book-keeping and accounting should not be taken in isolation, but should be considered as part of the general role that agricultural elites (experts, politicians, large landowners, officials) took on as 'guardians' of the broader agricultural population. Accounting education and services were part of a broader provision of public goods to European farmers which were meant to improve productivity and the standard of living of farmers.[84] This educational effort was often deemed incompatible with double-entry book-keeping, which seemed impractical and cumbersome. If capitalist rationality was part of the modernization of the countryside, it came rather with single-entry simplified book-keeping.

The Swiss and the Dutch case show interesting parallels (the importance of the action of regional and national organizations, the separation

82 *Rapport sur la mission de M. Baumont à l'Assemblée de l'Institute International d'Agriculture, Mai 1938* (translated by the author from the French original), United Nations Library and Archives, Geneva, League of Nations Secretariat, Economic and Financial Section, File R4374/10A/944/944/Jacket2 – Agriculture – Collaboration between the Secretariat and the International Institute of Agriculture: general questions.

83 Regulation No. 79/65/EEC of the Council of 15 June 1965 setting up a network for the collection of accountancy data on the incomes and business operation of agricultural holdings in the European Economic Community, DD I § (1965). http://data.europa.eu/eli/reg/1965/79/oj/eng.

84 G. Federico, *Feeding the World: An Economic History of Agriculture, 1800–2000* (2005).

of accounting and book-keeping, the increasing role of government), but also important differences: in Groningen and Leeuwarden cooperative models prevailed, with a higher degree of commercialization of the service; in Switzerland the government played a bigger role in funding the accounting office of the SBV and Laur started very early on to use accountancy data to represent the interests of farmers in policy debates. Whereas Laur, from the very beginning, intended the farm accounting office of the *Schweizerisches Bauernsekretariat* to be an observatory of general economic trends, the *Cooperative Centrale Landbouwboekhouding* of the Friesland Society of Agriculture and the Central Bureau of the Groningen Society of Agriculture initially responded only to the farmers' direct needs for precise accounting. Yet, even in the Dutch case, the main function of such accounting offices was not to equip farmers with better management techniques but to help them respond to the needs of the government and of the farmers' organizations for data.

The polarity became even less pronounced in the inter-war period, when government support for agriculture acquired a dominating role, and Dutch farmers' organizations integrated their accounting offices into a national network to turn account books into data. The generalization of book-keeping went hand in hand with the integration of family farms within a network of institutions and with extensive state support, as the standard form of agricultural production. It was precisely farmers' organizations that – with the support of governments – provided farmers with specific accounting services. The representative function of farm accountancy data became crucial for the State and the farmers' organizations that collected the data, to the point that farm accountancy officers spread across Europe. Switzerland and the Netherlands thus provide an outline of the experience of other European countries, and show how accounting offices arose either to meet the needs of private consulting or policy-making.

10

Agricultural Book-keeping in Switzerland: Adaptations, Institutionalisation and its Impact on the Perception of Gender Roles on the Farm

Peter Moser

Growth was a central sign of socio-economic change in the late eighteenth and early nineteenth centuries.[1] The invention of the steam engine made it possible to power machinery in industrial manufacturing by consuming fossil fuels from the lithosphere instead of the previous use of biotic resources from the biosphere. Since the energy resources in industry no longer had to be reproduced, the manufacturing of goods in factories could now be organised continuously, largely independent of seasonal fluctuations. This allowed a strict division of labour and led to a continuous growth of the economy. In agriculture, the innovations of the first agricultural revolution also resulted in increased production.[2] But the new growth in agriculture was still based on the use of biotic resources, i.e. animals and plants that had to be reproduced in the production process. Growth in agricultural production therefore

1 This chapter is based on J. Auderset and P. Moser, 'Die numerische Zergliederung des Agrarischen. Landwirtschaftliche Buchhaltung und Statistik', *Die Agrarfrage in der Industriegesellschaft. Wissenskulturen, Machtverhältnisse und natürliche Ressourcen in der agrarisch-industriellen Wissensgesellschaft (1850–1950)* (2018), pp. 49–102.

2 For an overview of the historiography of the 'agricultural revolutions', see Paul Bairoch, 'Les trois révolutions agricoles du monde développé. Rendements et productivité de 1800 à 1985', *Annales E.S.C.* 44 (1989), pp. 317–53; Peter Moser and Tony Varley (eds), *Integration through Subordination. The Politics of Agricultural Modernisation in Industrial Europe* (2013); Paul Brassley *et al.*, *The Real Agricultural Revolution. The Transformation of English Farming, 1939–1985* (2021).

remained cyclical and seasonally limited. In winter, the land still lay fallow. Cows only gave milk after they had produced calves which needed a share of the cows' milk for themselves.

The spatial and temporal idiosyncrasies resulting from these differences between industrial *manufacturing* and agricultural *production* were increasingly perceived as a problem in the emerging industrial societies in which the terms 'modern' and 'industrial' became seen as one and the same. Therefore, from the middle of the nineteenth century onwards, modernising farming practices primarily meant seeking to emulate the new mode of industrial production by re-organising agricultural production. But since the primary resource base of agricultural production remained the use of living animals and plants, the results of the modernising measures introduced in farming were often significantly different from those in industry. While, for example, the combustion engine rapidly displaced draught animals in industrial manufacturing, horses, oxen, cows and dogs became even more important in agriculture as can be observed by the increase in the number of working animals on farms from the middle of the nineteenth century onwards.[3] The same applies to wage labour. While it became a constitutive element in industry, it began to decline in agriculture towards the end of the nineteenth century, when large farms were displaced by family farms.[4] Therefore, agriculture, and quite often those engaged in it, became increasingly perceived as deviating from what was now the industrially defined norm. This perception strengthened the pre-existing resolve to modernise farming and those working the land along industrial lines. One attempt at doing this was to convert peasants into farmers who conformed to the standards that were set by the manufacturing industry. This normative ideal was succinctly formulated by the Swiss politician Zacharias Gysel, a farmer himself, who in 1854 (anonymously) published a book with the revealing title: 'The [...] peasant as he should be, and is not, and how he is and should not be'.[5]

Gysel was not an isolated figure. Rather, he was part of a growing number of scientists, civil servants, politicians and progressive farmers who became dedicated to modernising agriculture according to the norms followed in manufacturing industry. Many representatives of

3 J. Auderset and H-. U. Schiedt, 'Arbeitstiere. Aspekte animalischer Traktion in der Moderne', *traverse* 28 (2021), pp. 27–42; P. Moser and H-. U. Schiedt, 'Arbeitstiere im langen 19. Jahrhundert. Empirische Evidenzen und soziale Kontexte', *Schweizerisches Jahrbuch für Sozial- und Wirtschaftsgeschichte* (2022), pp. 199–226.

4 N. Koning, *The Failure of Agrarian Capitalism: Agrarian Politics in the United Kingdom, Germany, the Netherlands and the USA, 1846–1919* (1994); H. Levi, *Entstehung und Rückgang des landwirtschaftlichen Grossbetriebes in England* (1904).

5 Z. Gysel, *Der Schaffhauser Bauer, wie er sein sollte, und wie er nicht ist, wie er ist, und wie er nicht sein sollte* (1854).

the emerging 'agrarian-industrial knowledge society'[6] identified book-keeping as a particularly effective instrument for achieving this goal. For book-keeping was not only an instrument through which 'the world was disenchanted', as Max Weber put it,[7] it was also an instrument through which the 'cosmos' of the industrial capitalist world could be opened up, as Werner Sombart pointed out. With double-entry book-keeping, the idiosyncrasies of the agrarian world had to be reduced by definition to their monetary value, that is, in a capitalist society, their price.[8] There is hardly another instrument that guides actors with similar rigidity and simultaneously forces them to reduce the social, economic, biochemical and ecological processes to numbers and thus to an apparent uniqueness. Double-entry book-keeping was a mathematised language in which representatives of the industrial capitalist world, who were not interested in the peculiarities of agricultural reproduction, could talk about agrarian issues.[9] Not surprisingly, it subsequently was 'numbers, not narrative, that became the dominant language of agricultural knowledge' in industrial societies.[10]

However, before the book-keeping method that had been developed in commercial and industrial spheres could successfully be applied on a substantial number of farms in the twentieth century, it had to be adapted to the peculiarities of agricultural reproduction. This chapter, therefore, first deals with the process of adapting the book-keeping methods to the realities of the agricultural world at the end of the nineteenth century. The second part then focuses on the efforts to institutionalise the accounting system in Switzerland, where in the first half of the twentieth century a substantial number of male and female farmers began keeping accounts on their farms. The third and finalpart asks who was actually performing the book-keeping work and how this practice affected gender relations on the farms.

6 Auderset and Moser, *Die Agrarfrage in der Industriegesellschaft*, pp. 15–48.

7 M. Weber, 'Wissenschaft als Beruf', in M. Sukale (ed.), *Schriften zur Wissenschaftslehre* (1991), p. 250.

8 W. Sombart, *Der moderne Kapitalismus* (1917), p. 120.

9 P. Miller, 'Governing by Numbers. Why Calculative Practices Matter', *Social Research* 68 (2001), p. 381; T. M. Porter, 'Making Things Quantitative', in M. Power (ed.), *Accounting and Science. Natural Inquiry and Commercial Reason* (1994), p. 44.

10 D. Fitzgerald, *Every Farm a Factory. The Industrial Ideal in American Agriculture* (2003), p. 35.

I

In the second half of the nineteenth century chemists developed a particular affinity for accounting terminology.[11] They were convinced that by using this language they could measure, calculate, compare and describe agricultural production which is characterised by biochemical metabolic processes and, therefore, hardly possible to describe in static terms. Inspired by the German chemist Justus von Liebig, agronomists urged their contemporaries to understand agricultural material flows as transactions analogous to the monetary flows in accounting. Thus, accounting became the 'master metaphor' between agriculture, chemistry and economics.[12] Joseph Schild, a student of Liebig's, already spoke in the title of his first publication of an 'increase in the agricultural economy and a decrease in the alpine economy', when he wanted to address the unequal development of the agricultural production in Switzerland. Schild also saw 'the liquid capital' of agriculture as equivalent to the 'soluble material' from the mineral components of the soil that were taken up by the plant.[13] His colleague Rudolf Theodor Simler, who had worked as a chemist at the universities of Breslau and Bern before he began teaching chemistry to young farmers in agricultural colleges, even more explicitly used a terminology inspired by accounting in his publications.[14]

The relevance of accounting for the perception of agriculture in industrial societies far exceeds its practical dissemination on farms in the nineteenth century. Accounting was not only a calculative practice on the farm, it also shaped the relationship between industrial society and agriculture.[15] The introduction of book-keeping on farms had the effect of viewing the modern world exclusively through the lens of the social sciences modelled on industrial capitalist relations.

11 E. Pawley, 'Accounting with the Fields. Chemistry and Value in Nutriment in American Agricultural Improvement, 1835–1860', *Science as Culture* 19 (2010), pp. 461–82.

12 A. Klamer and D. McCloskey, 'Accounting as the Master Metaphor of Economics', *The European Accounting Review* 1 (1992), pp. 145–60; N. Jas, *Au carrefour de la chimie et de l'agriculture. Les sciences agronomiques en France et en Allemagne, 1840–1914* (2001).

13 J. Schild, *Die Zunahme der Land- und die Abnahme der Alpen-Wirthschaft der Schweiz* (1863), p. 3. For Joseph Schild (1824–66), see https://www.histoirerurale.ch/pers/personnes/Schild,_Joseph_(1824_1866)__DB3100.html. (viewed 28 July 2024).

14 R. T. Simler, *Ueber die Nothwendigkeit landwirthschaftlich-chemischer Laboratorien und Versuchsstationen in der Schweiz* (1864), p. 46. For R. T. Simler (1833–73), see https://www.histoirerurale.ch/pers/personnes/Simler,_Rudolf_Theodor_(1833_1873)__DB3342.html. (viewed 28 July 2024).

15 Miller, 'Governing by Numbers', p. 379.

> Accounting was one of the foundations for the emerging social sciences, helped economists to construct their analyses of the economy, and lit Marx's way in understanding the capitalist system; his analysis, reworked by Sombart, would later lead to the concept of capitalism.[16]

It is therefore not surprising that, when farmers began to keep accounts on their farms, they not only encountered solutions, but distortions as well. They encountered two problems in particular. The first concerned the valuation of products such as hay or young stock which resulted from production processes on the farm itself. Since they were neither bought nor sold (but kept as fodder or for replacing older animals), they had no price in accounting terms, even though they were absolutely necessary for the farm economy.[17] Comparable difficulties arose when it came to the valuation of the land which farmers did not want to sell, but to cultivate.

Those who advocated a widespread implementation of book-keeping in the agricultural sector had, therefore, to be willing and able to adapt the accounting templates to the idiosyncrasies of agriculture. Adolf Kraemer, an early advocate of book-keeping in agriculture, admitted in the expanded version of his book *Die Buchhaltung des Landwirts* ('The Farmer's Accounting') that one would only 'make progress' with the spread of double-entry book-keeping on farms if one recognized that agricultural activities were 'a *special* form of industrial activity'.[18]

As a solution to the problem of valuing products which were produced on the farm not for sale, but for internal use on the farm itself, Kraemer suggested that the farmer should take the market price, i.e. the price which one would have realized or paid in case of a sale or purchase.[19] As convincing as this proposal sounded at a first glance, it was precisely the method that farmers like Albert von Fellenberg-Ziegler explicitly rejected, because it produced 'arbitrarily assumed' values and figures for the individual farm which neither bought nor sold these products. In this matter, the progressive practical farmer Fellenberg-Ziegler adhered more clearly than the scientist Kraemer to the accounting principle that 'all book-keeping and accounting methods that were not based on cash' were

16 E. Chiapello, 'Accounting and the Birth of the Notion of Capitalism', *Critical Perspectives on Accounting* 18 (2007), pp. 263–96 at p. 283.

17 This point was also raised in other countries. For the discussion in France see Y. Lemarchand *et al.*, 'Schisme à Grignon autour de la comptabilité agricole, durant les années 1870', *Entreprises et histoire* 88 (2017), pp. 37–52.

18 A. Kraemer, *Die Buchhaltung des Landwirts* (1881), p. v. For Adolf Kraemer (1832–1910), see https://www.histoirerurale.ch/pers/personnes/Kraemer,_Adolf_(1832_1910)__DB2000.html. (viewed 28 July 2024).

19 Kraemer, *Die Buchhaltung des Landwirts*, p. 59.

'wrong in their fundamentals'. For only what was 'received and spent by cash' could, in accounting terms, 'produce a correct balance sheet'.[20]

It was the young agronomist Ernst Laur who set about adapting the double-entry book-keeping method to agricultural conditions in the 1890s.[21] Together with colleagues, Laur developed a method for determining the *value of output* for land that farmers wanted to cultivate. This was particularly urgent because since the late 1870s the value of output for land for agricultural production began to diverge significantly from the *market value* of land, i.e., the price paid for land when it was sold.[22] Albert Thaer was the first who proposed to differentiate between the value of output and the market value of land in the early nineteenth century.[23] But because industry and agriculture grew at more or less an equal rate in the first half of the nineteenth century, the value of output of agricultural land and the market price for land hardly differed and therefore Thaer's insight was not taken up by scientists and politicians. It was not until the transport revolution, industrialisation and population growth in the second half of the century that the value of output of agricultural land and the price for land began to diverge substantially in many parts of Europe. Thus, prices for agricultural land began to rise not because of an increase in demand for land for agricultural production, but because the price for land for the construction of factory buildings, roads, railroads, housing and other infrastructures of the industrial societies began to rise sharply.[24]

The agronomist Heinrich Abt has argued that ever since the late 1870s farmers had been paying too much for the land they were acquiring for cultivation since even the price for land they acquired by inheritance had become increasingly based on prices paid for land acquired for non-agricultural development. Abt was convinced that not only had overseas competition contributed to the agricultural crisis of the late nineteenth century, but also so had the lack of suitable accounting

20 A. Fellenberg-Ziegler, 'Über landwirthschaftliche Buchhaltung', *Bernische Blätter für Landwirtschaft* 15 (1861), p. 88.

21 For E. F. Laur (1871–1964), see https://www.histoirerurale.ch/pers/personnes/Laur,_Ernst_Ferdinand_(1871_1964)__DB2092.html. (viewed 28 July 2024).

22 A. Kraemer, 'Reinertrag und Einkommen aus der Landwirthschaft-Ertragswerth, Verkehrswerth und Preis des Grundbesitzes', *Landwirtschaftliches Jahrbuch der Schweiz* 4 (1890), p. 210.

23 E. Jaggi, *Methodik und Technik der Ertragswertschätzung landwirtschaftlicher Betriebe und Grundstücke unter spezieller Berücksichtigung der Verwendbarkeit der Einheitsbewertung für schweizerische Verhältnisse* (1945), p. 10.

24 P. Moser, 'Unterschiedliche Entfaltungsmöglichkeiten. Stadt und Land in Irland und der Schweiz 1800–1989', in W. Kersting and C. Zimmermann (eds), *Stadt-Land-Beziehungen im 20. Jahrhundert. Geschichts- und kulturwissenschaftliche Perspektiven* (2015).

methods for measuring the real costs of agricultural production.[25] Together with Ernst Laur, Abt has argued that a method of calculating the value of output for agricultural land was needed as long as there was a difference between the value of output of agricultural land and the price paid for land for non-agricultural purposes. On the other hand, the German agricultural economist Friedrich Aereboe has argued uncompromisingly against the value of output principle. In economics, Aereboe insisted, there is only 'one value, namely the estimated, attainable or payable price'.[26] Laur in turn has argued that this might well be true for those who were trading in land, but not for those who wanted to make their living by cultivating it. Farmers wanted primarily to 'cultivate their land, derive income and net income from it'. In his view, the market price only became important to them when they were selling their land to the next generation – in other words: when they no longer wanted to cultivate it themselves.[27]

On the other hand, young farmers who took over their parents' farm were particularly in favour of introducing a method of calculation that was capable of defining the value of output for agricultural land in order to avoid excessive levels of debt.[28] (Old) farmers who gave up agricultural production were, logically, less enthusiastic. For them, an introduction of the value of output principle could lead to a massive restriction in their power of disposal over their property. Equally opposed to the introduction of a value of output were economists and banks, because it effectively limited the security for mortgage debts.[29]

In Switzerland, the view that the value of output should be applied to both the taxation of agricultural land as well as for defining the value of land in the process of inheritance gained the upper hand. The Swiss Farmers' Union (SFU), founded in 1897–8 under the leadership of Ernst Laur, was instrumental in integrating the principle of value of output into the newly created Swiss Civil Code (ZGB). From now on, young heirs who were regarded as able to run a farm properly were entitled to acquire the farm undivided and for a price determined by the value of output of the land.[30]

25 H. Abt, *Der Reinertrag der Landwirthschaft, die Grundsteuerschatzung, Hypothekar- und Erbrechtsgesetzgebung. Ein Beitrag zur Förderung des Landwirthschaftsgewerbes* (1890), pp. 5–7. For Heinrich Abt (1854–1937), see https://www.histoirerurale.ch/pers/personnes/Abt,_Heinrich_(1854_1937)__DB7.html.

26 F. Aereboe, *Agrarpolitik. Ein Lehrbuch* (1928), p. 75.

27 cf. Ernst Laur on Friedrich Aereboes' *Agrarpolitik*, in *Archivbestand Schweizerischer Bauernverband*, Teil 1 (AfA Nr. 110), Dossier 161.1-03.

28 F. Zaugg, *Die Rentabilitätserhebungen des schweizerischen Bauernsekretariates. Eine monographische Darstellung* (1923).

29 *Schweizerische Landwirtschaftliche Zeitschrift* 21 (1893), pp. 728–31.

30 Auderset and Moser, *Die Agrarfrage in der Industriegesellschaft*, p. 68.

II

Ernst Laur not only made a significant contribution to identifying the problems that arose when accounting methods which were originally developed for commercial and industrial companies were applied to farms. He also played a crucial role in devising solutions to these specific problems and disseminating them to the scientific and agricultural world. Based on his practical experience as a book-keeping estate manager in the early 1890s, Laur came to the conclusion that the double-entry book-keeping method could only be practised on large farms by managers or specially trained book-keepers who had sufficient time and the necessary professional knowledge. He saw no justification for such a specialised division of labour on the overwhelming majority of small and medium-sized family farms. For these, Laur advocated the keeping of simple accounts which produced information about the overall results of the farm only, not about the profitability of its individual branches. In order to make the advantages of both methods of book-keeping widely available, in the 1890s Laur urged the existing agricultural organisations and state institutions to increase their commitment to the promotion of scientific publications on accounting systems. He developed and published a guide to double-entry book-keeping.[31] He tried to convince the Swiss Agricultural Association (SAA) to reward the accounting work on those farms that tried to keep double-entry book-keeping by offering prizes for good quality work.[32] In order to evaluate the figures obtained on farms with single-entry book-keeping, Laur suggested that the federal state should establish book-keeping survey stations at the regional level, modelled on the already existing state-supported agricultural experimental stations.

According to Laur's plan, the book-keeping survey stations would be linked with each other via a federal central bureau. Such a network, he hoped, would create close contacts and an exchange of knowledge between farmers and trained agronomists. And, equally important, it would make the establishment of costly institutions specifically designated to produce the required data material obsolete. The book-keeping survey stations were intended to provide theoretical training on book-keeping methods for farmers who, in turn, would supply the data created on their farms to the survey stations. Laur's proposed survey stations were then meant to calculate the profitability of individual branches of production on farms in order to explain to the ordinary farmer what was more profitable, forage or cereal production, artificial or natural

31 E. Laur, *Die Buchhaltung des Schweizerbauern* (1898).

32 Ernst Laur, 'Vorschläge für Massnahmen zur allgemeinen Verbreitung der landwirthschaftlichen Buchhaltung', *Schweizerische Landwirtschaftliche Zeitschrift* 23 (1895), pp. 433–42.

pastures, livestock or milk production, butter or cheesemaking. Because such cost calculations depended on cultural and natural characteristics, Laur advocated the setting up of regional survey stations for calculating the different production costs of the individual products. In this way, the decentralised structure of the survey stations would have acted as an intermediary between the regional diversity of agricultural production and the homogeneous quantitative data collection and accounting system in the central bureau. This structure was not unlike the one which Gustave Martinet established a few years later in the French-speaking part of Switzerland where he organised the wheat-breeding activities of local farmers in cooperation with scientists working in the research station of Mont-Calme in Lausanne.[33]

Ernst Laur presented his concept of regionally based survey stations as accounting knowledge centres to the Swiss Agricultural Association in 1895. He hoped that the Swiss Agricultural Association would adopt and propagate it, but he met with no interest. Nor was the plan adopted by either the existing agricultural organisations or the authorities or the scientific community. But Laur was not discouraged by this setback. When he was elected managing director of the newly founded Swiss Farmers' Union three years later, the 27-year-old Laur seized the (accounting) opportunity and established a scientific department to promote his book-keeping ideas. The Swiss Farmers' Secretariat (also, the Secretariat) soon became an internationally acclaimed scientific institution. In line with the functional link between accounting and statistics he advocated, Laur declared that the creation of a 'Swiss agricultural statistic' should also be part of the scope of the Secretariat.[34]

A few months after the creation of the Swiss Farmers' Union, the federal state commissioned the Secretariat to prepare an agricultural survey as part of a broader trade survey planned by the state. In a trial survey, the agricultural conditions in one specific municipality were to be statistically recorded. In addition, Laur advocated the analysis of the data gained from a simple book-keeping exercise conducted on eight farms which should be representative for the whole of Switzerland. In fact the survey planned for an entire municipality was never implemented because the Federal Assembly suspended the trade survey and thus the funding for the agricultural survey was lost. But Laur insisted on proceeding with the planned accounting analysis of eight individual farms by arguing that the work had already begun in the Secretariat and, therefore, expenses had already been incurred. Amongst the preparatory work claimed by Laur was the training of farmers who were interested in keeping accounts on their farms. Ten farmers had indeed attended a course that lasted several

33 Auderset and Moser, *Die Agrarfrage in der Industriegesellschaft*, pp. 155–200.

34 H. Franck, *75 Jahre Buchhaltungserhebungen beim Schweizerischen Bauernsekretariat* (1976), p. 8.

days at the headquarters of the Secretariat in February 1899. Particular emphasis was placed in their training on inventory taking and a uniform valuation method to elicit production costs. The subsequent surveys on the farms, which lasted for a whole year, were then exclusively concerned with 'testing the method' developed by the Secretariat. The closing of the first series of accounts was set for the end of March 1900.

After evaluating these data and adapting the content of the forms and guidelines, the Secretariat started the actual data collection throughout Switzerland in the spring of 1901. For financial reasons, it was originally planned to collect data from only 20 farms and to compensate the farming families for their efforts. But when a total of 180 farmers responded to the Secretariat's call, it was decided to enlarge the sample and cancel the promised compensation. In the end, 131 farmers were willing to take part in one of the introductory courses held in German or French at the headquarters of the Secretariat. On 1 April 1901, they started keeping accounts on their farms.

Over the next six years, Ernst Laur visited all the farming families that kept accounts for the Secretariat, often on Sundays, when he was also giving lectures in the villages. The visits enabled Laur, the son of a city dweller from Basel, to immerse himself in agricultural conditions. According to the assessment of the Secretariat, 108 of the first 131 checked accounts were 'well' or 'very well' kept, 16 were considered insufficient, and 7 as inadequate for a scientific analysis. As director of the Swiss Farmers' Union, Laur was simultaneously engaged in battles over the question of tariffs and price negotiations with cheese makers and consumer cooperatives. Therefore, it was not surprising that he was accused of mixing policies with science when he combined his visits to the book-keeping farms with giving public lectures which usually covered all kinds of topics. He countered the objections by the food industry and the labour movement by arguing that the value and importance of the federally subsidized secretariats lay precisely in the fact that they were 'closely related to their professional groups'. Such secretariats had been set up by the federal state for the industrial and trade sector as well as the labour movement before the Swiss Farmers Secretariat was founded. However, Laur argued, these secretariats should not simply be 'the mouthpiece of their interest groups', they should moreover have an 'educational effect on their professional comrades'. In this respect Laur distinguished the secretariats 'from the purely official bureaux of the federal administration'. While the latter had to attempt to 'show how it was', the former had the obligation to educate its members in order to enable them to change things for the better.[35]

[35] *Mitteilungen des Schweizerischen Bauernsekretariates* 13 (1902), p. 28.

The relationship between the Swiss Farmers' Secretariat and the book-keeping farmers was both confidential and hierarchical. For the farmers it was important that they could be sure that the data they provided were treated confidentially. The SFS, in turn, depended on the accountants to treat the returns from the farms rigorously. It therefore made sense for the preparatory courses to be held centrally at the headquarters of the Swiss Farmers' Union and for the farmers to be advised, inspected and respected by representatives of the Secretariat. The Secretariat assumed that the book-keeping farmers had to be subjected to a certain 'moral and financial constraint' as well as to an intellectual recognition in order to keep them in line. Before the (male and female) farmers completed the course, they had to sign a contract detailing their mutual rights and obligations.[36] Amongst their undertakings was one that those who did not keep records for at least one, later two successive years for the SFS, had to repay the cost of attending the preparatory course. The fact that the book-keeping was carried out in close cooperation with the Secretariat and involved rights and obligations for both sides led to a special relationship between the Swiss Farmers' Union and its book-keeping farmers. Many of them identified themselves as active elements of an umbrella association which had no individual membership.

Each of the accounts sent to the Secretariat was checked. In order to bring the calculations of the individual farms to uniform standards, some 30,000 calculations had to be carried out each year. This was made easier from 1902 onwards when a calculating machine was acquired.[37] For the elaborate evaluations, the Swiss Farmers' Union subsequently set up a separate department for profitability surveys, the so-called Renta. Academics, farmers and auxiliary staff were recruited as employees; eight to ten people worked on the compilations of figures and their statistical evaluation at any one time. These activities were financially supported by the federal government. The state contribution rose from an initial 5,000 to about 40,000 Swiss francs in the 1920s. This accounted for about two-thirds of the costs incurred by the Secretariat from their accounting activities.[38] From 1903 onwards the results of the surveys were published yearly in the *Agricultural Yearbook of Switzerland*, a publication of the Swiss Department of Trade, Industry and Agriculture. On the international level it also gained a solid reputation, attracting visitors from all over the world. One of the most renowned was the Russian agricultural economist

36 Printed in F. Zaugg, *Die Rentabilitätserhebungen des schweizerischen Bauernsekretariates*, p. 10.

37 *Mitteilungen des Schweizerischen Bauernsekretariates* 17 (1902), p. 33.

38 F. Zaugg, *Die Rentabilitätserhebungen des schweizerischen Bauernsekretariates*, pp. 18–19.

Alexander Cajanov (1888–1937) who spent several months at the Swiss Farmers' Union, studying the methods applied there.[39]

The farmers' interest in book-keeping was not diminished by the problems that arose in the 1890s by defining the value of land and the value of animals and plants which were neither bought nor sold. These problems were gradually solved, not least due to the numerous publications Laur himself contributed. His *Buchhaltung für den Schweizerbauer* ('Accounting for the Swiss Farmer'), first published in 1898, was reprinted in 1903 in a revised form as *Landwirtschaftliche Buchhaltung für bäuerliche Verhältnisse* ('Agricultural Accounting for Farmers') and then revised again and again. In 1907 Laur's book *Landwirtschaftliche Betriebslehre* (Agricultural Business Management) was published by the Association of Teachers at Agricultural Colleges and was used in agricultural colleges throughout the country. Over the following fifteen years it appeared in seven new editions. When Laur took over the lectures on agricultural economics at the Technical University in Zürich (ETH) in 1908, he gained direct contact with the future teachers at the agricultural colleges in the cantons since all teachers there had to have a degree from the ETH. By this time Laur no longer visited the book-keeping farmers himself but invested his energy in the further development of the accounting method on an international level.[40] His *Grundlagen und Methoden der Bewertung, Buchhaltung und Kalkulation in der Landwirtschaft* ('Principles and Methods of Valuation, Accounting and Calculation in Agriculture') was published in 1911 in Berlin. The longer Laur worked on the subject of valuation, the more convinced he became that his method could, after all, now adequately capture the complex 'organism' of the farming enterprise. 'The scepticism with which I had hitherto viewed double-entry book-keeping in some respects', Laur wrote in the preface of his standard work in 1911, has 'increasingly given way'. In October 1910, Laur wrote, that he had 'laid down his pen with the hope' that he had 'contributed to the rehabilitation of double-entry book-keeping' with this work.[41]

III

The analytical dissection of the farm in the process of book-keeping was accompanied by a strict separation of household and farm on the

39 W. Baumann and H. Haumann, '... um die Organisation des typischen Arbeitsbetriebes kennenzulernen. Zu Aleksandr Cajanovs Schrift "Bäuerliche Wirtschaft in der Schweiz"', *Schweizerische Zeitschrift für Geschichte* 47 (1997), pp. 1–26.

40 cf. for example: Archiv für Sozialwissenschaft und Sozialpolitik; Fühlings landwirtschaftliche Zeitung; Thünen-Archiv.

41 For Laur's international contribution see the chapter by D'Onofrio, Chapter 9, pp. 176–97 above.

analytical level. Already in his earliest accounting works, Laur had insisted that a cash book be kept on every farm. This was the most efficient way to ensure that men and women on the farm learned to separate the spheres of the household and the farm, spheres which were anything but separated in their everyday life. This analytical separation required a high level of abstraction on the part of the farming family which had to be learnt somewhere. Crucial in that respect were the agricultural colleges and the rural home economics schools, where the subject of book-keeping was taught by graduates of the ETH from the early twentieth century onwards. Here, young farmers of both sexes had the opportunity to familiarise themselves with the pitfalls of keeping accounts. Those who wanted to practise an accounting system to be evaluated by the Secretariat on their farm had to attend the introductory course organised by them. While in the beginning it was almost exclusively men who attended these training courses, women soon took part either in their capacity as widows (thus replacing their deceased husbands) or as female farmers in their own right. In the mid-1950s, the course conducted in German was attended by eight women and 60 men. In the 1960s, the proportion of women increased to about one-third of all participants.[42] Amongst early book-keeping female farmers were the well-known figures of Mina Hofstetter and Marianne Sulzer.[43] Laur, who like many of his contemporaries was known to be rather ambivalent about matters of legal and political equality, was obviously impressed by both of them. In his opulent volume *Der Schweizerbauer* ('The Swiss Farmer'), Laur included a photograph of Marianne Sulzer working with account sheets on her desk.[44] And he publicly praised Mina Hofstetter, the pioneer of livestock-free organic farming, who kept simple accounts on her farm in collaboration with the Secretariat from the early 1920s onwards. Hofstetter had 'put her farm at the service of agricultural experimentation', Laur informed the readership of the *Bauernzeitung* ('Farmers' Journal') in October 1928: 'We can only endorse her wish that her experimental work will also be supported by the authorities.'[45]

On the farms using book-keeping, women were directly involved in the practical work of account-keeping. Even if they did not keep accounts for the household itself, they had to collect and standardise data in their

42 E. Dettwiler, 'Die Buchhaltungserhebungen des Schweizerischen Bauernsekretariates', *Die Grüne. Schweizerische Landwirtschaftlichen Zeitschrift* 93 (1965), pp. 1475–81, 1511–19 at p. 1479.

43 P. Moser, *Mina Hofstetter. Eine ökofeministische Pionierin des biologischen Landbaus. Texte und Korrespondenz* (2024).

44 E. Laur, *Der Schweizerbauer, seine Heimat und sein Werk* (1947), p. 737; W. Baumann, 'Aus-Schnitt aus der Wirklichkeit? Eine Fotografie als historische Quelle', *traverse* 5 (1998), pp. 157–67.

45 *Schweizerische Bauernzeitung* (1928), p. 39.

fields of activity. The same instrument that made their productive activities effectively invisible at the analytical level paradoxically contributed significantly to the visibility of the 'working couple'[46] on the farm.[47] The Secretariat always reminded farmers interested in attending the introductory course that they had to ensure that no difficulties would arise for them from those who ran the household in carrying out the book-keeping.[48] For if their wife, mother, daughter or housekeeper did not make the relevant household figures available to him, the farmer would not be able to keep accurate accounts.

The accounting-based analytical separation of farm and household also had an impact on the perception and ordering of gender relations on the farm. On the basis of the numerical relationships between farm and household, the family farm, experienced by men and women in their everyday life as a unit of production and consumption, was split into two commensurate, but highly asymmetrical units, in their valuation. Although the effects of book-keeping on gender relations on the farms were complex and changing over time, it cannot be overlooked that it led to a reinforcement of gender segregation and that the need for an analytical separation of farm and household caused a one-sided conceptual reduction of the household to its consumption function. Already in the manual *Die hauswirtschaftliche Buchführung auf dem Lande* (Household accounting in the countryside), published in 1892, the agronomist Gottlieb Stalder explicitly recalled that on a book-keeping farm 'a very sharp boundary' would have to be drawn 'between the husband's field of activity and that of the wife'.[49]

The interlockings of production and reproduction, of household and farm were also reflected architecturally. In most farmhouses the economic area and the living quarters were united under the same roof. From the point of view of an industrialised society, where work and living became, generally speaking, systematically separated with the establishing of factories, the spatially connected arrangement of living and working space on the farm was increasingly felt to be alien (and, in the event of fire, too costly for the insurance companies), so that repeated attempts were made to change this in agriculture as well.[50] The extent to which the

46 H. Wunder, *Er ist die Sonn', sie ist der Mond: Frauen in der Frühen Neuzeit* (1992), pp. 97–109. Agronomists used the term 'working community', cf. E. Dettwiler, 'Die Buchhaltungserhebungen des Schweizerischen Bauernsekretariates', p. 1,479.

47 Ibid., p. 1,479.

48 cf. *Schweizerische Bauernzeitung*, Jan. 1911 and Jan. 1926.

49 G. Stalder, *Die hauswirtschaftliche Buchführung auf dem Lande. Praktische Anleitung zum Betriebe der Buchführung im landwirtschaftlichen Haushalte* (1892), p. 10.

50 W. Baumann and P. Moser, *Bauern im Industriestaat. Agrarpolitische Konzeptionen und bäuerliche Bewegungen in der Schweiz 1918–1968* (1999).

agrarian reality of close interaction between women and men, children and labourers, farm managers and employees, old and young, and, no less importantly, between humans and (often working) animals, resisted this tendency to modularise can be seen in the fact that the separation of residential and farm buildings required by authorities and insurance companies for new buildings was repeatedly torpedoed in practice by the construction of a connecting corridor. Men and women generally performed specific tasks and functions on the farm, but their activities were so closely linked functionally that it was more efficient within the family economy to spatially link household and business, specifically living, eating, cooking, catering, educating and agricultural work, rather than to separate them.

With the introduction of book-keeping, the household, which in the vast majority – but by no means all cases[51] – was headed by women, was explicitly reduced to its consumption function. Thus, the insight into the 'negative' monetary value of the household gained on the basis of an 'objective' method of measuring, distorted the economic reality of the family farm in the area of gender relations. The practice of book-keeping on the farms literally wrote women and many of their value-creating activities in the household out of the perception of the family-farm economy, in which they held a central function, as the very practice of the book-keeping couple illustrates.[52] At the same time, the fact that the expenditures caused by the household (but not the values created by household activities) could now be determined in francs and centimes with book-keeping brought it into a comparison with the monetary value of the yield of the farm. Under certain circumstances, this may have led to an objectification of the discussions about the necessity of expenses incurred in the fields, stables and households.

IV

The calls for accounts to be kept on farms sharply increased in the second half of the nineteenth century. Scientists, agronomists and politicians were convinced that an introduction of book-keeping would transform 'peasants' into farmers and make agriculture what industry had already become. However, the efforts to introduce book-keeping on farms were not met with enthusiasm by the farming population. Their scepticism was not based on an anti-modernist attitude or the alleged reluctance of male and female farmers to write things down. The distrust of the farming population was rather based on the fact that the accounting

51 There were always pairs of brothers who (temporarily) ran a farm together, where one was responsible for the household and the other for the farm.

52 Dettwiler, 'Die Buchhaltungserhebungen des Schweizerischen Bauernsekretariates', p. 1,477.

methods that were developed in commercial and industrial spheres did not adequately reflect the idiosyncrasies of agriculture. It was, therefore, not until accounting methods were adapted to agrarian conditions that farmers on farms large and small, female and male, as well as their organisations, began to propagate accounting on farms. In Switzerland, it was often women who kept the accounts on the farm in cooperation with their husbands, brothers, sons or fathers who managed the farm. The evaluation of the figures and their aggregation was carried out by the scientific department of the Swiss Farmers' Union, the Swiss Farmers' Secretariat with financial support of the federal state which was interested in gathering information on the sector as a whole.

However, it is important to remember that the introduction of book-keeping did not simply lead to a more accurate picture of the economic success or failure of individual farms and a better overview of the situation of agriculture as a whole. It also had unintended consequences. The separation of farm and household, for example, led to a situation in which many of the areas of women's responsibilities were largely reduced to their consumption function. What was indispensable in the everyday life of family farms was reduced to an expense in the book-keeping accounts. The work in the household by women, who also performed a particularly large part of the accounting work, was literally written out of the agricultural economy by the introduction of book-keeping.

It is therefore important that we do not only ask questions about the process of diffusion of book-keeping practices or try to measure its contribution for a more reliable calculation of the gains and losses on farms. Equally important is to search for the unintended consequences of the triumph of book-keeping on farms because it is significantly more than a rational instrument for gaining useful information. Book-keeping has had many different effects, depending on the time and circumstances in which it was applied.

11

Conclusion

Nathalie Joly and Federico D'Onofrio

The invention of the accounting farmer, as described in the chapters collected in this volume, is a twofold concept. On the one hand, it encompasses common traits shared by prescriptive models elaborated by agricultural experts and ideologues in the early modern and modern periods. Writers of agricultural handbooks, teachers, and politicians addressing rural constituencies imagined that the future of agriculture had no place for ignorant peasants and idle landowners. Only those who accurately managed their land would survive and thrive.

On the other hand, the emergence of the accounting farmer was a historical phenomenon that saw growing numbers of farmers keep increasingly formalized records of their businesses. Despite the relative paucity of the archives and the risks of their incompleteness, we have access to a wide range of valuable documentation, from large estates to small sharecroppers, tenants, and owner-farmers. The relationship between expert knowledge on the one hand and practices has been questioned, especially for the early modern period. The importance of books and printed media has been widely discussed but how far they were read and acted upon is unclear.[1] This book though shows how, through a variety of channels and conduits, at different times, models elaborated by experts stimulated and shaped practices of recording and, in all likelihood, of reasoning.

According to agricultural authors in the eighteenth, nineteenth, and twentieth centuries, counting and recording were essential for accurate management. As Hopper *et al.* emphasized, the claim that accounting was merely a neutral enabling device is not a sustainable one. Accounting was embedded in a global rhetoric about an organization's goals. It was

1 Here, we only mention the recent book by James D. Fisher, *The Enclosure of Knowledge: Books, Power and Agrarian Capitalism in Britain, 1660–1800* (2022).

'a symbolic device used by certain social actors to mark out a direction in which they would like to see effort and other resources directed'.[2] In practice, there are many and complex reasons why accounting techniques have become an integral part of farm management throughout modern Europe.

The link between the commercialization of farming and accounting has been stressed by previous writers, starting with Robert Brenner and Rob A. Bryer, both of whom insisted on a specific causality chain.[3] Notably, Brenner paid particular attention to 'the presence throughout the economy of a systematic, continuous and quasi-universal drive on the part of the individual direct producers to cut costs in aid of maximizing profitability via increasing efficiency and the movement of means of production'.[4] The accounting farmer, being encouraged or compelled by his own interest to maximize the gains from trade through specialization, accumulation and innovation, or reallocation of the means of production in response to changing demand, was forced to develop skills to measure his productivity and profit. Bryer's articulated theory attributed to accounting an even more central role. He saw an agricultural revolution emerging in England from the spread of a calculative mentality among farmers, rather than from a 'technological upheaval' or from increased market demand.[5] According to the new mentality – he claims – farmers calculated 'the rate of return on capital as capitalist profit (revenues minus expenses) divided by the capital employed in production'.[6] This became their guiding principle and thus a new type of accounting (but not double-entry book-keeping) revealed a new way of extracting surplus from labour.

2 Trevor Hopper, John Storey, and Hugh Willmott, 'Accounting for Accounting: Towards the Development of a Dialectical View', *Accounting, Organizations and Society*, 12 (1987), p. 441.

3 Robert Brenner, 'Agrarian Class Structure and Economic Development in Pre-Industrial Europe', *Past & Present*, 70 (1976), pp. 30–75; Robert Brenner, 'The Agrarian Roots of European Capitalism', *Past & Present*, 97 (1982), pp. 16–113; Ellen Meiksins Wood, 'Capitalism, Merchants and Bourgeois Revolution: Reflections on the Brenner Debate and Its Sequel', *International Review of Social History*, 41 (1996), pp. 209–32; R. A. Bryer, 'The History of Accounting and the Transition to Capitalism in England, Part One: Theory', *Accounting, Organizations and Society*, 25 (2000), pp. 131–62; idem, 'The History of Accounting and the Transition to Capitalism in England, Part Two: Evidence', *Accounting, Organizations and Society*, 25 (2000), pp. 327–81; idem, 'The Genesis of the Capitalist Farmer: Towards a Marxist Accounting History of the Origins of the English Agricultural Revolution', *Critical Perspectives on Accounting*, 17 (2006), pp. 367–97.

4 Robert Brenner, 'The Low Countries in the Transition to Capitalism', *Journal of Agrarian Change*, 1 (2001), p. 172.

5 Bryer, 'Genesis of the Capitalist Farmer', p. 372.

6 Bryer, 'History of Accounting and the Transition to Capitalism in England, Part One', p. 139.

In fact, the relationship between accounting and capitalism or accounting and increased commercialization does not seem linear, although the agricultural literature of the early twentieth century already insisted on this connection.[7] Giraudeau holds that detailed accounting was not systematically correlated with productivity growth in eighteenth-century England.[8] More, 'in some settings, the rise of a market economy for agricultural products, and increases in agricultural productivity, were associated with a decrease in the sophistication of accounting systems used' as can be observed in the late eighteenth-century United States.[9] The necessity for accounts did not grow automatically with the increased involvement of farmers in markets.

Moreover, the literature has broadly discussed the hypothesis that the end of the nineteenth century marked 'the failure of agrarian capitalism', with the increasing integration of farmers in co-operatives and their growing dependency on government subsidies, credit institutions, and extension offices.[10] While this process gradually shielded individual farmers from markets, it also imposed on them rapidly growing demands for recording, accounting, and reporting.

The chapters of this book do not stress, therefore, as much the impact of marketization as they shed light on the various and concomitant goals accounting served in different periods and places. Three periods or phases emerge throughout the book. The chapters devoted to the seventeenth and eighteenth centuries highlight the importance of accounting for establishing the control of landowners and gentlemen farmers over the administrators of estates and farms. They explore different models by illustrious agricultural authors, and actual practices which show processes of rationalization and standardization. The second part of the

7 Ernest Laur, *Landwirtschaftliche Betriebslehre für Bäuerliche Verhältnisse* (1912), p. 13. Laur insisted that the necessity for accounts had been growing with the entanglement of farmers in markets. 'Thus, in the course of a few decades, the farmer has moved from the ancient barter economy to the modern monetary economy. The local independence of his activity has been lost, and his farm has now become a link in international trade and the world economy.'

8 Martin Giraudeau, 'The Farm as an Accounting Laboratory: An Essay on the History of Accounting and Agriculture', *Accounting History Review*, 27 (2017), pp. 201–15. He cites Mark Overton, *Agricultural Revolution in England: The Transformation of the Agrarian Economy 1500 – 1850* (1996). See also, Michael Turner, John V. Beckett, and Bethanie Afton, *Farm Production in England 1700–1914* (2001).

9 Giraudeau, 'The Farm as an Accounting Laboratory', pp. 204–5. The claims are based on Naomi R. Lamoreaux, 'Rethinking the Transition to Capitalism in the Early American Northeast', *Journal of American History*, 90 (2003), pp. 437–61; Martin Bruegel, *Farm, Shop, Landing: The Rise of a Market Society in the Hudson Valley, 1780–1860* (2002).

10 Niek Koning, *The Failure of Agrarian Capitalism: Agrarian Politics in the UK, Germany, the Netherlands and the USA, 1846–1919* (1994).

book stresses how accounting was inserted in a narrative of economic improvement. Agricultural authors described it as a tool to involve farmers in the process of capital accumulation and extend to them the advantages of national, and soon international, markets. The final chapters of the book show from different perspectives how accounting became not just an instrument for transforming the mentality of individual farmers, but also, from the end of the nineteenth century, an element of policy-making and political mobilization.

The evolution of accounting in agriculture, therefore, does not appear here merely as a product of a growing entanglement of farms in markets, but also as the result of growing needs for control and discipline, by owners as well as governments.

Agrarian capitalism?

While the debate continues around the pace of change during the eighteenth century in various parts of Europe and its causes, the chapters collected here show that in some circumstances accounting emerged as a means to increase control over both workers and managers. Its rising importance appears to be linked to the redefinition of the roles of owners and managers. The professionalization of estate managers and bailiffs, on the one hand, and the growing involvement of aristocratic owners in the fine detail of farm administration on the other required an increasing demand for records and documents. These records tracked production and sales, but their primary function seems to be establishing control and setting the relationships between landowners and managers, between landowners and tenants, and between managers and workers.

The form of accounting during this phase does not seem systematically different from that of commercial accounting, neither in the practice of manorial households nor in theory. There does not seem to be a specific adaptation of accounting models to farming. Double-entry bookkeeping was mentioned as an ideal by the great agronomists of the early nineteenth century but did not play a prominent role in actual practices, where other systems of accounting dominated. In fact, Arthur Young considered double-entry too cumbersome for farmers. These findings confirm the historiography, which has pointed out the limited spread of double-entry in various European countries well into the nineteenth century.[11]

11 Paul D. A. Harvey, 'Manorial Accounts', in R. H. Parker and B. S. Yamey (eds), *Accounting History: Some British Contributions* (1994), pp. 91–115; Richard Macve, 'Insights to Be Gained from the Study of Ancient Accounting History: Some Reflections on the New Edition of Finley's *The Ancient Economy*', *European Accounting Review*, 11 (2002), pp. 453 – 72; Riccardo Mussari and Michela Magliacani, 'Agricultural Accounting in the Nineteenth and

The relationship between accounting and the increasing entanglement of agriculture in urban and long-distance markets, questioned by Giraudeau, was perhaps indirect. It was maybe the growing reliance of owners on monetary income that induced landowners and gentlemen farmers to exert a greater degree of control over expenses and resort to accounting records. As observed by other authors, increasingly frequent exchanges of letters and instructions between the managers on the farm and the owners was the context in which accounts were kept in this period, thus enabling the increased control.

The book also underlines the crucial role played by accounting in farming experiments during a period – such as the eighteenth century – when such experiments were becoming a driver of agricultural change. In this context, accounting was indeed centred on profit!

In the period of the agricultural enlightenment, the embodiment of the accounting farmer, according to the writers of the time, was essentially a gentleman farmer or the administrator of a large estate reporting to the aristocratic owner. This does raise the question of what the generality of owner-occupying or tenant farmers (Young's 'common farmers') kept in the way of accounts in the eighteenth century (and later). It is possible that they fell back on mental accounting of the sort identified amongst the Dutch farmers.[12]

Overall, it seems likely that 'common farmers' kept pocket books, or made entries in almanacs. If they kept accounts at all, they were simple charge and discharge ones, perhaps totalled at the end of the year to see how the farmer stood. They were functional, but contemporaries like Young sneered at them, as do the modern accounting historians.

Early Twentieth Centuries: The Case of the Noble Rucellai Family Farm in Campi', *Accounting, Business & Financial History*, 17 (2007), pp. 87–103; Valerio Antonelli et al., 'The Roles of Accounting in Agro-Pastoral Settings: The Case of the Landed Estates of Prince Sambiase in the mid-Eighteenth Century', *Accounting Historians Journal*, 46 (2019), pp. 1–18; Ramon Garrabou, Enric Saguer Hom, and Pere Sala López, 'Formas de gestión y evolución de la renta a partir del análisis de contabilidades agrarias: Los patrimonios del Marqués de Sentmenat en el Vallés y Urgell (1820–1917)', *Noticiario de historia agraria: Boletín informativo del Seminario de Historia Agraria*, 5 (1993), pp. 97–125; Jordi Planas and Enric Saguer, 'Accounting Records of Large Rural Estates and the Dynamics of Agriculture in Catalonia (Spain), 1850–1950', *Accounting, Business & Financial History*, 15 (2005), pp. 171–85.

12 Daan Hendrikx and Oscar Gelderblom, 'Accounting for Agricultural Development? The Case of the Netherlands, 1840–1940', *Agricultural History Review*, 70 (2002), pp. 23–48.

Disciplining through calculation

As this book documents, the situation changed over the course of the nineteenth century. The educational literature examined here shows the spread of a different model and the rise of different practices. Every farmer should be capable of calculating, nineteenth-century writers seemed to say, in order for agriculture to become a profitable, modern, and productive branch of the national economy. Accounting records, therefore, were part of a constellation of other records, ranging from diaries of crop rotations to genealogical books for cattle. The emphasis was on ending waste and making good use of natural resources and national capital by all farmers, as if preparing for what Jan Luiten van Zanden called 'Europe's first green revolution', namely the tumultuous growth of Europe's agriculture driven by family farms in the late nineteenth century.[13]

The accounting or calculating farmer thus partook in a broader ideal of economic improvement fostered through the general school system and specific forms of apprenticeship. Reading–writing–counting became the new historical ground from which rural classes evolved. A new relationship with money was emerging, which was indissociably a relationship with time, opening up the possibility of savings and investments. Present and future could both be improved through the reformulation of the work ethic. More precisely, what was at stake was the acquisition of social, behavioural, and organizational characteristics. In fact, there was a striking similarity between the disciplining imagined by this literature and the 'school formatting' that spread throughout Europe in the nineteenth century which, through writing, arithmetic, and the clock, produced a new framework for thought and action.[14] Teaching accounting to women, even in the sense of disciplining ancient practices, became thereby crucial to completing the attempt to establish an agrarian accounting family and invent the accounting farmer.

This effort, often led by governments, relied on publishers who brought to market an increasing variety of manuals, pre-printed forms, booklets, and almanacs, targeting and adapted to a rural population. Such printed material contributed to the codification of calculative practices that differed from the prescriptions of accounting manuals of the time. As Eisenstein has argued, we should pay greater attention to this printed

13 Jan Luiten van Zanden, 'The First Green Revolution: The Growth of Production and Productivity in European Agriculture, 1870–1914', *Economic History Review*, 44 (1991), pp. 215–39.

14 Bernard Lahire, Daniel Thin, and Guy Vincent, 'Sur l'histoire et la théorie de la forme scolaire', in Guy Vincent (ed.), *L'Education prisonnière de la forme scolaire? Scolarisation et socialisation dans les sociétés industrielles* (1994), pp. 11–48.

form which played an important role in setting the stage for the rising accounting farmer.[15]

The government, the farmers' unions, and accountancy data

Across Europe, over the course of the century, agricultural expertise became increasingly professionalized: agricultural schools appeared at all levels of education, together with research centres, experimental stations, extension offices, and private consultants. As the chapters in the third part of the book show, experts tried to discipline and regiment the calculative practices of farmers in order to channel them in simplified but 'approved' formats. Thus, we observe a growing specialization of accounting models and teachings aimed at relatively small farmers.

Since the 1870s, especially in central and northern Europe, the accounting farmer could also resort to the assistance of accounting offices, institutions especially designed to reduce the cost and trouble of accounting. By the beginning of the twentieth century, this had led to a growing separation between book-keeping, done at the farm by the farming family, and accounting (and the analysis of accounts), conducted by professionals at the accounting offices.

In this context, experts and teachers emerged who were not directly serving agricultural entrepreneurs, but worked for the government or for business associations, such as farmers' unions. Such experts often played a leading role in designing, selecting, and promoting accounting practices. The methods they designed could be taught, the corresponding forms and instructions printed and sold at discounted prices, thanks to the support of the government or unions. Next to a private market of accounting models, therefore, the beginning of the twentieth century witnessed the rise of subsidized accounting.

The goal was not only, as it had been for most of the nineteenth century, to help farmers improve the management of their farms, but to appropriate accountancy data for various collective ends. Governments and unions – either in cooperation or in competition – used accountancy data not only to create benchmarks against which farmers could assess their own farms (or be assessed), but also in order to produce measures of profitability, productivity, indebtedness, etc.

Since the early twentieth century, the accounting farmer, thus, has been seen not only as someone capable of effectively managing the available resources but also as a data provider, and at the frontline in the construction of agricultural policy. This broader social role was confirmed in the common agricultural policy of the European Economic Community in the 1950s.

15 Elizabeth L. Eisenstein, *The Printing Press as an Agent of Change* (1980).

What remains to be done?

Many issues worthy of consideration remain outside of the scope of this book. The fundamental and always open question of the materiality of accounting, with the growing role of pre-printed forms and methods, and the related issue of accounting costs, have been but cursorily discussed. Similarly, the chapters collected here say very little about vernacular calculative practices and their connection to book-keeping, especially in the early modern period. The role of schools in standardizing practices has been barely alluded to.

While it is not easy to establish the economic impact of accounting practices on farms, this volume provides us with a few advances on their impact. Accounting is one of Goody's 'basic technologies of intellect'. What are accounting records other than lists of expenses and receipts and cash flow statements, two basic technologies of intellect Goody highlighted and that give rise to deliberation?[16] Accounting 'changes the nature of mental life, because it makes visible and recurrently inspectable what is otherwise a transient speech signal that rapidly fades from recall'.[17] It extends the nature of communication on farm data over space and time. Crucial for us is that this technology operates not only at the level of the farm but also at the level of polities. As we have seen in this volume, accumulation of knowledge and expertise on accounting opened up the possibility of integrating farming into what Moser and Auderset call the 'agro-industrial science society' of modern Europe.[18]

To gain access to these complex and multifaceted consequences, we need to get closer to everyday farming life, drawing on a wide range of disciplines (history, sociology, anthropology, sciences of management, psychology, codicology ...). We also need theories of action and acting. In the meantime, this volume demonstrates the importance of accounting and sketches a framework for further studies on farm accounting in early modern and modern Europe.

16 Jack Goody, *The Interface between the Written and the Oral* (1987), p. 151.

17 Stephen C. Levinson, *On 'Technologies of the Intellect': Goody Lecture 2020* (2020), p. 7.

18 Auderset and Moser, *Die Agrarfrage in der Industriegesellschaft.*

BIBLIOGRAPHY

Aargauische landwirtschaftliche Gesellschaft (ed.), *Die Landwirtschaft im Kanton Aargau: Festschrift zur Feier des 100jährigen Bestehens der Aargauischen landwirtschaftlichen Gesellschaft* (Aarau, 1911)

Abt, H., *Der Reinertrag der Landwirthschaft, die Grundsteuerschatzung, Hypothekar- und Erbrechtsgesetzgebung: ein Beitrag zur Förderung des Landwirthschaftsgewerbes* (1890)

Achilles, W., 'Betriebswirtschaftliche Leitbilder in der ostdeutschen Gutswirtschaft seit dem Ende des 19. Jahrhunderts', *Ostelbische agrargesellschaft im Kaiserreich und in der weimarer Republik: Agrarkrise – junkerliche Interessenpolitik – Modernisierungstrategien*, ed. Heinz Reif (Berlin, 1994), pp. 190–212

—— *Landwirtschaft in der frühen Neuzeit* (München, 2010)

Ackermann, I., M. Hans-Moëvi, I. Roland and D. Zumkeller, *Les maisons rurales du canton de Genève* (Geneva, 2006)

Addens, N. G. and H. D. Louwes, *Gedenkboek, 1837–1937* (Groningen, 1937)

Aereboe, F., *Buchführung: Anleitung für den praktischen Landwirt* (Berlin, 1896)

—— *Agrarpolitik. Ein Lehrbuch* (Berlin, 1928)

Afton, B., 'Investigating Agricultural Production and Land Productivity: Methodology and Opportunities using English Farm Records', *Histoire & Mesure* 15 (2000), 233–45

Alparslan, A., *Strukturalistische Prinzipal-Agent-Theorie: Eine Reformulierung der Hidden Action Modelle aus der Perspektive des Strukturalismus* (Wiesbaden, 2006)

Ammannati, F. (ed.), *Religion and Religious Institutions in the European Economy, 1000–1800* (Florence, 2012)

Andersen, T., *Oversigt over Regnskabsresultaterne i de danske Kontrolforeninger (15 Oversigt) 1946–47* (Slagelse, 1948)

Antoine, A., 'Entre macro et micro: Les comptabilités agricoles du XVIIIe siècle', *Histoire & Mesure* 15 (2000), 247–70

—— 'La légende noire du métayage dans l'ouest de la France (XVIIIe–XXe siècle)', *Exploiter la terre: Les contrats agraires de l'Antiquité à nos jours*, ed. G. Béaur, M. Arnaux and A. Varet-Vitou (Rennes, 2003), pp. 457–70

Antonelli, V., E. Cafaro, R. D'Alessio and M. Bigoni, 'The Roles of Accounting in Agro-Pastoral Settings: The Case of the Landed Estates of Prince Sambiase in the mid-Eighteenth Century', *Accounting Historians Journal* 46,1 (2019), 1–18

Auderset, J. and P. Moser, *Die Agrarfrage in der Industriegesellschaft: Wissenskulturen, Machtverhältnisse und natürliche Ressourcen in der agrarisch-industriellen Wissensgesellschaft (1850–1950)* (Cologne, 2018)

Auderset, J. and H.-U. Schiedt, 'Aspekte animalischer Traktion in der Moderne', *traverse* 28 (2021), 27–42

Bang, I., 'Regnskabsføring i Landbruget, med særligt Henblik paa Skatteansættelsen', *Nationaløkonomisk Tidsskrift III* 31 (1923), 194–205

Barbier, J.-M., *Le quotidien et son économie* (Paris, 1981)

Barton, D. and U. Papen (eds), *The Anthropology of Writing: Understanding Textually Mediated Worlds* (London, 2010)

Baumann, W., 'Aus-Schnitt aus der Wirklichkeit? Eine Fotografie als historische Quelle', *traverse* 5 (1998), 157–67

Baumann, W. and H. Haumann, '... um die Organisation des typischen Arbeitsbetriebes kennenzulernen: Zu Aleksandr Cajanovs Schrift "Bäuerliche Wirtschaft in der Schweiz"', *Schweizerische Zeitschrift für Geschichte* 47 (1997), 1–26

Baumann, W. and P. Moser, *Bauern im Industriestaat: Agrarpolitische Konzeptionen und bäuerliche Bewegungen in der Schweiz 1918–1968* (Zürich, 1999)

Bay, H., 'Hvilket Resultat giver et gennemført Regnskab efter 30 Aars Forløb', *Ugeskrift for Landmænd 1942*, 59–61

Beardmore, C., 'Landowner, Tenant and Agent on the Marquis of Englesey 's Dorset and Somerset Estate, 1814–44', *Rural History* 26,2 (2015), 181–99

Béaur, G. and J.-M. Chevet, 'Les incertitudes de la croissance: Y-a-t-il eu un modèle français du développement agricole?', *L'histoire rurale de l'Europe: XVIe–XXe siècle*, ed. L. Herment (Paris, 2019), pp. 271–96

Beauvalet, S., 'Les femmes dans le monde rural à l'époque moderne, XVIe–XVIIIe siècles', *Ruralité française et britannique, XIIIe–XXe siècles: Approches comparées*, ed. N. Vivier (Rennes, 2002), pp. 89–11

Beckert, S., 'American Danger: United States Empire, Eurafrica, and the Territorialization of Industrial Capitalism, 1870–1950', *The American Historical Review* 122,4 (2017), 1137–70

Beckett, J. V., 'Absentee Landlordism in the Late Seventeenth and Early Eighteenth Centuries: The Case of Cumbria', *Northern History* 19 (1983), 87–107

— *The Aristocracy in England 1660–1914* (Oxford, 1986)

— 'Landownership and Estate Management', *The Agrarian History of England and Wales*, ed. G. E. Mingay (Cambridge, 1989), pp. 1750–850

—— 'Estate Management in Eighteenth-Century England: The Lowther-Spedding Relationship in Cumberland', *English Rural Society, 1500–1800*, ed. J. Chartres and D. Hey (Cambridge, 1990), pp. 55–72

Berghmans, S., 'The Management of the Estates of the Duke of Arenberg in the 18th and 19th Century', Unpublished paper, presented at the *Rural History Conference Leuven* (Leuven, 2017)

Berry, J. W., 'The Acculturation Process and Refugee Behavior', *Context* 10,75 (1989), 1–12

—— 'Immigration, Acculturation, and Adaptation', *Applied Psychology* 47,1 (1997), 5–68

Bertholet, A. B. and B. Kapossy, *La physiocratie et la Suisse: Études sur la correspondance du Marquis de Mirabeau et Marc Charles Frédéric de Sacconay (1731–1787)* (Geneva, 2023)

Bickerton, D. M., *Marc-Auguste and Charles Pictet, the Bibliothèque Britannique (1796–1815), and the Dissemination of British Literature and Science on the Continent* (Geneva, 1986)

Biéler, A., *La pensée économique et sociale de Calvin* (Geneva, 1959)

Bjerke, K., '[Review of] Jørgen Pedersen, *En Undersøgelse af Indtægtssvingningerne i Landbruget i Perioden 1922–36 og deres Indflydelse paa andre Erhverv* (Studier fra Aarhus Universitets økonomiske Institut 2, Kbhvn. 1938) ', *Nationaløkonomisk Tidsskrift* III,46 (1938), 345–7

Bloos, G., 'Die Rentmeister von Düsseldorf', *Beiträge zur Geschichte des Niederrheins* 7 (1893)

Boberg-Fazlic, N., P. S. Jensen, M. Lampe, P. Sharp and C. V. Skovsgaard '"Getting to Denmark": The Role of Agricultural Elites for Development', *Journal of Economic Growth* 28 (2023), 525–69

Bodinier, B., 'Un journal paysan du XVIIIe siècle: Le livre de recettes et dépenses de François Jacques Maret, laboureur et vigneron à Bueil (Eure), de 1730 à 1761. 1ère partie', *Histoire & Sociétés Rurales* 40 (2013), 97–154

Boje, P. V., *Vejen til velstand: Marked, stat og utopi, II: Hvorvor blev Danmark riget – og ikke rigere. Tiden 1850–1930* (Odense, 2020)

Boltanski, L. and E. Chiapello, *Le nouvel esprit du capitalisme* (Paris, 1999)

Bouche, P., 'Vulgariser, convaincre: Les "femmes économistes" en Angleterre dans les années 1830. Économie et littérature', *France et Grande-Bretagne 1815–1848*, ed. F. Vatin and N. Edelman (Paris, 2007), pp. 141–59

Bourde, A.-J., *Agronomie et agronomes en France au XVIIIe siècle* (Paris, 1967)

Bourrigaud, R., *Le développement agricole au 19e siècle en Loire-Atlantique* (Nantes, 1994)

Boyns, T., J. R. Edwards and M. Nitkitin, 'The Development of Industrial Accounting in Britain and France before 1880: A Comparative Study of Accounting Literature and Practice', *European Accounting Review* 6,3 (1997), 393–437

Bracht, J. and U. Pfister, *Landpacht, Marktgesellschaft und agrarische Entwicklung* (Münster, 2020)
Brandt, K., 'Land Valuation in Germany', *Journal of Farm Economics* 19,1 (1937), 173–87
Braun, R., *Le déclin de l'Ancien Régime en Suisse: Un tableau de l'histoire économique et sociale du 18e siècle* (Lausanne, 1988)
Bremer, J., *Die reichsunmittelbare Herrschaft Dyck der Grafen, jetzigen Fürsten zu Salm-Reifferscheidt* (Grevenbroich, 1959)
Brenner, R., 'Agrarian Class Structure and Economic Development in Pre-Industrial Europe', *Past & Present* 70,1 (1976), 30–75
—— 'The Agrarian Roots of European Capitalism', *Past & Present* 97,1 (1982), 16–113
—— 'The Low Countries in the Transition to Capitalism', *Journal of Agrarian Change* 1,2 (2001), 169–241
Bro Pedersen, T., 'Driftsøkonomisk Vejledning paa Grundlag af Regnskabsresultater', *Ugeskrift for Landmænd* 1942, 318–21
Broad, J. and R. Ford, 'Quand les fermiers anglais prennent la plume: Une littérature diversifiée (1600–1850)', *La plume et la terre*, ed. Fulgence Dellaux (Namur, 2022)
Bruegel, M., *Farm, Shop, Landing: The Rise of a Market Society in the Hudson Valley, 1780–1860* (Durham, 2002)
Bryer, R. A., 'The History of Accounting and the Transition to Capitalism in England. Part One: Theory', *Accounting, Organizations and Society* 25,2 (2000), 131–62
—— 'The History of Accounting and the Transition to Capitalism in England. Part Two: Evidence', *Accounting, Organizations and Society* 25,4–5 (2000), 327–81
—— 'The Roots of Modern Capitalism: A Marxist Account of the Origins and Consequences of Capitalist Landownership in England', *Accounting Historians Journal* 31,1 (2004), 1–5
—— 'The Genesis of the Capitalist Farmer: Towards a Marxist Accounting History of the Origins of the English Agricultural Revolution', *Critical Perspectives on Accounting* 17,4 (2006), 367–97
—— 'Accounting and Control of the Labour Process', *Critical Perspectives on Accounting* 17,5 (2006), 551–98
Bryer, R. A., R. Fleischmann and R. Macve, 'Smith, Marx or Foucault in Understanding the Early British Industrial Revolution? A Re-examination of the Management and Accounting of Capital and Labor at the Carron Company', *Proceedings of the 28th European Accounting Association Conference* (2005)
Bujault, J., *L'agriculture populaire ou méthode générale et nouvelle pour l'enseignement et l'amélioration de l'agriculture* (Niort, 1831)

Burchell, S., C. Clubb, A. Hopwood., J. Hughes and J. Nahapiet, 'The Roles of Accounting in Organizations and Society', *Accounting, Organizations and Society* 5,1 (1980), 5–27

Burnette, J., 'Seasonal Patterns of Agricultural Day-Labour at Eight English Farms, 1835–1844', *Seven Centuries of Unreal Wages: The Unreliable Data, Sources and Methods that Have Been Used for Measuring Standards of Living in the Past*, ed. J. Hatcher and J. Stephenson (London, 2018)

Bustarret, C., 'Usages des supports d'écriture au XVIIIe siècle: Une esquisse codicologique', *Genesis. Manuscrits – Recherche – Invention* 34 (2012), 37–65

Buus, N. P. J., 'Om Køernes Udbytte i 1864', *Ugeskrift for Landmænd* I (1865), 179–93

Candaux, J.-D., S. Capdeville, M. Grenon, R. S. Somov and V. Sonov (eds), *Deux astronomes genevois dans la Russie de Catherine II: Journaux de voyage en Laponie russe de Jean-Louis Pictet et Jacques-André Mallet pour observer le passage de Vénus devant le disque solaire, 1768–1769* (Ferney-Voltaire, 2005)

Callon, M. (ed.), *The Laws of the Markets* (Malden/Oxford, 1998)

Carruthers, B. G. and W. N. Espeland, 'Accounting for Rationality: Double-Entry Bookkeeping and the Rhetoric of Economic Rationality', *American Journal of Sociology* 97,1 (1991), 31–69

Cazeaux, P.-E., *Du rôle des femmes dans l'agriculture: Esquisse d'un institut rural féminin* (Paris, 1869)

Chajanov, A., *Bjudzhetnie Issledovanija: Istorija i Metodi* (Moscow, 1929)

Charmasson, T., A.-M. Lelorrain and Y. Ripa, *L'enseignement agricole et vétérinaire de la révolution à la libération* (Paris, 1992)

Cherkaoui, M., 'Le réel et le rationnel: Rationalités et conséquences inattendues chez Max Weber', *Revue européenne des sciences sociales* 42,129 (2004), 73–86

Chiapello, È., 'Accounting and the Birth of the Notion of Capitalism', *Critical Perspectives on Accounting* 18,3 (2007), 263–96

Chiapello, È. and P. Gilbert, *Sociologie des outils de gestion* (Paris, 2020)

Cianferoni, R., 'Gli antichi libri contabili delle Fattorie quali fonti della storia dell'agricoltura e dell'economia toscana: metodi e problemi della loro utilizzazione', *Storia dell'agricoltura* 13 (1973), 47–76

Clarke, C., *The True Theory and Practice of Husbandry* (London, 1777)

Clarke, L. L., *Schooling the Daughters of Marianne: Textbooks and the Socialization of Girls in Modern French Primary Schools* (New York, 1984)

Congost, R. and E. Sauger, 'Mémoires humbles: Les écrits des travailleurs agricoles comme témoignages du changement social (région de Gerone, Catalogne, XVIIIe siècle)', *La plume et la terre*, ed. F. Delleaux (Namur, 2022)

Connor, R. E., *Women, Accounting and Narrative: Keeping Books in Eighteenth-Century England* (London, 2004)

Cop, R., 'Travaux céréaliers et assolements aux montagnes du XVIIe au début du XIXe siècle', *Musée Neuchâtelois* 27,1 (1990), 85–103

Coquery, N., F. Menant and F. Weber, *Ecrire, compter, mesurer: Vers une histoire des rationalités pratiques* (Paris, 2006)

Cuin, C.-H., 'Émotions et rationalité dans la sociologie classique: Le cas de Weber et Durkheim', *Revue européenne des sciences sociales* 120 (2001), 77–100

D'Onofrio, F., 'Making Variety Simple: Agricultural Economists in Southern Italy, 1906–9', *History of Political Economy* 44,1 (2012), 93–113

—— 'Knowing to Transform: Three Ways for Agricultural Economists to Observe Italy 1900–1940', PhD dissertation, Universiteit Utrecht (2013)

—— *Observing Agriculture in Early Twentieth-Century Italy: Agricultural Economists and Statistics* (London/New York, 2016)

—— 'The Microfoundations of Italian Agrarianism: Italian Agricultural Economists and Fascism', *Agricultural History* 91 (2017), 369–96

D'Onofrio, F. and N. Mignemi. 'The International Institute of Agriculture and the Information Infrastructure of World Trade (1905–1946)', *Histoire & Mesure* XXXVIII,1 (2023), 13–38

De Certeau, M., *L'invention du quotidien: 1. Arts de faire* (Paris, 1990)

De Gasparin, A., *Cours d'agriculture* (Paris, 1848)

Delleaux, F., 'L'Astronome aux champs: Le journal de Jacques-André Mallet sur son domaine d'Avully en Genevois (1773–1789)', *Histoire et sociétés rurales* 31 (2009), 141–94

—— 'L'Astronome aux champs: Le journal de Jacques-André Mallet sur son domaine d'Avully en Genevois (1773–1789)', *Histoire et sociétés rurales* 32 (2009), 135–97

—— *Les censiers et les mutations des campagnes du Hainaut français: La formation originale d'une structure socio-économique, fin XVIIe–début XIXe siècle* (Namur, 2012)

—— 'La grande exploitation, la ville et les agronomes: Dynamiques et stratégies de production au domaine d'Avully en Genevois à la fin du XVIIIe siècle', *Histoire, Économie & Société* 34,4 (2015), 5–26

—— 'De la paille à la grappe: Mesurer le progrès agricole d'un domaine genevois au XVIIIe siècle', *Revue Suisse d'Histoire* 68,2 (2018), 240–73

—— (ed.), *La plume et la terre: Écrire sur son exploitation agricole en Europe occidentale (1650–1850)* (Namur, 2021)

—— *Inquiétude dans les champs: Essai sur la gestion des exploitations agricoles dans l'espace francophone, vers 1730–vers 1830* (Louvain-la-Neuve, 2022)

Densmore, C. 'Understanding and Using Early Nineteenth-Century Account Books', *The Midwestern Archivist* 5,1 (1980), 5–19

Depecker, T., 'La loi des tables: Quantification du besoin alimentaire et réforme des conduites de vie (XIXe–XXe siècles)', PhD dissertation, EHESS Paris (2014)

Depecker, T. and N. Joly, 'Agronomists and Accounting: The Beginnings of Capitalist Rationalization on the Farm (1800–1850)', *Historia Agraria* 65,1 (2015), 75–94

—'La terre et ses manufacturiers: L'introduction d'une raison gestionnaire dans les domaines agricoles (1800–1850)', *Entreprises et histoire* 79,2 (2015), 12–23

Depecker, T. and F. Vatin, 'Taking Stock to Yield a Return: Agricultural Accounting, Agronomy, and Chemical Statistics in the Early Nineteenth Century', *Accounting History Review* 26,2 (2016), 107–29

Det Landøkonomiske Driftsbureau, *25 Aars Undersøgelser over Landbrugets Driftsforhold, 1918–43* (Copenhagen, 1943)

Detienne, M., 'L'art de construire des comparables: Entre historiens et anthropologues', *Critiques internationales* 1 (2002), 68–78

Dettwiler, E., 'Die Buchhaltungserhebungen des Schweizerischen Bauernsekretariates', *Die Grüne Schweizerische Landwirtschaftliche Zeitschrift* 93 (1965), 1476–81, 1511–19

Dierkes, S. and U. Schäfer, 'Prinzipal-Agenten-Theorie und Performance Measurement', *Zeitschrift für Controlling & Management* (2008), 19–27

Donzelot, J., *La police des familles* (Paris, 1977)

Dupin, C., *Le petit producteur français* (Paris, 1827)

Ecklin, S., *Le journal de Daniel Sandoz, 1770–1779: Essai de lecture critique* (Neuchâtel, 1990)

— 'Le journal de Daniel Sandoz, 1770–1779: Chronique d'un système rédactionnel complexe', *Lire et écrire en Europe (1500–1900): Perspectives comparées*, ed. R. Chartier and A. Messerli (Basel, 2001), pp. 139–49

Edwards, E. E., 'Agricultural Records: Their Nature and Value for Research', *Agricultural History* 13,1 (1939), 1–12

Edwards, J. R., 'Accounting on English Landed Estates during the Agricultural Revolution – A Textbook Perspective', *Accounting Historians Journal* 38,2 (2011), 1–45

Edwards, J. R. and T. Boyns, *A History of Management Accounting: The British Experience* (London, 2016)

Edwards R. S., 'A Survey of French Contributions to the Study of Cost Accounting during the Nineteenth Century', *Accounting in France: Historical Essays/études historiques*, ed. Y. Lemarchand and R. Parker (London, 1996), pp. 155–90

Eisenstein, E. L., *The Printing Press as an Agent of Change* (Cambridge, 1980)

El Amrani-Boisseau, F., *Filles de la terre: Apprentissages au féminin (Anjou 1920–1950)* (Rennes, 2012)

Engel, E., 'Die vorherrschenden Gewerbszweige in den Gerichtsämtern mit Beziehung auf die Productions- und Consumtionsverhältnisse des Königreichs Sachsen', *WISTA – Wirtschaft und Statistik* 73,2 (2021 [1857]), 126–36

—— *Das Rechnungsbuch der Hausfrau und seine Bedeutung im Wirthschaftsleben der Nation: Ein Vortrag* (Berlin, 1882)

—— 'Die Lebenskosten belgischer Arbeiter-Familien früher und jetzt – Ermittelt aus Familien-Haushaltrechnungen und vergleichend zusammengestelt', *Bulletin de L'Institut International de Statistique* IX,1 (1895), 1–124

Esch, A., 'Chance et hasard de transmission', *Le problème de la représentativité et de la déformation de la transmission historique: Les tendances actuelles de l'histoire du Moyen Âge en France et en Allemagne. Actes des colloques de Sèvres*, ed. J.-C. Schmitt and O. G. Oexle (Paris, 1997)

Federico, G., *Feeding the World: An Economic History of Agriculture 1800–2000* (Princeton, 2005)

Fellenberg-Ziegler, A., 'Über landwirthschaftliche Buchhaltung', *Bernische Blätter für Landwirtschaft* 15 (1861), 88–9

Fisher, J. D., *The Enclosure of Knowledge: Books, Power and Agrarian Capitalism in Britain, 1660–1800* (Cambridge, 2022)

Fitzgerald, D., *Every Farm a Factory: The Industrial Ideal in American Agriculture* (New Haven, 2003)

Fletcher, T. W., 'The Great Depression of English Agriculture 1873–1896', *The Economic History Review* 13,3 (1961), 417–32

Foucault, M., *The Archaeology of Knowledge and the Discourse on Language* (New York, 1972)

Franck, H., '75 Jahre Buchhaltungserhebungen beim schweizerischen Bauernsekretariat', *Mitteilungen des schweizerischen Bauernsekretariates* 194 (1976)

Freear, J., 'Robert Loder, Jacobean Management Accountant', *Abacus* 6,1 (1970), 25–38

French, H. and R. W. Hoyle, *The Character of English Rural Society: Earls Colne, 1550–1750* (Manchester, 2007)

Furet, F. and J. Ozouf, *Lire et écrire: L'alphabétisation des Français de Calvin à Jules Ferry* (Paris, 1977)

Gaboriaux, C., 'Entre innovations agronomiques et pratiques paysannes: La figure de "l'agriculteur pratique" au 19e siècle', *Sciences, chercheurs et agriculture: Pour une histoire de la recherche agronomique*, ed. C. Bonneuil, G. Denis and J.-L. Mayaud (Paris, 2008), pp. 45–60

Gacon-Dufour d'Humières, M.-A.-J., *Recueil pratique d'économie rurale et domestique* (Paris, 1804)

Gandhi, N. M., 'The Emergence of the Post-Industrial Society and the Future of the Accounting Function', *Journal of Management Studies* 13,3 (1976), 199–212

Garrabou, R., J. Planas and E. Saguer, 'The Management of Agricultural Estates in Catalonia in the Nineteenth and Early Twentieth Century', *The Agricultural History Review* 60,2 (2012), 173–90

Garrabou, R., E. Saguer Hom and P. S. López, 'Formas de gestión y evolución de la renta a partir del análisis de contabilidades agrarias: Los patrimonios del Marqués de Sentmenat en el Vallés y Urgell (1820–1917)', *Noticiario de historia agraria: boletín informativo del Seminario de Historia Agraria* 5 (1993), 97–125

Gervais, P., 'Why Profit and Loss Didn't Matter: The Historicized Rationality of Early Modern Merchant Accounting', *Merchants and Profit in the Age of Commerce, 1680–1830*, ed. P. Gervais, Y. Lemarchand and D. Margairaz (London, 2014), pp. 33–53

—— 'Comptabilité et profit: Comment saisir les pratiques comptables de l'époque Moderne', *Comptabilités* 14 (2021)

Geurts, H. M. L., 'Herman Derk Louwes (1893–1960): Burgemeester van de Nederlandse landbouw', *Historia agriculturae* 32 (Groningen, 2002)

Gibson, M. A., 'Immigrant Adaptation and Patterns of Acculturation', *Human Development* 44 (2001), 19–23

Giorgio, M., 'La bonne catholique', *Histoire des femmes en Occident: Le XIXe siècle*, ed. G. Fraisse and M. Perrot (Tome IV, 1991), pp. 203–39

Giraudeau, M., 'The Farm as an Accounting Laboratory: An Essay on the History of Accounting and Agriculture', *Accounting History Review* 27,2 (2017), 201–15

Glennie, P. and N. Thrift, 'Reworking E. P. 'Thompson's "Time, Work-Discipline and Industrial Capitalism"', *Time & Society* 5,3 (1996), 275–9

Goody, J., *The Domestication of the Savage Mind* (Cambridge/London/New York, 1977)

—— *The Interface between the Written and the Oral* (Cambridge, 1987)

Greyerz, K., 'Écriture de soi et lecture religieuse chez les protestants du monde germanophone en perspective confessionnelle', *Appel à témoins: Écrits personnels et pratiques socioculturelles, XVIe–XXe*, ed. D. Tosato-Rigo (Lausanne, 2016), pp. 39–61

Gubin, E., 'Un rempart contre le désordre: Les paysannes belges au tournant du XXe siècle', *Enquêtes rurales* 10 (2004), 137–58

Gyllembourg, C. F., *Forsøg til et Landbrugs-Bogholderie* (Copenhagen, 1908)

Gysel, Z., *Der Schaffhauser Bauer, wie er sein sollte, und wie er nicht ist, wie er ist, und wie er nicht sein sollte* (Schaffhausen, 1854)

Haas, P. M., 'Introduction: Epistemic Communities and International Policy Coordination', *International Organization* 46,1 (1992), 1–35

Hailwood, M., 'Time and Work in Rural England, 1500–1700', *Past & Present* 248,1 (2020), 87–121

Hainsworth, D. R. S., 'The Estate Steward and his World in Later Stuart England', *Cambridge Studies in Early Modern British History* (Cambridge, 2008)

Hansen, K., 'Regnskabsføring for Landbrug', *Ugeskrift for Landmænd* (1922)

Harvey, P. D. A, 'Manorial Accounts', *Accounting History: Some British Contributions,* ed. R H. Parker and B. S. Yamey (Oxford, 1994), pp. 91–115

Harwood, J., *Europe's Green Revolution and Others Since* (London, 2016)

Hashimzade, N., G. Myles and J. Black, 'Principal–Agent Problem', *A Dictionary of Economics,* Oxford Reference (Oxford, 2017)

Haumann, H. and W. Baumann, '"... um die Organisation des typischen Arbeitsbetriebes kennenzulernen": Zu Aleksandr Čajanovs Schrift "Bäuerliche Wirtschaft in der Schweiz"', *Schweizerische Zeitschrift für Geschichte/Revue Suisse d'histoire/Rivista storica Svizzera* (1997), 1–26

Hébrard, J., 'La lettre représentée: Les pratiques épistolaires dans les récits de vie ouvriers et paysans', *La correspondance: Les usages de la lettre au XIXème siècle,* ed. R. Chartier (Paris, 1991), pp. 279–365

Hendrikx, D. and O. Gelderblom, 'Accounting for Agricultural Development? The Case of the Netherlands, 1840–1940', *Agricultural History Review* 70,1 (2022), 23–48

Henriksen, I., M. Lampe and P. Sharp, 'The Role of Technology and Institutions for Growth: Danish Creameries in the Late Nineteenth Century', *European Review of Economic History* 15 (2011), 475–93

—— 'The Strange Birth of Liberal Denmark: Danish Trade Protection and the Growth of the Dairy Industry since the Mid-Nineteenth Century', *Economic History Review* 65,2 (2012), 770–88

Henriques, S., P. Sharp, X. Tsoukli and C. Vedel, 'Resilience, Adaptability and Transformability: Danish Butter Factories in the Face of Coal Shortages', *EHES Working Paper 220* (2021)

Herment, L., 'Mesurer les performances céréalières des petites exploitations du bassin parisien durant le premier XIXe siècle', *Histoire et Sociétés Rurales* 36,2 (2011), 97–136

—— *Les fruits du partage: Petits paysans du bassin parisien au XIXe siècle* (Rennes, 2012)

—— 'Un capitulo poco conocido sobre la historia de la patata en la region Parisina durante el sigle XIX', *Obradoiro de Historia Moderna* 27 (2018), 209–33

—— *La plus belle firme du monde ne peut offrir que ce qu'elle a* (Paris, 2021)

Herment, L. and A. Antoine, 'Specialisation in Rural History: Towards a Definition', *Agricultural Specialisation and Rural Patterns of Development in Rural History in Europe,* ed. A. Antoine (Turnhout, 2016), pp. 13–45

Herment, L. and N. Mignemi, 'La especialización agrícola en la historia rural europea: Recursos, mercados y espacios (siglos XVIII–XX)', *Mundo Agrario* 22,49 (2021)

Hertel, H., *Det Kgl. Danske Landhusholdningsselskabs Historie, II: Selskabets Historie i Tiden fra 1869–1918* (Copenhagen, 1920)

Hiler, D., 'Permanences et innovations alimentaires: L'évolution de la consommation des Genevois pendant le XVIIIe siècle', *Bulletin de la Société d'Histoire et d'Archéologie de Genève* 18 (1984)

—— 'Le vin genevois au XVIIIe siècle: Vente et consommation', *Revue du Vieux Genève* (1984)

Hobsbawm, E., *L'ère du capital (1848–1875)* (Paris, 1994).

Hofman Bang, N. E., 'Om Meieriregnskaber og Forpagtningsforhold', *Ugeskrift for Landmænd* (1862), 213–28

Hofstee, E. W., 'De ontwikkeling van de groote der landbouwbedrijven in de provincie Groningen', *Tijdschrift voor economische geographie* 38,6–7 (1947), 134–51

Hoggart, R., *The Uses of Literacy: Aspects of Working-Class Life* (The Hague, 1967)

Hont, I. 'Correcting Europe's Political Economy: The Virtuous Eclecticism of Georg Ludwig Schmid', *History of European Ideas* 33,4 (2007), 390–410

Hopf-Droste, M.-L., 'Vorbilder, Formen und Funktionen ländlicher Anscreibebücher', *Alte Tagebücher und Anschreibebücher: Quellen zum Alltag der ländlichen Bevölkerung in Nordwesteuropa*, ed. H. Ottenjann and G. Wiegelmann (Münster, 1982), pp. 61–84

Hopper, J. S. and H. Willmott, 'Accounting for Accounting: Towards the Development of a Dialectical View', *Accounting, Organizations and Society* 12,5 (1987), 441

Hopwood, A. G., 'Accounting and Everyday Life: An Introduction', *Accounting, Organizations and Society* 19,3 (1994), 299–301

Horn, P., *William Marshall (1745–1818) and the Georgian Countryside* (Abingdon, 1982)

Hoskin, K. and R. Macve, 'Writing, Examining, Disciplining: The Genesis of Accounting's Modern Power', *Accounting as Social and Institutional Practice*, ed. A. Hopwood and P. Miller (Cambridge, 1994), pp. 67–97

Hubscher, R., 'La petite exploitation en France: Reproduction et compétitivité (fin XIXe siècle–début XXe siècle)', *Annales ESC* 1 (1985), 3–34

Hyden-Hanscho, V., *Herrschaftsvermittlung in den österreichischen Niederlanden. Léopold Philippe Arenberg zwischen Karl III./VI. und Maria Theresia*, ed. V. Hyden-Hanscho and W. D. Godsey (Regensburg, 2019)

Inhetveen, H., 'Women Pioneers in Farming: A Gendered History of Agricultural Progress', *Sociologia Ruralis* 38,3 (1998), 265–84

Institut International d'Agriculture, 'Séances plénières de l'Assemblée Générale – Séance du samedi 10 Mai', *Actes de la quatrième Assemblée Générale 6–12 Mai 1913* (Rome, 1913)

—— *Les offices de comptabilité agricole dans les différents pays* (Rome, 1924)

—— *The First World Agricultural Census* (Rome, 1939)

Jack, L., 'Agriculture', *The Routledge Companion to Accounting History*, ed. J. R. Edwards and S. Walker (Abingdon, 2020), pp. 389–409

Jacob, G., *The Country Gentleman's Vade Mecum* (London, 1717)

Jacobsen, A. P., 'Regnskabsfører og Driftskonsulent', *Ugeskrift for Landmænd* (1932)

Jaggi, E., 'Methodik und Technik der Ertragswertschätzung landwirtschaftlicher Betriebe und Grundstücke unter spezieller Berücksichtigung der Verwendbarkeit der Einheitsbewertung für schweizerische Verhältnisse', PhD dissertation, ETH Zürich (1945)

Järvelä, H. and A.-M. Aarnio, 'The Development of Bookkeeping Activities', *Maatalouden kannattavuustutkimus 75 vuotta* (Helsinki, 1987)

Jas, N., 'Les enjeux scientifiques, techniques et commerciaux du contrôle de la qualité des engrais au XIXe siècle', *Réseaux* 18,102 (2000), 165–94

— 'Au carrefour de la chimie et de l'agriculture: Les sciences agronomiques en France et en Allemagne 1840–1914', ed. Archives contemporaines (Paris, 2001)

Jeannin, P., 'La diffusion des manuels de marchands: Fonctions et stratégies éditoriales', *Revue d'histoire moderne et contemporaine* 45,3 (1998), 515–57

Jensen, E., *Danish Agriculture: Its Economic Development. A Description and Economic Analysis Centering on the Free Trade Epoch, 1870–1930* (Copenhagen, 1937)

Jensen, M. C. and W. H. Meckling, 'Theory of the Firm: Managerial Behavior, Agency Costs and Ownership Structure', *Journal of Finance Economics V* 3,4 (1976), 305–60

Jensen, S., '[Review of] Det landøkonomiske Driftsbureau: 25 Aars Undersøgelser over Landbrugets Driftsforhold 1918–43. I Kommission hos fh. August Bangs Forlag, Ejvind Christensen. København 1943. 173 Sider. Kr. 4,00', *Handelsvidenskabeligt Tidsskrift* 8 (1943), 83–4

Jensen, S. P., 'Landbrugets systemskifte 1870 til 1914 belyst gennem dagbøger og regnskaber fra en enkelt gård', *Fra stilstand til vækst: Studier i dansk landbrugs udvikling fra 1682 til 1914*, ed. S. P. Jensen (Auning, 2007), pp. 215–49

Jervelund, C., 'Hvilke Fordele har jeg som praktisk Landmand haft af ca. 40 Aars Regnskabsføring', *Ugeskrift for Landmænd* (1942), 321–3

Joly, N., 'Écritures du travail et savoirs paysans: Aperçu historique et lecture de pratiques: les agendas des agriculteurs', PhD dissertation, Université de Paris X (Nanterre, 1997)

— 'Écrire l'événement: Le travail agricole mis en mémoire', *Sociologie du travail* 46 (2004), 511–27

— 'Vaches et blés sur le papier: Socialisations à l'écrit du monde agricole', *Communication et langages* 1 (2009), 77–90

— 'Tracing Cows: Practical and Administrative Logics in Tension', *The Anthropology of Writing: Understanding Textually Mediated Worlds*, ed. D. Barton and U. Papen (London, 2010), pp. 90–105

—— 'Shaping Records on the Farm: Agricultural Record Keeping in France from the Nineteenth Century to the Liberation', *The Agricultural History Review* 59,1 (2011), 61–80

—— 'Educating in Economic Calculus: The Invention of the Enlightened Peasant via Manuals of Agriculture, 1830–1870', *Accounting History Review* 26,2 (2016), 131–60

—— 'L'organisation comptable dans les grandes exploitations françaises (XVIIe s.-milieu XIXe s.)', *Dictionnaire historique de comptabilité des entreprises*, ed. D. Bensadon, N. Praquin and B. Touchelay (Villeneuve d'Ascq, 2016), pp. 438–41

—— 'Comme le sang dans le corps des animaux: Le capital circulant expliqué à la jeunesse rurale par Louis Gossin (1838)', *Entreprises et histoire* 88,3 (2017), 182–8

Joly, N., R. Bourrigaud and F. Knittel, 'Administrer une ferme-modèle au XIXe siècle: Deux expériences d'agronomes entrepreneurs ruraux, Mathieu de Dombasle et Rieffel', *Entreprises et histoire* 3,88 (2017), 21–36

Joly, N., T. Depecker and J. Labatut, 'L'entreprise agricole et sa gestion: Ethos, structures et instruments (XIXe–XXe siècle)', *Entreprises et histoire* 88,1 (2017), 6–20

Jones, P. M., *Agricultural Enlightenment: Knowledge, Technology, and Nature, 1750–1840* (Oxford, 2016)

Jost, P., *Die Prinzipal-Agenten-Theorie in der Betriebswirtschaftlehre* (Stuttgart, 2001)

Juchau, R., 'Agricultural Cost Accounting Development in Britain: The Contributions of Three Men from Wye: A Review Note', *Accounting, Business and Financial History* 8,2 (1998), 165–74

—— 'Early Cost Accounting Ideas in Agriculture: The Contributions of Arthur Young', *Accounting, Business & Financial History* 12,3 (2002), 369–86

Kaak, H. and M. Schattkowsky, *Herrschaft: Machtentfaltung über adligen und fürstlichen Grundbesitz in der Frühen Neuzeit*, ed. J. Peters (Cologne, 2003)

Kalaora, B. and A. Savoye, *Les inventeurs oubliés: Le Play et ses continuateurs aux origines des sciences sociales* (Seyssel, 1989)

Kalberg, S., 'La sociologie des émotions de Max Weber', *Revue du MAUSS* 40,2 (2012), 285–99

Kalma, J. J., 'Rauwerda, Anne Melles', *Biografisch Woordenboek van het Socialisme en de Arbeidersbeweging in Nederland*, vol. 4 (Amsterdam, 1990), pp. 169–71

Klamer, A. and D. McCloskey, 'Accounting as the Master Metaphor of Economics', *The European Accounting Review* 1,1 (1992), 145–60

Knittel, F., 'L'Europe agronomique de C-J-A Mathieu de Dombasle', *Revue d'histoire moderne et contemporaine* 57,1 (2010), 119–38

Koning, N., *The Failure of Agrarian Capitalism: Agrarian Politics in the United Kingdom, Germany, the Netherlands and the USA 1946–1919* (London/New York, 1994)

Kooijmans, T. and J. Jonker, 'Chained to the Manor? Payment Patterns and Landlord–ǀTenant Relations in the Salland Region of the Netherlands around 1750', *Tijdschrift Voor Sociale en Economische Geschiedenis* 12,4 (2015), 89–116

Kotsonis, Y., *Making Peasants Backward* (London, 1999)

Kraemer, A., *Die Buchhaltung des Landwirts* (Bonn, 1881)

—'Reinertrag und Einkommen aus der Landwirthschaft – Ertragswerth, Verkehrswerth und Preis des Grundbesitzes', *Landwirtschaftliches Jahrbuch der Schweiz* (1890), p. 210

Kristensen, K. J., '(Review of) Det landøkonomiske Driftsbureau: Undersøgelser over Landbrugets Driftsforhold I. Nogle Regnskabsresultater fra danske Landbrug i Aaret 1916—17 ved J. C. Overgaard. 38 S', *Nationaløkonomisk Tidsskrift* III,27 (1919), 587–90

Krusius-Ahrenberg, L., 'Carl Fredrik Gyllembourg-Ehrensvärd som dansk lantbruksekonom', *Svenska litteratursällskapet i Finland historiska och litteraturhistoriska studier* 23 (1947), 284–369

Kuperus, J. A., 'Boekhoudingen op nederlandse Landbouwbedrijven voor 1900', *Ceres en Clio: Zeven variaties op het thema landbouwgeschiedenis: geschreven ter gelegenheid van het vijfentwintigjarig bestaan van de Studiekring voor de Geschiedenis van de Landbouw*, ed. N.G. Addens (Wageningen, 1964), pp. 89–111

L. O., 'Kursus i Regnskabsføring i Hadsten og Omegns Landboforening', *Ugeskrift for Landmænd* 63 (1918), 280–2

Labardin, P., 'L'émergence de la fonction comptable en France', PhD dissertation, Université d'Orléans (Orleans, 2008)

— 'Accounting Prescription and Practice in Nineteenth Century France: An Analysis of Bankruptcy Cases', *Accounting History Review* 21,3 (2011), 263–83

Labardin, P. and P. Gervais, 'Marketing the Past over the Long Run: Uses of the Past in French Accounting Textbooks, 17th–19th C.', *Journal of Historical Research in Marketing* 14,1 (2022), 90–110

Labardin, P. and M. Nikitin, 'Accounting and the Words to Tell it: An Historical Perspective', *Accounting, Business and Financial History* 19,2 (2009), 149–66

Labardin, P. and P. Robic, 'Épouses et petites entreprises: Permanence du XVIIIe au XXe siècle', *Revue française de gestion* 8–9,188–9 (2008), 97–117

Ladurie, E. L. R., 'Les comptes fantastiques de Gregory King', *Annales. Économies, Sociétés, Civilisations* 23,5 (1968), 1086–102

Lahire, B., D. Thin and G. Vincent, 'Sur l'histoire et la théorie de la forme scolaire', *L'Education prisonnière de la forme scolaire? Scolarisation et socialisation dans les sociétés industrielles*, ed. G. Vincent (Lyon, 1994), 11–48

Lambrecht, T., 'Reciprocal Exchange, Credit and Cash: Agricultural Labour Markets and Local Economies in the Southern Low Countries during the Eighteenth Century', *Continuity and Change* 18,2 (2003), 237–61

Lampe, M. and P. Sharp, 'Just Add Milk: A Productivity Analysis of the Revolutionary Changes in Nineteenth Century Danish Dairying', *Economic History Review* 68,4 (2015), 1132–53

—— 'A Quest for Useful Knowledge: The Early Development of Agricultural Accounting in Denmark and Northern Germany', *Accounting History Review* 27,1 (2017), 73–99

—— '"Rational" Farmers and the Emergence of Modern Accounting in Danish Dairying', *EHES Working Papers in Economic History* 115 (2017)

—— 'Accounting for the Wealth of Denmark: A Case Study of Smithian Growth Using the Emergence of Modern Accounting in Danish Dairying', *European Journal of the History of Economic Thought* 26,4 (2019), 659–97

—— A *Land of Milk and Butter: How Elites Created the Modern Danish Dairy Industry* (Chicago, 2019)

Lamoreaux, N., 'Rethinking the Transition to Capitalism in the Early American Northeast', *Journal of American History* 90,2 (2003)

Lampland, M., 'False Numbers as Formalizing Practices', *Social Studies of Science* 40,3 (2010), 377–40

—— *The Value of Labor: The Science of Commodification in Hungary, 1920–1956* (Chicago, 2016)

Landbrugskandidat, N., 'Skovduen eller Skaden?', *Ugeskrift for Landmænd* 62 (1916), 451–4

Landes, D. S., 'Culture Makes Almost All the Difference', *Culture Matters: How Values Shape Human Progress*, ed. L. E. Harrison and S. P. Huntington (2000), pp. 1–13

Lando, Z. D., 'Landøkonomisk Oplysningarbejde', *Handelsvidenskabeligt Tidsskrift* 4 (1940), 188–207

Larsen, O. H., 'Det landøkonomiske Driftsbureau og dets Arbejde gennem de første 10 Aar', *Ugeskrift for Landmænd* 73 (1928), 769–72, 785–8

Larsen, O. H. and I. Dokken, *Undersøgelser over Landbrugets Driftsforhold II: Regnskabsresultater fra danske Landbrug i Aaret 1917–18* (Odense, 1919)

—— *Vejledning ved Landbrugs-Regnskabsføringen i Tilslutning til det landøkonomiske Driftsbureau* (Copenhagen, 1926)

Latour B., 'Visualization and Cognition', *Knowledge and Society* 6,1 (1986), 1–40

Laur, E., *Die Buchhaltung des Schweizerbauern* (Aarau, 1898)

—— *Grundlagen und Methoden der Bewertung, Buchhaltung und Kalkulation in der Landwirtschaft* (Berlin, 1911)

—— *Landwirtschaftliche Betriebslehre für bäuerliche Verhältnisse* (Aarau, 1912)
—— 'Basis of International Statistics of Agricultural Book-Keeping', *Monthly Bulletin of Agricultural Intelligence and Plant Diseases* 5,2 (1914), 171–85
—— *Der Schweizerbauer, seine Heimat und sein Werk* (Bern, 1947)
Laurence, E., *The Duty of a Steward to his Lord* (London, 1727)
Le Texier, T., 'Homemade Economics: The Managerial Rationalization of Women's Everyday Life in America, 1820–1920' (2012), http://www.letexier.org/article.php3?id_article=107
Lecouteux, É., 'Notice sur le manuel de comptabilité agricole de Saintoin-Leroy', *Journal d'agriculture pratique* Tome 1 (1861), 62
Lee, G. A. and R. H. Osborne, 'The Account Book of a Derbyshire Farm of the Eighteenth Century', *Accounting, Business and Financial History* 4 (1994), 147–62
Lemarchand, Y., *Du dépérissement à l'amortissement: Enquête sur l'histoire d'un concept et de sa traduction comptable* (Nantes, 1993)
—— 'Double Entry Versus Charge and Discharge Accounting in Eighteenth-Century France', *Accounting, Business and Financial History* 4,1 (1994), 119–45
—— 'Style mercantile ou mode des finances: Le choix d'un modèle comptable dans la France d'Ancien Régime', *Annales histoire, sciences sociales* 50,1 (1995), 159–82
—— 'Journal-livre journal (XVIIIs.)', *Dictionnaire historique de comptabilité des entreprises*, ed. D. Bensadon, N. Praquin and B. Touchelay (Villeneuve d'Ascq, 2016), pp. 389–90
——'The Birth of Industrial Accounting in France: Some Curious Paradoxes', *Accounting History Review* 29,2 (2019), 221–41
Lemarchand, Y., Y. Levant and H. Zimnovitch, 'Schisme à Grignon: Autour de la comptabilité agricole durant les années 1870', *Entreprises et histoire* 88,3 (2017), 37–52
Lemarchand, Y. and R. Parker (eds), *Accounting in France: Historical Essays/Etudes historiques* (London, 1996)
Levant, Y. and H. Zimnovitch, 'Overview of Cost Accounting Practices in France from the Early Nineteenth Century to the 1880s', *Accounting History* 27,4 (2022), 576–606
Levi, H., *Entstehung und Rückgang des landwirtschaftlichen Grossbetriebes in England* (Berlin, 1904)
Levinson, S., *On 'Technologies of the Intellect': Goody Lecture 2020* (Halle, 2020)
Licoppe, C., *La formation de la pratique scientifique: Le discours de l'expérience en France et en Angleterre (1630–1820)* (Paris, 2013)
Linnemeier, B.-W., *Ein Gut und sein Alltag: Neuhof an der Weser* (Münster, 1992)

Loer, R. C., 'Farmers' Diaries: Their Interest and Value as Historical Sources', *Agricultural History* 12,4 (1938), 313–25

Lorenzen-Schmidt, K. J. and B. Poulsen (eds), *Bäuerliche Anschreibebücher als Quellen zur Wirtschaftsgeschichte* (Neumünster, 1992)

Lyautey M., L. Humbert and C. Bonneuil, 'Introduction', *Histoire des modernisations agricoles au XXe siècle*, ed. M. Lyautey, L. Humbert and C. Bonneuil (Rennes, 2021), pp. 5–26

Maas, H., 'Letts Calculate: Moral Accounting in the Victorian Period', *History of Political Economy* 48,1 (2016), 16–43

——'Monitoring the Self: François-Marc-Louis Naville and his Moral Tables', *History of Science* 58,2 (2020), 117–41

MacKenzie, D., *An Engine, Not a Camera: How Financial Models Shape Markets* (Cambridge/London, 2006)

Macve, R., 'Insights to Be Gained from the Study of Ancient Accounting History: Some Reflections on the New Edition of Finley's *The Ancient Economy*', *European Accounting Review* 11,2 (2002), 453–72

Madeline, P. and J.- M. Moriceau, *Un paysan et son univers de la guerre au marché commun: À travers les agendas de Pierre Lebugle, cultivateur en Pays d'Auge* (Paris/Berlin, 2010)

Manuel de la Jeune Fermière ou dialogue campagnard entre le curé-laboureur et la mère Matinotte sur l'économie domestique agricole (Niort, 1850)

Marenghi, E., 'Organizzazione ed importanza degli uffici di contabilità per lo studio dell'economia dell'azienda agraria', *Rivista italiana di ragioneria* 4, 5, 6, 7, 8, 9 (1914), 162–75, 201–4, 241–6, 289–301, 329–38, 386–90

—— 'Gli uffici di contabilità agraria nei diversi paesi', *Atti della Reale Accademia dei Georgofili* 99,2 (1921), 100–12

Marenghi, E. and A. Gabba (ed.), *Aspetti evolutivi della scienza estimativa: Seminario in onore di Ernesto Marenghi* (Florence, 1995)

Markham, G., *Markhams Farwell to Husbandry* (London, 1620)

Marshall, W., *Minutes of Agriculture, Made on a Farm of 300 Acres* (London, 1778)

—— *On the Landed Property of England* (London, 1804)

Mayaud, J.-L., *La petite exploitation triomphante* (Paris, 1999)

McCloskey, D., *The Bourgeois Virtues: Ethics for an Age of Commerce* (Chicago, 2006)

McLean, T., 'The Measurement and Management of Human Performance in Seventeenth Century English Farming: The Case of Henry Best', *Accounting Forum* 33,1 (2009), 62–73

Meager, L., *The Mystery of Husbandry: Or, Arable, Pasture, and Wood-Land Improved* (London, 1697)

Michel, P., 'La maison rustique des dames, ou l'édification domestique', *L'édification: Morales et cultures au XIXe siècle*, ed. S. Michaud (Paris, 1994), pp. 105–15

Mignemi, N., *Coopératives et mondes agricoles* (Rennes, 2017)
Mikkelsen, J. and E. Nørr, *Efter bemyndigelse: Kilder til dansk forvaltningshistorie, 1920–1970* (Copenhagen, 2008)
Miller, P., 'Governing by Numbers: Why Calculative Practices Matter', *Social Research* 68,2 (2001), 379–96
Miller, P. and T. O'Leary, 'Accounting and the Construction of the Governable Person', *Accounting, Organizations and Society* 12,3 (1987), 235–65
— 'Governing the Calculable Person', *Accounting as Social and Institutional Practice*, ed. A. G. Hopwood and P. Miller (Cambridge, 1994)
Miller, P., T. Hopper and R. Laughlin, 'The New Accounting History: An Introduction', *Accounting, Organizations and Society* 16,5–6 (1991), 395–403
Millet-Robinet, C.-É., *La maison rustique des dames*, tome 1 (Paris, 1845)
— *La maison rustique des dames*, tome 2 (Paris, 1856)
— *Guide pratique du fermier et de la fermière: La routine vaincue par le progrès. Histoire agricole et morale: Annexe à La maison rustique des dames* (Poitiers and Paris, 1860)
Milthers, A., 'M. Pedersen', *Dansk Biografisk Leksikon*, ed. S. C. Bech (Copenhagen, 1979)
Mingay, G. E., 'The Eighteenth Century Land Steward', *Land, Labour and Population in the Industrial Revolution: Essay Presented to J. D. Chambers*, ed. E. L. Jones and G. E. Mingay (Chatham, 1967), pp. 163–74
— *Rural Life in Victorian England* (London, 1976)
— 'Marshall, William (Bap. 1745, d. 1818)', *Oxford Dictionary of National Biography* (Oxford, 2004)
Mochard, M., 'Essai sur la meilleure méthode pour l'éducation du paysan, relativement à l'agriculture', *Mémoires et observations recueillies par la Société oeconomique de Berne* 5,3 (1764), 65
Mokyr, J., 'The Intellectual Origins of Modern Economic Growth', *Journal of Economic History* 65,2 (2005), 285–351
Molema, M., 'Collective Organisation of Knowledge in the Early Phase of the Dutch–Friesian Dairy Industry (c. 1880–1914)', *Historia Agraria* 73,4 (2017), 91–118
Mordant, J., *The Complete Steward: or, The Duty of a Steward to His Lord*, 2 (London, 1761)
Mordenti, R., *I libri di famiglia in Italia*, II, *Geografia e Storia* (Rome, 2001)
— 'Les livres de famille en Italie', *Annales, Histoire, Sciences Sociales* 59,4 (2004), 785–804
Moriceau, J.-M., *Les fermiers de l'Île-de-France: L'ascension d'un patronat agricole, XVe–XVIIe siècle* (Paris, 1994)
— *Les grands fermiers: Les laboureurs de l'Île-de-France (XVe–XVIIIe siècle)* (Paris, 2017)

—— 'A travers les comptes des grands fermiers du bassin parisien (1689–1884): Modèle de gestion ou mémorial familial?', *La plume et la terre*, ed. F. Delleaux (Namur, 2022), pp. 99–124

Moriceau, J.-M. and G. Postel-Vinay, *Ferme, entreprise, famille: Grande exploitation et changements agricoles, XVIIe–XIXe siècles* (Paris, 1992)

Mortimer, J., *The Whole Art of Husbandry* (London, 1707)

Moser, P., 'Stadt und Land in Irland und der Schweiz 1800–1989', *Stadt-Land-Beziehungen im 20: Jahrhundert. Geschichts- und kulturwissenschaftliche Perspektiven*, ed. F.-W. Kersting and C. Zimmermann (Paderborn, 2015), pp. 289–322

Moser, P., J. Auderset and B. Baechi, 'Die agrarisch-industrielle Wissensgesellschaft im 19./20. Jahrhundert: Akteure, Diskurse, Praktiken', *Geschichte im virtuellen Archiv: Das Archiv für Agrargeschichte als Zentrum der Archivierung und Geschichtsschreibung zur ländlichen Gesellschaft*, ed. B. B. Baden, M. Ineichen and T. Schibli (Baden, 2012), pp. 21–38

Moser, P. and H.-U. Schiedt, 'Arbeitstiere im langen 19. Jahrhundert: Empirische Evidenzen und soziale Kontexte', *Schweizerisches Jahrbuch für Sozial- und Wirtschaftsgeschichte* (Zürich, 2023)

Mouysset, S., *Papiers de famille: Introduction à l'étude des livres de raison (France, XVe–XXe siècle)* (Rennes, 2007)

—— 'Penser/classer: La passion de la liste dans quelques livres de raison du Midi de la France à l'époque moderne', *Les écrits du for privé: Objets matériels, objets édités: Actes du colloque de Limoges, 17 et 18 novembre 2005*, ed. M. Cassan, J.-P. Bardet and F.-J. Ruggiu (Limoges, 2007), 151–66

—— 'Pourquoi laisser trace de sa vie ordinaire? France-Catalogne (XVe–XIXe siècle)', *Memòria personal: Construcció i projecció en primera persona a l'època moderna*, ed. P. O. Jané and P. Poujade (Madrid, 2015), pp. 63–75

Mussari, R. and M. Magliacani, 'Agricultural Accounting in the Nineteenth and Early Twentieth Centuries: The Case of the Noble Rucellai Family Farm in Campi', *Accounting, Business & Financial History* 17,1 (2007), 87–103

Napier, C. J., 'Aristocratic Accounting: The Bute Estate in Glamorgan, 1814–1880', *Accounting and Business Research* 21 (1991), 163–74

—— 'Historiography', *The Routledge Companion to Accounting History*, ed. J. R. Edwards and S. Walker (2020), pp. 32–53

Nimmo, R., 'Auditing Nature, Enacting Culture: Rationalisation as Disciplinary Purification in Early Twentieth-Century British Dairy Farming', *Journal of Historical Sociology* 21,2 (2008), 272–302

North, R., *The Gentleman Accomptant: Or, an Essay to Unfold the Mystery of Accompts* (London, 1714)

Nõu, J., *The Development of Agricultural Economics in Europe* (Uppsala, 1967)

Nourse, T., *Campania Felix, or a Discourse of the Benefits and Improvements of Husbandry* (London, 1700)

O'Rourke, K. H., 'The European Grain Invasion, 1870–1913', *The Journal of Economic History* 57,4 (1997), 775–801

Ohmstede, V. S., *Wet op de inkomstenbelasting 1914, benevens wet op de vermogensbelasting, wet op de dividend- en tantièmebelasting, wet op de raden van beroep voor de directe belastingen* (Woerden, 1918)

Oldroyd, D., 'Through a Glass Clearly: Management Practice on the Bowes Family Estates c. 1700–70 as Revealed by the Accounts', *Accounting, Business & Financial History* 9,2 (1999), 175–201

— *Estates, Enterprise and Investment at the Dawn of the Industrial Revolution: Estate Management in the North-East of England, c. 1700–1780* (Farnham, 2017)

Oldroyd, D. and A. Dobie, 'Bookkeeping', *The Routledge Companion to Accounting History*, ed. J. R. Edwards and S. Walker (Abingdon/New York, 2008), 95–120

Overgaard, J. C., 'Kejsernes nye Klæder', *Ugeskrift for Landmænd* 61 (1916), 161–2

— *Undersøgelser over Landbrugets Driftsforhold I: Nogle Regnskabsresultater fra danske Landbrug i Aaret 1916–17* (Kolding, 1918)

Overton, M., *Agricultural Revolution in England: The Transformation of the Agrarian Economy 1500–1850* (Cambridge, 1996)

Park, K., 'Observation in the Margin 500–1500', *Histories of Scientific Observation*, ed. L. Daston and E. Lunbeck (Chicago, 2011), pp. 15–44

Parker, R. H., 'Reckoning, Merchants' Accounts, Book-Keeping, Accounting or Accountancy? The Evidence of the Long Titles of Books on Accounting in English, 1543–1914', *External Financial Reporting*, ed. B. Carsber and S. Dev (London, 1984), pp. 109–22

— 'Finding English Words to Talk about Accounting Concepts', *Accounting, Auditing and Accountability Journal* 7 (1994), 70–85

—'Roger North: Gentleman, Accountant and Lexicographer', *Accounting History* 2 (1997), 31–51

Pawley, E., 'Accounting with the Fields: Chemistry and Value in Nutriment in American Agricultural Improvement, 1835–1860', *Science as Culture* 19 (2010), 461–82

Pazzagli, R., 'Scuole d'agricoltura e poderi sperimentali: Agronomia, istruzione e progresso tecnico nella prima meta dell'800', PhD dissertation, European University Institute (Florence, 1989)

Pedersen, E. H., *Det danske landbrugs historie IV: 1914–1988* (Odense, 1988)

Pedersen, J., 'Det landøkonomiske Driftsbureaus Beretning', *Nationaløkonomisk Tidsskrift* III,35 (1927), 90–101

— *En Undersøgelse af Indtægtssvingningerne i Landbruget i Perioden 1922–36 og deres Indflydelse paa andre Erhverv* (Copenhagen, 1938)

Pedersen, M. C., *Beretning om Andelsmælkerivirksomheden i Vestjylland 1884–85*, ed. C. Bjørn (Esbjerg, 1918)

—— 'Landbrugets Regnskabsføring', *Ugeskrift for Landmænd* 64 (1919), 415–16

Piñeiro, M. V., 'Readings for Farmers: Agrarian Almanacs in Italy from the Eighteenth to the Twentieth Century', *Agricultural History Review* 63,2 (2015), 243–64

Pérez Picazo, M. T., 'Riqueza territorial y cambio agrícola en la Murcia del siglo XIX: Aproximación al estudio de una contabilidad privada (circa 1800–1902)', *Agricultura y sociedad* 61 (1991), 39–96

Perrenoud, A., *La population de Genève (XVIe–XVIIIe siècles)* (Geneva, 1979)

Perrot, J.-C., 'La comptabilité des entreprises agricoles dans l'économie physiocratique', *Annales: Économies, Sociétés, Civilisations* 33,3 (1978), 567

Perrot, M., 'La jaciste: Figure emblématique', *Celles de la terre. Agricultrice: l'invention politique d'un métier*, ed. R.-M. Lagrave (Paris, 1987), pp. 34–60

Pervushin, S. A., 'O Budzhetnikh Izsledovanijakh', *Trudy Vol'nogo-Ekonomicheskogo Obshestva* 1 (1912), 13–35

Petersen, T., *Optimale Anreizsysteme: Betriebswirtschaftliche Implikationen der Prinzipal-Agenten-Theorie* (Wiesbaden, 1989)

Piètrement, M., *Le bonheur au foyer domestique: Livre de lecture courante pour les jeunes filles* (Paris, 1887)

Pilat, D., *Dutch Agricultural Export Performance (1846–1926)* (Groningen, 1989).

Pintus, R., 'La main d'œuvre d'une ferme du pays d'Ath: Le livre de comptes des Martin-Scaillez (fin XVIIIe–XIXe siècle)', *La plume et la terre*, ed. F. Delleaux (Namur, 2022), pp. 167–81

Piuz, A.-M., 'Un aspect de l'économie genevoise au XVIIe siècle: La fabrique de dorures d'Élisabeth Baulacre', *Mélanges offerts à Paul Martin* (Geneva, 1961), pp. 523–40

—— *L'économie genevoise de la réforme à la fin de l'Ancien Régime, XVIe–XVIIIe siècles*, ed. L. Mottu-Weber (Geneva, 1990)

Planas, J. and E. Sauger, 'Accounting Records of Large Rural Estates and the Dynamics of Agriculture in Catalonia (Spain), 1850–1950', *Accounting, Business & Financial History* 15,2 (2005), 171–85

Polanyi, K., *The Great Transformation: The Political and Economic Origins of Our Time* (Boston, 2001)

Porter, T. M., 'Making Things Quantitative', *Science in Context* 7,3 (1994), 389–407

——'The Engineer and the Sage: Le Play's Quest for Social Renewal and the Reconstruction of Observation', *History of Observation in Economics Working Paper Series* 2 (2009)

Postel-Vinay, G., *La rente foncière dans le capitalisme agricole: Analyse de la voie 'classique' du développement du capitalisme dans l'agriculture à partir de l'exemple du Soissonnais* (Paris, 1994)

— *La terre et l'argent: L'agriculture et le crédit en France du XVIIIe au début du XXe siècle* (Paris, 1998)

Prass, R., 'Les écrits personnels de paysans et l'histoire économique: Un tour d'horizon dans l'historiographie de l'Allemagne préindustrielle', *La plume et la terre*, ed. F. Delleaux (Namur, 2022), pp. 27–46

Quattrone, P., 'Is Time Spent, Passed or Counted? The Missing Link between Time and Accounting History', *Accounting Historians Journal* 32,1 (2005), 185–208

Radeff, A., *Du café dans le chaudron: Économie globale d'Ancien Régime. Suisse occidentale, Franche-Comté et Savoie* (Lausanne, 1996)

Raffnsøe, S., A. Mennicken and P. Miller, 'The Foucault Effect in Organization Studies', *Organization Studies*, 40,2 (2019), 155–82

Reddy, W. M., *La traversée des sentiments: Un cadre pour l'histoire des émotions, 1700–1850* (Dijon, 2019)

'Réflexions sur les moyens proposés pour faire fleurir l'agriculture en Suisse', *Mémoires et observations recueillies par la Société oeconomique de Berne* 3,2 (1762), 89–90

Reif, H., *Westfälischer Adel 1770–1860: Vom Herrschaftsstand zur regionalen Elite* (Göttingen, 1979)

Rhodes, J., 'Subletting in Eighteenth-Century England: A New Methodological Approach', *Agricultural History Review* 66,1 (2018), 67–92

Richter, N., *Du conditionnement à la culture: L'offre de lecture des Lumières à la Troisième République* (Bernay, 2003)

Rieffel, J., *Œuvres de Jacques Bujault* (Paris, 1845)

Rilliet, N., *Le Reposoir, histoire d'un domaine genevois* (Geneva, 2012)

Robson, K., 'Accounting Numbers as "Inscription": Action at a Distance and the Development of Accounting', *Accounting, Organizations and Society* 17,7 (1992), 685–708

Roiger, M. B., *Gestaltung von Anreizsystemen und Unternehmensethik: Eine norm- und wertbezogene Analyse der normativen Prinzipal-Agent-Theorie* (Wiesbaden, 2007)

Roll, S., 'De la ménagère parfaite à la consommatrice engagée: Histoire culturelle de la ménagère nouvelle en France au tournant des XIXe–XXe siècles', PhD dissertation, Université de Marc Bloch Strasbourg (2008)

Rose, L., *La bonne fermière ou éléments économiques utiles aux jeunes personnes destinées à cet état* (Lille, 1767)

Rossi, M.- L., 'Une comptabilité industrielle: L'entreprise agricole du Pô à l'Arno (1826–1922)', *Twelfth Accounting and Management History Conference* (2007), 29–30

—— 'Une entreprise agricole à la recherche du profit optimum: La Casa Spalletti en Italie au XIXe siècle', *Comptabilités. Revue d'histoire des comptabilités*. Online: https://journals.openedition.org/comptabilites/1349 (2013)

—— 'Les archives agricoles de la Casa Spalletti en Italie (1821–1922): Conserver pour entreprendre', *Gazette des archives* 213 (2009), 103–17

Roth, W. J., 'Farm Accounting Investigations in Switzerland', *Journal of Farm Economics* 13,4 (1931), 554–72

Sammenvirkende Landboforeninger, *1895–1920. Kontrolforeningerne og deres Arbejde gennem fem og tyve Aar* (Copenhagen, 1920)

Sargiacomo. M., L. Ianni, A. d'Andreamatteo and L. d'Amico, 'Accounting and the Government of the Agricultural Economy: Arrigo Serpieri and the Reclamation Consortia', *Accounting History Review* 26,3 (2016), 307–31

Schattkowsky, M., 'Ein kursächsischer Hofmarschall als Gutsherr: Christoph von Loß auf Schleinitz (1574–1629)', *Gutsherrschaftsgesellschaften im europäischen Vergleich*, ed. J. Peters (Berlin, 1997), pp. 295–309

—— Zwischen Rittergut, Residenz und Reich, *Die Lebenswelt des kursächsischen Landadligen Christoph von Loß auf Schleinitz (1574–1620)* (Leipzig, 2007)

Schild, J., *Die Zunahme der Land- und die Abnahme der Alpen-Wirthschaft der Schweiz* (Bern, 1863)

Schilke, O., M. Reimann and K. S. Cook, 'Trust in Social Relations', *Annual Review of Sociology* 47,1 (2021), 239–59

Schlumbohm, J., '"Zu Schreiben und die ganze Beschaffenheit der Sache": Signierfähigkeit und Schriftgebrauch bei Bauern und Heuerleuten des Kirshspiels Belm, ca. 1770–1840', *Alphabetissierung und Literalisierung in Deutschland in der Frühern Neuzeit: Wolfenbüttler Studien zur Aufklärung*, ed. H. E. Bödeker and E. Hinrichs (Tübingen, 1999), pp. 163–80

Schnakenbourg, C., *Histoire de l'industrie sucrière en Picardie (1810–2006)* (Paris, 2010)

Scholten-Buschhoff, F., 'Verkaufen – Verschenken – Lagern. Adelige Getreidewirtschaft in Rheinland und Westfalen, 1650–1850', PhD dissertation, Universität Münster (Münster, 2020)

Schulde, U., 'Cultiver selon "les bonnes règles et avec profit": La création d'un savoir agricole à la cour de l'électeur et de l'électrice de Saxe à Dresde', *Élites et progrès agricole*, ed. N. Vivier (Rennes, 2009), pp. 59–81

Schulte, M., 'Rationalisierung in der Landwirtschaft: Johann Friedrich von Reden auf Wendlinghausen (1731–1791)', *Adel und Innovation: Industriepioniere aus der Familie von Reden* (Dettmold, 1996), pp. 21–5

Schuurman, A., 'Het Nederlands Landhuishoudkundig Congres van 1846–1896: Forum en showroom van de Agrarische Republiek', *Levenslopen in transformatie: Liber amicorum bij het afscheid van prof. dr.*

Paul M.M. Klep, ed. T. Engelen, A. Janssens and O. Boonstra (Nijmegen, 2011), pp. 318–35

— 'Agricultural Policy and the Dutch Agricultural Institutional Matrix during the Transition from Organized to Disorganized Capitalism', *Integration through Subordination: The Politics of Agricultural Modernisation in Industrial Europe*, ed. P. Moser and P. Varley (Turnhout, 2013), pp. 65–84

— 'The Agricultural Enquiry of 1890 in the Netherlands. Bringing the State Back In', *The Golden Age of State Enquiries: Rural Enquiries in the Nineteenth Century. From Fact Gathering to Political Instrument*, ed. N. Vivier (2014), pp. 239–54

Secrétariat des Paysans Suisses, *Statistiques et évaluations agricoles* (Brougg, 1923)

Ségalen, M., *Mari et femme dans la société paysanne* (Paris, 1980)

Sharp, P., S. Henriques, E. McLaughlin, X. Tsoukli and C. Vedel, 'A Microlevel Analysis of Danish Dairy Cooperatives: Opportunities for Large Data in Business History', *Enterprise and Society* (2023), 1–29

Shaw-Taylor, L., 'The Rise of Agrarian Capitalism and the Decline of Family Farming in England', *The Economic History Review* 65,1 (2012), 26–60

Simler, R.T., *Ueber die Nothwendigkeit landwirthschaftlich-chemischer Laboratorien und Versuchsstationen in der Schweiz* (Bern, 1864)

Slicher van Bath, B. H., 'Accounts and Diaries of Farmers before 1800', *Afdeling Agrarische Geschiedenis Bijdragen* 8 (1962), 5–33

Solterbeck, S., *Blaues Blut und rote Zahlen* (Münster, 2018)

Sombart, W., *Der moderne Kapitalismus* (Munich/Leipzig, 1917)

Staatscommissie tot onderzoek naar de toestand van de Landbouw, *Uitkomsten van het onderzoek naar den toestand van den landbouw in Nederland* (Den Haag, 1890)

Stalder, G., *Die hauswirtschaftliche Buchführung auf dem Lande: Praktische Anleitung zum Betriebe der Buchführung im landwirtschaftlichen Haushalte* (Bern, 1892)

Stapelbroek, K. and J. Marjanen, 'Political Economy, Patriotism and the Rise of Societies', *The Rise of Economic Societies in the Eighteenth Century: Patriotic Reform in Europe and North America*, ed. K. Stapelbroek and J. Marjanen (Basingstoke, 2012), pp. 1–25

State Historical Society of Wisconsin, 'Henry C. Taylor Papers, 1896–1968'

Statistics Denmark, *Agriculture and Danish Farm Returns through 100 years: 1916–2015* (Copenhagen, 2017)

Stieger, G., 'Moeglichkeit und Bedeutung landwirtschaftlicher Produktionskostenberechnungen', *Jahrbuch der Deutschen Landwirtschafts-Gesellschaft* 24 (1909), 950–81

Schweizerischer Verband für Wohnungswesen, 'Die Rentabilitätserhebungen des schweizerischen Bauernsekretariates im Lichte statistischer Wissenschaft', *Wohnen* 27,7 (1952)

Taylor, H. C., 'The Objectives in Agricultural Cost Accounting', *Journal of Farm Economics* 5,2 (1923), 65–78

Tesdorpf, E., 'Er det rigtig at give Malkeqvæget et kraftigt Foder?', *Ugeskrift for Landmænd* (1856), 81–5

Theobald, J., 'Distant Lands: The Management of Absentee Estates in Woodland High Suffolk, 1660–1860', *Cambridge Rural History* 12,1 (2001), 1–18

Thompson, E. P., 'Time, Work-Discipline, and Industrial Capitalism', *Past & Present* 38,1 (1967), 56–97

Thordal, P. K., 'Udviklingerne i Landbrugets Regnskabsføring og dertil hørende Konsulentvirksomhed', *Ugeskrift for Landmænd* 88 (1942), 315–17

Todeschini, G., 'La comptabilité à partie double et la rationalité économique occidentale: Max Weber et Jack Goody', *Écrire, compter, mesurer: Vers une histoire des rationalités pratiques*, ed. N. Coquery, F. Menant and F. Weber (Paris, 2006), pp. 67–76

Tomo, S., 'The Epistemology of Macroeconomic Reality: The Keynesian Revolution from an Accounting Point of View', *Accounting, Organizations and Society* 28,5 (2003), 471–517

—— 'Capitalism', *The Routledge Companion to Accounting History*, ed. J. R. Edwards and S. Walker (London, 2020), pp. 427–42

Tribe, K., *Land, Labour and Economic Discourse* (London, 1978)

—— *Genealogies of Capitalism* (London, 1981)

Turner, M. E., J. V. Beckett and B. Afton, *Farm Production in England, 1700–1914* (Oxford, 2001)

—— *Agricultural Rent in England, 1690–1914* (Cambridge, 2004)

Uekötter, F. (ed.), *Die Wahrheit ist auf dem Feld: Eine Wissensgeschichte der deutschen Landwirtschaft, Umwelt und Gesellschaft* (Göttingen, 2010)

Valarché, J., 'L'influence des physiocrates en Suisse', *Revue d'histoire économique et sociale* 35,4 (1957), 337–46

Van de Grift, L. and A. R. Forclaz (eds), *Governing the Rural in Interwar Europe* (New York/Abingdon, 2017)

Van der Burg, B., 'Een en ander over zuivelbereiding in Nederland: Openbare voordracht gehouden ter opening van de lessen in de zuivelbereiding aan de Rijks Hoogere Land-, Tuin- en Boschbouwschool te Wageningen den 28 September 1914', *Mededeelingen van de Rijks Hoogere Land-, Tuin- en Boschbouwschool en van de daaraan verbonden instituten* 7,3 (1914), 101–21

Van der Poel, J. M. G., *Heren en boeren* (Wageningen, 1949)

Van Zanden, J. L., *De economische ontwikkeling van de Nederlandse landbouw in de negentiende eeuw, 1800–1914* (Wageningen, 1985)

— 'The First Green Revolution: The Growth of Production and Productivity in European Agriculture, 1870–1914', *The Economic History Review* 44,2 (1991), 215–39

Varese, F., 'Principal–Agent Problem', *A Concise Oxford Dictionary of Politics and International Relations*, ed. G. W. Brown, I. McLean and A. McMillan (Oxford, 2018)

Vitting Andersen, H., *Landbrugets økonomi i 50 år: 1918–1968* (Copenhagen, 1968)

Vivier, N., 'L'âge d'or des grandes enquêtes agricoles: Le XIXe siècle', *Annales du Midi: Revue de la France méridionale* 284 (2013), 495–510

Vivier, N. (ed.), *Élites et progrès agricole: XVIe–XXe siècle* (Rennes, 2009)

Von Frauendorfer, S., *Ideengeschichte der Agrarwirtschaft und Agrarpolitik im deutschen Sprachgebiet: Von den Anfängen bis zum ersten Weltkrieg* (Munich, 1957)

Walker, S. P., 'How to Secure your Husband's Esteem: Accounting and Private Patriarchy in the British Middle Class Household during the Nineteenth Century', *Accounting, Organizations and Society* 23,5/6 (1998), 485–514

— 'Accounting Histories of Women: Beyond Recovery?', *Accounting, Auditing and Accountability Journal* 21,4 (2008), 580–610

— 'Accounting and Rural Rehabilitation in New Deal America', *Accounting, Organizations and Society* 39,3 (2014), 208–35

— 'Revisiting the Roles of Accounting in Society', *Accounting, Organizations and Society* 49 (2016), 41–50

Ward, C., 'Thinking outside the Berry Boxes: New Perspectives on Identity, and Intercultural Relations', *International Journal of Intercultural Relations* 32,2 (2008), 105–14

Weber, M., *L'éthique protestante et l'esprit du capitalisme* (Paris, 1964)

— 'Wissenschaft als Beruf', *Schriften zur Wissenschaftslehre*, 'Wissenschaft als Beruf' (Stuttgart, 1991)

— *Économie et société. Tome 1: Les catégories de la sociologie* (1st edn 1956, Paris, 1995)

— *Wirtschaft und Gesellschaft: Grundriss der verstehenden Soziologie* (Frankfurt am Main, 2005)

Webster, S., 'Estate Improvement and the Professionalization of Land Agents on the Egremont Estates in Sussex and Yorkshire, 1770–1835', *Rural History* 18,1 (2007), 47–69

Weulersse, G., *Le mouvement physiocratique en France de 1756 à 1770* (Paris, 1910)

Whittle, J., *The Development of Agrarian Capitalism: Land and Labour in Norfolk, 1440–1580* (Oxford, 2000)

— 'Le travail des femmes dans les ménages ruraux anglais, 1450–1650: Trois approches alternatives', *Ruralité française et britannique, XIIIe–XXe siècles: Approches comparées*, ed. N. Vivier (Rennes, 2002), pp. 77–87

Wood, E. M. 'Capitalism, Merchants and Bourgeois Revolution: Reflections on the Brenner Debate and Its Sequel', *International Review of Social History* 41,2 (1996), 209–32

Woodward, D., *The Farming and Memorandum Books of Henry Best of Elmswell, 1642* (Oxford, 1984)

Wunder, H., *Er ist die Sonn', sie ist der Mond: Frauen in der Frühen Neuzeit* (Munich, 1992)

Young, A., *The Farmer's Guide in Hiring and Stocking Farms* (London, 1770)

—— *Rural Oeconomy or, Essays on the Practical Parts of Husbandry* (London, 1770)

Zaugg, F., *Die Rentabilitätserhebungen des schweizerischen Bauernsekretariates: Eine monographische Darstellung* (Brugg, 1923)

Zumkeller, D., *Le paysan et la terre: Agriculture et structure agraire à Genève au XVIIIe siècle* (Geneva, 1992)

—— 'Les patriciens genevois aux champs et leurs écrits: Les améliorations viticoles au domaine de Villette (XVIIIe siècle)', *La plume et la terre*, ed. F. Dellaux (Namur, 2022), pp. 253–67

Zwarts, H., 'Knowledge, Networks, and Niches: Dutch Agricultural Innovation in an International Perspective, c. 1880–1970', PhD dissertation, Wageningen Universiteit (2021)

INDEX

Boydell Studies in Rural History

The Real Agricultural Revolution: The Transformation of English Farming, 1939–1985
Paul Brassley, David Harvey, Matt Lobley and Michael Winter

Agricultural Knowledge Networks in Rural Europe, 1700–2000
Edited by Yves Segers and Leen Van Molle

Landless Households in Rural Europe, 1600–1900
Edited by Christine Fertig, Richard Paping and Henry French

Agriculture, Economy and Society in Early Modern Scotland
Edited by Harriet Cornell, Julian Goodare and Alan R. MacDonald

The Tithe War in England and Wales, 1881–1936: A Curious Rural Revolt
John Bulaitis

Farming the North Sea Coast, 900–2000: Managing Water, Reclaiming the Land
Piet van Cruyningen

Printed and bound by CPI Group (UK) Ltd, Croydon, CR0 4YY

13/09/2026

14961005-0006